Criminal Justice
Contemporary Literature in Theory and Practice

Series Editors

Marilyn McShane
Frank P. Williams III
California State University – San Bernardino

GARLAND PUBLISHING, INC.
New York & London
1997

Contents of the Series

Law Enforcement Operations and Management

Edited with introductions by
Marilyn McShane
Frank P. Williams III
California State University – San Bernardino

GARLAND PUBLISHING, INC.
New York & London
1997

Library of Congress Cataloging-in-Publication Data

Law enforcement operations and management / edited with
introductions by Marilyn McShane and Frank P. Williams III.
    p.   cm. — (Criminal justice ; v. 1)
    Includes bibliographical references.
    ISBN 0-8153-2508-8 (alk. paper)
    1. Police—United States. 2. Police administration—United
States. 3. Law enforcement—United States. I. McShane, Marilyn
D., 1956–   . II. Williams, Franklin P. III. Series: Criminal
justice (New York, N.Y.) ; v. 1.
HV8141.L416 1997
363.2'0973—dc21   96-39143
                                                        CIP

Printed on acid-free, 250-year-life paper
Manufactured in the United States of America

Contents

Series Introduction

At the turn of the century the criminal justice system will be confronting many of the same demons, although the drugs of choice, the technology of crime fighting, and the tools and techniques of management have evolved. Despite the enhancements of twenty-first century technologies, funding, crowding, and public concerns about effectiveness continue to be discussed in "crisis" terminology, and criminal justice scholars remain somewhat cynical about the ability to reform the criminal justice system. This pessimistic attitude may be fueled, at least in part, by the drama of real-life crime that plays itself out in courtrooms, newspapers, and talk shows across America every day. The combination of emotional political maneuvering and campaigning on punitive rhetoric assures us of a steady stream of legislation designed to reflect a zero tolerance for crime.

Testing the constitutional limits of our times, we have devised even more ways of imposing severe punishments, seizing assets, reinstituting corporal punishment, and penalizing the parents of delinquents. We have also created new offenses, such as recruiting someone into a gang, transmitting "indecent" images on the Internet, and knowingly passing along a disease. Despite these politically popular solutions to crime, problems of enforcement, equity, and affordability remain. The public's preoccupation with "what works?" and quick fixes to crime problems have never been reconciled with the more realistic ideas of "what can we live with?" and long-range preventive solutions.

Ironically, despite public perceptions that crime has been getting worse, statistics seem to indicate that the rates for virtually all offenses are either no worse than they were in 1980 or are now lower. Drug-related arrests and the rates for most forms of adult crime (in particular, most violent crimes) have actually decreased. Against this general backdrop, the rate of violent juvenile crime appears to be the sole increasing trend, leading to a situation in which risks of victimization by violent crime have also increased for juveniles. The contrary public perception of a massive and growing crime problem has created a situation in which the number of cases of juveniles transferred to adult court has increased, as has the proportion of inmates facing life sentences, life in prison without parole, and death sentences. On the other hand the risk of incarceration also appears to have increased for minorities, directing attention to questions of racial and economic disparity in the quality of protection and justice available in this country today.

While all this has been happening over the past two decades, academia has rather quietly developed an entire discipline dedicated to the study of crime and the criminal justice system. Though crime policy is still dominated largely by political interests swayed by public opinion, crime scholars have begun to have an impact on how crime is viewed and what can be done about it. While this impact is not yet a major one, it continues to gain weight and shows promise of some day achieving the influence that economists have come to wield in the realm of public policy-making.

Simultaneously with this growing scholarship comes an irony: academic journals, the major repository of scholarly wisdom, are being discontinued by libraries. Access, although ostensibly available in an electronic form, is decreasing. In many academic libraries, only a few select, "major" journals are being retained. Clearly, there is so much being done that the few "top" journals cannot adequately represent current developments (even if these journals were not focused in particular directions). Thus, the knowledge of the field is being centralized and, at the same time, more difficult to obtain. The multitude of criminal justice and criminology degree programs now face an interesting dilemma: how do students and faculty access current information? Or put differently, how does the field distribute its hard-gained knowledge to both assure quality of education and pursue efforts to offset the often ill-informed myths of public opinion?

Electronic access would appear to be one possible answer to the problem, especially with libraries facing yet another squeeze, that of space. On-line and media-based (CD-ROM) services promise quick availability of periodical literature, but remain futuristic. The costs associated with downloading articles can approximate the cost of the journal subscriptions themselves and many libraries cannot afford to participate in on-line periodical services. In addition, there is the inconvenience of translating the electronic images into the user's still-preferred paper-based format. Moreover, the paper-based serendipitous value of "browsing" decreases as only specific articles appear on-line, without surrounding materials.

An alternative solution is to review the range of journals and collect the "best" of their articles for reprinting. This is the approach this criminal justice periodical series has taken. By combining both depth and scope in a series of reprints, the series can offer an attractive, cost-effective answer to the problem of creating access to scholarship. Moreover, such a compact format yields the added advantage that individuals searching for a specific topic are more likely to experience the serendipity of running across related articles. Each of the six volumes presents a comprehensive picture of the state of the art in criminal justice today and each contains articles focused on one of the major areas of criminal justice and criminology: Police, Drugs, Criminological Theory, Corrections, Courts, and Victimology. Each volume contains approximately twenty articles.

The Article Selection Process

The articles appearing in the series represent the choices of the editors and a board of experts in each area. These choices were based on four criteria: (1) that the articles were from the time period of 1991–1995, (2) that they represent excellent scholarship, (3) that collectively they constitute a fair representation of the knowledge of the period, and (4) that where there were multiple choices for representing a knowledge area, the articles appeared in journals that are less likely to be in today's academic library holdings. We believe the selection criteria and the board of experts were successful in compiling truly representative content in each topical area. In addition, the authors of the selected articles constitute a list of recognizable experts whose work is commonly cited.

Finally, there is one other advantage offered by the volumes in this series: the articles are reprinted as they originally appeared. Scholars using anthologized materials are commonly faced with having to cite secondary source pages because they do not have access to the original pagination and format. This is a difficulty because mistakes in reprinting have been known to alter the original context, thus making the use of secondary sources risky (and synonymous with sloppy scholarship). In order to overcome this problem, the series editors and the publisher made the joint decision to photoreproduce each article's original image, complete with pagination and format. Thus, each article retains its own unique typesetting and character. Citations may be made to pages in confidence that the reproduced version is identical in all respects with the original. In short, the journal article is being made available exactly as if the issue had been on a library shelf.

We believe this series will be of great utility to students, scholars, and others with interests in the literature of criminal justice and criminology. Moreover, the series saves the user time that would have otherwise been spent in locating quality articles during a typical literature search. Whether in an academic or personal library, the only alternative to this collection is having the journals themselves.

Volume Introduction

Contemporary law enforcement presents a host of complex social and management problems. This volume presents the latest research and commentary on the major issues facing law enforcement agencies today. While some problems like corruption and use of force continue to demand legal and philosophical scrutiny, we are perhaps able to address them with more sophisticated administrative responses. This work addresses some of the creative approaches to the traditional as well as to the new dilemmas facing not only large urban departments but smaller, more rural agencies, which are often overlooked. Staffing challenges that range from shiftwork and diversity in hiring, to increased liability and decentralized decision-making generate opportunities to experiment with structural and procedural solutions. Confronting public criticisms often means implementing community-based strategies such as citizen-advisory boards and community policing, and opening communication lines between consumers and providers of police services. The readings in this collection reflect what the experts are saying about the controversies and the realities of modern American law enforcement.

Reform

Videotapes, tape recorders, and eyewitness news-cameras have changed the face of policing forever, but then again, so have liability lawsuits, civilian oversight boards, and affirmative action. As policing moves into the twenty-first century, it is shaped by a number of forces and reforms that seek to improve management efficiency and the overall effectiveness of daily procedures. Susan Martin empirically examines the effects of affirmative action, particularly the integration of women into the ranks of policing. Using questionnaire and case-study data from municipal police departments in 1986, she finds that some 10 percent of police officers are women. While this percentage is not particularly high, it represents a real increase in the hiring of female officers. The same cannot be said, however, of promotions. On the basis of these data, Martin argues that affirmative action programs have had an effect and should be continued.

Sam Walker and Vic Bumphus discuss some of the issues related to civilian review of police departments, based on a survey of 34 departments with civilian review boards. Such boards appear to have become the latest trend and many departments have implemented them in the past ten years. Boards differ mostly in the degree of review they are allowed to pursue, with some participating at all levels of complaint investigation and others only reviewing the police chief's decisions. The authors caution that there is inadequate information to allow for a determination of the boards' effectiveness.

Research

In order to assess the relevance of these recent writings in the area of law enforcement, readers must examine their own perceptions about the nature of change in police organizations and, ultimately, what we want police to do. Calculated into that mandate would be considerations of what we are willing to pay for and whether police should take on increasing demands for services. Pamela Jackson discusses police expenditures as they relate to urban decline and gang problems. Analyzing 60 cities over a ten-year period, she concludes that expenditures in declining cities increase even when crime rates are stabilized. Gang problems also contribute heavily to city spending. Thus, declining cities appear to pay more for law enforcement, which may help perpetuate the decline.

David Hirschel, Ira Hutchinson, Charles Dean, and Anne-Marie Mills review police response to a specific offense type: domestic violence. Because the historical approach has been to minimize the importance of spouse abuse, they argue that police reluctance to enforce abuse laws is, in part, due both to historical precedent and to perceptions of what police work should be. Even though legislatures have strengthened abuse laws, the research shows that police remain reluctant to intervene. They conclude that more research is necessary to determine appropriate intervention strategies.

Another form of police response is the controversial practice of automobile pursuits. Some agencies have considered abandoning them altogether. Michael Blankenship and James Moneymaker analyze the issue from both crime control and order-maintenance perspectives. Clearly, from the crime control perspective, police pursuits are valuable in that they demonstrate the tenacity and long arm of the law. From a order-maintenance perspective, however, their utility is doubtful and perhaps even counterproductive, conflicting with community policing goals.

Corruption and Abuse

While lawsuits certainly highlight some of the "worst case scenarios" for police, controversial incidents have introduced terms like "problem officers" and "rogue cops." The cumulative effects of the consecutive commissions studying the Los Angeles Police Department and Los Angeles Sheriff's Department following the Rodney King beating have focused on the "code of silence," racism, and a department's responsibility to discipline and weed out those who have proven to be ill-suited for high-stress public encounters. Corruption investigations in several large cities, and a series of high-profile stings have once again raised concerns about the ability of managers to monitor the amount of discretion used on the job. An article by Dorothy Bracey explores the impact of police corruption on community policing. Noting that previous attempts to stem police corruption stressed professionalism, Bracey points out that those reforms embraced an impersonal approach to the job. Unfortunately, that approach is now at odds with the personal one required by community policing. As a result, she sees greater opportunities for minor forms of corruption and new challenges for police administrators.

Like corruption, police abuse of citizens (arrested or not) is a recurrent phenomenon. Intentional abuse and use of force is clearly not the norm among police officers, yet it happens with enough frequency to suggest that it is not an individual problem but a structural and organizational one. According to David Rudovsky, judicial responses to police abuse have been to perceive it as individually based and therefore best rectified with individual action. Structural problems have been ignored by police departments, commissions, and by the judiciary. Rudovsky provides several suggestions to remedy these perceptions and proposes an agenda for reform.

Abraham Tennenbaum looks at the influence of one specific Supreme Court decision on the police use of deadly force. Reviewing *Tennessee* v. *Garner*, he notes that state laws authorizing the use of deadly force to apprehend fleeing, unarmed, nonviolent felony suspects were unconstitutional, violating the Fourth Amendment. Tennenbaum's analysis of data on police homicides after the 1985 decision shows that an average 16 percent reduction has occurred, with an even greater drop attributable to states where laws had to be changed. Thus, it appears that judicial intervention may indeed affect structural and individual behavior.

Police abuse is not necessarily intentional; it may also occur when police interact with those from cultures that are substantively different from the mainstream. In these cases, abuse can result from misunderstandings of gestures or speech inflection and from differences in approach to authority. For these reasons, David and Melissa Barlow explore the return of human relations to police work and suggest integrating cultural sensitivity training into the police curriculum. Using two different police training programs, they review the critical issues involved in sensitivity training and provide specific curriculum suggestions for such training.

Richard Lumb looks toward standards of professionalism as a way of gauging police performance. Defining professionalism as a composite of five standards of knowledge and skill, with commensurate updating over time, he examines state education and training standards for their compliance. Lumb concludes that police professionalism ranges from very low levels to high levels, with most departments needing quite a bit of improvement.

Management

Over the last few years, scholars have examined and critiqued the way police organizational structures, as well as other internal and external forces, enhance or inhibit reforms. Traditional paramilitary models have been questioned, as the tenets of modern management point out the weaknesses in such organizations and the need for adaptive management styles and techniques. Decentralized decision-making has been an experiment in some departments with mixed results.

Malcolm Sparrow discusses the problem of having an either/or approach to proactive or reactive policing and argues that police managers should create an organization capable of doing either. The problem is to balance the organization (with planning, training, assignments, etc.) so that both can be integrated. He provides some practical suggestions of how this might be done.

Regardless of what is implied by many discussions of management, police managers do not operate in a vacuum. They must respond to outside influences in deciding what management strategies would benefit the organization. In researching one of these outside influences, Ken Tunnel and Larry Gaines point out the role that political pressures continue to play on police executives. They collected survey data from police chiefs in Kentucky, asking about perceived political influence. Findings include political affects on length of time in the job, operational decisions, and personnel decisions. Mayors and members of the city council appear to unduly interfere in police departments, resulting in a decrease in the quality of service provided to the municipalities.

Jack Greene, Geoff Alpert, and Paul Styles answer a question that arises when police departments attempt organizational change via lessons from the research literature: to what extent are metropolitan and smaller police agencies similar? Examining one department of each size as they attempt to reshape organizational values and behavior, Green, Alpert, and Styles conclude that there are many similarities between the two.

Robert Pursley discusses the impact on police agencies of diminishing fiscal resources within local governments. Using data from a survey of municipal police departments from 1989 to 1991, he concludes that those departments largely reacted to fiscal scarcity in an unproductive fashion. Rather than pursue new methods of greater productivity and efficiency, the departments were simply undertaking cost-reduction measures. Pursley notes that the traditional, public nature of policing serves to limit the ability to pursue more productive strategies.

Carl Klockars' and Peter Manning's contributions in this volume are separate essays (actually an essay and a commentary) examining reasons for police conservatism, a major structural influence in police management and organization. Klockars argues that police conservatism is mostly apolitical and believes that their focus on street crime has more to do with their competencies and skills. Therefore, those who argue that police unfairly focus on the less-powerful in society fail to see the police as they are designed, choosing to critique on the basis of what they want the police to be. Manning argues in response that police could still deal with crimes of the state if those crimes represent symbolic violence. He presents a practical approach to defining such forms of violence.

Community Policing

Of all the police reforms suggested, community policing seems to have become the national elixir, prescribed in various forms and doses all around America. Defining community policing itself turned out to be so controversial that much of the research and literature was not able to go beyond discussions of the fundamental differences in designing and implementing this concept. Terms such as partnerships, networks, exchanges, and goal-oriented interactions all attempt to describe ways that police and the community can work together more effectively. Community involvement seems to range on a continuum from citizen education sessions, where police direct and control information, to citizen-controlled police commissions. The median appears to be some type of citizen advisory board.

John Crank argues that both conservative and liberal advocates have contributed to the institutionalization of community policing we see today. His essay posits that the dual historical myths of the police "watchman" and of "community" have done much to influence the community-policing movement, although neither represents reality. Crank argues that the strategies that have been implemented in community policing draw more from ideologies of crime control than from evidence.

In another essay that uses police history to illuminate current practice, Samuel Walker draws comparisons between 1970s team policing and today's community policing. As with today's strategies, team policing was an effort to reorganize the police, define new roles, and change community perceptions. Walker concludes that, because the problems faced by team policing are similar to those that will affect community policing, advocates of the current approach would do well to examine the evaluation literature of that earlier period.

Ralph Weisheit, Edward Wells, and David Falcone interview rural sheriffs and police chiefs in order to examine community policing in rural America. They find that community policing is almost second nature for rural departments, drawing on long-standing traditions. The major difference in community policing and rural policing is in the degree of formality: the authors believe community policing attempts formal accountability and rural policing tends toward informal practices.

Steve Brandl, James Frank, Robert Worden, and Tim Bynum attempt to distinguish among different types or levels of public attitudes (global and specific) toward police. Surveying about 400 people in a panel study of a midwestern city, they find that while both attitudes affect each other the stronger affect is global on local. Thus, it appears that generalized perceptions of the police may have important ramifications for individual officers as community policing is developed. Indeed, they imply that community policing strategies may be hampered by the negative stereotypical images of police that dominate some neighborhoods.

Frank Williams and Carl Wagoner explore the historical purpose of the police in their analysis of the future of community policing. Because urban police originally developed as agents of government and business, they conclude that police are organizationally sensitive and respond to power structures. Williams and Wagoner speculate that community policing will be implemented largely in lower class areas and may ultimately be viewed as an intrusive method of control. Therefore, there is some question whether community policing can, or will, become the police organizational style of the future.

* * * * * *

We would like to thank the board members of this volume who assisted us in the selection of articles. Because only a limited number of pieces could be selected for this volume, an expanded bibliography is included to provide additional materials. Articles marked with an asterisk (*) are included in this anthology.

Alpert, Geoffrey, William Smith, and Daniel Watters (1992). Law Enforcement: Implications of the Rodney King Beating. *Criminal Law Bulletin* 28(5): 469–78.

Arthur, John and Charles Case (1994). Race, class, and support for police use of force. *Crime, Law, and Social Change* 21(2): 167–82.

*Barlow, David and Melissa Barlow (1994). Cultural sensitivity rediscovered: Developing training strategies for police officers. *Justice Professional* 8(2): 97–116.

Bayley, David (1994). *Police for the future.* New York: Oxford University Press.

*Blankenship, Michael and James Moneymaker (1991). Unsafe at any speed: The utility of police pursuits. *American Journal of Police* 10(2): 53–59.

Blount, William, Bonnie Yegidis, and Randolph Maheux (1992). Police attitudes toward preferred arrest: Influences of rank and productivity. *American Journal of Police* 11(3): 35–52.

*Bracey, Dorothy (1992). Police corruption and community relations: Community policing. *Police Studies* 15(4): 179–83.

*Brandl, Steven, James Frank, Robert Worden, and Timothy Bynum (1994). Global and specific attitudes towards the police: Disentangling the relationship. *Justice Quarterly* 11(1): 119–34.

Cloninger, Dale (1991). Lethal police response as a crime deterrent. *American Journal of Economics and Sociology* 50(1): 59–70.

*Crank, John (1994). Watchman and community: Myth and institutionalization in policing. *Law and Society Review* 28(2): 325–51.

Crank, John (1993). Legalistic and order-maintenance behavior among police patrol officers: A survey of eight municipal police agencies. *American Journal of Police* 12(4): 103–26.

Crank, John, Robert Regoli, and John Hewitt (1993). An assessment of work stress among police executives. *Journal of Criminal Justice* 21(4): 313–24.

Crank, John, Robert Regoli, John Hewitt, and Robert Culbertson (1995). Institutional and organizational antecedents of role stress, work alienation, and anomie among police executives. *Criminal Justice and Behavior* 22(2): 152–71.

Crank, John and Robert Langworthy (1992). An institutional perspective of policing. *Journal of Criminal Law and Criminology* 83(2): 338–63.

Dantzker, Mark (1993). An issue for policing educational level and job satisfaction. *American Journal of Police* 12(2): 101–18.

Davis, Michael (1991). Do cops really need a code of ethics? *Criminal Justice Ethics* 10(2): 14–28.

Dugan, John and Daniel Breda (1991). Complaints about police officers: A comparison among types and agencies. *Journal of Criminal Justice* 19: 165–71.

Felkenes, George, Paul Peretz, and Jean Schroedel (1993). An analysis of the mandatory hiring of females: The Los Angeles Police Department experience. *Women and Criminal Justice* 4(2): 31–63.

Frank, James and Steven Brandl (1991). The police attitude-behavior relationship: Methodological and conceptual considerations. *American Journal of Police* 10(4): 83–103.

Fridell, Lorie and Arnold Binder (1992). Police officer decision-making in potentially violent confrontations. *Journal of Criminal Justice* 20(5): 385–99.

Geis, Gil, Ted Huston, and Joseph Wells (1991). Rewards by business for crime information: The views of law enforcement. *American Journal of Police* 10(3): 69–81.

*Greene, Jack, Geoffrey Alpert, and Paul Styles (1992). Values and culture in two American police departments: Lessons from King Arthur. *Journal of Contemporary Criminal Justice* 8: 183–207.

Guffey, James (1992). The police and the media: Proposals for managing conflict productively. *American Journal of Police* 11(1): 33–51.

Hamilton, Henry and John Smykla (1994). Guidelines for police undercover work: New questions about accreditation and the emphasis of procedures over authorization. *Justice Quarterly* 11(1): 135–51.

Heffernan, William and Richard Lovely (1991). Evaluating the 4th Amendment Exclusionary Rule: The problem of police compliance with the law. *University of Michigan Journal of Law Reform* 24(2): 311–69.

Hirschel, David, Charles Dean, and Richard Lumb (1994). The relative contribution of domestic violence to assault and injury of police officers. *Justice Quarterly* 11(1): 99–117.

Hirschel, David and Charles Dean (1995). The relative cost effectiveness of citation and arrest. *Journal of Criminal Justice* 23(1): 1–12.

*Hirschel, David, Ira Hutchinson, Charles Dean, and Anne-Marie Mills (1992). Review essay on the law enforcement response to spouse abuse: Past, present, and future. *Justice Quarterly* 9(2): 247–83.

Hirschel, David, Ira Hutchinson, and Charles Dean (1992). The failure of arrest to deter spouse abuse. *Journal of Research in Crime and Delinquency* 29(1): 7–33.

Ho, Taiping (1994). Individual and situational determinants of the use of deadly force: A simulation. *American Journal of Criminal Justice* 18(1): 41–60.

Homant, Robert and Daniel Kennedy (1994). The effect of high speed pursuit policies on officers' tendency to pursue. *American Journal of Police* 13(1): 91–111.

Homant, Robert and Daniel Kennedy (1994). Citizen preferences and perceptions concerning police pursuit policies. *Journal of Criminal Justice* 22(5): 425–35.

Independent Commission on the Los Angeles Police Department (1991). *Report of the Independent Commission on the Los Angeles Police Department.* Los Angeles, Calif.

*Jackson, Pamela (1992). The police and social threat: Urban transition, youth gangs and social control. *Policing and Society* 2(3): 193–204.

Jacobs, Bruce (1993). Undercover deception clues: A case of restrictive deterrence. *Criminology* 31(2): 281–99.

Jacobs, Bruce (1993). Getting narced: Neutralization of undercover identity discreditation. *Deviant Behavior* 14(3): 187–208.

Kappeler, Victor (1993). *Critical Issues in Police Civil Liability.* Prospect Heights, Ill: Waveland.

Kappeler, Stephen and Victor Kappeler (1992). A research note on section 1983 claims against the police: Cases before the federal district courts in 1990. *American Journal of Police* 11(1): 65–73.

Kavanagh, John (1994). The occurrence of violence in police-citizen arrest encounters. *Criminal Justice Abstracts* 26(2): 319–30.

Kennedy, Daniel, Robert Homant, and John Kennedy (1992). A comparative analysis of police vehicle pursuit policies. *Justice Quarterly* 9(2): 227–46.

Kessler, David (1993). Integrating calls for service with community and problem-oriented policing: A case study. *Crime and Delinquency* 39(4): 485–508.

Klinger, David (1994). Demeanor or crime? Why "hostile" citizens are more likely to be arrested. *Criminology* 32(3): 475–93.

*Klockars, Carl (1993). The legacy of conservative ideology and police. *Police Forum* 3(1): 1–6.

Lasley, James (1994). The impact of the Rodney King incident on citizen attitudes toward police. *Policing and Society* 3(4): 245–55.

*Lumb, Richard (1994). Standards of professionalization: Do the American police measure up? *Police Studies* 17(3): 1–19.

Lundman, Richard (1994). Demeanor or crime? The Midwest city police-citizen encounters study. *Criminology* 32(4): 631–56.

Lurigio, Arthur and Dennis Rosenbaum (1992). The travails of the Detroit police-victims experiment: Assumptions and important lessons. *American Journal of Police* 11(3) 1–34.

Manning, Peter (1992). Technological dramas and the police: Statement and counterstatement in organizational analysis. *Criminology* 30(3): 327–46.

Manning, Peter (1992). Economic rhetoric and policing reform. *Criminal Justice Research Bulletin* 7(4): 1–8.

*Manning, Peter (1993). Violence and symbolic violence. *Police Forum* 3(1): 1–6.

*Martin, Susan (1991). The effectiveness of affirmative action: The case of women in policing. *Justice Quarterly* 8(4): 489–504.

Martin, Susan (1994). Outside within the station house: The impact of race and gender on black women police. *Social Problems* 41(3): 383–400.

Marx, Gary (1992). Under-the-covers undercover investigations: Some reflections on the state's use of sex and deception in law enforcement. *Criminal Justice Ethics* 11(1): 13–24.

*Marx, Gary (1992). When the guards guard themselves: Undercover tactics turned inward. *Policing and Society* 2(3): 151–72.

Mastrofski, Stephen and Richard Ritti (1992). You can lead a horse to water... a case study of a police department's response to stricter drunk driving laws. *Justice Quarterly* 9(3): 465–91.

McShane, Marilyn (1992). Sixty-two bad cops don't spoil the whole bunch? An analysis of the analyses of the LAPD and LASD. Paper presented at the annual meeting of the Academy of Criminal Justice Sciences, Kansas City, Mo.

Miller, Mitchell and Kevin Bryant (1994). Predicting police behavior: Ecology, class, and autonomy. *American Journal of Criminal Justice* 18(1): 133–51.

Miller, Mitchell and Lance Silva (1994). Drug enforcement's double-edged sword: An assessment of asset forfeiture programs. *Justice Quarterly* 11(2): 313–35.

Nalla, Mahesh (1992). Perspectives on the growth of police bureaucracies 1948–1984: An examination of three explanations. *Policing and Society* 3(1): 51–61.

Nalla, Mahesh and Graeme Newman (1994). Is white-collar policing, policing? *Policing and Society* 3(4): 303–18.

Nalla, Mahesh and Graeme Newman (1991). Public versus private control: A reassessment. *Journal of Criminal Justice* 19(6): 537–47.

Penegor, Janice and Ken Peak (1992). Police chief acquisitions: A comparison of internal and external selections. *American Journal of Police* 11(1): 17–32.

Pogrebin, Mark and Eric Poole (1993). Vice isn't nice: A look at the effects of working undercover. *Journal of Criminal Justice* 21(4): 383–94.

*Pursley, Robert (1993). Local government fiscal scarcity: Its context and an examination of the productivity issue among municipal police departments. *Journal of Crime and Justice* 16(2): 109–38.

Quinn, James and William Downs (1993). Police perceptions of the severity of gang problems: An analysis of noncriminal predictors. *Sociological Spectrum* 13(2): 209–26.

Quint, Thurman, Andrew GiaComazzi and Phill Bogen (1993). Research note: Cops, kids, and community policing: An assessment of a community policing demonstration project. *Crime and Delinquency* 39(4): 554–64.

Rasmussen, Cecilia (1994). City settlements. *Los Angeles Times* April 20, A:23.

Reichel, Philip (1992). The misplaced emphasis on urbanization in police development. *Policing and Society* 3(1): 1–12.

Rosenbaum, Dennis (1991). The pursuit of "justice" in the United States: A policy lesson in the war on crime and drugs? *Canadian Police College Journal* 15(4): 239–55.

Ross, Jeffrey Ian (1994). The future of municipal police violence in advanced industrialized democracies: Towards a structural causal model. *Police Studies* 17(2): 1–27.

Ross, Jeffrey Ian (1992). The outcomes of public police violence: A neglected research agenda. *Police Studies* 15(1): 1–12.

*Rudovsky, David (1992). Police abuse: Can the violence be contained? *Harvard Civil Rights-Civil Liberties Law Review* 27(2): 467–501.

Schneid, Thomas and Larry Gaines (1991). The Americans with Disabilities Act: Implications for Police Administrators. *Police Liability Review* 3(Winter) 1–4 (also in *Journal of Police* 10(1): 47–58).

Sherman, Lawrence (1995). The Police. Chapter 14 of *Crime*, edited by James Q. Wilson and Joan Petersilia. San Francisco: ICS Press.

Sherman, Lawrence, Janell Schmidt, Dennis Rogan, Douglas Smith, Patrick Gartin, Ellen Cohn, Dean Collins, and Anthony Bacich (1992). The variable effects of arrest on criminal careers: The Milwaukee domestic violence experiment. *The Journal of Criminal Law and Criminology* 83(1): 137–69.

Sloan, John (1991). The "new" female criminal revisited: Police officer attitudes about female criminality. *American Journal of Police* 10(4): 105–28.

Smith, Michael (1995). Law enforcement liability under section 1983. *Criminal Law Bulletin* 32(2): 128–50.

Sparger, Jerry and David Giacopassi (1992). Memphis revisited: A re-examination of police shootings after the *Garner* decision. *Justice Quarterly* 9(2): 211–25.

*Sparrow, Malcolm (1993). Integrating distinct managerial styles: The challenge for police leadership. *American Journal of Police* 12(2): 1–16.

Stotland, Ezra (1991). The effects of police work and professional relationships on health. *Journal of Criminal Justice* 19(4): 371–79.

*Tennenbaum, Abraham (1994). The influence of the *Garner* decision on police use of deadly force. *Journal of Criminal Law and Criminology* 81(1): 241–60.

*Tunnell, Kenneth and Larry Gaines (1992). Political pressures and influences on police executives: A descriptive analysis. *American Journal of Police* 11(1): 1–16.

Vinzant, Janet and Lane Crothers (1994). Street level leadership: The role of patrol officers in community policing. *Criminal Justice Review* 19(2): 189–211.

*Walker, Samuel (1993). Does anyone remember team policing? Lessons of the team policing experience for community policing. *American Journal of Police* 12(4): 33–55.

*Walker, Samuel and Vic Bumphus (1992). The effectiveness of civilian review: Observations on recent trends and new issues regarding the civilian review of police. *American Journal of Police* 11(4): 1–26.

Walker, Samuel and Lorie Fridell (1992). Forces of change in police policy and the impact of *Tennessee v. Garner. American Journal of Police* 11(3): 97–112.

Webster, Barbara and Edward Connors (1993). Police methods for identifying community problems. *American Journal of Police* 12(4): 75–101.

*Weisheit, Ralph, Edward Wells, and David Falcone (1994). Community policing in a small town and rural America. *Crime and Delinquency* 40(4): 549–67.

Welsh, Wayne (1993). Changes in arrest policies as a result of court orders against county jails. *Justice Quarterly* 10(1): 89–120.

*Williams, Frank and Carl Wagoner (1992). Making the police proactive: An impossible task for improbable reasons. *Police Forum* 2(2): 1–5.

Worden, Alissa (1993). The attitudes of women and men in policing: Testing conventional and contemporary wisdom. *Criminology* 31(2): 203–41.

Worden, Robert (1993). Toward equity and efficiency in law enforcement: Differential police response. *American Journal of Police* 12(4): 1–32.

CULTURAL SENSITIVITY REDISCOVERED: DEVELOPING TRAINING STRATEGIES FOR POLICE OFFICERS

by

David E. Barlow

and

Melissa Hickman Barlow

Abstract

The most important issue in law enforcement for the 1990s is the rediscovery of human relations in police work. In many ways, the mood of the nineties is reminiscent of the urgency of the 1960s with regard to instilling in the police officer a greater sensitivity to diverse cultures and lifestyles. Two decades of focus on technology, professionalism, and war-like strategies in law enforcement has left a void in policing in the area of human relations. This article reviews the history of police-minority relations and compares the development of cultural sensitivity training in a southern state and in a large midwestern city in order to outline the critical issues involved in human relations training for police. Finally, it provides a practical guide for constructing lesson plans and instructing such seminars.

Introduction

In the summer of 1992, the eyes of the nation were focused on scenes of violence and despair in South Central Los Angeles, in the wake of the acquittal of four police officers on charges of police brutality against Rodney King. Across the United States, consumers of news from all walks of life, who had witnessed the video taped police beating Mr. King, were now faced with comprehending the significance of the acquittals for our national life. For days it appeared from the visual images of destruction on our television screens that our country was coming apart, and that a principal malefactor in this destruction was the extreme tension in relations between police and racial minorities.

An earlier version of this paper was presented at the 1992 Academy of Criminal Justice Sciences meetings in Pittsburgh, Pennsylvania.

1

A recurring theme in comments from both citizens and experts, called upon by news reporters to offer their observations, was that problems in police-minority relations are not unique to Los Angeles. The riots in South Central Los Angeles were viewed as evidence that racial tensions are at a boiling point and that, in particular, relations between police and minorities are at a critical juncture. Certainly this is not the first such moment in U.S. history. As recently as the 1960s, the same concerns about police brutality, and the pressing need to make police officers more sensitive to diverse cultures and lifestyles, were voiced in response to police treatment of student protesters and civil rights activists. Yet law enforcement policy in the two decades between the end of the 1960s and the onset of the 1990s has been characterized by a focus on technology, professionalization, and a war-on-crime approach which has left a void in policing in the area of human relations.

In the aftermath of events in Los Angeles, and in relation to incidents and circumstances in cities throughout the United States, criminal justice professionals are demonstrating a renewed interest in human relations and cultural sensitivity training in law enforcement. The first section of this paper presents a brief history of police-minority relations in the United States. This is followed by discussion of two contemporary initiatives in the development of human relations and cultural sensitivity training with which the authors have personally been involved. The first two sections provide a foundation for the third, which outlines issues which we view as central to the development of cultural diversity awareness training if it is to learn from the past, directly address the valid concerns of both police and minorities in the present, and improve relations between police and the multicultural community for the future.

History Of Police-Minority Relations

Problematic relations between police and minorities have a long tradition in the United States (Barlow, Barlow, and Chiricos, 1993). The mission of the first relatively modern-style municipal police department, established in the 1740s in Charleston, South Carolina, was to catch runway slaves (Walker, 1980). In the early half of the 19th Century, when small municipal police departments were being formed in Boston, New York and Philadelphia, private police agencies dominated the scene. Private police were hired to protect the private property of industry, break strikes, attack labor organizers, and quell riots. The people most likely to be involved in these conflicts were the poor, working class immigrants who labored in these industries. Not only were police responsible for workplace control, both public and private police also played a major role in regulating the recreational activities of the working class. They enforced vagrancy, Sunday closing, liquor, gambling and prostitution laws, which were by design extremely discriminatory against the poor, urban working class. These activities brought the police into direct conflict with Irish, Italian, and German immigrants in the major urban, seacoast and industrial areas (Harring, 1983).

Interestingly, the very immigrant communities which were the targets of much police control were recruiting pools for both private and public police. The concept of hiring minorities to police minorities was an important strategy of social control. Immigrant recruits knew the people and the community. They could gather information more easily and could communicate more effectively in their communities than could nonindigenous officers. Their presence on the police force helped to conceal the inherently discriminatory nature of police work, as members of immigrant minorities occupied the front lines in the social control of the working poor (Harring, 1983; Spitzer, 1981). The social control strategy of minorities policing minorities is a phenomenon which suggests the usefulness of viewing the police as occupying a "contra-dictory class location" (Wright, 1979). While police themselves typically belong to non-propertied working classes, a primary function of police in U.S. history has been to protect the interests of propertied classes.

In the latter half of the 19th century, the municipal police replaced private police as the primary social control agency in the United States. Public police experienced a major transformation which included efforts to centralize authority and supervision, to increase employee discipline, to improve technology, and to improve working conditions and benefits. The two primary goals in police agencies of this period were to remove politics from policing and to make police officers more professional. The outcome of these efforts was the creation of large municipal police departments, with greatly improved technology and with civil service protection for police officers. However, protecting industry property, breaking strikes, attacking labor organizing activities, and suppressing riots, as well as regulating the recreational activities of the working poor remained the central activities of police work. The strategy of drawing police recruits from within minority immigrant groups continued. At the same time, the shift from private police, employed by private industry, to public police, employed by local governments, lent considerable legitimacy to police in their role as social regulators (Harring, 1983).

3

Throughout the 20th century, professionalization continued to be a popular theme in connection with modern policing. The professional model focused on creating police officers who are legalistic, emotionally detached and apolitical (Goldstein, 1990). Part of this process included removing from police officers any sense of loyalty to their own ethnic groups. Professionalism was also sought in order to reduce police corruption, brutality, favoritism, differential treatment, and selective enforcement. For the professional police officer, emotions and personal prejudices had no place in police work (Walker, 1980; Richardson, 1980).

Since the 1940s, dramatic demographic changes have occurred in the large urban areas of the United States. Heavy African-American and Hispanic migration, combined with white flight into the suburbs, has transformed the racial composition of urban communities. The racial and ethnic compositions of urban police forces, however, have not reflected these demographic changes (U.S. Department of Commerce, 1991). The connection between urban police and the communities in which they work is no longer cemented by commonly shared experiences, cultural traditions and language. In a sense, alien cultures have been thrust together in an inherently antagonistic situation.

Spitzer (1981) notes that, as racial and ethnic minorities begin the process of self-empowerment through political and social movements, many of their activities bring them into direct conflict with the police. According to Friedman (1981), as protests and demonstrations are met with the long arm of the law, subordinate groups seeking to produce fundamental change are under increasing pressure to enhance their side of the power relationship through the threat of violence and damage to property owned and controlled by the powers that be. As the most visible and accessible symbol of the repressive social structure which is so resistant to the desired social change, police are often the force with which subordinate groups seeking more power must contend (Bittner, 1980). In this context, police officers are frequently discourteous and even violent in their interactions with insurgent groups. Police and minority activists each view themselves as victims of deteriorating relations and violent confrontations. Conflicts between police and minorities became particularly explosive within the civil rights movement as it progressed into the 1960s (Goldstein, 1990; Walker, 1980; Harris and Wicker, 1988).

The ineffectiveness of the police in controlling the riots of the 1960s led to the implementation of a number of strategies to improve police

Barlow, Barlow 101

operations (Barlow, Barlow, Chiricos, 1993). For a time, local law enforcement was inundated with funds, particularly from the federal government. Much of this money went into technological developments as well as specialized training in the use of force, criminal investigation, and officer survival strategies. In the early 1960s, programs and training blocks were developed to improve police community relations, especially with groups who were involved in confrontations with the police. Some of this training focused on dealing with all types of civil disturbances, but the most critical issue was clearly the relationship between the police and the black community (Platt et al., 1982).

Although police departments began to implement police-community relations training and programs in the 1960s, efforts were often half-hearted and, in fact, were soon abandoned, as new technology and training on the "hard" side of policing were emphasized (Walker, 1980; Brown, 1973). In the 1970s, community relations programs were transformed into small-budget crime prevention units and DARE programs. Technological advancements and an increasing number of law suits against police resulted in the funneling of large proportions of training budgets to firearms training, officer survival training, defensive tactics instruction, computer and equipment seminars, and legal instruction. Human relations took a back seat to numerous other law enforcement concerns. There was an almost unquestioned acceptance of the professional model in policing, which, while it purports to reduce the degree to which the personal prejudices of police officers will affect policing, also is in direct conflict with goals of creating more friendly and personal relations between police and community members (Goldstein, 1990; Brown, 1973).

Although there appeared to be some improvement in police-minority relations in the 1970s, the situation deteriorated significantly in the decade of the 1980s (Goldstein, 1990). What took place in the 1980s to reignite tensions between police and minorities? Given the history and development of police departments as organizations charged with controlling marginalized groups, perhaps the most fundamental answer is that the strategies of the 1960s and 1970s were simply not successful. A number of factors appear as more specific explanations. First, African-Americans as a group did not experience the anticipated improvements in their social and economic conditions following the civil rights movement. Disparity between the median black income and the median white income was not reduced and the criminal justice system continues to deal with disproportional numbers of Blacks and Hispanics (U.S.

5

Department of Commerce, 1991; Flanagan and Maguire, 1990). Police agencies were originally created to regulate working class activities and to police those people who are in the streets. As long as racial minorities are disproportionately represented in lower income groups, they will bear the brunt of crime and the criminal justice system (Spitzer, 1981). The success of specific strategies to improve police-minority relations is likely to be short lived within this context.

An important factor in the objective economic conditions of racial minorities in the United States, as well as in their relations with the criminal justice system, is the degree to which racism operates within social and economic relations. Presidential leadership in the 1980s and early 1990s has virtually legitimized racism in the United States, by identifying affirmative action, welfare mothers, hiring and promotion quotas, and illegal aliens as primary contributors to our country's political and economic problems. Many consider the 1988 Bush campaign's use of the visual image of Willie Horton, a black offender who committed violent crimes while on parole, as a flagrant manipula-tion of racial fears for political purposes. More recently, speakers at the 1992 Republican National Convention declared war on multiculturalism in the United States. The Reagan and Bush administrations legitimized apprehensions about homosexuals by responding slowly to the AIDS crisis, by refusing to openly recognize their lifestyle as acceptable, and by attacking the National Endowment for the Arts for its support of art which featured homosexual activities. They alienated many women, by supporting restrictions on the freedom of choice in the area of abortion rights, by being slow to give women equality in the armed forces, and by undermining the Equal Rights Amendment. At this writing, the effects of the new Clinton Administration on the multi-cultural agenda remain to be seen. Within this political climate, racial and ethnic minorities, gay and lesbian activists and women's groups seek to transcend their marginalized status and gain greater political and economic power. A critical component of such efforts toward empowerment is gaining equal treatment and protection from the police.

Two Contemporary Initiatives In Human Relations/Cultural Sensitivity Training

Events and conditions have, in the past few years, given rise to numerous initiatives in the development of human relations and cultural diversity awareness training across the United States. The authors have been directly involved with such initiatives in two separate regions of the country. In each of these circumstances, very specific events prompted community leaders concerned with the civil rights of racial and ethnic minorities and homosexuals, to call into question police-minority relations. While the heightened public focus on police-minority relations was precipitated in each instance by specific incidents, community leaders in both areas were careful to emphasize that these incidents are indicative of long-term problems in police-minority relations. Examination of the circumstances surrounding efforts to develop human relations and cultural sensitivity training in South Carolina beginning at the onset of the 1990s, and in the Milwaukee area in 1991/92, provide a number of insights into critical issues in the development of such training.

In both South Carolina and Milwaukee, the push for sensitivity training has come from grassroots community organizations. A police shooting of a young, African-American man in South Carolina prompted the South Carolina Chapter of the National Rainbow Coalition to call for an evaluation of police training in the areas of human relations, racism, crisis intervention, and use of force. The shooting was viewed not as an isolated incident, but as indicative of widespread problems throughout the state in police relations with African-Americans. In response to the concerns of the Rainbow Coalition and other groups, the executive director of the South Carolina Criminal Justice Academy (SCCJA) created a Human Relations Curriculum Committee to develop human relations training for police officers throughout the state of South Carolina.

In Wisconsin, the problem is viewed primarily as a problem of the city of Milwaukee and the close outlying suburbs, although cultural diversity training initiatives are being developed in other parts of the state as well. The impetus for the development of cultural sensitivity training for police officers in Milwaukee came from incidents related to the Jeffrey Dahmer serial murder case. Two police officers were fired after it was discovered that they released a 14 year old Laotian boy back into Dahmer's custody after Dahmer convinced them that the problem was a "lovers quarrel." Not only did this interaction occur in a predominately African-American community, but most of Dahmer's victims were African-American, and all were gay (or bisexual) men of color. Reports concerning police handling of the earlier incident involving Dahmer and his young victim, as well as their disregard for the concerns of three African-American women who had attempted to alert them to the fact that the young Laotian boy was, indeed, a boy, inflamed the Asian, African-American,

7

Hispanic, and gay communities. This case brought to a boiling point long standing tensions between the police and Milwaukee's multicultural community. In response, the Mayor appointed a Blue Ribbon Commission on Police-Community Relations, the Milwaukee Police Department issued a Request for Proposals for Cultural Diversity Awareness Training, and efforts to develop and implement cultural diversity training for criminal justice personnel are emerging in Milwaukee and in other parts of Wisconsin (Barlow, Barlow, and Stojkovic, 1992).

Initial efforts to develop human relations and cultural sensitivity training in these two regions have involved different logistic and political concerns. As a statewide criminal justice academy, SCCJA is responsible for basic and in service training for all police officers in South Carolina. With the approval of the South Carolina Training Council, this academy has the authority to impose training requirements upon police officers throughout the state. The focal point for training issues, therefore, is located in the state police academy, rather than within particular police departments.

The situation in Wisconsin is much more decentralized, with training for police officers taking place in a combination of basic training academies, employer based training institutes and within technical colleges throughout the state. The Wisconsin Law Enforcement Training and Standards Board, through its staffing arm in the Department of Justice Training and Standards Bureau, sets employment standards for police officers in the state and sets the content for basic recruit training. Beyond setting the content for basic training, they simply act in an advisory capacity and oversee annual training requirements.

Although all police departments in the Milwaukee area are currently under scrutiny, the Milwaukee Police Department (MPD) is receiving the brunt of indictments regarding police treatment of diverse groups within the community. The Milwaukee Police Department is faced with policing a multi-ethnic community in the context of an onslaught of complaints by a variety of community groups who are calling for a police department that is more responsive to all of its citizens.

In contrast, concerns in South Carolina are more directly focused on relations between police and African-Americans. The Jesse Jackson presidential campaign in 1988 brought together diverse groups of African-American activists, community leaders and public officials, transforming them into a viable political force in the state. Gays and

Lesbians, Hispanics, Asians, and Women's organizations in South Carolina do not presently have the political presence in the state to have a significant impact on state-wide policing. In fact, African-Americans in South Carolina, outside the context of a phenomenon such as the Jackson campaign, are not nearly as politically active and visible as community groups in Milwaukee.

For this reason, the SCCJA received only limited political pressure to deal with police-minority tensions in the state. The director of the academy, however, made a conscious and decisive effort to take the lead in addressing this issue for all police agencies in the state. As mentioned above, faced with the Rainbow Coalition's concerns following the police shooting of a young African-American man in the late 1980s, and in the context of a number of other incidents indicative of growing racial tensions in the state, the director established a permanent committee composed of community representatives and experienced minority police executives to develop, implement, guide and evaluate Human Relations Training at the basic, in-service and supervisory levels. This Human Relations Curriculum Committee's mission is to:

> assist the South Carolina Criminal Justice Academy in the development and evaluation of a Human Relations curriculum that will enable South Carolina Law Enforcement to perform its duties so that, each citizen is accorded his or her civil and human rights in accordance with the law.

Public forums and media releases were conducted in order to get community input and support. The curriculum development process began late in the summer of 1990 and is still continuing.

In contrast, the Milwaukee Police Department did not take the initiative in developing human relations training until community sentiment reached a boiling point and a blue ribbon commission was appointed to examine police-community relations in connection with the Jeffrey Dahmer case. The Mayor of Milwaukee established a Citizen's Commission on Police-Community Relations to:

> examine the Milwaukee Police Department's performance of service to the public, particularly in the areas of responsiveness and sensitivity to diversity within the community and to make recommendations for improved police-community relations (Mayor's Citizen Commission on Police-Community Relations, 1991: ii).

The Commission concluded that "good relationships and effective policing are best fostered by community-oriented policing with appropriate training, in a Department which values both its own diversity and the community's (Mayor's Citizen Commission on Police-Community Relations, 1991: i). In response, the Milwaukee Police Department issued a request for proposals for developing and conducting cultural diversity awareness training, emphasizing that it should integrate the philosophy of community policing (Koleas, 1991: 1).

Curriculum Development

Drawing from the history of police-minority relations in the United States, personal experiences in conducting cultural diversity awareness training, and interaction with other individuals involved in such training, a number of common obstacles and key strategies emerge as significant. Many of these strategies have been around in theory, if not always in practice, for a number of years (Cizon and Smith, 1970).

Key Strategies

Know the audience. First of all, the instructor must know his or her audience and be sympathetic to the difficulties faced by police officers. Approaching topics as sensitive as police-minority relations from a purely academic standpoint makes it all too easy for officers to dismiss the training as irrelevant to life in the real world of policing.

Create a positive learning environment. Once again, the sensitive nature of the topic makes it particularly important that participants in the training not be alienated by a setting in which they feel they are under attack. For this reason, the use of community activists as instructors should be avoided. A basic lack of understanding on both sides of the training relationship is likely to occur when community activists are utilized as trainers. The simple maxim that intimidated and infuriated officers are not in a trainable state is fundamental to the training process. Likewise, it is important to avoid mixing community members with officers in training, to decrease the potential for accusations and misunderstandings. Trainees should be as much like each other as possible, so that they feel safe and unthreatened by individuals in the training group. The nature of the training is threatening enough. Conducting it within an already threatening environment will block the communication process.

10

Establish the practical relevance of the training. The instructor should make every effort to illustrate the relevance of the course material for the daily activities and concerns of police officers. Demonstrating the significance of cultural diversity awareness for such concerns as officer safety, issues of legal liability, and law enforcement effectiveness is an important part of assuring police officers of the relevance of the training. Techniques such as relating personal experiences and providing every-day examples of concepts go a long way toward making the information intelligible to the audience.

Include lectures and group work. General teaching strategies should include a mix of lectures, in which scholarly knowledge is presented, and group activities, such as group discussion and practical skills development through exercises and role play. Reviews of previous sensitivity training programs have shown that they are often too academic or lecture-oriented (St. George, 1991). Combining lectures with group work serves to create multiple avenues through which students can get beyond the natural resistance to new ideas. Conferencing allows trainees to interact with the ideas presented in the lectures, to question and reflect upon their validity, and to develop unique personal solutions to problems.

Know and express the limits of the training. Cultural diversity is a subject which is best handled through an exchange of ideas, careful thought and self-reflection. Unlike traditional police training courses on matters of a more technical nature, cultural sensitivity training cannot provide simple answers. This is an area of contention for police officers, because they are looking for specific guidelines and universal formulae, which, when applied, will immunize them against complaints and law suits. Obviously, these cannot be provided. This message should be conveyed to trainees early on, so that their expectations are realistic.

Emphasize human relations skills. It should also be pointed out that the material is not radically new and that each officer possesses the essential skills within him or herself. The instructor's role should be that of a facilitator rather than an educator. It is hoped that through an exchange of information between the officers and the instructor, and among the officers themselves, knowledge and understanding of people will be enhanced. It is important to stress to participants that the purpose of the class is simply to fine tune the human relations skills that they already possess. The intent will be to make them conscious of their own personal biases, how these biases affect their behavior, and how that

11

behavior may be interpreted by others. As a matter of fact, the goal of the training seminar is to help police officers perform their job in a way that is less likely to alienate any member of society, not just members of particular groups. The atmosphere should be as non-threatening as possible. The instructor plays a critical role in assuring the officers that it is not the purpose of the course to place blame or to condemn them.

Use trainers committed to the training. In addition, a good human relations skills instructor must be highly committed to the subject. She or he must convey to officers that this a worthwhile course and that it is in their own best interest to fully embrace the subject matter. At the same time, trainers should be prepared for anger and distrust among the officers and willing to do the work required to move the groups to a more positive state. Cultural diversity training is often implemented in response to incidents or allegations of discrimination. Thus, officers may view the training session as a demonstration that they are being blamed for problems in police-minority relations.

Recognize the importance of terminology. Part of the difficulty in getting officers to be receptive and listen to what the cultural sensitivity instructor has to say originates in the title of the training seminar itself. The key buzz words are "sensitivity" and "culture." Both these terms alienate the officers and place them in a defensive posture. For example, "sensitivity" is inherently accusatory, because the assumption is that officers are insensitive. The very concept of sensitivity runs counter to the image which many police officers hold of their role in society — as enforcers of the law. In addition, framing the discussion in terms of issues of "culture" results in the training being viewed as "just another affirmative action program." Police officers generally do not respond well to courses designed to give special treatment to minority cultures or to promote affirmative action. They maintain that their job is to enforce the law uniformly, without regard to race, class, or gender. For this reason, it is important to not let the focus of the training appear to be toward any one group. Human relations training should be presented as a universal issue that can help the officers deal with all segments of the population more effectively.

Training Blocks

With these key strategies in mind, it is possible to outline a model set of training blocks for cultural diversity awareness, or, preferably, human relations training. The training blocks discussed below incorporate what are suggested here as critical components of such training.

First block: Selling the training. After trainees have been introduced to the topic, the goal of the first block of training is to sell the program to the officers. Women and minority instructors will face additional difficulties in selling the training to white, male officers, who may dismiss them as simply "crying racism" or "blaming sexism" for their own personal failures. The course objectives should focus on positive police improvement and emphasize the practical importance of developing good community relations, such as reducing law suits and enhancing safety and effectiveness. The following are some sample course objectives:

1. Increase the students' knowledge base in reference to the history and special concerns of various segments of the civilian and police population;
2. Develop and enhance human relations skills;
3. Reduce the frequency of inflammatory language used by practitioners on the radio, the phone, or while interacting with the public;
4. Reduce the number of citizen complaints;
5. Reduce the number of law suits filed;
6. Reduce the frequency of injuries accrued by police officers and civilians.

The ability to motivate trainees to embrace such objectives is the key to being an effective instructor. It is critically important for the instructor to avoid accusatory, derogatory and condemning language (St. George, 1991). The material, especially the group discussion assignments and role plays, must be relevant and realistic (St. George, 1991; Cizon and Smith, 1970). The instructor should reinforce objectives by allowing the officers to form groups and develop their own ideas and present them to the rest of the class. In support of this, the first group assignment should be to identify why human relations skills training is beneficial to police officers. It must demonstrate that the training will:

1. Improve law enforcement effectiveness;
2. Enhance officer safety;
3. Reduce officer liability;
4. Focus closely on what police actually do;
5. Improve performance evaluations;
6. Make a line officer a better candidate for promotion;

13

7. Reduce internal and external stress;
8. Increase understanding of the historical contribution of cultural diversity to America culture.

The focus should be on human dignity, individual rights and justice. It is this author's position that police officers respond well to these issues.

Second block: Recognizing personal prejudices. The goal of the second training block is to help officers recognize and accept their own personal prejudices while reflecting on how these prejudices affect behavior. This is an extremely sensitive and difficult part of the training. It is best if the instructor begins this process by providing a very neutral definition of prejudice or bias and then uses examples which reflect the instructor's own personal prejudices throughout the presentation. Groups can then search for examples in each of the following categories:

1. Assumptions and prejudices are necessary for social functioning, communication, etc.;
2. Certain prejudices are a vital part of officer safety and law enforcement;
3. Police officers' prejudices and attitudes are reflective of those of U.S. society in general;
4. Prejudices and attitudes differ from behaviors and action;
5. Identification of inner prejudices aids the officer in gaining control of his or her actions;
6. Fear, emotions, stereotypes and prejudices have a potential negative impact on police behavior/action.

The groups play a vital role in facilitating self-reflection and self-awareness. Again, honesty and open class discussions during group presentations must be encouraged. This lesson plan attempts to accomplish this task by removing bad connotations from such terms as prejudice and bias. The purpose is to move from exploring productive prejudices, to neutral ones and finally to examining the destructive ones that may negatively affect officer behavior.

Third block: Police-minority relations. The purpose of the third lesson block is to provide information on the general relationship between minority communities and the police. The instructor must play his or her most active role as a lecturer during this part of the training. The instructor must provide information on the historical relationship between police and immigrant minority groups and the poor working class

14

in order to demonstrate the *inherently* discriminatory nature of police work, and to take some of the pressure off the officers as individuals. Also, current research should be presented concerning the public's perceptions of the police, and police perceptions of the public, to demonstrate the lack of understanding and communication between the two. Statistics on the discriminatory outcomes in criminal justice for minorities and the poor may be presented in order to help explain the fear and hostility which minority groups may harbor against police. As much as possible data presented should come from the jurisdictions policed by participants in the training. This information is especially critical for young white officers who have grown up in suburban environments, who may have no direct knowledge of the context in which problems in police-minority relations arise. Finally, this session should be followed by a discussion of the potential impact of fears, emotions, stereotypes, and prejudices on the public's behavior toward the police.

It should be stressed by the instructor that these data are presented for the purpose of helping officers to better understand the tension between themselves and certain segments of the community. It is a natural tendency for the officers to interpret the presentation of such data as an assault on officers, and as blaming them for discriminatory outcomes. They must be assured that the data are presented to help them understand the roots of fear and hostility toward police among certain segments of the population.

Fourth block: Specific skills training. The goal of the fourth lesson block is to teach specific human relations skills which can help police officers reduce tension and conflict in interactions with community members. The focus here is on improving basic communication between the police and the community. Traditional lessons on barriers to interpersonal communication and strategies for improving communication are presented. Since most of the officers will have heard of many of strategies before, they should be presented in a way that does not insult the officers' intelligence. For instance, they might be described by the instructor as a refresher course. In addition, the officers should be allowed to develop some of their own strategies for good communication within their discussion groups.

At the departmental level, community-oriented policing is suggested as probably the best way to improve communication between police and minority groups. As discussed above, community policing is in direct conflict with many of the precepts of the professional model (Goldstein,

1990). This fundamental contradiction is a source of confusion for many officers. They are unsure about what the public wants. This exasperation is heightened by the information that African-Americans, Hispanics, juveniles, homosexuals and other segments of the community have two primary concerns in relation to the police: being over-policed and being under-protected. These groups often feel that they are over-policed, because they perceive that the police are harassing them and are too involved in their personal lives. On the other hand, they also feel that they are not receiving adequate police protection, as evidenced by their proportionately high levels of victimization (Walker, 1992; Barlow, 1992). When police officers express their understandable confusion about what the community wants them to do, it is a good time to reiterate the importance of communication between the police and the community.

Role play is vitally important here to allow officers to demonstrate human relations skills. Video-taping the role play allows for self-critique. An example of a useful role play situation is to set up a mock community-oriented policing initial meeting. This provides an opportunity for trainees themselves to verbalize the concerns of community members, as they understand them, as well as giving them the opportunity to practice skills which foster good communication.

A critical component of this segment of the training is impressing upon participants the power of language. This point cannot be over-empha-sized. A major facet of police work is what has been referred to as a "working language" (Reiss, 1971). According to Walker (1992), some studies have interpreted racial and sexist jokes as being "in good humor," maintaining that such jokes release stress and do not result in differential treatment. However, this author contends that these jokes and comments in everyday conversation among police or on radio transmissions are serious and need to be dealt with in an aggressive manner. Whether these jokes are in good humor or are mean spirited, their impact on fellow officers and on community members is the same. Such jokes place minority and women police officers in hostile and unjustly uncomfortable working conditions. Regardless of the intention of the offending party, discriminatory jokes and language result in law suits for harassment from other officers and from citizens. When these incidents are made public, citizen perceptions of the police are seriously tarnished. The suggestion that discriminatory language and jokes are relatively benign does not take into account that language has long been used as a propaganda tool to facilitate the persecution of certain groups of people. To the degree that language reduces human beings to some aspect of their physical being (i.e. to body parts, skin color, or specific sexual practices) it dehumanizes them and desensitizes the speaker to their feelings. This makes it easier to harm them or to ignore their rights as human beings.

It can be anticipated that the discussion of jokes and offensive language, and other seemingly mild forms of discrimination, will likely produce a defensive attitude on the part of the officers. It is in this area, however, that much of the training should be concentrated. Blatant and violent forms of discrimination are easily identified and quickly condemned by most police officers. They occur primarily among a fringe group of police whose behavior is not likely to be altered by any amount of training. Most officers would agree that the only way to deal with this fringe is simply to remove them from law enforcement.

The issues upon which the training should focus are the more subtle forms of racism, sexism, and prejudice. Evidence of these is found not only in language but also in arrest decisions and "attitude tests," which officers give to suspects. For example, important factors in arrest decisions include both the demeanor of the suspect and that of the victim (Walker, 1992). To what extent is this demeanor, and the outcome of the attitude test, affected by prejudice, stereotypes, cultural differences or fear of the unfamiliar? To what extent are police-citizen interactions heightened to unnecessary levels of anxiety, tension and possibly even violence because of fear? Other factors affecting arrest decisions are the characteristics of the neighborhood or the family. Again, to what extent are decisions based on cultural biases? It is important for participants to explore their decision-making to answer these questions on their own. This process is very difficult because of the naturally defensive attitude that police officers have with regard to issues of discrimination. This attitude develops in response to the perceived challenge to the officers' level of fairness and professionalism. Addressing these issues touches a sensitive nerve because it opens the door to the possibility that officers may ultimately have to admit that some of their beliefs and feelings in fact produce discrimination.

Fifth block: Management issues. A final lesson block concentrates on management issues and is intended for police executives, managers and supervisors. The purpose of this block is to provide information on the critical role of chief executives and to offer management strategies for improving police-community interactions. Police managers need to receive this training first for a number of reasons (St. George, 1991). First, this sends a clear message to the rank-and-file, and to the public, that the administration does not perceive the line officer as "the problem." Second, in order for cultural diversity/human relations training to have any impact whatsoever it must be fully supported, in both actions and words, by administration. Third, in order for the training program to have an impact it must be part of a comprehensive strategic plan to build better police-community relations and to provide better law enforcement.

This training block includes several topics, but the overall purpose is to hammer home the above three points. One topic is the impact of management style on officers' policing style. For example, when officers are treated by supervisors with mistrust, with demeaning language, or disrespect the officers may transfer that approach to their interactions with the public. Managers must lead by example. To be successful in improving police-community relations the department needs a full, action-oriented administrative commitment from the police chief on down to the sergeants and field training officers. This commitment involves a critical review of management strategies, the award system, the general orders, recruiting, training, performance evaluations, and promotions so that they can be brought in line with the values of good community relations and possibly community-oriented policing. In addition an environment of intolerance for discrimination, mistreatment or improper police actions at every supervisory level must be established.

Police administrators also play an important direct role in creating good police-community relations through their own interaction with the community. Part of this role includes creating a citizen complaint system which is proactive and provides automatic feedback. A second important role is building good media relations. Good police officers are not enough. Police administrators must take an active role in marketing a positive image of their officers to the public. Another important role for management is to enhance the recruitment, hiring, and retention of women and minority police officers and, more generally, officers who demonstrate an appreciation for the concerns of diverse segments of the population. The police administrator sets the tone for the entire police department and human relations skills training must be part of a comprehensive package that actively seeks to develop a police department and a community which are responsive to each other's needs.

In sum, human relations training is a complex and difficult enterprise. The instructor is in constant danger of losing his or her audience by producing the appearance that they are blaming the officers. Officers attending training of this kind want to be dazzled by an interesting and upbeat session. Training in human relations and cultural diversity awareness does not lend itself to a dazzling approach because there are no set answers that are universal for all police officers or for all members of the public. The overall goal is to encourage officers to be aware, to listen, to speak clearly, to respect other human beings, and, most of all, to be able to empathize with human troubles.

Conclusion

This paper has addressed the need for police departments to develop human relations training and it has provided ideas concerning how this can be accomplished. However, one very important factor in this process should not be overlooked: the responsibility of college-level criminal justice and criminology programs. Several studies have provided evidence that college educated police officers are no more likely to be understanding of human suffering or less prejudiced than those with only a high school education (Worden, 1990). The college professors who conduct these studies are quick to blame the police subculture and other social factors for this phenomenon. If college education has no significant impact on a police officer's level of tolerance and sensitivity, then our criminal justice programs have failed. It is unreasonable to expect police academies to effectively teach cultural diversity awareness and appreciation, if college programs in criminal justice neglect these issues. Programs do exist in which classes encourage, support and demand tolerance of human differences, empathy for human suffering, and appreciation for human diversity. Criminal justice programs are well advised to adopt this approach to their unique subject matter, for human relations skills are more important to the real issues in policing than all the computer, firearm and defensive tactics skills combined.

References

Barlow, D. E., Barlow, M. H., and Chiricos, T. G. (1993). Long economic cycles and the criminal justice system in the U.S. *Crime, Law and Social Change, 19*, 143-169.

Barlow, M. H. (1992). "A youth activities plan for the city of Kenosha, Wisconsin." Unpublished research report sponsored by the Kenosha Mayor's Youth Commission.

Barlow, M. H., Barlow, D. E., and Stojkovic, S. (1992). The media, the police and the multicultural community. An unpublished paper presented at the annual meetings of the Society for the Study of Social Problems in Pittsburgh, Pennsylvania.

Bittner, E. (1980). *The functions of the police in modern society.* Cambridge, MA: Olegeschlager, Gunn, and Hain.

Brown, L. P. (1973). *The death of police community relations.* Washington, D.C.: Institute for Urban Affairs and Research.

Cizon, F. A. and Smith, W. H. T. (1970). *Some guidelines for successful police-community relations training programs.* Washington, D.C.: U.S. Government Printing Office.

Flanagan, T. J. and Maguire, K. (Eds.) (1990). *Sourcebook of criminal justice statistics.* Washington, D.C.: U.S. Department of Justice.

Friedman, L. M. (1981). "History, social policy and criminal justice." In Rothman and Wheeler (Eds.) *Social History and Social Policy.* New York: Academic Press.

Goldstein, H. (1990). *Problem-oriented policing.* New York: McGraw-Hill Publishers.

Harring, S. L. (1983). *Policing a class society: The experience of American cities, 1865-1915.* New Brunswick, New Jersey: Rutgers University Press.

Harris, F. R. and Wicker, T. (1988). *The Kerner report: The 1968 report of the National Advisory Commission on Civil Disorders.* New York: Pantheon Books.

Koleas, J. W. (1991). *Request for proposals: Diversity training for the city of Milwaukee Police Department.* Milwaukee: Milwaukee Police Department.

Mayor's Citizen Committee on Police-Community Relations. (1991). *A report to Mayor John O. Norquist and the Board of Fire and Police Commissioners.* Milwaukee: Fire and Police Commission.

Platt, T., Frappier, J., Ray, G., Shauffler, R., Trujillo, L., Cooper, L., Currie, E., and Harring, S. (1982). *The iron fist and the velvet glove: An analysis of the U.S. police.* (3rd ed.). San Francisco: Crime and Social Justice Associates.

Reiss, A. J. (1971). *The police and the public.* New Haven, CT: Yale University Press.

Richardson, J. F. (1980). "Police in America: Functions and control." In Inciardi and Faupel (Eds.), *History and Crime: Implications for Criminal Justice Policy.* Beverly Hills: Sage Publications.

Spitzer, S. (1981). "The political economy of policing." In Greenberg (Ed.) *Crime and Capitalism: Readings in Marxist Criminology.* Palo Alto, California: Mayfield Publishing Company.

St. George, J. (1991). "'Sensitivity' training needs rethinking." *Law Enforcement News.* New York: John Jay College of Criminal Justice/CUNY.

U.S. Department of Commerce. (1991). *Statistical abstracts of the United States: 1971-1988.* Washington, DC: U.S. Government Printing Office.

Walker, S. (1980). *Popular justice: A history of American criminal justice.* New York: Oxford University Press.

Walker, S. (1992). *The police in America: An introduction.* (2nd ed.) New York: McGraw-Hill Publishers.

Worden, R. E. (1990). "A badge and a baccalaureate: Policies, hypotheses, and further evidence." *Justice Quarterly, 7*(3), 565-592.

American Journal of Police Vol. 10 No. 2 1991   *53*

UNSAFE AT ANY SPEED: THE UTILITY OF POLICE PURSUITS

Michael B. Blankenship
James M. Moneymaker
Memphis State University

INTRODUCTION

Traditional thinking about the police has generally been confined to descriptions or prescriptions about either their purpose or their form. As a result, the literature regarding police functions is voluminous. Yet it is only recently that the focus has begun to shift from discerning the activities of the police towards understanding how they go about their task.

Bittner (1980) and Klockars (1985a; 1985b) advocate an abandonment of the "ends of policing" approach in favor of one that assesses the means by which the ends are achieved. As Klockars (1985b:9) so cogently argues, any "definition" of the police "must be based on the fundamental tool police use to do their work rather than on what they use that tool to do." That tool is the right to use non-negotiable coercive force to resolve problems that confront the police.

However, this definition is problematic because it fails to consider the value conflict between order maintenance and the enforcement of law. While the conventional wisdom may be that enforcing the law is essential to the preservation of order, law and order are not synonymous (Skolnick, 1975). The events leading to the decision in *Tennessee v. Garner* (471 U.S. 1) serve as a prime example. The annals of policing are replete with other instances in which the enforcement of law in such areas as narcotics interdiction, traffic enforcement, and vice repression have undermined respect for the rule of law, and consequently threatened the civil order.

Such actions by the police demonstrate the relationship between the means and the ends of policing. When viewed from a crime control (Packer, 1968) perspective, the ends justify the means; however, from a

21

due process viewpoint, the means employed can subvert the ends, thus placing them in competition with each other.

In the following sections, the utility of automobile pursuits of fleeing suspects is examined in terms of the conflict between enforcement of the law and order maintenance. Our analysis suggests that because of the potential for death, injury, and property loss, automobile pursuits offer efficacious opportunities for enforcing the law, but pose a continuing threat to order maintenance.

APPLICATION OF AN ETHICAL CONCEPT

The problem confronting us is a determination of whether the maintenance of order has priority over the enforcement of law. In effect, we are asking which goal, and which means to achieve it, are in the best interests of society. This question is a value judgment, and we would prefer a rational comprehensive method of resolving the conflict.

The term *ethics* is heard with increasing frequency with regard to attempts at regulating the conduct of individuals. For example, it is currently in vogue to speak of ethics laws or codes of ethics that regulate the behavior of government officials. Use of the term ethics in this manner presupposes that a determination of what constitutes "good" and "bad" behavior has already been made.

However, ethics has a much broader meaning. In Plato's dialogue, the *Crito*, Socrates appealed to a set of moral principles (i.e., never harm anyone) in making his decision whether to escape from prison or to remain and face his punishment. In essence, Socrates applied a set of moral principles to his circumstances in order to decide between right and wrong behavior. Therefore, we should think of ethics, in the broader sense, as a framework for decision making.

Richards (1985) argues that the application of ethics to policing allows researchers to focus on how the police should act, especially in conflicting circumstances. His plea for applied ethics rests on the belief that

it raises questions about the values served by an occupation and focuses upon how those ends are to be legitimately achieved. Logically it demands, therefore, that policing's key concepts, such as "authority," "consent," "impartiality," "discretion," and "professionalism," are carefully unraveled

and defined so that value commitments and moral requirements are made explicit (p. 13).

One of the more popular ethical "frameworks" that can be used to
"unravel and define the value commitments" is utilitarianism. This ethical position is typically thought of as "the greatest good for the greatest
number." Frankena (1973:15) defines a utilitarian as someone who takes
the position that "....an act or rule of action is right if and only if it is, or
probably is, conducive to at least as great a balance of good over evil."

Using this ethical concept, the utility of an act or rule can be determined based on its actual or potential outcome for maximizing the greatest amount of good for the greatest number. However, before this determination can be made, *good* must first be defined. We suggest three basic principles that maximize the value commitments (i.e., good) between
the police and society. First is the principle that *all* human life is valuable. The second principle is that no one should be physically harmed.
And third, the only reason for interfering in the affairs of a group or an
individual, including the use of force, is to prevent physical harm to others.

Assuming that these three principles establish a minimum value
commitment, we can then decide if an act or rule has utility. For example, policies that permit the use of deadly force in defense of property
would be morally unacceptable because such a level of force would violate two of the three basic principles of our value commitment. On the
other hand, sobriety checkpoints should be permitted because they generally produce a greater "balance of good over evil." The inconvenience
of brief detainment is outweighed by the need to remove alcohol-im-
paired motorists from our streets and highways.

It is apparent then, that decisions by the police, especially those involving the use of deadly force, must be considered in terms of the consequences to the police and to society. Instances such as those in the
Garner decision suggest that adherence to existing case and statutory law
in formulating policies and procedures can be an insufficient safeguard to
ensure that civil liberties are maintained. Instead, it is necessary to analyze the value commitment in order to determine the utility of any act
undertaken by the police.

In the following section, the value commitments between the police
and society are more closely examined in terms of the utility of automobile pursuits by the police. While the use of firearms and other lethal
weapons available to the police has been the subject of increasing

scrutiny by the courts and the community, the lethal potential of police pursuits has only recently attracted similar attention.

THE UTILITY OF POLICE PURSUITS

The topic of police pursuit of suspects fleeing in automobiles has recently gained much notoriety. Automobiles rather than firearms may be the deadliest weapon in the police arsenal (Alpert & Anderson, 1986).

One study revealed that the greatest number of pursuits occurred after officers observed a traffic violation. Pursuits in these instances resulted in 30 percent of the total number of crashes, while approximately 50 percent of chases involving felons result in vehicular crashes (Alpert & Anderson, 1986). A similar pattern was present in a later study of police pursuits in Dade County, Florida (Alpert & Dunham, 1988). Thus, the data suggest that a significant number of police pursuits involve individuals accused of misdemeanor offenses, while most chases resulting in crashes involve fleeing felons.

However, the utility of pursuit in all circumstances must be questioned, given that a significant number of chases involve individuals accused of non-serious types of offenses. When viewed from an order maintenance perspective, we may conclude that the benefit derived from pursuing misdemeanants is not worth the possible endangerment of the public, the police officers, and the suspect. Therefore, a policy that allows pursuit in all circumstances may not be in the best interests of those involved, or of society in general. We maintain this position despite the evidence that most pursuits do not end in crashes resulting in either injury or injury (Alpert & Dunham, 1988), because the potential for a crash to occur is always present.

Because of the relatively low number of deaths, injuries, and amounts of property damage, Alpert and Dunham (1988) suggest that benefits derived from pursuits, such as deterrence, generally outweigh the actual costs. Their attitude reflects the value conflict between the ends and the means of policing, as Alpert and Dunham seem to treat crime repression as the superordinate goal of policing. We do not agree with the priority given that goal over others, but instead, are concerned with the means that are used to achieve that particular end. The likelihood of a beneficial outcome is reduced given the potential risk to the police, the suspect, and the public in order to capture a misdemeanor violator.

However, we must consider the exceptions, such as pursuits involving fleeing felons. Resolution of the value conflict between the means and ends of policing becomes more problematic because the pursued felon who is not apprehended poses a greater threat to the public than would most misdemeanants. On the other hand, the available data suggest that the probability of crashes during pursuits increases if the suspect is a fleeing felon. Yet, as in the case of misdemeanants, not every fleeing felon poses the same potential risk if not captured.

We maintain that the same proscription regarding pursuit of misdemeanants should apply to all non-violent offenders. We remain unconvinced of the utility of jeopardizing life and property solely for the sake of fulfilling the goal of crime control. However, an additional distinction must be made between pursuing all felons and only those that present a clear and present danger to the community if not apprehended immediately.

There is insufficient data to determine if more crashes result from the pursuit of violent felons than non-violent felons. However, we still suggest that pursuit of even the most violent felons should be limited in certain circumstances. For example, pursuit of an armed-robbery suspect at high speeds through heavily congested city streets during rush-hour traffic should usually be terminated in most circumstances.

In the preceding discussion, we have couched our argument in terms of a cost or benefit to society. However, such comparisons should be undertaken with caution. For example, the argument could be made that the benefit of apprehending a violent felon would usually outweigh the cost of any property damage or minor physical injuries that result from a crash during pursuit. Yet such conclusions may be incorrect because actual outcomes cannot be planned. As previously noted, it is the potential for a particular outcome that is of concern to us. Therefore, we maintain that the potential for serious injury or death still surpasses any benefit derived from the apprehension of a dangerous felon in these *very limited* situations.

In arriving at a solution to the problems posed by police pursuits, we suggest that future policies conform to case law regarding the use of deadly force (e.g., *Garner*). Policies outlining procedures for pursuits, like those regulating the use of firearms, should limit pursuits to those circumstances in which the suspect presents a clear and present danger to the community if not apprehended. However, the main reason for adopting and enforcing a stringent pursuit policy should not be based solely on the desire to avoid litigation. Instead, all police activities should be motivated by the utility of their actions.

CONCLUSIONS

Bittner (1980) warns that using the analogy between "war" and efforts to control crime creates unreasonable expectations, not the least of which is the expectation of winning. The war analogy may also inure us to the harm that results from crime control policies predicated on the enforcement of law. Anyone who suffers a loss, either financial or physical, resulting from enforcement of the law may be regarded as simply a victim of "war." In effect, this is seen as one of the costs paid by society in the effort to repress crime.

The preceding discussion of police pursuits exemplifies the problem; when viewed from a crime control perspective, all pursuits seem to have utility (e.g., specific or general deterrence, or incapacitation). However, on the basis of their utility, we suggest that many police pursuits are counterproductive. The broader aspect of our argument is that liberal pursuit policies are the antithesis of order maintenance.

Skolnick (1975) has noted that too much effort has been expended in reforming the police (e.g., professionalization) while scant attention has been paid to revising their philosophy. Society and the police may have fallen into an epistemological trap by believing that the enforcement of law is the only prescription for maintaining order. However, concepts such as community-oriented policing offer the hope of revitalizing the value commitment between society and the police by emphasizing the utility of police policies.

Yet we must remember that policy decisions are extremely complex and that our discussion of the problem has occurred within a limited context. There is no panacea to resolving conflicts between the police and the policed. Instead, we must continue to balance the need for ordered liberty while accommodating the desire to control crime. While empirical inquiry is essential to policy formulation, as has been illustrated, ethics as a framework for decision making also has a role in our understanding of the police function in our society.

26

NOTE

An earlier draft of this paper was presented at the annual meeting of the American Society of Criminology, November 8, 1989 in Reno, Nevada.

REFERENCES

Alpert, G.P. & P. Anderson (1986) "The Most Deadly Force: Police Pursuits." *Justice Quarterly* 3:1-14.

Alpert, G.P. & R.G. Dunham (1988) "Research on Police Pursuits." *American Journal of Police* 7:123-131.

Bittner, E. (1980) *The Functions of Police in Modern Society.* Cambridge, MA: Oelgeschlager, Gunn & Hain.

Frankena, W.K. (1973) *Ethics*, 2nd ed. Englewood Cliffs, NJ: Prentice-Hall.

Klockars, C.B. (1985a) "The Dirty Harry Problem." In F. Elliston & M. Feldberg (eds.) *Moral Issues in Police Work.* Totowa, NJ: Rowman & Allanheld.

_____ (1985b) *The Idea of Police.* Beverly Hills, CA: Sage Publications.

Mill, J.S. (1978) *On Liberty.* Indianapolis, IN: Hacket. (Original work published in 1859).

Packer, H.L. (1968) *The Limits of the Criminal Sanction.* Stanford, CA: Stanford University Press.

Richards, N. (1985) "A Plea for Applied Ethics." In J.R. Thackrah (ed.) *Contemporary Policing: An Examination of Society in the 1980s.* London: Sphere.

Skolnick, J. (1975) *Justice Without Trial*, 2nd ed. New York: John Wiley & Sons.

27

Police Corruption and Community Relations: Community Policing

Dorothy H. Bracey, *John Jay College of Criminal Justice, U.S.A.*

A while ago I listened to two school teachers introducing themselves. "I teach biology," said the secondary school teacher. "And you?" The primary school teacher answered, "I teach third graders."

This incident led to the reflection that an integral part of what we have been calling "professionalism" or "the professional attitude" has to do with impersonality. Teachers teach intellectual disciplines, not students. Doctors treat broken legs or cancerous tissue — not patients. Lawyers tackle legal issues, rather than solve clients' problems. And professional police officers enforce the law and control crime instead of helping people in trouble.

This aspect of professionalism was particularly attractive to police reformers concerned with eliminating corruption. By insisting that the police job consisted of the impersonal, non-discretionary enforcement of the criminal law, administrators could require police officers to eliminate "unnecessary" interaction with citizens, all of whom were viewed as potential corruptors.

Just as patients and clients have become dissatisfied with the impersonality of medicine and law — as they have demanded more caring and humane attitudes from professionals in these areas — citizens have become dissatisfied with the impersonality of professional policing. They have decided — and have often convinced police executives and other policy makers — that effective policing requires lengthy, stable, *personal* involvement of police officers in the community and with its residents. Community policing, problem-oriented policing, preventive policing, unit beat policing, neighborhood policing — all of these are responses to this decision and all of them are retreats from some of the most important tenets of police professionalism. For the pur-

poses of this gathering, the most important thing about this situation is that many of the anti-corruption measures of the past decades have been based on the concept of impersonal administration of the law and on the practices that follow logically from that concept. Community policing means that many of those practices will have to be changed. Let us examine some of them.

Perhaps the most important of these practices is the attempt to eliminate — or at least reduce — discretion. The most extreme form of this attempt is the doctrine — or the myth — of full enforcement. This doctrine, which follows from the assertion that law enforcement is the main component of the police job, holds that police officers have the duty to issue a summons or make an arrest whenever they see a violation of the criminal law. In its less extreme form, it acknowledges that full enforcement is not always possible, but asserts that discretion is properly exercised only in the making of policy and that lower-ranking officers must consistently carry out that policy; even where these doctrines are honored mainly in the breach, they still exert influence on the behavior of members of the organization and also provide administrators with a tool to discipline those officers whose use of discretion proves offensive or embarassing to the department.

But community policing holds that law enforcement is only a part of the police task and that in providing services, maintaining order and solving problems, street-level officers and first-line supervisors are encouraged to use their initiative and ingenuity, i.e., to use discretion, constrained only by department policies which are expressed in terms of broad principles rather than minute regulations. In so holding, community policing opens pos-

179

sibilities for corruption consisting of inducements to use that discretion illegitimately.

An underlying assumption of professional policing seems to be that justice consists of applying the same law to everyone. Community policing is forced to consider the view that treating different groups in the same way may actually result in injustice in some cases. It can certainly result in misunderstanding, resentment and, at worst, disruption or public order. Should the community police officer or police team be empowered to consider the ethnic, cultural, or economic background of individuals or groups when making decisions as to the use of police powers or the distribution of police services? If so, some individuals or groups may see in this an opportunity to influence those decisions through the use of corrupt means.

Professional policing also demanded that officers deal only with facts, laws, and department regulations — not with emotions, hunches or people. At its most rigorous, this philosophy saw people as complainants, witnesses, criminals or sources of information — not as individuals whose practical and emotional needs have to be met. This called for as little interaction as possible — only that which was required to extract the information necessary to carry out the law. There was no reason to spend any time with people who were not sources of information. Even brief contacts with people seen as morally dubious were to be reported (preferably ahead of time) to superior officers. The less time spent with members of the community — the more impersonal the relationship — the less the opportunities for corruption.

Sustained interaction with members of the community is the essence of community policing — community leaders and community representatives, but also residents, businesspeople, visitors and people whose identity is not quite clear. While visits with some of these people can be scheduled ahead of time, others are spontaneous and casual, arise from the circumstances of the moment, and cannot be cleared with superiors, at least not until after they have taken place. At least some of these relationships will be intense and of long duration, leading to the very type of personal interaction that provided corruption opportunities in the past.

At the very least, sustained participation in the community will lead to what professional police reformers considered minor forms of corruption. This is because human relationships consist to a large extent of mutual exchange. When relationships are impersonal, exchange can be impersonal and indirect. Members of the community pay taxes to the government and from this tax money comes the salary of the police officer, in return for which the officer provides police services to the community. Particularly when that service consists largely of law enforcement, all participants in the situation — at least, all honest participants — find this satisfactory. But when police and members of the community have warm personal relationships — when police services are customized to fit the expressed needs of the community and its residents — this indirect exchange may no longer prove satisfactory. Even honest members of the community may wish to express and strengthen what they see as a personal relationship with personal gifts. Simply forbidding such exchange may weaken the very relationships community policing is designed to produce. But methods of handling this in ways that promote police-community solidarity, do not insult members of the community, and yet do not lead to improper behavior or the perception of improper behavior will be a new challenge to police administrators.

A final aspect of police professionalism was a departmental organization that was strongly bureaucratic, with a high degree of centralization and clear chain of command. Community policing calls for a flatter organizational chart with few layers of bureaucracy between the lowest and highest ranks. This implies that much decision-making power will be removed from the office of the commissioner and will be given to commanders at the community level. These commanders — no longer minutely regulated and supervised by headquarters — will be seen as targets for corruption by individuals and groups with an interest in illegitimately influencing police activity.

What are the implications of closer community ties for corruption? First, it is entirely possible that better ties with the community and the changes in police organization that support such efforts may well promote a lower incidence of corruption than was true with previous situations. This is not to say that greed and human frailty will disappear; it is to suggest that some types of corruption stemmed from frustration with the police organization. The professional bureaucratic style implied that members of the organization were either stupid or corrupt, probably both. By regarding its employees with suspicion, without giving them an opportunity to use their ingenuity, by positively discouraging initiative, this style ran the danger of actually breeding hostility; by insisting on impersonal relationships with the majority of citizens, it created a situation in which most police contacts were with deviants and a resulting police world-view which saw all of society as deviant and corrupt. Finally, the combination of all these factors brought about a situation in which the only challenges and excitement came from car chases and corruption. By creating a job that is professionally and personally satisfying, closer relationships with the community may actually prevent corruption.

Secondly, policy makers may have to look again at small gifts and other offerings. Traditionally, such items, beginning with the notorious free cup of coffee, have either been blanketly forbidden or else have been tacitly ignored. It has been suggested elsewhere that the appropriateness of gifts of food can be measured by examining the time and place of the consumption, i.e., anything eatable, drinkable or smokable within 24 hours is not corrupt. While this may be a good rule of thumb, what I am suggesting here is that it is even better to appraise these instances in terms of their context and their meaning to the participants and onlookers. The context for such appraisal is reciprocity, the knowledge that gift giving and exchange both create and reflect the personal relationships that are the currency of community policing. Factors to be considered include the value of the gift, the perceived intent of both donor and recipient, whether the offering is made freely or is the result of even the mildest form of extortion, whether it is a single incident or part of a series, whether it is meant for the individual or the organization, whether it is made openly or

secretly, whether it might be demeaning to policing as an occupation, and the cultural context in which it is offered.

Terms such as reciprocity and exchange mean that the gifts flow in both directions. Let's look at some of the implications of this.

Gifts of small monetary value may be seen as not corrupt, but as demeaning; they are a form of tip, totally at the discretion of the tipper. But they are converted into reciprocity between equals when the police officer gives a return gift. It is this which leads to the concern about corruption, large or small, for if the gift is not to make the recipient indebted to the giver, it demands a return gift. The assumption has always been that the only thing that the officer had to give in return — that the only thing in which the donor was interested — was some sort of misuse of official position, of power or authority.

But if the officer can legitimately give a return gift, then an obligation is converted into an exchange relationship of equals which is strengthened by the exchange. The community policing-oriented organization may encourage such exchanges, which may be personal to the officer but might also involve legitimate small services which the organization approves. In such an organization, an officer may come to be rated on how *many* — not how few — exchanges she participates in.

Let me give three examples — all essentially based on actual incidents, but all heavily disguised — to illustrate the type of situation about which I am thinking.

A woman living alone calls the police several times because she thinks someone is trying to break into her house. Each time, the police come, treat her politely, search the premises, but can find nothing to account for the frightening noises she is reporting. Finally, a police officer realizes that the noise is being made by a tree rubbing against the roof of the house. Grateful but embarrassed, the woman bakes an elaborate cake and brings it to the police station. The young officer on duty thanks her courteously, but explains that the police are not permitted to accept gratuities of any kind and that in responding to her calls they were simply doing their duty. Feeling rebuffed, she prepares to leave with her cake when a sergeant who has overheard the conversation comes out, accepts the cake with thanks, and promises her that everyone in the station will enjoy having it with that afternoon's tea.

A police officer working in a poor community organizes a sports club for the neighborhood's young people, many of whom have been or are on the verge of being in trouble with the law. The youngsters react positively to the club, finding it an outlet for their energies, and they enjoy the contact with the police officer and the other young adults she has recruited to take part. Since the club is short of money for equipment, the officer organises a fund-raising event, putting a great deal of her own time into this effort. She sends a letter of invitation to potential donors, explaining the purpose of the event and signing it "Police Officer Jane Doe, Marley Street Police Station." Department regulatons forbid members to use their department affiliation in any solicitation for funds. Officer Doe is reprimanded and reassigned to matron duty in the jail.

A community which includes a large amusement park has become crime-ridden, disorderly and dangerous. Many of the long-time residents move out, while those who stay, including those who work in the park, are terrified. A new area commander works tirelessly with community and business groups, calming their fears, identifying problems and finding solutions, and acting as liaison between older residents and members of minority groups who have recently moved in. His efforts pay off in a lower crime rate, greater confidence, and a growing sense of understanding among the various ethnic and racial groups. On several occasions, the commander brings his family to the amusement park, where owners of many of the stalls ply them with food, offer free rides, and give them handfuls of coins so they may operate the various games (the commander is careful to spend all the coins before leaving the park.) On one occasion, the commander has trouble with his car, which a local garage owner repairs without charge. These incidents come to the attention of the commander's superiors, who request his resignation.

Finally, if reaching out to the community is to represent a major change in organizational philosophy and not, as so many suspect, another exercise in public relations, education and training will have a major role to play.

182

Police professionalism is based on a low-trust model of human resource management. Such a model is closely akin to Theory X views of human nature and assumes that members of the organization — left to their own devices — will shirk their duty, conspire to undermine the goals of the organization, take advantage of any corruption opportunities that come their way, and work to create opportunities for corruption if not enough exist naturally. Such a model emphasizes supervision at all levels, orders spelled out in careful detail, and penalties for misbehavior. Community policing, on the other hand, is most compatible with a high-trust model. This assumes that members of the organization, if properly prepared and led, will take pleasure and satisfaction in doing their tasks honestly and well, are capable of applying broad principles to particular situations, and are a source of knowledge and ideas that are capable of enriching the organization. It emphasizes innovation, tolerates failure resulting from a sincere effort to implement the organizations's policies, and rewards those who take responsibility at all levels. A low-trust model pays little attention to education, especially for its lower-ranking members, since following detailed instructions under closely supervised conditions does not call for highly educated personnel. Indeed, experience has shown that placing highly educated people in highly structured organizations can lead to frustration, stress, and a high rate of turnover.

High-trust models, by contrast, rely heavily on education for all ranks. Since members at the lowest levels of the organization exercise discretion and take responsibility, they must be prepared to do these things wisely. In community policing, it is often the lowest-ranking police who have the greatest responsibility for cultivating acquaintance with various members of the community; collecting, sorting, and analyzing information; identifying problems and proposing solutions; and organizing and working with voluntary, private and government agencies. A broad base of knowledge, the ability to acquire and evaluate information, and sharply honed analytic skills — the end products of a good education — are clearly necessary for successfully carrying out such responsibilities. But those members of the organization who provide leadership and support for these activities; who obtain resources, formulate and articulate policy; persuade the public that the organization's vision of itself and its place in the community is viable, just, and effective — they also need an education that assists them in performing leadership and administrative duties that are very different from those performed in a more bureaucratic agency.

Part of the education at all ranks can provide help in maintaining integrity in an organization that can no longer rely on the most prominent methods of integrity maintenance it has used in the past.

Whether or not honesty can be taught in an educational setting remains a subject of debate. But educational settings can make a contribution to ethical behavior. In the United States, a country with a long tradition of ethical problems, there is a growing body of research that demonstrates that police officers with higher education not only have superior field performance, but also that they have better relations with the community, use discretion wisely, and are less likely to be charged or found guilty in disciplinary hearings.

Education and training are an ideal place to communicate the agency's concern for ethical behavior. All instructors can point out the moral components of their subjects, admit that ethical dilemmas can be difficult, and use scenarios and case studies to explore them. An agency's Code of Ethics is a good starting place, but only if it is indeed used as a starting place. Discussing its ramifications and implications in various settings and situations can reveal its real meaning. Ranking and experienced officers can visit training establishments to convey their concern for integrity, reminding trainees that the agency trusts them and that it is up to them to

preserve that trust. Language outside of the classroom, attitudes, and body language must be consistent with the lessons being taught; trainees are quick to pick up insincerity.

Much academy training is undermined in the field. Field training officers and others who accompany and supervise young police officers should be picked for their integrity as much as for their experience. They should understand that ethical training is a part of their job and they should be given preparation for carrying out that part of their job. They should understand that ethical lapses on the part of the trainees should be included in their reports and evaluations.

While much attention in recent years has focused on recruit training, it is important to remember that a change to a philosophy of community outreach and its corresponding organizational changes will necessitate new training for more senior members of the organization also. Discussion of the support integrity and of ways in which the department can support integrity in its members under a high-trust model of organization should be an important part of such training. And higher-ranking officers should be reminded that temptation does not exist only on the street — they too will be interacting with members of the community. Compared to the contacts of street-level officers, their community contacts may have even greater reasons to buy police discretion — and greater means with which to do so.

Finally, there is good reason to believe that greater community outreach will result in an organization that is both more effective and more honest. This will be true, however, only when the organization realizes that both the challenges to integrity and the means of meeting those challenges are different from those that existed before.

GLOBAL AND SPECIFIC ATTITUDES TOWARD THE POLICE: DISENTANGLING THE RELATIONSHIP*

STEVEN G. BRANDL
University of Wisconsin—Milwaukee

JAMES FRANK
University of Cincinnati

ROBERT E. WORDEN
The University at Albany, State University of New York

TIMOTHY S. BYNUM
Michigan State University

Since the 1960s, a substantial body of research has focused on citizens' attitudes toward the police. These studies tap a rather wide variety of outlooks: some ask about specific assessments of the police (e.g., satisfaction with the police in particular incidents), while others ask about more global assessments (e.g., satisfaction with the police in general, police in the community, or police in the neighborhood). Using data obtained through a panel survey of 398 residents of a large midwestern city, we compare specific assessments of police performance with more global attitudes toward the police. We also examine the effects of global and specific attitudes on one another. The results show that the two measures produce similar levels of support for the police. The results reveal further that global attitudes have substantial effects on specific assessments of police performance, and that the effects of specific assessments of police performance on global attitudes are modest by comparison.

Since the turbulent and riotous 1960s, many efforts have been made to measure and analyze citizens' attitudes toward the police. The role of the police in precipitating civil disorders and, more generally, the tensions between the police and minorities initially directed attention toward the racial and ethnic correlates of citizens' attitudes. Over the past two decades, as evaluators and police practitioners have come to see citizens' support both as an important

* The authors are grateful for the comments and suggestions of the *JQ* referees. The data on which this article is based were collected under Grant 89-DD-CX-0049 from the National Institute of Justice, U.S. Department of Justice. The analyses and interpretations presented here are not intended to reflect the views of the U.S. Department of Justice.

JUSTICE QUARTERLY, Vol. 11 No. 1, March 1994
© 1994 Academy of Criminal Justice Sciences

outcome in its own right and as an essential element in the "coproduction" of public safety, surveys of citizens have been incorporated increasingly into evaluations of police strategies (e.g., community policing). In the absence of market mechanisms whereby the public value of police services is established through consumers' willingness to pay, surveys are one medium through which the police can obtain feedback—both positive and negative—on police practices.

The studies that have examined citizens' attitudes toward the police tap a rather wide variety of outlooks. Some surveys inquire about respondents' satisfaction with the police in their communities or neighborhoods; others elicit respondents' degree of satisfaction with their own contacts with the police. Unfortunately, we think, too little effort has been made to better understand these different outlooks as elements of citizens' systems of beliefs about the police. Existing research does not permit us to draw definitive inferences about how these attitudes differ in their valences (positive or negative) or in their degree of intensity. Moreover, because the cross-sectional designs of previous research preclude the necessary analyses, previous research has not yet established the nature of the relationship between these attitudes: whether they are causal or spurious and, if they are causal, the direction of causality. Consequently analysts often claim that citizens' assessments of their contacts with the police influence their more general attitudes toward the police, but they rarely acknowledge that more general attitudes might influence assessments of individual contacts.

In this paper we report the results of analyses that extend our understanding of the structure of citizens' attitudes toward the police. We compare specific attitudes about police performance in individual contacts with more global or general attitudes toward the police in the neighborhood. We also examine the effects of global and specific attitudes on one another, using panel data that enable us to disentangle these effects. This research offers empirical evidence where only assumptions existed before. Insofar as the findings prove to be generalizable, the study may suggest that we reject some of those assumptions.

GLOBAL ATTITUDES AND SPECIFIC ATTITUDES

Easton (1965) provides at least a general foundation for analyses of global and specific attitudes toward the police. He identified two forms of public support associated with political systems: diffuse and specific. Easton defined diffuse support as "that which continues independently of the specific rewards which the member may feel he obtains from belonging to the system" (p. 125). Specific support refers to "input to a system that occurs as a return for the specific benefits and advantages that members of a system experience as part of their membership. It represents or reflects the satisfaction a member feels when he perceives his demands as having been met" (p. 125).

Dennis (1976) further defined and elaborated on Easton's framework. As he explained, specific support refers to an evaluation of a particular role incumbent within the institution, whereas "diffuse support involves a generalization of support for the institution . . . it is a reservoir of good will normally directed toward the institution rather than particular incumbents. It is a regime-level sentiment and support or rejection of institutional authority" (p. 50). Dennis hypothesized, first, that the levels of diffuse and specific support normally differ substantially; the former is higher than the latter. Further, he suggested that specific support can affect the level of diffuse support for the institution.

At best, only weak evidence for the veracity of Dennis's first hypothesis can be gathered from the "attitude toward police" literature. White and Menke (1982) compared measures that purportedly capture general and specific support for police and found, in support of this hypothesis, that the general items produced more favorable attitudes than did the specific.[1] Beyond White and Menke's study, we can only compare the results of studies that measured either specific or more global attitudes in order to draw inferences about the disparity between the two constructs. Several studies that measured global attitudes toward the police found very favorable attitudes (e.g., Benson 1981; Homant, Kennedy, and Fleming 1984; Koenig 1980); other studies which measured specific attitudes—that is, assessments of individual contacts with the police—often found attitudes to be less favorable (e.g., Percy 1980; Poister and McDavid 1978). At the same time, however, some studies report quite positive specific attitudes (e.g., Shapland 1983), while others reveal less favorable global attitudes (e.g., Carter 1985; Thomas and Hyman 1977; Zamble and Annesley 1987).

---

[1] One could question, however, the extent to which the analyses presented by White and Menke actually parallel Dennis's (1976) hypothesis. Specifically, White and Menke (1982) measure *general* support in terms of responses to the statement "Most police are competent in their work," while they measure *specific* support in terms of responses to "A lot of criminals get off free because the police are not doing their jobs effectively." Although the second item may be more specific than the first in that it asks about a particular type of police "competence," the object of the judgment ("the police") is the same in both cases. A seemingly more valid measure of specific support would focus on a particular role incumbent, and thus on the police in a particular contact situation.

These inconsistencies should not be surprising given other variations across the studies (e.g., wording and format of questions, nature of the sample and sample characteristics, study site).
Consequently we are left with little more than speculative conclusions about the disparity between specific and more global attitudes
toward the police.

Equally weak are the inferences that we can draw about the
causal relationship between specific and global attitudes. Several
studies have concluded, on the basis of empirical analyses, that citizens' evaluations of police actions in particular incidents strongly
influence citizens' global assessments of police performance (Dean
1980; Scaglion and Condon 1980).[2] These (cross-sectional) studies,
however, do not (indeed, cannot) control for global attitudes toward
the police that existed before the measured contact. Instead they
assume that specific attitudes affect global attitudes, and they do
not test the opposite causal relationship: that preexisting global attitudes (i.e., attitudes that exist before the measured contact) affect
specific assessments. Koenig (1980) captures this dilemma when
he states:

> It is debatable whether perceived police rudeness and un-
> fairness [in a specific incident] lead to less favorable public
> evaluations of local police, or whether less favorable evalu-
> ations of local police lead to the perception of neutral be-
> haviors as incidents of rudeness or unfairness (p. 248).

The only study to date that controls for prior global attitudes (Skogan 1991) is able to estimate only the effects of police- and citizen-
initiated contacts, but not the effects of citizens' assessments of
those contacts, on global attitudes toward the police. The effects of
such contacts presumably are mediated by citizens' reactions,
which—as we show below—are not unanimous: not everyone who
is stopped by the police is dissatisfied with the contact, and (of
course) not everyone who calls the police is satisfied. Moreover, the
effects of global attitudes on (the unmeasured) specific attitudes are
not estimated.

A theoretical basis exists for the proposition that global attitudes toward the police influence specific assessments. If the cognitive processes associated with stereotyping characterize the
formation of citizens' attitudes toward the police, we would expect
that information received during a contact with a police officer
would be processed in accordance with the citizen's existing beliefs
or attitudes (Hamilton 1981). Existing stereotypes may even bias
the processing of information so that that information which is
processed appears to reinforce the existing belief system (Hamilton

---

[2] See Hero and Durand (1985) for an example outside the police context.

and Rose 1980). In addition, evidence that confirms a stereotype may be more cognitively available, and thus may be recalled more easily (Synder, Tanke, and Berscheid 1977). The data collected here allow us to examine the extent to which global attitudes affect specific assessments of police performance, as well as the reverse.

METHOD

Sample

Data for this study were collected through a three-wave panel survey that was conducted as part of a larger study of narcotics enforcement. To minimize the effects of panel mortality, we use only the second and third waves for the analyses described here. Respondents were drawn from four areas (each consisting of several census tracts) in a large midwestern city. A cluster sampling procedure was used to ensure that all or most blocks within the areas were represented; households were selected randomly from each block in each area and were contacted by telephone. For the Wave 1 interviews, the interviewer asked to speak with someone age 18 or older who had lived in the home for at least six months.[3] Efforts were made to contact the same individual for Waves 2 and 3. If the respondent from the previous wave could not be recontacted, a replacement household was selected. The Wave 2 interviews, which for our purposes are called Time 1(T_1), were conducted in October 1990 and had a response rate of 75 percent (N=571). Wave 3, which we call Time 2(T_2), was conducted in April 1991 and had a response rate of 74 percent (N=560). The panel contains 398 respondents.

Table 1 illustrates the demographic composition of the Wave 3 sample, the panel, and on the basis of 1990 census data, the four areas from which the sample was drawn; these are similar to the city in race, gender, age, and other demographic characteristics. The panel is similar to the Wave 3 sample; this fact suggests that the findings are not distorted by panel mortality. The panel differs from the larger population, however, in that the panel contains larger proportions of whites, females, and individuals who own their own homes. These areas were not selected because they are representative of any larger population; thus even a perfectly representative sample of their residents would form the basis for only limited generalization. The more telling points to be made with reference to Table 1 are that these areas are predominant black and of low to moderate income, as are the panel respondents. Therefore

---

[3] If a person possessing these characteristics was not at home, a return call was scheduled; this process was repeated until a refusal was received or until several contacts had been attempted without success.

the generalizability of the findings we report below may be limited to such neighborhoods. We will return to this issue in our discussion.

Table 1.   Demographic Characteristics of Wave 3, Panel, and Sample Areas[a]

Characteristic	Wave 3		Panel		Sample Areas	
Totals (N)	560		398		65,084	
Race						
White	187	(33.8)	146	(36.9)	13,530	(20.8)
Black	338	(61.0)	228	(57.6)	48,316	(74.2)
Native American	8	(1.4)	5	(1.3)	247	(.3)
Asian	3	(.5)	3	(.8)	391	(.6)
Hispanic	4	(.7)	2	(.5)	1,663	(3.0)
Other	14	(2.5)	12	(3.1)	939	(1.4)
Gender						
Male	164	(29.3)	115	(28.9)	30,348	(46.6)
Female	396	(70.7)	283	(71.1)	34,737	(53.4)
Age						
18-24	65	(11.9)	40	(10.2)	8,026	(19.1)[b]
25-44	218	(39.8)	147	(37.6)	19,726	(47.0)
45-64	149	(27.2)	112	(28.6)	8,871	(21.2)
65+	116	(21.2)	92	(23.5)	5,309	(12.7)
Household Type						
Own	394	(70.6)	291	(73.5)	—	(48.1)
Rent	164	(29.3)	105	(26.5)	—	(51.9)
Median Income		$15,001 - $25,000[c]			$15,318	
Education						
Elementary	49	(8.8)	35	(8.8)	4,276	(12.9)[d]
Some high school	109	(19.5)	82	(20.6)	10,382	(31.4)
High school graduate	189	(33.8)	133	(33.4)	9,026	(27.3)
Some college	153	(27.4)	105	(26.4)	6,109	(18.5)
College graduate	59	(10.6)	43	(10.8)	3,299	(10.0)

[a] Percentages are in parentheses.
[b] N = 41,932.
[c] Income was collected as a categorical variable. The $15,001-$25,000 category was the median category for Wave 3 and for the panel.
[d] N = 33,092 because the census includes only individuals who are age 25 and over for the education measure.

Data

The same questions were asked at both T_1 and T_2. For analyses concerning the disparity between specific and more global attitudes (Table 2), we use only the T_1 data. For the causal analyses (Tables 3 and 4), we use the panel data to provide the proper temporal order of variables.

We measured citizens' global attitudes toward the police according to their responses to this question: "In general, how satisfied are you with the police? Are you very satisfied, somewhat satisfied, somewhat dissatisfied, or very dissatisfied?" This question was prefaced with the statement "Now let's talk about the police in your neighborhood."

We measured four specific attitudes, each involving a different type of contact with the police: when requesting information ("How satisfied were you with how the police handled the problem?"), when requesting assistance ("How satisfied were you with the way the police handled the problem?"), when stopped and questioned ("How satisfied were you with the way you were treated?"), and when victimized ("How satisfied were you with the police in their handling of the incident?"). Respondents who had each type of contact within the past year were asked about their most recent contact of that type.[4] For all of the specific attitude items, the response options were the same as in the global measure: "Were you very satisfied, somewhat satisfied, somewhat dissatisfied, or very dissatisfied?"

Items that potentially could confound the relationship between specific attitudes and more global attitudes toward the police are included as control variables in the multivariate analyses. These variables are the citizen's age, education, race, income, and gender.[5]

RESULTS

To assess the disparity between specific and global attitudes toward the police, and to explore the association between the two, we compare the two measures across types of contact: first, by computing differences in mean item scores with t-tests of statistical significance; second, by examining the joint distribution of scores; and third, by estimating correlations.[6]

As shown in Table 2, the mean level of satisfaction expressed by individuals with each specific contact is equal to or greater than

---

[4] The Wave 2 and Wave 3 interviews were six months apart, but in the Wave 3 interview, respondents were asked about contacts that occurred within the past year. To ensure proper temporal order of contacts and (global) satisfaction, those respondents who stated during the Wave 3 interview that their most recent contact with the police occurred before the Wave 2 interview are either coded as not having a contact (Table 3) or excluded from the analyses (Table 4).

[5] We used the following coding schemes: education (1 = less than high school, 2 = some high school, 3 = completed high school, 4 = some college, 5 = completed college/some advanced college); race (1 = nonwhite, 2 = white); income (1 = 0 – $8,000, 2 = $8,001 – $15,000, 3 = $15,001 – $25,000, 4 = more than $25,000); gender (1 = male, 2 = female). Age was coded in its raw form.

[6] All of the respondents included in these analyses (N=262) had had either an "information," a "help," a "victimization," or a "stopped and questioned" contact with the police. Only two (of 262; .8%) had had all four types of contact, 22 (8.4%) had three types of contact, and 66 (25.2%) had two types of contact. The remaining 172 (65.6%) had just one type of contact. Therefore, because well over half of the sample only had one type of (measured) contact with the police, the possibility of confounding experiences is of little concern.

their mean level of global satisfaction, although none of the differences achieves a conventional (.05) level of statistical significance. Thus we find no support in these data for the hypothesis that general support for the police is greater than specific support.

Table 2.   Relationships between Global Satisfaction and Specific Satisfaction Measures

Specific Satisfaction Measures	r	N	Global Satisfaction 1=vd	2=sd	3=ss	4=vs
Satisfaction/Info	.50	160	39	42	60	19
1=very dissatisfied		66	33	15	16	2
2=somewhat dissatisfied		15	1	6	8	0
3=somewhat satisfied		25	2	8	13	2
4=very satisfied		54	3	13	23	15
Global mean = 2.37						
Specific mean = 2.42						
t-value = -.53; p=.60						
Satisfaction/Assistance	.58	103	23	21	41	18
1=very dissatisfied		26	12	7	7	0
2=somewhat dissatisfied		13	4	4	5	0
3=somewhat satisfied		28	7	5	15	1
4=very satisfied		36	0	5	14	17
Global mean = 2.52						
Specific mean = 2.72						
t-value = -1.91; p=.06						
Satisfaction/Stopped	.24	56	10	12	25	9
1=very dissatisfied		15	6	1	7	1
2=somewhat dissatisfied		10	1	4	3	2
3=somewhat satisfied		12	1	3	6	2
4=very satisfied		19	2	4	9	4
Global mean = 2.59						
Specific mean = 2.63						
t-value = -.20; p=.85						
Satisfaction/Victimization	.43	49	15	18	11	5
1=very dissatisfied		16	8	4	4	0
2=somewhat dissatisfied		9	5	4	0	0
3=somewhat satisfied		11	0	6	3	2
4=very satisfied		13	2	4	4	3
Global mean = 2.12						
Specific mean = 2.43						
t-value = -1.82; p=.08						

Notes: Missing data are excluded from the analyses. Raw frequencies are presented in cross-tabulations.

Although the means of these attitude measures do not differ widely, an examination of the joint distribution shows some divergence. In each cross-tabulation in Table 2, more than half of the cases (53.4% to 64.3%) fall off the main diagonal. In addition, a sizable percentage of respondents (28.2% to 41.1%) in each cross-tabulation are "very" or "somewhat" satisfied on one attitudinal measure but "very" or "somewhat" *dis*satisfied on the other. Moreover, the correlations range only from .24 to .58. Thus, although

42

individuals who are satisfied ("very" and "somewhat" combined) with the police in a particular contact are also more likely to be satisfied than dissatisfied with the police overall, *and* although individuals who are dissatisfied ("very" and "somewhat") with the police in a particular contact are more likely to be dissatisfied than satisfied with the police overall, the association is only moderately strong. It would be an error to conclude that the global and the specific attitudinal measures are statistically indistinguishable.

With reference to Table 2, we would add that satisfaction with specific types of contacts varies markedly among citizens who had the same types of contacts. More than half of those who had been stopped by the police were satisfied with the way they were treated, whereas half of those who requested information and more than one-third of those who had requested assistance were dissatisfied with the police response. Analyses of global attitudes toward the police should estimate, if possible, the effects of specific attitudes, not of contacts as such, because citizens are so diverse in their assessments of seemingly similar types of experiences.

To test the hypotheses that assert a causal relationship between the global and the specific attitudes, we perform ordinary least squares (OLS) regression analyses.[7] Table 3 displays findings concerning the hypothesis that specific attitudes influence global attitudes. Here the dependent variable is T_2 global satisfaction. The independent variables are T_1 global satisfaction, the specific satisfaction measures, and (as controls) the demographic items. By including *prior* (T_1) global satisfaction in the analyses, and thus controlling for its impact on T_2 global satisfaction, we can more accurately identify the effects of specific attitudes on general attitudes. Table 3 shows, in parentheses, the estimated effects of specific satisfaction and demographic characteristics when T_1 global satisfaction is omitted from the model; these are the results of a cross-sectional analysis that makes the customary assumption about causal direction.

In both sets of analyses presented in Table 3 (with and without T_1 global satisfaction), each of the four specific attitudes appears as two variables that are coded to represent degrees of positive (satisfied) or negative (dissatisfied) evaluations of each experience ($2=very$ satisfied or *very* dissatisfied; $1=somewhat$ satisfied or *somewhat* dissatisfied; $0=$did not have a contact of that type). For example, a respondent who was "somewhat satisfied" with the officer in a

---

7 The purpose of the regression analyses is to test the hypotheses concerning the causal effects of global and specific satisfaction on one another. The analyses are not intended to explain satisfaction levels. Therefore the proportion of variance explained in the models is of secondary importance.

Table 3.   OLS Regression Analyses of T_2 Global Satisfaction

Variable	Coefficient	Standard Error	t-ratio	Beta
T_1 Global Satisfaction	.50	.05	10.92**	.50
Education	.08	.04	1.81*	.09
	(.10)	(.05)	(2.17)*	(.12)
Sex	−.03	.10	− .32	−.01
	(.00)	(.11)	(−.03)	(.00)
Race	−.14	.09	−1.48	−.07
	(−.28)	(.11)	(−2.69)**	(−.14)
Income	−.01	.04	− .24	−.01
	(−.04)	(.05)	(−.82)	(−.05)
Age	.01	.00	1.93*	.09
	(.01)	(.00)	(2.89)**	(.16)
Positive Info	.01	.06	.12	.01
	(−.02)	(.07)	(−.35)	(−.02)
Negative Info	−.21	.07	−3.16**	−.14
	(−.36)	(.07)	(−4.90)**	(−.25)
Positive Assistance	.26	.08	3.20**	.14
	(.28)	(.09)	(3.06)**	(.15)
Negative Assistance	−.21	.11	−1.96	−.09
	(−.28)	(.12)	(−2.35)	(−.12)
Positive Stop	.01	.11	.05	.00
	(−.01)	(.12)	(−.07)	(.00)
Negative Stop	.03	.13	.20	.01
	(−.14)	(.15)	(−.98)	(−.05)
Positive Victimization	−.17	.15	−1.12	−.05
	(−.13)	(.17)	(−.74)	(−.04)
Negative Victimization	−.38	.25	−1.51	−.06
	(−.68)	(.30)	(−2.29)**	(−.11)
Constant	1.23	.33	3.67**	
	(2.59)	(.36)	(7.18)**	
R^2	.42			
	(.20)			
Adjusted R^2	.39			
	(.17)			
N	314			
	(327)			

* $p < .05$; ** $p < .01$ (one-tailed test)
Notes: Missing data are excluded from analyses. Results in parentheses do not include T_1 global satisfaction.

request for information contact is coded 1 on the Positive Info variable, while another respondent who was "very dissatisfied" in the same type of contact is coded 2 on the Negative Info variable. This treatment is necessary because previous research has shown that negative evaluations have a stronger impact than positive evaluations on overall attitudes (see Dean 1980) and because a single variable would not allow us to examine the differential impacts of negative and positive assessments.

The results of these analyses show, first, that T_1 global satisfaction has a substantial effect on T_2 global satisfaction; this coefficient, even without a correction for attenuation due to measurement error, suggests that the global attitude is fairly stable over at least a six-month period. Second, the results show that T_2 global satisfaction is affected by three specific attitudes, namely positive and negative assessments of assistance contacts and negative assessments of information contacts, even when prior (T_1) global satisfaction is controlled. Third, because a cross-sectional analysis—the results of which appear in parentheses— cannot control for T_1 global satisfaction, it somewhat overestimates the impact of specific satisfaction on T_2 global satisfaction. The cross-sectional analysis yields an estimate of the impact of citizens' negative assessments of victimization contacts which is substantively and statistically significant, and which falls to 0 when T_1 global satisfaction is controlled. This analysis also produces inflated estimates of the effects of other specific attitudes: positive and negative assessments of information contacts, positive and negative assessments of assistance contacts, and negative assessments of stopped and questioned contacts.

To examine the hypothesis that global attitudes influence specific attitudes, we estimate OLS regression equations once again. The dependent variable in each equation is the specific satisfaction measure (1=very dissatisfied; 4=very satisfied); T_2 global satisfaction and the demographic characteristics are explanatory variables. As shown by the results in Table 4, global satisfaction has a substantively and statistically significant effect on specific satisfaction with each of three types of contact (the "victimization" contact is the exception). Moreover, in these three equations, the *strongest* impact on specific satisfaction is that of T_1 global satisfaction. The effect of global satisfaction in victimization-related contacts is substantially large but does not achieve statistical significance, perhaps because of the small size of the subsamples on which the estimate is based. One then might infer that global attitudes toward the police influence evaluations of police in particular contact situations.

DISCUSSION

This study represents an attempt to understand more clearly the relationship between specific and more global attitudes toward

45

Table 4. OLS Regression Analyses of Specific Satisfaction (T₂)

	Type of Contact															
	Information				Assist				Stop				Victim			
Variable	Coeff.	SE	t	Beta	Coeff.	SE	t	Beta	Coeff.	SE	t	Beta	Coeff.	SE	t	Beta
T₁ Global Satisfaction	.36	.13	2.73**	.26	.30	.17	1.73*	.24	.57	.28	2.03*	.45	.31	.24	1.27	.25
Education	.18	.14	1.27	.13	.05	.18	.28	.04	.16	.29	.54	.11	-.22	.24	-.90	-.19
Sex	-.04	.29	-.14	-.01	-.44	.37	-.19	-.18	.22	.53	.41	.09	-.10	.47	-.21	-.04
Race	-.73	.27	-2.74**	-.26	-.52	.31	-1.71*	-.22	-.12	.53	-.23	-.04	-.92	.50	-1.85*	-.39
Income	.15	.13	1.17	.12	.21	.15	1.45	.20	.01	.22	.05	.01	.28	.21	1.38	.29
Age	-.01	-.01	-1.54	-.15	-.01	.01	-.66	-.02	.01	.02	.58	.12	.00	.01	-.14	-.03
Constant	1.21	.92	1.30	—	2.72	1.11	2.45*	—	1.14	1.48	.77	—	3.27	1.43	2.29*	—
R²	.22				.17				.21				.30			
Adjusted R²	.17				.08				.03				.09			
N	100				59				32				25			

*p<.05; **p<.01 (one-tailed test)
Note: Missing data are excluded from the analyses.

the police. The comparison of specific with global attitudes shows that *most* of the differences—in means and in proportions—are neither substantively large nor statistically significant; insofar as global and specific attitudes differ, respondents who have had a contact with the police tend to be more satisfied with their individual contact than with the police more generally. These findings are contrary to the hypothesis offered by Dennis (1976) and to White and Menke's (1982) conclusion.

Furthermore, this study suggests that global and specific attitudes toward the police are causally related, and that the causal effects are asymmetrically reciprocal. That is, citizens' global attitudes toward the police affect their assessments of specific contacts with the police, and citizens' assessments of specific contacts affect their global attitudes, but the former effect is stronger than the latter. These findings are consistent with the proposition that citizens' evaluations of their personal experiences with the police are affected by stereotyping and selective perception; those who hold generally favorable views of the police are more likely to evaluate their contacts with the police favorably, and those who hold generally unfavorable views are more likely to evaluate their contacts unfavorably. The findings also support propositions about the effects of specific attitudes on global attitudes. They indicate, however, that these effects might have been overestimated in previous research, which did not control for the confounding effects of prior global attitudes.

These results have important implications for community policing reforms, which are directed toward building police-citizen partnerships to address community problems. One objective of community policing, especially in neighborhoods whose residents traditionally have regarded the police with skepticism or hostility, is to improve citizens' views of the police in order to establish a firmer foundation for cooperation. Inasmuch as citizens' assessments of their contacts with police are influenced by their existing global attitudes more strongly than the reverse, the police may face a particularly difficult—though perhaps not insuperable—barrier to forming closer police-community relationships. The failure to overcome citizens' preconceptions of police may contribute to the differential outcomes that Skogan (1990:104-107) found in Houston, where some forms of community policing benefited some social groups— minorities, renters, low-income households—less (if at all) than they benefitted higher-status groups.

Whether the findings of our research are generalizable is a question that invites replication of this research. The survey respondents whose attitudes we analyzed live in neighborhoods that are predominantly black and of low to moderate income— neighbor-hoods in which global attitudes toward the police may be least favorable, and in which cultural forces may have pronounced effects on residents' (global and specific) attitudes toward the police (Erez 1984; Jacob 1971). The relationship between global and specific at-titudes among different populations in different social contexts may differ from those found here. Future research should collect panel data in various neighborhoods in various cities, and from larger samples.[8]

Future research also should be directed toward understanding more clearly how global attitudes toward the police are formed, and how (if at all) global or specific attitudes can be influenced by the quality of police contacts. One potentially informative direction for such research would be analyses of socialization, focusing especially on the forces—including familial and peer attitudes and exper-iences—that influence youths' attitudes toward the police. Another potentially useful approach would involve intensive interviews with small samples of selected social groups. Most research on citizens' attitudes toward the police has been based on responses to closed-ended items on highly structured survey instruments; these items provide data on outlooks that the researchers conceived. More loosely structured interviews that provide for more open-ended re-sponses (see, e.g., Hochschild 1981; Lane 1962) could permit deeper insights into the form and nature of citizens' views of the police: their definitions of the police role, their expectations of their local police, their perceptions of police practices, the criteria by which they evaluate the police, and so on. Such research might form the basis for survey instruments which are designed to capture the ele-ments of citizens' belief systems more completely and more accu-rately, and on which more informative quantitative analyses could be based.

In another logical extension of this study, researchers would examine the consequences of citizens' attitudes toward the police. It is a common but untested assumption that citizens who are satis-fied with the police are more likely to engage in behaviors which support the police (e.g., reporting crimes, providing information to the police, engaging in crime prevention activities). Citizens with more favorable attitudes presumably are more likely to become

---

[8] It is worthwhile to highlight the methodological difficulties associated with providing larger sample sizes in a panel survey with the purposes intended here. To do so, one must obtain a (representative) sample of people who will have a certain form of contact with the police within some period in the future. On the assumption that 30 percent of the general population has such contacts with the police in a six-month period, the addition of 100 respondents in the Wave 1 survey would yield only 30 additional respondents for the subsample analyses.

"coproducers" (Goldstein 1987) of crime prevention. An empirical examination of this assumption could prompt additional inquiries into the complexities of citizens' attitudes toward the police.

REFERENCES

Benson, P.R. (1981) "Political Alienation and Public Satisfaction with Police Services." *Pacific Sociological Review* 24:45-64.

Carter, D.L. (1985) "Hispanic Perception of Police Performance: An Empirical Assessment." *Journal of Criminal Justice* 13:487-500.

Dean, D. (1980) "Citizen Ratings of the Police: The Difference Contact Makes." *Law and Policy Quarterly* 2:445-71.

Dennis, J. (1976) "Who Supports the Presidency?" *Society* 13:48-53.

Easton, D. (1965) *A Framework for Political Analysis.* Englewood Cliffs, NJ: Prentice-Hall.

Erez, E. (1984) "Self-Defined 'Desert' and Citizens' Assessment of the Police." *Journal of Criminal Law and Criminology* 75:1276-99.

Goldstein, H. (1987) "Toward Community-Oriented Policing: Potential, Basic Requirements, and Threshold Questions." *Crime and Delinquency* 33:6-30.

Hamilton, D.L. (1981) *Cognitive Processes in Stereotyping and Intergroup Behavior.* Hillsdale, NJ: Erlbaum.

Hamilton, D.L. and T.L. Rose (1980) "Illusory Correlation and the Maintenance of Stereotypic Beliefs." *Journal of Personality and Social Psychology* 39:832-45.

Hero, R.E. and R. Durand (1985) "Explaining Citizen Evaluations of Urban Services: A Comparison of Some Alternative Models." *Urban Affairs Quarterly* 20:344-54.

Hochschild, J.L. (1981) *What's Fair? American Beliefs about Distributive Justice.* Cambridge, MA: Harvard University Press.

Homant, R.J., D.B. Kennedy, and R.M. Fleming (1984) "The Effect of Victimization and the Police Response on Citizens' Attitudes toward the Police." *Journal of Police Science and Administration* 12:323-32.

Jacob, H. (1971) "Black and White Perceptions of Justice in the City." *Law and Society Review* 6:69-89.

Koenig, D.J. (1980) "The Effect of Criminal Victimization and Judicial or Police Contacts on Public Attitudes toward Local Police." *Journal of Criminal Justice* 8:243-49.

Mastrofski, S. (1981) "Surveying Clients to Assess Police Performance." *Evaluation Review* 5:397-408.

Lane, R.E. (1962) *Political Ideology: Why the American Common Man Believes What He Does.* New York: Free Press.

Parks, R.B. (1984) "Linking Objective and Subjective Performance." *Public Administration Review* 44:118-27.

——— (1986) "In Defense of Citizen Evaluations as Performance Measures." *Urban Affairs Quarterly* 22:66-83.

Percy, S.L. (1980) "Response Time and Citizen Evaluation of Police." *Journal of Police Science and Administration* 8:75-86.

Poister, T.H. and J.C. McDavid (1978) "Victims' Evaluation of Police Performance." *Journal of Criminal Justice* 6:133-49.

Scaglion, R. and R.G. Condon (1980) "Determinants of Attitudes toward City Police." *Criminology* 17:485-94.

Shapland, J. (1983) "Victim-Witness Services and the Needs of the Victim." *Victimology* 8:233-37.

Skogan, W.G. (1990) *Disorder and Decline: Crime and the Spiral of Decay in American Neighborhoods.* Berkeley: University of California Press.

——— (1991) "The Impact of Routine Encounters with the Police." Paper presented at the annual meeting of the American Society of Criminology, San Francisco.

Snyder, M., E.D. Tanke, and E. Berscheid (1977) "Social Perception and Interpersonal Behavior: On the Self-Fulfilling Nature of Social Stereotypes." *Journal of Personality and Social Psychology* 9:656-66.

Thomas, C.W. and J.M. Hyman (1977) "Perceptions of Crime, Fear of Victimization, and Public Perceptions of Police Performance." *Journal of Police Science and Administration* 5:305-17.

White, M.F. and B.A. Menke (1982) "On Assessing the Mood of the Public toward the Police: Some Conceptual Issues." *Journal of Criminal Justice* 10:211-30.

Zamble, E. and P. Annesley (1987) "Some Determinants of Public Attitudes towards the Police." *Journal of Police Science and Administration* 15:285-90.

Watchman and Community:
Myth and Institutionalization in Policing

John P. Crank

The author uses a conceptual framework grounded in theory of institutional process to assess developments in the theory of community-based policing. He suggests that two contemporary myths in policing—the myth of the police watchman and the myth of community—provide core elements the theory. Both liberal and conservative advocates for reform have drawn on these myths to support reinstitutionalizing police as community protectors with broad authority, including authority to arrest, unconstrained by law enforcement or due process considerations. He also discusses fundamental differences in the ways in which liberal and conservative reform advocates perceive the relationship between the myths.

[C]ertain ideas burst upon the intellectual landscape with a tremendous force. They solve so many fundamental problems at once that they seem also to promise that they will resolve all fundamental problems, clarify all obscure issues.

—Clifford Geertz 1973:3

Clifford Geertz thus described the force with which the idea of culture energized the development of the field of anthropology. It is with such dynamic vigor that the idea of community-based policing currently envelops police work (Manning 1984; Trojanowicz & Bucqueroux 1990; Walker 1992b). Community-based policing has emerged as the articulation of a police reform movement that addressed a central problem confronting police in the 1960s—the problem of legitimacy (Mastrofski 1991). By invoking two powerful myths—the myth of the 18th-century morally invested "small-town" American community and the myth of police officers as community watchmen—community-based policing provided a source of legitimation for police activity in terms of community protection when legitimacy in terms of police professionalization had been lost (Klockars 1991).

Address correspondence to John P. Crank, Department of Criminal Justice, 4505 Maryland Parkway, Box 455009, Las Vegas, NV 89154-5009.

Law & Society Review, Volume 28, Number 2 (1994)

The police had failed by many accounts to do much in the way of controlling sharply increasing crime; moreover, they were implicated by the 1967 Kerner and 1968 Crime Commissions in the devastating urban riots of the 1960s.[1] Police practice following the reports of these commissions began to change from structures and activities associated with the police professionalism movement and toward the adoption of structures and policies that would forge relationships between police and communities. This change coalesced under the rubric of community policing by the 1980s.

Community policing involved the adoption of elements of structure, activity, and policy designed to make the police look like an organization should look that was responding to problems associated with police professionalism (among them, abrasive enforcement practices that alienated minority communities and police inability to do much about crime). By the 1980s community-based policing was rapidly being institutionalized. Its popularity stemmed from its seeming potential to alleviate a broad range of social and moral dilemmas overwhelming contemporary urban society (Mastrofski 1991).

I argue that the diffusion of the philosophy and programmatic elements of community-based policing across the political landscape of the United States from the early 1970s to the present was an institutional process aimed at restoring legitimacy to the police (Crank & Langworthy 1992). In this essay on institutionalization in the policing sector, I adopt the perspective that institutionalization is a process guided by myth construction, and I hold that the community policing movement is guided by powerful myths of community and watchman (Klockars 1991). By looking at how these two myths developed, we gain insight into how community-based policing is becoming institutionalized as the way police organizations should organize and accomplish their work, independent of the efficiency or effectiveness of community-based strategies and tactics to accomplish the prevention of crime and the production of arrests.

Integral to the process of institutionalization is the entrepreneurial activity of individuals with broad influence within the institutional field (DiMaggio 1988:15). Consequently, the assessment of the process of institutionalization of community-based policing takes into consideration how particular institutional entrepreneurs have influenced the development of the myths of watchman and community.

Finally, I suggest that, because the process of institutionalization for the police occurs within a broad political environment,

---

[1] Throughout, the report of the National Advisory Commission on Civil Disorders (1967) is cited as "Kerner Commission"; the report of the U.S. President's Commission on Law Enforcement & Administration of Justice (1967) is cited as "Crime Commission." The References include cross-references from the informal names to the official reports.

elements of community policing can and should be described in terms of conservative and liberal crime-control conceptions (Walker 1989a). The implementation of particular strategies under the rubric of community policing in specific police organizations does not indicate how efficient or effective they are in dealing with crime; instead, such implementation reveals the dominant crime-control theology at that place and at that time.

Legitimacy and Community Policing

Legitimacy Lost

Within highly institutionalized environments, particular organizational structures, policies, and behaviors take the form they do because of prevailing values and beliefs that have become institutionalized (Hall 1982:313). Random preventive patrol, rapid police response systems, the importance of technology in the investigation of criminal suspects, organizational elaboration in crime-fighting areas, and a militaristic system of rank are aspects of policing that, under the banner of the police professionalism movement, have been institutionalized (Crank & Langworthy 1992).

Prevailing values and beliefs, however, may have their legitimacy challenged. Legitimacy crises may emerge of such severity that they bring into question the fundamental purpose of the organization itself (Meyer & Scott 1983). Such a crisis occurred for policing in the late 1960s. This crisis was precipitated by several factors. The presidential elections of 1964 and 1968 elevated street crime to national attention for the first time. In part, this stemmed from the public perception that crime was sharply increasing (Walker 1980). However, regardless of how crime was measured, police were unable to improve on their performance (Kelling & Moore 1989). Widespread protests against the Vietnam War and the violent urban riots of 1963–67 fostered a public image of police forces ill prepared to accomplish their primary mandate—preserving and protecting the citizenry (Walker 1985).[2] The assassinations of President John Kennedy, his brother Robert Kennedy, and Martin Luther King and the emergence of crime as a topic of national political interest contributed to a broad-based concern over lawlessness and a sharp increase in fear of crime (Michalowski 1985).

This era also witnessed an increasing public mistrust of the police, brought about by such events as the killings of Black Panther leaders by the Chicago police and the Knapp Commission

---

2 Walker (1985:356) describes the "challenge of the 1960's" as the growing momentum of the civil rights movement, problems of police behavior in black neighborhoods, the dramatic increases in crime between 1963 and 1973 resulting in heightened public fear, and urban riots and militant protests against the Vietnam war.

findings of pervasive police corruption in New York City (Manning 1977). A series of Supreme Court decisions, such as *Miranda v. Arizona* (1966), contributed to a public climate of concern over the tendency of the police to engage in illegal behavior (Walker 1980). The reports of the 1950s American Bar Foundation (ABF) Survey of the Administration of Criminal Justice published in the 1960s had a far-reaching impact throughout the criminal justice system (Walker 1992a). The ABF survey reports brought an end to the idea that the police performed their task in a nondiscretionary, ministerial fashion and documented the absence of controls over discretionary police behavior. These events coalesced in the 1967 Kerner and Crime Commissions' reports.

Crank and Langworthy (1992) state that loss of legitimacy is a ceremonial process marked by rituals of public degradation and absolution through the adoption of a new legitimating mandate. Their research focused on police organizations only, but I suggest that a similar ceremonial process also occurred for policing at the national level. For the police, public degradation and revocation of legitimacy occurred ceremonially through two blue-ribbon panels of prominent citizens, acting in the name of elected leadership, and convened to investigate crime control in the United States—the Kerner Commission and the Crime Commission, both issuing reports in 1967—sharply questioned then-current police strategies and related structures. Not only did these commissions cite problems of lawlessness unresolved by current police practices, but they implicated the police in the riots of the late 1960s.

Both commissions called for police reform, to be accomplished through operational strategies and organizational structures that addressed what were described as profound problems of police-community relations. The Kerner Commission noted that in 40% of the riots, police actions triggered the riot (Greene 1989). Institutionalized racism was seen as the underlying problem, but aggressive and violent police behavior was identified as the direct cause. The commission commented on the atmosphere of hostility and cynicism, reinforced by a widespread belief among minorities in rampant police brutality and in a double standard of justice for blacks and whites. This reservoir of grievances, they contended, created an explosive atmosphere where an incident, often involving the police, would spark a riot. Moreover, the commission noted that the most severe disorders were in communities with highly professionalized police agencies.[3] Recommendations included the elimination of abrasive police practices, the establishment of contacts with minority communi-

---

3 The Kerner Commission (1967:158) noted: "many of the [most] serious disturbances took place in cities whose police are among the best led, best organized, best trained and most professional in the country."

ties, increased hiring of minority members, effective grievance mechanisms, and the creation of the position of community service officer.

The Crime Commission (1967) focused more heavily on the sharp increase in crime through the 1960s. Their criticism struck at the heart of the professionalism movement: The police, in spite of adopting a law enforcement mandate, had failed to stem a rising tide of crime. This commission's recommendations were much like those of the Kerner Commission. It encouraged the creation of police community relations units, the recruitment and promotion of more minority members, experimentation with team policing (a precursor of community policing), and the creation of a new police position, the community service officer, who would be drawn from members of the local community and would provide community liaison work.

Professionalism Reconsidered

Central to the findings of both commission reports were the citation and discussion of profound problems with police-community relations. Following the reports, many observers of the police noted that traditional sources of police legitimacy, grounded in law enforcement activity and described by an aloof and legalistic "professional" police, should be reconsidered (Moore & Kelling 1983; Fogelson 1977). The police professionalism movement, with its narrow view of police legitimacy in terms of law enforcement, had failed by all accounts to accomplish its self-chosen mandate—victory in the war on crime (Walker 1992b; Skolnick & Bayley 1986). Moreover, the quasi-military and bureaucratic organizational structure advocated by crime-control-oriented reformers at the beginning of the 20th century was itself an impediment to the production of law enforcement activity. It was even a source of enduring problems such as a "you cover my ass and I'll cover yours" line-officer mentality (Klockars 1985), line-level discontent (Brown 1981), and police officer corruption (Manning & Redlinger 1977).

The police professionalism movement was admonished for its failure to adapt to a changing urban milieu, particularly changes that involved minority emigration (Walker 1977). That the police professionalism movement advocated forms of police organization and behavior that alienated minority populations has been widely noted (Walker 1992b). Founded in the conflict between political machines and urban progressives at the end of the 19th century (Fogelson 1977), the movement, encouraged by police executives and supported in 1893 by the fledgling International Association of Chiefs of Police, represented the interests of the progressives. Structures associated with the movement—for example, a militaristic rank structure, civil service personnel system, and centralization of authority—provided police organizations with autonomy from local political machines.

The latent consequences of such "professionalized" organizational structures, critics argued, was a fundamental separation of police from community—civil service conflicted with efforts to hire minorities from within the service community, a militaristic rank structure contributed to a "we-them" siege mentality in which the "them" became the local community, and centralization of authority was inconsistent with the need to tailor police delivery of service to the needs of particular neighborhoods.

Following the commission reports, reform advocates promulgated a new police mission, a mission that legitimized police work in terms of protecting neighborhoods and communities (Kelling & Moore 1989; Alpert & Dunham 1988). Yet, whether reform efforts would have coalesced into the community-based policing movement of the 1980s without the support of the federal government by way of the Law Enforcement Assistance Administration (LEAA) is questionable. The history of the LEAA is a widely told story (Duffee 1980; Michalowski 1985). LEAA's contribution to the process of police relegitimation lay in its investment in police experimentation. As Feeley and Sarat (1980) noted, the federal government provided, even required, block grants for program and policy innovation in the Omnibus Safe Streets and Crime Control Act of 1968. As they said, "The message of the act was . . . simple—money would be given, innovation produced" (p. 92).

The LEAA supported widespread experimentation in the delivery of police services.[4] Team policing experiments, popular during the late 1960s and early 1970s, involved a "team" of officers assigned to a permanent geographical location and given the discretionary authority to develop their own solutions to crime problems. Team police were expected to identify with the local community, which would make them more sensitive to developing local crime problems. As many as 40 departments adopted some form of team policing in this period (Walker 1992b).

A second strategy was to reorganize the police into a less militaristic rank structure. For example, the city of Longmont, Colorado, abandoned traditional militaristic rank and insignia for civilian dress and less threatening titles and changed its name to

---

[4] This is not to imply that the LEAA was an advocate of community-oriented policing in favor of more traditional police practices. Only a relatively small percentage of the LEAA money was spent for community-oriented experimentation. Michalowski (1985:182) notes that the bulk of LEAA funds for policing went for crime control by supporting strategies for apprehension of criminals and deterrence. In 1973, for example, 29.4% of the monies that went to policing were provided for "soft" crime prevention or community relations programs. What was fortunate for the evolving community-based policing movement was that *any* federal money was being spent for experimentation into crime prevention or community-based programs.

56

the Longmont Department of Public Safety (Guyot 1979). Third, traditional ideas of police patrol were reconsidered. In what has been called the most significant experiment in policing in the 1970s, the Kansas City Police Department evaluated the efficacy of random preventive patrol, a cornerstone of traditional police patrol practices, and concluded that variations in the level of patrol had no effect on crime (Kelling et al. 1974).

Fourth, a function of police patrol was shifted from the gathering of incident-based statistics to the identification and analysis of problem areas, as proposed by Herman Goldstein (1979). Traditional ideas of random preventive patrol overlooked the fact that crime events were not distinct incidents but tended to be grouped together in problem areas. The proper focus of police patrol, said Goldstein, should not be on providing a broad deterrent by dispersing patrol across the community but rather on identifiable problem areas. Other strategies included "storefront" police stations—small, typically one-person offices scattered around a community providing a restricted range of services—and expanded foot patrol. Both these strategies were aimed at elevating the quality of police-community interaction and lowering citizens' fear of crime (Eck & Spelman 1987).

The 1970s thus witnessed the development of organizational structures and strategies aimed at reinvolving the police in the life of the community. It is against the backdrop of these organizational innovations that the mythos of community and watchman took root. The notions that cities were made up of moral communities, and that police could act as watchmen to protect these communities, were consistent with both the recommendations of both commissions and many of the structural and operational innovations in policing following the commission reports (Eck & Spelman 1987). The myths of watchman and community were to emerge as the foundational myths of the movement to institutionalize community-based policing.

Before examining the specific characteristics of the myths of the watchman and community, I will review the concept of myth and its foundational relationship to institutions and to the process of institutional development.

The Concept of Myth

That myth may take diverse forms in the service of a broad array of social and ceremonial purposes has been noted (Kirk 1974; Day 1984). One of these purposes, the functional role of myth, provides the foundation for institutional analysis of myth as it is used here. Functional perspectives of myth are grounded in the perspective that social customs and institutions are validated by myths. In a word, myths legitimate social institutions and imbue them with meaning (Kirk 1974).

57

The idea that myth provides a function for society may be traced to the writings of Durkheim (1955). Myth, Durkheim argued, establishes, maintains, and expresses social solidarity. The ritual acting out of myth is in its essence a ceremonial validation of social institutions (Day 1984:249). Durkheim's influence was evident in the work of Malinowski, who extended the functional analysis of myth. Myth, according to Malinowski, was not a reflection of cosmic events or of mysterious impulses in the human soul but acted as a *charter* for social institutions and actions. As a charter, myths validated traditional customs, attitudes, and beliefs (Kirk 1974:32).[5] Thus, myth imbued social institutions with legitimacy. The idea that myth performed important ceremonial functions for particular social groups was extended to police work by Manning (1977).[6]

Myth and Institutional Change

The idea that myth can be an agent of institutional change can be traced to the writings of Georges Sorel (1916), who wrote that myths were ideas carried by particular groups seeking social change. Myths, according to Sorel, had the following properties. They were social, that is, they were held by participants in some collective action. They were political in that they aimed at achieving a change in human affairs. They were intentional, acting on social structure rather than reflecting it. Finally, they were magical, that is, they were beyond the realm of rational choice and consequently could not be evaluated and falsified (Strenski 1987:164).[7]

Contemporary investigation into the function of myth for social institutions is typically traced to the work of Meyer and Rowan (1977). These authors contended that for organizations in highly institutionalized environments, organizational struc-

---

[5] Malinowski (1954:73) described the myth as a "vital ingredient of human civilization" that fulfills "an indispensable function: it expresses, enhances, and codifies belief; it safeguards and enforces morality."

[6] Myth, Manning suggested, served six purposes for the police. The first was to reinterpret events into integrated and holistic units, where police-citizen encounters are transformed into a confrontation between forces of good and evil. Second, police myths removed police activity from the realm of special interest. Third, myth provided an explanation of otherwise inextricable events (e.g., the myth that police enforce the law equally to all obscures the underlying reality that the probability of arrest for violent crime is actually very low). Fourth, mythical actors are provided with human attributes, placed in dramatic events, and given predictable outcomes. Fifth, myths drew public attention to the stability of the police, even in times of change. Sixth, police myths gave the police a symbolic and heightened authority over that which they oppose.

[7] Similar ideas have been used to describe the ideology as a political device. Swidler (1986) noted that highly charged beliefs may emerge in competition with existing cultural frameworks. Systems of such beliefs are ideologies, in which ideology is conceptualized as a highly articulated and organized systems of ideas carried by individuals who aim at fundamental institutional change (Drucker 1974). Crank, Payn, and Jackson (1993) referred to the police professionalism movement in its early days as such a system of highly charged and articulated beliefs.

tures, and formal activities did not serve purposes of efficiency or effectiveness. Instead, forms of organizational structure and activity were highly institutionalized and conformed to widely held ideas about the way organizations should act and work—ideas that were mythic in that they were perceived to be beyond the ability of any particular actor to change.

Organizations that conformed to institutional myths of structure and activity received legitimacy from other institutional actors, thereby facilitating access to resources and improving the prospects of organizational survival (Meyer & Rowan 1977:345). The influence of the institutional environment over organizational structure and behavior was particularly important for public sector organizations that tended to be low on technological development and high on institutional development (Dobbin et al. 1988; Meyer & Scott 1983).

Ritti and Silver (1986) extended Meyer and Scott's ideas to the process of institutionalization. They examined the ways in which a new organization, the Bureau of Consumer Services (BCS) in Pennsylvania, attained legitimacy in a highly institutionalized organizational environment. If, they argued, organizations embodied in their structure and policies prevailing institutional myths in the organizational environment, then "myth making must be a first step in the process of institutionalization" (p. 27). In their analysis, the BCS had to demonstrate that it was a legitimate public representative of consumer concerns, while at the same time insuring a fair return to the industry. Structural innovations, described in their research as formal organizational ties and ceremonial interactions with the electricity, gas, and telephone companies, allowed the BCS to acquire legitimacy in its institutional environment while demonstrating to the public and legislature that it was indeed acting as a legitimate protector of the public interest. Thus, Ritti and Silver suggested, for highly institutionalized sectors such as the one in which BCS was participating, the process of organizational innovation was an institutional solution to the need to attain organizational legitimacy.

Crank and Langworthy (1992) looked at myth and institutionalized environments among police organizations.[8] These authors presented a discussion of three powerful myth-building processes: coercive legitimacy stemming from rules, law, and licensing; the elaboration of relations networks in their organizational and institutional environment; and organizational-institutional reactivity, in which the organization or powerful individuals representing it were recognized as powerful actors in

---

[8] Applying the Meyer & Rowan (1977) perspective of institutionalized organizations to police agencies, the authors argued that police organizations were not "mere engines" of bureaucratic efficiency (Selznick 1957:15) but embodied in their formal structures and activities "widespread understandings of social reality," called myths (Meyer & Rowan 1977:343).

their environments. The incorporation of widely held myths into structure and activity, they suggested, demonstrated to other powerful actors within the institutional sector that a police organization looked and behaved appropriately. When organizations conformed to institutional expectations, they received organizational legitimacy and thus were provided with continuing accesses to resources.

The Properties of Institutional Myths

Four elements common to myths can be drawn from the previous discussion. First, myths, as institutional elements, have *power*. This means two things. On the one hand, they convey a sense of permanence and importance above and beyond the influence of particular actors (DiMaggio 1988; Meyer & Rowan 1977). On the other, myths that invoke history do not derive their power from the historical accuracy of their premises but from the way metaphorical images conjured by myth enables an organization to provide a satisfactory public account of its behavior (Klockars 1991).

Second, a myth contains within it implications regarding features of the environment affected by the myth (Trice & Beyer 1984; Ritti & Silver 1986).[9] That is, the myth is contextualized by a social or physical geography. For the police, this refers to their beat area and the dangers that inhere in that area. Third, contained within a myth is the emergence or transformation of something. For the police, this transformation is from danger to safety (Manning 1977). For example, ideas of community are set against ideas of urban society, with its seeming absence of morality and host of social ills.

The fourth component is specific to the process of institutionalization—the idea that foundational myths are tied to particular powerful individuals or political interest groups within the institutional environment. Traditionally, institutional theorists have looked at how a coercive institutional presence obstructs individual goal-directed behavior (DiMaggio & Powell 1983). The influence of individual actors over particular institutional processes is being increasingly recognized (Powell 1991; Crank & Langworthy 1992). The myth-building process itself may stem from individual goal-directed behavior and may reflect the political influence of "institutional entrepreneurs" (DiMaggio 1988: 13).[10] Because institutionalized myths become "part of the stock

---

9 Ritti and Silver (p. 26) note that myths convey "unquestioned beliefs not only about the origins, functions, and technical efficacy of the innovation, but also about the features of the environment that require adoption of the innovation."

10 In DiMaggio's words, while the *product* of institutionalized environments may place "organizational structures and practices beyond the reach of interest and politics," the *process* of institutionalization "is profoundly political and reflects the relative power of organized interests and the actors who mobilize around them."

of 'things taken for granted' within the prevailing organizational culture" (Ritti & Silver 1986:26), the influence of moral entrepreneurs over the myth-building process may be both powerful and long term, affecting both organizational structure and activity.[11] Thus, elements of police procedure and structure introduced in the current era may extend well into the future, independent of their efficiency or effectiveness in terms of law enforcement or crime prevention.

This review of myth and institutional process provides the framework for discussing the myths of watchman and community and for understanding how those myths contribute to the process of institutionalization of the community policing movement. I argue that community policing as a new legitimating mandate worked because it evoked powerful metaphors of democracy, small-town morality, and local autonomy (Manning 1984). The strength of the metaphorical image of policing as a community-based enterprise derived from its evocation of two powerful myths—the myth of the watchman and of community (Mastrofski 1991; Walker 1989a).

The Mythos of Community Policing

The myth of the watchman is as follows. The primary tasks of the police who do community-based policing are the maintenance of the public order and protection of the community from criminal invasion. To accomplish these tasks, the police mandate is to reinforce the informal social control mechanisms already present in communities (Wilson & Kelling 1982). By adopting strategies and tactics appropriate to the specific needs of particular communities, by dealing with underlying problems rather than incidents, and by generally becoming involved in the life of the community, police can do something about both crime and fear of crime and thus enhance the overall quality of community life (Skolnick & Bayley 1986; Goldstein 1979).

The police officer who does this work is not occupying a police role new to American cities but is a contemporary version of the friendly night watchman who served, in his walking beat, the immigrant masses and urban poor in the 19th century (Moore & Kelling 1983). Thus, there was already in place a historical model, called the "watchman," for the type of policing appropri-

---

[11] An example of the influence of an institutional entrepreneur is revealed in the works of August Vollmer, often cited as the patriarch of the police professionalism movement. One of his contributions to policing was the establishment of the Uniform Crime Reports (UCR) in 1929 (Carte 1986). Vollmer initially proposed the Uniform Crime Reports as a method to track crime in the United States. Today, the ritual of data collection for the UCR is accomplished by tens of thousands of reporting districts across the country, all of which use similar offense classifications for the labeling of crime.

ate for contemporary crime control problems (Wilson 1968; Wilson & Kelling 1982).[12]

The second myth, the myth of community, is a myth about what it is that the watchman protects. The community myth is that there is now, or ever has been, a "community" in the sense of groups of like-minded individuals, living in urban areas, who share a common heritage, have similar values and norms, and share a common perception of social order (see Mastrofski 1991). This image of moral community was presented by Tocqueville (1945:71) in his discussion of the relationship between a New England native and his community, and is used in Kelling's (1987) article advocating order-maintenance policing:

> [The community's] welfare is the aim of his ambition and of his future expectations . . . . [H]e acquires a taste for order, comprehends the balance of powers, and collects clear practical notions on the nature of his duties and the extent of his rights.

The relationship between the watchman and the community has provided the foundation for a mythos of community-based policing. The watchman was responsible for the preservation and protection of a conception of community that celebrated the traditions and values of traditional American society (Klockars 1991; Walker 1989a). Community-based policing "taps a nostalgia for the U.S. democratic grass-roots tradition of citizen initiative" (Mastrofski 1991:515). Thus, the watchman and his work reaffirmed an image of community morality of 19th-century America and provided a blanket of myth to shroud that powerful image in nostalgic imagery.

These myths are consistent with the previous discussion of foundational myths. First, they have power. On the one hand, they convey a sense of durability and permanence to ideas of communities and watchmen. On the other, their power derives not from their historical accuracy (Walker 1989b) but from recognition by the public and police alike that watchman and community are valid metaphors from which to model the organization and activity of police agencies.

Second, these myths provide a transformative image from dangerous urban environments into safe and orderly "communities." Communities destroyed by poverty and criminal predation are transformed by community police into moral communities with like-minded citizens preserving a common heritage. It is the watchman who enables this transformation to occur.

Third, the idea of community contains many implications of the environment encompassed by the myth. Geographically and ethnically identifiable groups become "neighborhoods," or

---

12 The recurring reference to the watchman in male gender is used instead of a gender-neutral phraseology to indicate the paternalistic quality of the watchman image implicit in early discussions of the watchman. Also, the use of the male gender specification in the word "watchman" is historically accurate.

moral entities characterized by a sense of belonging, a sense of common goals, involvement in community affairs, and a sense of wholeness (Poplin 1979).

Fourth, these myths are linked to particular individuals or political groups in the institutional environment of policing. The development of ideas regarding community-based policing can be traced to the writings of individuals who act as institutional entrepreneurs. The remainder of this article traces the development of the ideas of community policing and the particular influence of institutional entrepreneurs on the process of institutionalization of community-based policing.

The Watchman and the Law Enforcer: The Emergence of the Myth

The idea that police work contains watchman elements can be traced to Wilson's (1968) seminal study of police style in eight communities. His presentation of watchman-style departments provided a perspective for thinking about police work in terms of community protection. By contrasting watchmen and legalistic departments, Wilson provided an alternative to the idea that all police work is characterized by the police professionalism model.

The influence of Wilson's conception of police style stemmed not only from the content of his message but from its timeliness. That Wilson's writing coincided with the broad legitimation crisis that was occurring to the police nationally increased the likelihood that his cogent way of thinking about police would achieve recognition. In the 1960s, the field of criminal justice was undergoing a profound change, described by Walker (1992a) as a shift from a *progressive era* to a *systems* paradigm. An aspect of this new paradigm was a recognition of the wide discretion that police employ in the performance of their work. Although others (e.g., Goldstein 1963) had noted police use of discretion, Wilson (1968) provided a case affirming the centrality of discretion to the task of line-level police. Wilson's recognition of the discretionary quality of police work coincided with and complemented the paradigmatic shift across the field of criminal justice in the 1960s.

Breaking from the idea that police work simply amounted to efforts to maximize law enforcement activity, Wilson argued that there were different styles of police work. Integral to Wilson's presentation of styles of policing was a distinction between policing as a profession and policing as a craft. A craftsmanship style of policing was indicated by departments that displayed a "watchman" style of policing—one in which police activity was directed more toward maintaining the public order than enforcing the law. The watchman Wilson described was a metaphor for the traditions of the department, of the "good old days" when a police officer could, with skills learned through street sense and apprenticeship, solve problems without invoking the formal process of law. The watchman controlled his beat by relying on personal authority to solve problems on the street and used his practical knowledge of local culture as a *tool kit* to provide seemingly intuitive solutions to everyday problems of the citizenry.[13]

Philosophically opposed to craftsmanship was police professionalism, the guiding ideology of police reform from the end of the 19th century through the 1960s (Brown 1981; Berman 1987). Professionalism, as an explicit and articulated set of strategies for police occupational reform, emerged as an ideological challenge by police reformers to the big-city machine control of the police organization (Fogelson 1977). However, Wilson argued that order maintenance was central to the police role, and for that reason, professionalizing chiefs would always exist in an uneasy relationship with the rank and file. In sum, Wilson presented an image of police work that was by its nature dominated by highly discretionary order-maintenance interventions and an ethic of craftsmanship that infused this type of work with commonsense meaning. This image of police work provided the basis for the later development of the watchman myth.

Myth Transformation in the 1980s: From Description to Prescription

The 1980s witnessed a reconsideration of the federalization of the crime effort that marked crime-control strategy from the issuance of the Kerner and Crime Commission reports. This was an era of a "new federalism" in which fiscal responsibility for crime control was shifted onto the states. It was an era of crime control in which ideas of community were increasingly invoked in conjunction with crime-control strategy. The use of community-based alternative efforts to resolve disputes, for example, were given impetus by the Dispute Resolution Act of 1980. Alternative dispute resolution (ADR) sought to move disputes out of the decisionmaking apparatus of the criminal justice system and into community participation and neighborhood self-governance (Duffee 1980:230). Intermediate sanctions that placed offenders within the community became the centerpiece of the community corrections movement. Much of this movement was aimed at creating the appearance of a more severe criminal justice system while at the same time allowing offenders to be released from incarceration.[14]

---

[13] A cultural "tool kit" may be described as a set of cultural skills that direct and influence behavior. The notion of culture as a tool kit provides a perspective on the differential abilities of individuals to employ particular social actions or behaviors in the pursuit of similar goals (Swidler 1986).

[14] See Gordon (1991:92–144) for a discussion of community as prison. Duffee (1980:230) notes: "In corrections, intermediate punishments such as home incarceration, electronic monitoring, and intensive probation supervision have become the buzzwords in community programming."

In police work, the 1980s witnessed the coalescence of program innovations, structures, and policies into a full-fledged community-based policing movement. Skolnick and Bayley (1986) described how police departments in six major cities reorganized elements of organizational structure and patrol strategy in line with ideas of community-based policing. Trojanowicz and Bucqueroux (1990) provide an overview of community efforts in several communities and describe briefly community-police efforts in 9 cities. And Rosenbaum (1986) provides a detailed description of 11 community-policing evaluations in 14 U.S. cities.

If the 1980s were marked by a shift in police to an enterprise conceived in terms of ideas of community, they were also marked by a maturing of the philosophy of the police as community protectors. A broad dialogue on community-based reform was conducted among practitioners and academicians alike (Hartmann 1988; Sykes 1986; Moore & Kelling 1983). Perhaps the most influential of the new conceptualizations of police work was an article entitled "Broken Windows" (Wilson & Kelling 1982).

In 1982, the publication of "Broken Windows" marked a fundamental transformation in the watchman myth. The transformation was moral: The myth of the watchman shifted from a description of police style in particular types of urban departments to a prescription describing how police work should generally be. The watchman image evolved from that of a blue-collar craftsman who displayed an idiosyncratic, street-wise policing style to a standardbearer for the protection of urban communities in late 20th-century America.

The broken windows idea was a simple metaphor: If a broken window in an untended building was left unrepaired, the remainder of the windows would soon be broken. Similarly, untended behavior leads to the breakdown of community controls. The broken window was an analogy for untended behavior. Wilson and Kelling linked the broken-window analogy to what they perceived to be a contemporary cycle of urban decay that began with the presence of untended property (and by implication, "untended" behavior) and ended with the breakdown of community controls and the moral and economic destruction of neighborhoods via criminal invasion. The police could disrupt the process of urban decay by reinforcing the informal control mechanisms of the community itself. The responsibility of the police was to protect the rights of the community, even if sacrifices to individual liberties were incurred.

The police had only to look to their past to find a model for the watchman. Wilson and Kelling argued that a community protection style of policing was present prior to the end of the 19th century. This style, described by a community-oriented order-maintenance mandate, was present in the activity of the watchman in large urban departments through the latter half of the

65

19th century. Wilson and Kelling (ibid., p. 38) concluded: "Above all, we must return to our long-abandoned view that the police ought to protect communities as well as individuals." This article thrust Wilson and Kelling into the role of institutional entrepreneurs, providing contemporary police reform with a model of police style constructed from a powerful mythos derived from a historical era of policing and imbued with a "moral rightness" of the police role as community protector derived from that mythos.[15]

The Linkage to Community-based Policing

The linkage of the watchman to ideas of police reform had an inevitability that only retrospect can reveal. The idea of community invoked by proponents of community-based policing provided an appropriate environment for the work of the watchman (Klockars 1991). Simply put, community-based policing, with its emphasis on the maintenance of public order (as opposed to enforcing the law) was precisely the kind of work the watchman did. Mastrofski (1991:515) provided a clear statement of this linkage in his analysis of the community policing reform movement:

> [C]ommunity policing advocates propose a significant departure from the ways in which issues of role, control, and legitimacy are addressed. Order maintenance replaces law enforcement as the police mission; legalistic constraints on officer discretion are reduced, while direct linkages to the community are increased; and policies and actions are justified . . . in terms of the sense of peace, order, and security they impart to the public.

The myth of the watchman was thus joined to an image of community. Like the watchman myth, the community protected by the watchman was also mythic. The community-based policing movement capitalized on a "nostalgia for the U.S. democratic grass-roots tradition of citizen initiative" (ibid.) where "[c]ommunity relationships are based on status not contract, manners not morals, norms not laws, and understandings not regulations" (Klockars 1991:535). In the mythic reconstruction of the past, the image of community that emerged as corollary to the watchman was 19th-century small-town America, with citizenry of moral fiber, of common purpose, and value (Alpert & Dunham 1988). The watchman symbolized protection of small-town America from the profound social and economic dislocations that washed across the American municipal landscape in the 20th century. As a myth of police reform, the watchman promised a rebirth of the spirit of 19th-century small-town morality in

---

[15] See DiMaggio (1988:15) for a discussion of morality and institutional entrepreneurship.

66

the 21st-century urban metropolis. Thus, the conjoined myths of community and watchman became valid and powerful representations of what community-based policing should be and provided a powerful morality of police behavior that justified legal and extralegal tactics in the name of community preservation.

Watchmen and Arrest Authority

The emergent mythos of community-based policing proved adaptable to the new federalism of the 1980s, a period in which executive federal leadership sought to divest the government of fiscal responsibility for state and municipal problems. A conundrum of the new federalism was to balance the expensive, punishment-oriented crime-control policies characteristic of the 1970s and 1980s with a strategy in which the federal government played a sharply reduced role (Duffee 1980). On the one hand, all segments of the criminal justice system were abandoning rehabilitation in favor of punitive strategies emphasizing incapacitation, deterrence, and retribution (Gordon 1991; Walker 1980). On the other, the federal government was relinquishing its role as bankroller for local crime-control efforts. These trends created a crime-control dilemma at the local level: Legislators at all levels were seeking increasingly punitive crime legislation, while local municipalities were increasingly expected to pick up the cost (Feeley & Sarat 1980). For corrections, this problem has been phrased as a question: How can criminals be sentenced to probation or parole and at the same time the appearance be created that the criminal justice system is being more punitive toward them? The answer was to increase the use of intensive supervision and to stack the sheer number of programs required for probationers and parolees. Communities were thus made to look like prison in concept and in degree of control over offenders (Gordon 1991). But the urban police asked: How could reforms favorable to community-based policing be sustained while preserving politically popular law-and-order ideas of tough-minded, arrest-producing police work?

The answer was a sharp reversal in the conceptualization of the watchman style in the early 1980s, from a police officer who would infrequently invoke formal processes of law, even in the presence of law breaking, to one who would arrest to maintain community order, even in the absence of law breaking. A component of the style of the craftsman, as articulated by Wilson (1977; 1968), was the police tendency to underenforce the law. Arrest was invoked only as a last resort, when all other strategies for restoring order had failed.

By the mid-1980s, the paternalistic image of the police as tough and street-wise but fair underenforcers of the law had evolved into an image of the watchman as a no-holds-barred aggressive order-maintenance superenforcer who would arrest, even in legally ambiguous situations, in the name of protecting the community (Kelling 1985; Sykes 1986). Kelling (1987), citing civic responsibility, advocated police intervention in the public roller-skating activities of juveniles in Chicago. Aggressive order maintenance, including the use of arrest, was needed to provide the public with order and safety from threatening behavior. As Kelling (p. 91) asked, "Do we want police officers to develop a 'What the hell' attitude toward disorderly or dangerous behavior, even if it is not *technically* illegal?" (emphasis added). Wilson and Kelling (1982) similarly argued for the priority of community protection over individual due process protections. This aggressive police response to order-maintenance problems was often cited in the literature (Sykes 1989, Kelling 1985; Moore & Kelling 1983: Wycoff & Manning 1983). Thus, by the mid-1980s, the policing style associated with the watchman had shifted from infrequent intervention and underenforcement of the law, in the name of community preservation and protection, to frequent intervention and arrest even in legally ambiguous situations, again in the name of community preservation and protection.

The Political Dimensions of Institutional Myth Making

Nostalgia, we must make no mistake, is good politics.

—Robert Nisbet 1988:110

As a reform agenda, community-based policing has been tractable to both conservative and liberal ideas of crime control. Central elements of community-based policing—an emphasis on problem-oriented tactics, police-community partnership in crime prevention activities, geographical and command decentralization of authority to the line level, and an elevation of the importance of order maintenance and crime prevention activity (Skolnick & Bayley 1986; Kelling & Moore 1989)—are present in both conservative and liberal perspectives of police reform. By considering these two perspectives, we can begin to understand the power and mutability that sustains community-based policing as a reform movement.[16]

Institutional entrepreneurs representing the conservative political view advocate an aggressive order-maintenance style of policing in which due process considerations of individual liberties are less important than community protection (Wilson & Kelling 1982).[17] Aggressive order maintenance is an effective deter-

---

16 I am not suggesting that the individuals mentioned in this paragraph are either politically conservative or liberal. I am suggesting that the ideas mentioned in conjunction with their work are consistent with either conservative or liberal crime-control ideas (see Walker 1989a:10–17).

17 Walker (1989a) notes that in practice, the differences between liberal and conservative perspectives tend to become "muddy." The value of the liberal-conservative dis-

rent for crime (Kelling 1985). Community breakdown occurs not from underlying social or structural problems in those communities but from criminal invasion into those communities. The watchman, as the moral representative of the community, is provided with substantial discretion to deal with problems on the street, and may even use arrest when no law has been broken. The issue of discretion, according to this perspective, is about whether to observe an individual's due process protections when observing threats to "community rights" (Alpert & Dunham 1988). Appropriate police strategies to achieve these ends include vigorous enforcement of nuisance and order-maintenance laws, arresting people for violation of order-maintenance statutes, and field interrogations (Mastrofski 1991).

The liberal agenda describes a strikingly different view of community-based policing. The watchman is a community organizer (Skolnick & Bayley 1986) whose task is not aggressive order maintenance but crime prevention through community service. The watchman engages in the shoring up of community institutions through community and neighborhood organization. The watchman approaches crime not through aggressive patrol strategies—these are believed to alienate citizens—but by sponsoring community-based programs that aim at crime prevention and community service (Alpert & Dunham 1988). Consequently, the watchman constructs ties to the local community and develops local strategies that assist the community to repair itself (Guyot 1991). Strategies include newsletters, block watch, nonenforcement police-citizen encounters, and victim follow-up (Mastrofski 1991). Thus, from the liberal perspective, the watchman assists the community in self-repair, while from the conservative perspective, the watchman protects the community from the destructive influence of criminal invasion (Skolnick & Bayley 1986; Wilson & Kelling 1982).

Two examples, drawn from Skolnick and Bayley's (1986) research on contemporary police innovation, illuminate the distinction between the liberal and conservative organizational elements of community-based policing. The first, Detroit, developed innovative structures consistent with what I have described as the liberal conception of community policing. Mayor Coleman Young implemented the program to deemphasize traditional, reactive policing in favor of "intensive community mobilization for self-defense." This was accomplished through the implementation of two organizational units that did only crime prevention activity, a crime prevention section, and a mini-station command. The crime prevention section organized neighborhood watches, apartment watches, and business watches. Special attention was

tinction is that it enables policymakers to assess the assumptions that provide the basis of much current crime-control policy.

given to the needs of elderly citizens, including the maintenance of a senior citizen roster and transportation for personal needs. A mini-station command operating in 52 mini-stations scattered around the city was devoted exclusively to community mobilization. Officers assigned to these beats spent half their time in patrol and half their time in community organization. These officers also would organize citizen band patrols and would maintain regular ongoing contact with community leaders. A great deal of patrol time was devoted by both sections to the organization of and participation in citizen crime-prevention meetings, described as the lifeblood of crime prevention. Meetings were held at the neighborhood level, and each precinct had a police-community relations council. Officers in both sections did what Skolnick and Bayley described as creative, customized fieldwork; their responsibility was to tailor crime prevention efforts to the particular needs of local areas.

Organizational innovations in the Denver Police Department are consistent with conservative ideas of community-based policing. The approach to reducing fear of crime in Denver was in terms of improving patrol effectiveness, accomplished by specialized, proactive field units. This directed patrol strategy involved four elements: intensified coverage, delegation of command responsibility, team activity, and operational crime analysis. The assumption by the Denver command was that some types of crimes were "patrol preventable," where crime prevention was achieved through high patrol visibility. Through the use of crime analysis techniques, specialized squads were engaged in problem-solving activity.

One organizational innovation was the development of a Special Crime Attack Team that attacked the problem of burglary through saturation patrol. A Special Services Unit was also established that required skills in the specialized application of force, such as hostage situations. Another program, called ESCORT (Eliminate Street Crime on Residential Thoroughfares), was described as aggressive order-maintenance. As one officer described the program, their job was to "find a rock and kick it," to look for minor violations and seek out individuals with known reputations. ESCORT was, as Skolnick and Bayley (1986:139) noted, "deterrent policing with a vengeance."

The areas of innovation adopted by Denver represented not so much a change in the role of police as modifications and extensions of traditional patrol strategy. Denver, though adopting programmatic innovations aimed at decentralizing command authority, increasing emphasis on order-maintenance activity, and doing proactive, problem-oriented policing, continued to be wedded to traditional ideas of the centrality of police patrol for police work. Storefront police organizations and a crime-prevention-oriented community services bureau were initiated but were perceived as ineffective; they were not integrated into the ongoing field operations of the department. Thus, Denver implemented types of organizational innovation consistent with three of the ideas of community-based policing stated at the opening of this section—decentralization of authority for specialized patrol activities, an elevation of order-maintenance activity through the use of aggressive order-maintenance street tactics, and the implementation of problem-oriented evaluational strategies. But in operational strategy and organizational development, these innovations matched what I have described as the conservative branch of the community policing movement.

These two examples reveal the flexibility of the foundational myths of watchman and community. Given the right "spin," ideas of community-based policing are acceptable organizational theory for both conservative and liberal advocates of police change. Because legitimacy can be obtained from both conservative and liberal proponents of police change, community-based policing appears to be sufficiently adaptable to survive a changing and somewhat unpredictable political electorate. In other words, even given the mutable tides of American electoral politics, community policing continues to be a healthy and vigorous movement that is becoming institutionalized.

Institutional Change in the Occupation of Policing

The rapidity with which elements of community-based policing are currently diffusing across the municipal landscape is remarkable. By 1985, more than 300 police departments had adopted some form of community policing program (Walker 1992b). The state of Washington is currently exploring a strategy to convert over 50 municipal and county police agencies in the state to a community-based policing model. Support for community-based policing has been provided by the National Institute of Justice, with its allocation of a special grants category for research and experimentation on community-based policing. Textbooks and readers on policing in the United States today all contain sections on community-based policing. Experiments with community-based elements have been conducted in many major U.S. cities (Trojanowicz & Bucqueroux 1990; Skolnick & Bayley 1986). The chiefs of police of 10 major metropolitan police organizations in 1991 issued a position paper in support of community policing (Christopher Commission 1991:104).[18] The past commissioner of New York City, Lee Brown, developed a program to convert the entire New York City Police Department to a community-based model, a program that continues today. In

---

[18] The report of the Independent Commission on the Los Angeles Police Department (1991) is also referred to as "the Christopher Commission." The References include cross-references from the Christopher Commission to the Independent Commission.

short, community-based policing, with its core myths of community and watchman, is being institutionalized.

With the institutionalization of elements of community-based policing, legitimacy lost in the late 1960s becomes legitimacy restored in the current era. A new legitimating mandate, infused with powerful myths of community and watchman, appears to be steadily displacing the previous mandate of police professionalism. That this process is proceeding with fervor is illustrated by the Christopher Commission report (ibid.). That report, an investigation into police conduct in Los Angeles, called for sweeping changes in structure and procedure to refocus department resources in the direction of community-based policing (ibid., pp. 95–106). In microcosm, the Christopher Commission report enacted the drama laid out by the Kerner and Crime Commissions at the national level and affirmed the continuing vitality of the myths of community and police as community watchmen.

Conclusions

By the late 1980s, many scholars had raised important questions regarding community-based policing (Walker 1992b). Walker (1989b) cited problems of historical accuracy in Wilson and Kelling's (1982) discussion of watchman-style 19th-century patrol practices. Klockars (1985) challenged Kelling's (1985) linkage between aggressive order-maintenance patrol practices and the quality of urban life. Bohm (1984) questioned whether community-based institutions could represent the breadth of interests of a diverse citizenry or provide informal systems of control. Crank (1990) suggested that police are more likely to have a professional than a crafts-like view of their occupational activity. Positive, rather than negative, relationships were noted between aggressive order-maintenance behavior and victimization (Sherman 1986). Mastrofski (1991) provided a broad-ranging discussion of misconceptions of the concept of community and implications of those misconceptions for police activity. Klockars (1991) charged that the community-policing movement was a circumlocution whose purpose was to obscure the principal role of police as a mechanism for the distribution of nonnegotiable coercive force (Bittner 1970). Bayley (1988) cited a host of theoretical and practical issues seldom addressed by advocates of community-based policing. Thus, a large body of literature emerged to challenge many facets of the community policing movement.

These challenges to community-based policing, though thoughtful and important, have overlooked an important point regarding community-based policing (but see Klockars 1991). Although it is, of course, important to ask whether community-based structures and policies are efficient or effective in the achievement of crime control, it is also important to note that community-based policing provides police organizations with an organizational theory that is acceptable to other institutional actors, in Meyer and Scott's (1983) terms, whose opinions count. By adopting elements of community and watchman into their structures and formalized activities, police organizations ceremonially regain the legitimacy that was ceremonially withdrawn in the 1960s.

The rapid spread of elements of community-based reform across the institutional sector of policing suggests that the invocation of community is providing an acceptable legitimating theory for police organizations. Furthermore, images of watchman and community do not derive their power from historical accuracy and thus are not vulnerable to inaccuracies in historical reporting. They derive their power to mobilize sentiment from the mythic images of watchmen as community protectors and communities as enclaves of traditional American values. I have argued here that institutional entrepreneurs have latched onto these myths and have modified them in an effort to affect the direction of policing at the outset of the 21st century. This is evident in Wilson and Kelling's 1982 "Broken Windows" piece, in which the authors cast the mythos of the watchman in terms of conservative theology.

There are institutional entrepreneurs on both sides of the conservative-liberal debate, and at present neither side is recognized as the authoritative expression of community-based policing philosophy, policy, and strategy. This can be seen in the widespread popularity of community-based policing and the virtual absence of consensus over the definition of the term or the appropriate role of community-based police officers. Nevertheless, given the current spirit of change in policing, particular community-based strategies will undoubtedly diffuse across the urban vista. The types of organizational structures, policies, and operational strategies that emerge under the banner of community-based policing will, I suspect, depend on the advocacy of institutional entrepreneurs, whose efficacy will in turn reflect the relative prominence of conservative or liberal crime-control agendas in the wider sphere of American politics. However, community-based policing, guided by a powerful and surprisingly mutable mythos of police and community, will probably be with us in one form or another for many years to come.

References

Alpert, Geoffrey P., & Roger G. Dunham (1988) *Policing Multi-ethnic Neighborhoods.* New York: Greenwood Press.

Bayley, David H. (1988) "Community Policing: A Report from the Devil's Advocate," in J. R. Greene & S. D. Mastrofski, eds., *Community Policing: Rhetoric or Reality?* New York: Praeger.

Berman, Jay Stuart (1987) *Police Administration and Progressive Reform: Theodore Roosevelt as Police Commissioner of New York.* New York: Greenwood Press.

Bittner, Egon (1970) *The Functions of Police in Modern Society.* Chevy Chase, MD: National Institute of Mental Health.

Bohm, Robert (1984) Book Review, 1 *Justice Q.* 449.

Brown, Michael K. (1981) *Working the Street: Police Discretion and the Dilemmas of Reform.* New York: Russell Sage Foundation.

Carte, Gene Edward (1986) "August Vollmer and the Origin of Police Professionalism," in M. R. Pogrebin & R. M. Regoli, eds., *Police Administrative Issues: Techniques and Functions,* Millwood, NY: Associated Faculty Press.

Christopher Commission (1991) See Independent Commission on the Los Angeles Police Department (1991).

Crank, John P. (1990) "Police: Professionals or Craftsmen? An Empirical Assessment of Professionalism and Craftsmanship among Eight Municipal Police Agencies," 18 *J. Criminal Justice* 333.

Crank, John P., & Robert Langworthy (1992) "An Institutional Perspective of Policing," 83 *J. of Criminal Law & Criminology* 338.

Crank, John P., Betsy Payn, & Stanley Jackson (1993) "The Relationship between Police Belief Systems and Attitude toward Police Practices," 20 *Criminal Justice & Behavior* 199.

Crime Commission (1967) See U.S. President's Commission on Law Enforcement and Administration of Justice (1967).

Day, Martin S. (1984) *The Many Meanings of Myth.* Lanham, MD: Univ. Press of America.

DiMaggio, Paul (1988) "Interest and Agency in Institutional Theory," in Zucker 1988.

DiMaggio, Paul, & Walter Powell (1983) "The Iron Cage Revisited: Institutional Isomorphism and Collective Rationality in Organizational Fields," 48 *American Sociological Rev.* 147.

Dobbin, Frank R., Lauren Edelmen, John W. Meyer, W. Richard Scott, & Ann Swidler (1988) "The Expansion of Due Process in Organizations," in Zucker 1988.

Drucker, H. M. (1974) *The Political Uses of Ideology.* London: Macmillan, for the London School of Economics and Political Science.

Duffee, David (1980) *Explaining Criminal Justice: Community Theory and Criminal Justice Reform.* Cambridge, MA: Oelgeschlager, Gunn & Hain.

Dunham, Roger G., & Geoffrey P. Alpert, eds. (1989) *Critical Issues in Policing.* Prospect Heights, IL: Waveland Press.

Durkheim, Emile (1955) *The Elementary Forms of the Religious Life,* trans. J. W. Swain. New York: Free Press.

Eck, John E., & William Spelman (1987) "Who Ya Gonna Call? The Police as Problem-Busters," 33 *Crime & Delinquency* 31.

Feeley, Malcolm M., & Austin D. Sarat (1980) *The Policy Dilemma: Federal Crime Policy and the Law Enforcement Assistance Administration.* Minneapolis: Univ. of Minnesota Press.

Fogelson, Robert (1977) *Big-City Police.* Cambridge: Harvard Univ. Press.

Geertz, Clifford (1973) "Thick Description: Toward an Interpretive Theory of Culture," in C. Geertz, ed., *The Interpretation of Cultures.* New York: Basic Books.

Geller, William A., ed. (1985) *Police Leadership in America: Crisis and Opportunity.* New York: Praeger.

Goldstein, Herman (1963) "Police Discretion: The Ideal versus the Real," 23 *Public Administration Rev.* 140.

—— (1979) "Improving Policing: A Problem-oriented Approach," 25 *Crime & Delinquency* 25: 236-58.

Gordon, Diana R. (1991) *The Justice Juggernaut: Fighting Street Crime, Controlling Citizens.* New Brunswick, NJ: Rutgers Univ. Press.

Greene, Jack R. (1989) "Police and Community Relations: Where Have We Been and Where Are We Going?" in Dunham & Alpert 1989.

Guyot, Dorothy (1979) "Bending Granite: Attempts to Change the Rank Structure of American Police Departments," 7 *J. of Police Science & Administration* 253.

—— (1991) *Policing as Though People Matter.* Philadelphia: Temple Univ. Press.

Hall, Richard H. (1982) *Organizations: Structures, Processes, and Outcomes.* 3d ed. Englewood Cliffs, NJ: Prentice-Hall.

Hartmann, Francis X. (1988) *Debating the Evolution of American Policing.* Perspectives on the Police #5. Washington: National Institute of Justice.

Independent Commission on the Los Angeles Police Department (1991) *Report of the Independent Commission on the Los Angeles Police Department* ("Christopher Commission"). Los Angeles: The Independent Commission.

Kelling, George L. (1985) "Order Maintenance, the Quality of Urban Life, and Police: A Line of Argument," in Geller 1985.

—— (1987) "Acquiring a Taste for Order: The Community and the Police," 33 *Crime & Delinquency* 90.

Kelling, George, Tony Pate, Duane Dieckman, & Charles E. Brown (1974) *The Kansas City Preventive Patrol Experiment: A Technical Report.* Washington: Police Foundation.

Kelling, George, & Mark H. Moore (1989) *The Evolving Strategy of Policing.* Perspectives on Policing #4. Washington: National Institute on Justice & Harvard Univ.

Kerner Commission (1967) See National Advisory Commission on Civil Disorders (1967).

Kirk, G. S. (1974) *The Nature of Greek Myths.* New York: Penguin Books.

Klockars, Carl B. (1985) "Order and Maintenance, the Quality of Urban Life, and Police: A Different Line of Argument," in Geller 1985.

—— (1991) "The Rhetoric of Community Policing," in Klockars & Mastrofski 1991.

Klockars, Carl B., & Stephen D. Mastrofski, eds. (1991) *Thinking about Policing.* 2d ed. New York: McGraw-Hill.

Malinowski, Bronislaw (1954) *Magic, Science and Religion.* New York: Doubleday.

Manning, Peter K. (1977) *Police Work: The Social Organization of Policing.* Cambridge: MIT Press.

—— (1984) "Community Policing," 3 *American J. of Police* 205.

Manning, Peter, & Lawrence John Redlinger (1977) "Invitational Edges of Corruption: Some Consequences of Narcotic Law Enforcement," in P. E. Rock, ed., *Drugs and Politics.* New Brunswick, NJ: Transaction Books.

Mastrofski, Stephen D. (1991) "Community Policing as Reform: A Cautionary Tale," in Klockars & Mastrofski 1991.

Meyer, John W., & Brian Rowan (1977) "Institutionalized Organizations: Formal Structure as Myth and Ceremony," 83 *American J. of Sociology* 340.

Meyer, John W., & W. Richard Scott (1983) "Centralization and the Legitimacy Problems of Local Government," in J. W. Meyer & W. R. Scott, eds., *Organizational Environments: Ritual and Rationality.* Beverly Hills, CA: Sage Publications.

Michalowski, Raymond J. (1985) *Order, Law, and Crime.* New York: Random House.

Moore, Mark H., & George L. Kelling (1983) "'To Serve and Protect': Learning from Police History," 70 *Public Interest* 49.

National Advisory Commission on Civil Disorders (1967) *Report of the National Advisory Commission on Civil Disorder* ("Kerner Commission"). Washington: GPO.

Nisbet, Robert (1988) *The Present Age: Progress and Anarchy in Modern America.* New York: Harper & Row.

Poplin, Dennis E. (1979) *Communities: A Survey of Theories and Methods of Research.* New York: Macmillan

Powell, Walter (1991) "Expanding the Scope of Institutional Analysis," in W. W. Powell & P. J. DiMaggio, eds., *The New Institutionalism in Organizational Analysis.* Chicago: Univ. of Chicago Press.

Ritti, R. Richard, & Jonathan H. Silver (1986) "Early Processes of Institutionalization: The Dramaturgy of Exchange in Interorganizational Relations," 31 *Administrative Science Q.* 25.

Rosenbaum, Dennis P., ed. (1986). *Community Crime Prevention: Does It Work?* Beverly Hills, CA: Sage Publications.

Selznick, Philip (1957) *Leadership in Administration.* New York: Harper & Row.

Sherman, Lawrence (1986) "Policing Communities: What Really Works?" in A. Reiss & M. Tonry, eds., *Community and Crisis.* Chicago: Univ. of Chicago Press.

Skolnick, Jerome M., & David H. Bayley (1986) *The New Blue Line: Police Innovation in Six American Cities.* New York: Free Press.

Sorel, Georges (1916) *Reflections of Violence,* trans. by T. E. Hulme. London: Allen & Unwin.

Strenski, Ivan (1987) *Four Theories of Myth in Twentieth-Century History.* Iowa City: Univ. of Iowa Press.

Swidler, Ann (1986) "Culture in Action: Symbols and Strategies," 51 *American Sociological Rev.* 273.

Sykes, Gary W. (1986) "Street Justice: A Moral Defense of Order Maintenance Policing," 3 *Justice Q.* 497.

—— (1989) "The Functional Nature of Police Reform: The 'Myth' of Controlling the Police," in Dunham & Alpert 1989.

Tocqueville, Alexis de (1945) 1 *Democracy in America.* New York: Vintage.

Trice, Harrison M., & Janice M. Beyer (1984) "Studying Organizational Cultures through Rites and Ceremonials," 9 *Academy of Management Rev.* 653.

Trojanowicz, Robert, & Bonnie Bucqueroux (1990) *Community Policing: A Contemporary Perspective.* Cincinnati: Anderson Publishing Co.

U.S. President's Commission on Law Enforcement & Administration of Justice (1967) *The Challenge of Crime in a Free Society* ("Crime Commission"). Washington: GPO.

Vernon, Richard (1978) *Commitment and Change: Georges Sorel and the Idea of Revolution.* Toronto: Univ. of Toronto Press.

Walker, Samuel (1977) *A Critical History of Police Reform: The Emergence of Professionalism.* Lexington, MA: Lexington Books.

—— (1980) *Popular Justice: A History of American Criminal Justice.* New York: Oxford Univ. Press.

—— (1985) "Setting the Standards: The Efforts and Impact of Blue-Ribbon Commissions on the Police," in Geller 1985.

—— (1989a) *Sense and Nonsense about Crime: A Policy Guide.* 2d ed. Belmont, CA: Brooks/Cole.

—— (1989b) "'Broken Windows' and Fractured History: The Use and Misuse of History in Recent Police Patrol Analysis," in Dunham & Alpert 1989.

—— (1992a) "Origins of the Contemporary Criminal Justice Paradigm: The American Bar Foundation Survey, 1953–1969," 9 (1) *Justice Q.* 47.

—— (1992b) *Police In America.* 2d ed. New York: McGraw-Hill.

Wilson, James Q. (1968) *Varieties of Police Behavior: The Management of Law and Order in Eight Communities.* Cambridge: Harvard Univ. Press.

—— (1977) "Two Police Departments: The Influence of Structure on Operation," in D. B. Kenny, ed., *The Dysfunctional Alliance: Emotion and Reason in Justice Administration.* Cincinnati: Anderson Publishing.

Wilson, James Q., & George L. Kelling (1982) "Broken Windows," *Atlantic Monthly,* pp. 29-38 (March).

Wycoff, Mary Ann, & Peter K. Manning (1983) "The Police and Crime Control," in G. Whitaker & C. Phillips, eds., *Evaluating Performance in Police Agencies*. Beverly Hills, CA: Sage Publications.
Zucker, Lynne, ed. (1988) *Institutional Patterns and Organizations: Culture and Environment*. Cambridge, MA: Ballinger Publishing Co.

Case Cited

Miranda v. Arizona, 384 U.S. 436 (1966).

Journal of Contemporary Criminal Justice
Vol. 8 • No. 3 • August 1992

Values and Culture in Two American Police Departments: Lessons from King Arthur

by

Jack R. Greene, Ph.D., Geoffrey P. Alpert, Ph.D., & Paul Styles

Abstract

The changing nature of public and private management calls into question the role of managers in transmitting values to assist in guiding the actions of organizational members. Recently, in policing there has been a major value reorientation from traditional approaches to crime control and suppression, to community policing a philosophy that emphasizes greater police and citizen contact. This paper reports the findings from two qualitative analyses of value clarification and transmission, one in a large, metropolitan police department, and the other in a smaller police agency. Whereas past research has suggested that organization size greatly affects the value formation and communication process within such agencies, this paper identifies the similarities between these two agencies as the seek to re-shape values and to influence police officer and police organization behavior.

Institutional Values and Public Law Enforcement

When King Arthur appointed his Knights to the same rank and emphasized their equality by seating them at a round table, he created a legendary brotherhood of dedicated individuals with a distinct set of values and a singular identity. The Knights of the Round Table, in search of the Holy Grail, may have been legendary, but they exist as a literary example of social organization with high values and strong institutional identity. The Knights of the Round Table maintained their individual identity, however, even in the face of Arthur's charge. Each bore a distinct coat of arms, and each represented some external fiefdom's social, political and economic interests, for such was the nature of feudal society. Nonetheless, Arthur's Knights were little directed by complex rules and regulations; rather, personal and institutional norms converged, and the "sense of purpose" for which they were brought together guided individual and collective action.

79

In modern-day organizations, King Arthur's model might be referred to as the organizational culture, or "the values, beliefs, assumptions, perceptions, norms, artifacts, and patterns of behavior" that guide individual and group action (Ott, 1989: 1). As Kilmann, Saxton and Serpa (1985: ix) suggest "culture is to the organization what personality is to the individual a hidden yet unifying theme that provides, meaning, direction and mobilization". Cultures are powerful metaphors, for they focus our concerns on the internal symbols that channel organizational behavior (Morgan, 1986).

Progressive police administrators strive to create a sense of organizational identity for their departments and to set high individual values for their officers, similar to the efforts of King Arthur. In policing this has been referred to as "style", or the philosophies and values that guide police officer behavior, absent a rule (Slovak, 1986). And, it has been long recognized that the "style" of policing in any community results from a mixture of the values and attitudes of the community, the philosophy that the police chief instills in the police organization, and the relationships with citizens in which individual police officers find themselves engaged (Wilson, 1978, Brown, 1981). Despite a recognition of the important role that style or organizational culture plays in policing, the methods for creating this organizational culture, and the implications of competing cultures for police work, are not clearly understood, and less obviously practiced in modern day law enforcement agencies.

Organizational "image" can be created readily by the use of publicity and public relations, and police administrators can and do influence the institutional identity of a department by the control of their officers through strong guidance and direction generally in the form of supervisory and reporting control systems. Unfortunately, the achievement of such goals underlying the image namely institutional/individual identity congruence has more likely occurred within the realm of the legendary King Arthur than within many police departments of the 1990s. And, while there are OFTTIMES competing role identities and ideologies within police departments, the conflict between "street cops" and "management cops" (Reuss Iianni and Iianni, 1983) remains one of several tensions in values within modern day police organizations.

Values and organizational culture in policing are important to study beyond the issue of "image" or the general "stylistic" notions which are thought to condition police departments (Wilson, 1967; Brown, 1981). At the institutional level of policing, values and culture are most often associated with the "corporate strategy" being pursued by the organization as a whole (See, Kelling and Moore, 1988, and Moore and Trojanowicz, 1988). In the private sector such manifestations of corporate culture change are evident is the trend toward "value driven" organizations (Peters and Waterman, 1983; Morgan, 1986). As Morgan (1986: 121) notes;

Organizations are mini-societies that have their own distinctive patterns of culture and subculture. Such patterns of belief or shared meaning, fragmented or integrated, and supported by various operating norms and rituals, can exert a distinctive influence on the overall ability of the organization to deal with the challenges that it faces".

Current trends in policing toward the identification and publication of explicit organizational values can be viewed as illustrating the institutional connections between values, culture and corporate strategy. And, conflict between the internalized management culture of police organizations and the tactical culture of police operations, which has been identified by several researchers (Manning, 1977; Brown, 1981; Reuss Iianni and Iianni, 1983), can be viewed as evidence of an ongoing internal struggle for value clarification within police departments. Moreover, current efforts to shift police departments from "traditional" policing toward "problem oriented" policing (Goldstein, 1990) can also be viewed as explicitly addressing competing internal values within policing.

At the individual police officer level, however, clarity in the relationship between values, culture and institutional strategy have been less clear, and more often in conflict. Since the early 1950s when Westley (1953: 34-41) studied the Gary, Indiana Police Department, it has been documented that the "culture" of policing greatly shapes police and citizen interactions. Further, the underlying subcultural values associated with police work have often been found to be negative (See, for example: Neiderhoffer, 1967; Bittner, 1967; Westley, 1970; Reiss, 1971; Muir, 1977; and, Black, 1980). Such values are more often conditioned by the manner in which the police are occupationally socialized, the work performed, and to some lessor degree by the quality and focus of first line supervision (Van Mannen, 1973, 1974, 1983). How police officers see themselves, society and the police role they enact is equally powerful in shaping the individual styles of police officers (Muir, 1977).

Taken together extant, yet fragmented, research on police values and culture points to the problems confronted by King Arthur; how to instill a sense of ultimate purpose, without attempting to control individual action. This ancient concern is foremost on the agenda of American policing in the 1990s.

The purpose of this study is to qualitatively investigate systems of institutional identity and values specifically related to the relationships among officers, between officers and command staff and between officers and the public in two very different police departments one a large urban, metropolitan police agency in Philadelphia, and the other a medium sized police department in Columbia, South Carolina.

The Philadelphia Police Department represents a large scale bureaucracy, confederatively organized, having multiple power centers and gangling communications and decision systems. In struggling toward a new organizational corporate strategy, the Philadelphia Police Department administrative culture, and the politicalization of that culture within the department, were major factors shaping the transmission of values within the department. In fact, the central focus in Philadelphia was with changing values which were not serving the department, nor the community, well.

By contrast the Columbia Police Department is an agency that is small enough to be managed effectively, yet which is large enough to include levels of specialization and stratification. In Columbia the issue of value transmission was more a matter of communication and interaction between supervisors and police officers, partly due to the size of the organization, and partly due to confusion about the strategic direction of the department among those at the bottom of the hierarchy.

Each of these departments represent special, yet common, problems of value acquisition, transmission and maintenance in American law enforcement. As illustrations of these problems, both Philadelphia and Columbia represent opportunities for qualitatively understanding the dynamics of cultural change within police departments. Given their size differences, however, we first consider the impact of size on police agency culture.

Organizational Size and Police Agency Culture

The same power relationships that influence identities and relationships in other complex organizations exist in police departments (Etzioni, 1975). That is, all organizations seeking compliance between organizational and individual goals seek to influence an individual's basis for organizational participation and sustained organizational life. Such internal organizational systems manipulate power and authority, recruitment and entrance processes, occupational socialization, and internal reward and sanction systems, such that compliance is more or less assured. These processes are actively engaged in police departments as well, although their integration toward shaping organizational identities is not as thought out as it might be.

One major effect on this process of identity building is department size. Small departments are presumed to rely on consensus and the direct involvement of the street level officers in many facets of organizational life (Crank, 1989), while larger departments are thought to rely more on remuneration and more coercive or controlling influences (Etzioni, 1975). In either case the value base of the department is affected, albeit through differing means normative versus coercive compliance systems.

One of the toughest jobs of today's police administrator is to create relationships among officers that foster a positive "product" and "client" identity, including a supporting set of shared values. This "product" identify focuses on the effects of the services produced, not merely on the functional production of the services themselves (Greene, 1990). By focusing on products and clients (Peters and Waterman, 1983) organizations attempt to involve those within the organization in "seeing the big picture", the organization's goals and strategies, rather than focusing on some sub-optimal functions within the organization. In policing this shift is from focusing on patrol or investigation services, for example, to examining concerns with "the quality of city life" and public safety, most certainly those issues focusing on the police organization as a whole.

A method to achieve this working identity is the decentralization of authority to foster appropriate levels of peer influence under a controlled and supervised environment. In smaller police organizations decentralization is defacto, in that size may help to restrict over specialization and the problems of sub-optimization that accrue to specialized agencies. In major metropolitan police departments size and organizational complexity have pushed for much work segmentation, centralized decision making and extreme specialization within the work force.

Whereas in smaller police departments the patrol force may handle all types of citizen mobilizations, except, perhaps, for complicated criminal investigations, in large scale police departments patrol services are highly differentiated, such as separate units for 911 response, traffic enforcement, accident investigation and the like. And, although larger police agencies are geographically decentralized, the decision systems within these agencies remain close to the apex of the organization generally in the offices of the top commanders. Where decentralization occurs within large police departments it must be structured, rather than emerging from the nature of the work performed, as in smaller agencies.

In recent years there has been some movement toward greater decentralization within large and smaller police departments, and several are moving in that direction (Skolnick and Bayley, 1986; Kelling et al., 1988; Wilson and Kelling, 1989). This movement has been referred to as community and problem solving policing (Goldstein, 1990 and 1987; Eck et al., 1988), emphasizing analytic thinking and decentralized accountability among other things. The decentralization associated with problem or community oriented policing has generally taken two forms, one within smaller agencies, another within larger agencies. As noted above, smaller agencies are inherently likely to have less centralized functional operations, whereas larger police departments, while often geographically decentralized, are more likely to be functionally centralized. Community policing, therefore, is more likely to meet with internal value and cultural resistance within the larger, more complex police departments, owing in part to the decentralized and despecialized aims of this in the newest of policing corporate strategies. In smaller departments such resistance is more likely associated with value and cultural resistance stemming from beliefs about the fundamental nature of the police role itself, i.e., service orientation versus law enforcement orientation.

All estimates of police departments recognize that most are small, with fewer than 25 officers (Hoetmer, 1989, Sims, 1988 and Cordner, 1989). Victor Sims (1988: 22) provides a view of the impact of agency size on police department functioning;

> ...In other words, small is a function of direct and personal relationships and interactions among the officers and between the officers and citizens.... [T]he small town or rural police department is best defined ... by the presence of personal, direct, intimate, and informal interaction occurring regularly among all group members. This personal and informal social interaction among all group members remains a uniqueness of small town and rural police.

Small departments also lack specialization and stratification and the complex organizational structures of the larger departments, in part because the interactions they seek to manage are small in number and are not particularly overwhelming (Brown, 1981). Smaller departments, therefore are thought more normatively constrained by the limited set of interactions they confront and the personal involvement of citizens and police in those interactions. By contrast, Slovak (1986:129-130) argues that in large police departments:

> patrol officers receive less direction and control from their immediate supervisors, usually patrol sergeants, so that more room is left to the patrol officer for the exercise of discretion than is true of their counterparts in smaller agencies.

Police research in the United States has concentrated on the smaller in number but larger in membership big city, urban police departments (Alpert and Dunham, 1988). These studies tend to be more quantitative and empirical, providing little understanding of the context of policing confronted or enacted. The majority of research reported on the relatively small department generally includes narratives concerning personal experiences (Daviss, 1983; Pratt, 1979; Domonoske, 1978; Watson; 1977; but see Ostrom, Parks and Whitaker, 1978 and 1978; and Cordner, 1989).

Sims (1988) reports a number of variables which correlate with department size. Among the most interesting and positive relationships he points to are the strength of loyalty, beneficial human relations activities, noncriminal contacts with citizens, and percent of citizens receiving assistance from the police. In addition, Brown (1981) notes that officers in smaller departments have less freedom to make discretionary decisions. At least theoretically, then, the structural variations between larger and smaller agencies form the major functional differences between these police departments (Simms, 1988).

The structure of small departments also frequently rely on authority by group process, with patrol officers serving as generalists. Major city police departments usually reflect the traditional para military, bureaucratic model. This bureaucracy fosters dependence on authority by rank, specialization and supervision. Sims (1988: 143) notes that;

> "the goals and objectives of some small town and rural departments remain unconsidered and never discussed. Usually this results in status quo policing no experimentation, no innovation, and little or no improvement".

Values and Identity: Some Further Considerations

Values in policing are important because they represent the beliefs which guide the general perspective and mission of the department as well as the officers' specific actions and performance. In fact, values help form the officers' occupational identity. Conventional wisdom informs us that when values are not held and articulated by the command staff, officers on the street are not likely to be influenced by them. In fact, other structural and environmental conditions may be necessary before expressed values are taken seriously by the officers (see Alpert and Dunham, 1988; Wasserman and Moore, 1988; and Greene and Decker, 1989).

Without the foundation of a structure and environment that supports specific values, a departmental philosophy can be confusing and challenged by officers, while followed only when convenient. It can also lead to a department which is driven in multiple directions. Kelling et al. (1988:3) provide a classic example.

> ...loyalty to peers can conflict with the maintenance of high standards of professional practice. When police officers decide to close their eyes to the incompetence or corruption of colleagues and draw the 'blue curtain' around them, they choose the value of loyalty to peers over the other values, such as quality service to the community.

In many police departments, other values, some explicit and others implicit, can be identified that shape and drive police performance: 'stay out of trouble,' 'we are the finest,' 'machismo,' 'serve and protect,' and many others.

Such a dilemma can manifest itself in multiple approaches to policing without the presence of a dominant style or philosophy. Strengthening the values of a police department can, therefore, be an important management tool by creating consistency and predictability among all ranks and can help control discretionary decision making (Greene, 1990; Brooks, 1989; Alpert and Dunham, 1988; Brown, 1981). To accomplish this, however, police managers must provide persuasive and convincing leadership that represents the norms which they want to establish and maintain.

As there are different types of police agencies and assorted styles of policing, there are different value systems. It is both the strength of the message as well as its content which have important consequences. As Michael Brown (1981:223) explains what influences operational and individual styles of policing:

> A patrolman's operational style is based on his responses to ... the difficulties and dilemmas he encounters in attempting to control crime ... [and] the ways in which he accommodates himself to the pressures and demands of the police bureaucracy.

Thus, the officer's individual style is influenced by the departmental value system and its institutional identity. However, a desired identity designed at the top is not sufficient. It is necessary that the identity be transmitted to the officers through policy, training, control, supervision and accountability. Indeed, the public must be informed of the department's desired 'personality' to close the loop and maintain predictability. King Arthur provided the ultimate model and challenge to his Knights and to those who relied upon them, the citizens.

It has been noted that "the speed of the boss is the speed of the crew" (Alpert, 1985: 29). While this organizational premise may attach to police departments of all sizes, its meaning differs in relation to the demands of the police bureaucracy. An urban police department may have an infrastructure so complex that the formal lines of communication are clouded by custom and practice and influences are based upon incentive pay and peer pressure. Departments which are significantly smaller, have the advantage of a less complex structure and one in which communication can be more direct.

The Research Problem and Method

The general framework for this analysis is presented in two qualitative research projects, one conducted in Philadelphia and the other in Columbia, South Carolina. In Philadelphia, the information presented comes from an ongoing five year program of organizational development and institutional change.

Following on the heals of a major corruption scandal in 1984, and the bombing of the MOVE house in West Philadelphia in 1985, the Philadelphia Police Department set about to "change the way it did business." This has resulted in several programs aimed at adopting a community policing strategy, with the attendant change in values that come with such a strategy. Data reported here come from field observation, official departmental records, and numerous interviews conducted since 1987 (See, Greene, 1989; Greene and Decker, 1989; Greene 1990 and 1990b).

As part of a larger study of the Columbia, South Carolina Police Department, individual interviews were conducted with all members of the department above the rank of police officer. These officers were asked to complete questionnaires which included questions on values and identity. Specifically, they were asked about personal and shared values and how each affected their identification with the department. The results of the empirical analyses of responses to these questions are not reported in this study as we are concentrating on our interview data, but they are consistent with our findings.

Each of the 97 members of the department above the rank of officer was interviewed individually for 90 minutes during January, 1989. Each officer was asked a variety of questions and encouraged to discuss his or her opinions and perspectives on what structure and communication was useful, important or desirable to improve policing.

The "joining" of the results of these two research projects, may appear to some as problematic, in that each project was separated in time and space, and the dominant research questions varied somewhat. Furthermore, we recognize that these two agencies significantly differ from one another on such matters as size, complexity, and community environment, to but name a few.

Nonetheless, we believe that what were cast as two independent inquiries, nevertheless identify common themes of organizational value transmission and maintenance in law enforcement agencies practices and problems that are not as different as we might suppose. We do not proffer to be testing theory; rather through two qualitative approaches we seek to sharpen the lens of cultural assessment within police agencies.

Analysis
Changing Values in the Philadelphia Police Department.

The Philadelphia Police Department is the fourth largest police department in the United States. Philadelphia employees nearly 6500 police officers, having the highest number of officers per capita (4.3 per 1000 residents) of the 10 largest municipal police departments in the country. In calendar year 1985 the Philadelphia Police Department responded to more than 3 million calls, yet had the lowest reported crime rate for the nation's 10 largest cities (Police Study Task Force: 1987).

Despite the lower reported crime rate and higher density of police officers, Philadelphia has had mixed reactions in terms of community support. In a recent survey "two thirds of Philadelphia's citizens believe that their police use unnecessary force. One half thought the police took bribes [and] two fifths of the citizens thought that the police drank on duty" (Police Study Task Force, 1987: 23).

Furthermore, for a number of years the United States Commission on Human Relations had investigated police brutality complaints filed in Philadelphia. From the standpoint of image, then, the department has not enjoyed a favorable community climate, in the sense of its general reputation.

In May of 1985 that reputation was further damaged. At shortly after 5:27 pm a Philadelphia police lieutenant leaned out of a helicopter and dropped a satchel containing explosives on the roof of a row house in West Philadelphia. The row house was under siege for it housed the members of a socially disruptive group known as MOVE. The resulting fire leveled nearly three city blocks, left some 240 city residents homeless and incinerated 11 members of MOVE.

Shortly before the MOVE incident, the Federal Bureau of Investigation and the United States Attorney's Office announced the completion of a major corruption investigation. This federal investigation, and subsequent indictments, revealed an institutional pattern of corruption within the Philadelphia Police Department, reaching the highest levels of police management a Deputy Commissioner of Police, the second highest ranking officer in the City, was fully implicated in what was seen as a system of institutional graft.

An Outside Police Commissioner?

At the seeming height of the scandals confronting Philadelphia's police, a new police commissioner was appointed. This person, a former member of the Secret Service, was the first non-Philadelphia police officer appointed commissioner. He was touted as an effective administrator, politically savvy and visionary.

88

The new police commissioner was immediately faced with a hostile and turbulent internal and external environment. Throughout 1986 and into 1987 he slowly instituted changes in policies affecting the internal investigation of police corruption. He formed internal committees to study virtually all of the department's operational and strategic systems, changed the symbol of the department, and sent many of the commanders in the department packing to Harvard University for police managerial training.

He also commissioned a study of the Philadelphia Police Department. In March, 1987 the Police Study Task Force produced a 195 page department study making some 200 often scathing recommendations for change. This document became the change agenda for the police department, although reference to it in recent years has fallen off dramatically.

After approximately two years in office the "reform" commissioner resigned. Part of his resignation was no doubt due to fiscal problems confronting the city and his perception that many of the programs he sought to implement would not be funded. Faced with a growing fiscal deficit, and the likelihood that he would preside over the dismantling of the very programs he had proposed, he resigned. A power vacuum was created that resulted in the appointment of a new police commissioner, this time from within the department.

The Internal Police Commissioner

Shortly after the announcement of the "reform" commissioner's resignation, a new commissioner was appointed. The first black man to hold the rank of Police Commissioner in the city, the new commissioner was a career officer from within the department. Faced with the fiscal collapse of the Police Department the new commissioner spent nearly his first year in office "studying" problems, and reestablishing a commitment from the Mayor that police department personnel strength would be maintained. Furthermore, the new police commissioner faced other dilemmas.

First, as the first Black man to hold this office, the commissioner recognized that the shifting internal coalitions within the department were not supportive of his tenure. Second, the "symbols" of change that were created by his predecessor were themselves eroding. While, on the one hand, the initial "reform" commissioner had succeeded in changing the internal and external image of the police department from that of "war like" and "corrupt" to that of "community centered", these images were these philosophies and policies, the department was headed for a return to the "business as usual" reputation it had enjoyed in the past.

Third, internal competition with the previous reform commissioner had been intense, and the new commissioner wanted to distance himself from his predecessor, to avoid the intensity of this conflict, and to establish his own change agenda.

The Change Climate Actors and Perspectives

Philadelphia has a mayor/city council form of government. Historically, the mayor has been directly involved in the day to day management of the police department; city politics within Philadelphia are based on a strong ward system, that is visible in the political arena, the media, and to the "man on the street".

Economically, Philadelphia has suffered the same misfortune of many Eastern cities. The riots of the late 1960s left the city racially divided. Economic development in the city was decimated in the mid 1970s. It wasn't until the mid-1980s that service industries began to replace the eroded industrial base.

Police and community relations have often been strained in Philadelphia. While citizens globally evaluate the department as effective, the department's reputation for aggressive law enforcement has often pitted the community against the police; black citizens are less sanguine about Philadelphia's police than are white citizens. As the Police Task Force Study reported (1987: 23);

> "the Department labors under the burden of history. In the early years of this century, it was ridiculed for incompetence serving as the model for the 'Keystone Cops'. And in later years its reputation grew uglier, as allegations of brutality and corruption mounted. In the late 1960s the Philadelphia Police Department successfully resisted reforms that occurred in other parts of the country, and its failure to reform bore its painful fruit in the 1985 and 1986 corruption indictments, and ongoing investigations of police attacks against handcuffed prisoners."

For nearly two decades, commissioners of the Philadelphia Police Department has systematically centralized decision making. The "new commissioners" emphasized decentralized command with accountability being focused at the appropriate organizational level. For most commanders this new role was inconsistent with their management tenure and dominant perspectives within the department. Absent significant training most did not know how to function as decentralized managers.

Part of the complexity of introducing change in this police agency rests in the internal dynamics of shifting political and social coalitions within the department. The central command staff within the department is itself divided. Three groups emerge; appointed Deputy Police Commissioners, Civil Service Chief Inspectors, and lessor powerful commanders. The rank and file are also split on the basis of "reform" versus "returning to the good ole days."

A major problem for any police commissioner in Philadelphia is forming a "management team" for directing the department. Currently, there are but three (3) appointed positions among the police commissioner's staff. Two of these positions are at the Deputy Police Commissioner level, and one is a staff position. Given such inflexibility in appointing policy making staff, the exercise of authority in these positions tends to be idiosyncratic to the office holder. Consequently, deputy commissioners act largely in independent spheres of influence, and at times in opposition to one another. Despite the form of regularized "commissioners" meetings there is little communication among commissioners and much intrigue, all of which contributes to a perception among lower ranking officers that when direction comes from this level of organization it is generally punitive and rarely positively directed.

Long tenured commanders and those who grew up in the former police system in the city also send mixed messages about their support of the changes and values sought. These persons are generally positioned at the rank of Chief Inspector. Within the Department they are referred to as "dinosaurs", primarily in connection with their long tenure as well as their inability or unwillingness to change to new circumstances. Unlike the "dinosaurs" of the natural world, however, these "institutional dinosaurs" are not faced with an Darwinian "adapt or die" position. Rather they occupy powerful policy making positions, being directly responsible for the day-to-day operation of the functional activities of the department. They represent a formidable force for maintaining the status quo.

The immediate past and current commissioners have of necessity developed a cadre of junior command officers to assume some of the programmatic responsibilities suggested by the value change program, and as a way of "end running" the resistance of more senior level commanders. Whether these officers can provide the administrative support for the massive changes anticipated remains to be seen, as many are not in sufficiently high policy making positions to counteract the Chief Inspectors of the department. Given the "punishment centered" bureaucracy (See Gouldner, 1954) represented in current departmental operations, lessor senior officers pursuing a change agenda, do so at their own risk.

Philadelphia has been a long standing labor city. The police union (Fraternal Order of Police) has successfully resisted a number of programs that have been advanced by the past two Commissioners in support of value change within the department. The union has the largest membership within the department, and has resisted graduated employee evaluations and shift rotation programs among other issues central to the reforms anticipated.

In addition to this union, there is an association of black police officers, the Guardian Civic League. While less in number than the FOP, the Civic League has on occasion successfully opposed policies from the commissioner's office. Although they took no direct stance on a policy to

91

raise entry educational standards, the Civic League has ardently supported the department in its struggle to increase minority applicants. On several issues the FOP and Guardian Civic League are opposing forces generally attempting to enjoin the department from actions advocated by the other.

The general labor climate can best be described as apocalyptic; battle lines are drawn, minor policies are contested, and political rivalry is clearly evident.

Change Agenda

While the players and their agendas have been roughly defined, the agenda for change has not. Unlike Arthur's charge of the Knights to secure the Holy Grail, the purpose of change in Philadelphia has been unclear and unstructured from its inception.

The Police Study Task Force made 195 recommendations for change in the department. Three major themes connect many of these recommendations; administrative decentralization, the development of a community oriented policing philosophy, and an improvement in the training provided to personnel. Each of these themes involves affecting the compliance systems within the police department much like Arthur's need to obtain compliance from his Knights of the Round Table.

The department has only recently recognized the inter-dependency of these change strategies, however. To change philosophy (community policing) and structure (decentralization) without preparing people for their new roles (systematic training) and responsibilities (career development) would be to repeat the mistakes of the past. To change climate without a concurrent change in administration, would also pose serious implementation problems. Finally, to change people without a change in climate and structure would obviously reduce the effectiveness of such a strategy. In short, incremental change has not withstood the long standing insularity of this bureaucracy, and given the piecemeal approach to implementing this change, much of the "reform" has had marginal effectiveness.

Present programs of change include, the implementation of community policing in the patrol bureau (but not in investigative functions), revamping of the training system, upgrading police management through attendance at several police executive training programs, linking of the personnel system with career development and training, the re-deployment of personnel across Philadelphia's 23 police districts, and an unfocused administrative reorganization of the department and its major bureaus. Many of these programs have been tried and implemented elsewhere, but rarely have as many changes been implemented concurrently. Moreover, as the resistance to change is apparent in the command staff of this police department, so the pace of value change has been slowed to a glacial reform.

Communicating Values in the Columbia Police Department

The City of Columbia, South Carolina, has a population of approximately 105,000 and a police force of just over 200 officers. The department is divided into four districts created for quick response to calls for service and crime investigation. These districts are consistent with natural community boundaries. Residential policing in Columbia is differentiated by the socioeconomic status of the various neighborhoods. Observations made by Slovak a few years ago (1986: 156) remain accurate today;

> [A]reas containing high status populations receive relatively more aggressive and less watchman like police services than do their lower class counterparts; and black areas receive slightly more watchman like and noticeably less aggressive styles of policing than do their white counterparts."

From Slovak's earlier research and our interviews, the Columbia Police Department emerges as an agency with a collection of diverse internal territories. Policing appears as a method to maintain administrative status quo and to avoid any threat to have to change (Slovak 1986:157). The information revealed during the questionnaires and interviews, characterized each office and specialized squad as its own mini-department, standing independently from others. A small number of people reported that they desired to serve the goal of the administration, while the majority of officers described themselves as involved in a hierarchy of contacts and information sources quite independent of the formalized rank structure. Most officers, representing all ranks; had formal and informal communication with other governmental agencies or community organizations, and reported that these contacts were often seen as more beneficial to get things accomplished than the inadequate lines of communication within the department. One police investigator illustrated how a laissez faire attitude to the rank structure had developed when he informed us that he reported on some matters directly to his Captain by passing his Lieutenant, who was;

> ...relatively new as far as investigations goes. He had never been an investigator and he had never worked in investigations. It was his first time down there. The Captain didn't like things being relayed second and third hand. He had more or less an open door policy with me as far as incidents of this nature...

It would be true to say that policing attracts individuals who welcome conformity, feel at home with rules, have a clear sense of morals, yet wish to retain a certain level of individual freedom of action. There were the inevitable individuals who were merely serving their time for a pension, or who had become disgruntled and disillusioned. However, most of the respondents maintained an enthusiasm for their work. A typical attitude towards the job was provided by the youthful respondent who said:

> [Police work] is something I've always wanted to do since I was a kid. I set my goal to be here and it is a very challenging and rewarding job that I love. I've been here fifteen years and plan to be here until I retire. I enjoy being responsible for myself and doing the best job that I can. I am very self-motivated and take a pride in my job.

While this enthusiasm allied to contentment is, on the surface, quite commendable, it can also point to the inevitable stagnation that occurs in many small or medium sized police departments, lacking the resources to develop employees through extensive in-service training or appropriate incentives for advancement. Being in a small department with nowhere to go can contribute to a growing sense of frustration and an erosion in the service values supposed of the organization.

Moreover, many of the officers interviewed report that there is little opportunity to stand aside from the daily routine to question values, role or identity. In the course of describing their job tasks, without exception, the respondents exhibited a clear view of what their individual jobs entailed. Unfortunately, only a few individuals related their work objectives to any set of wider aims or overall mission. Indeed, when asked, the respondents revealed few, if any, indications of an overall mission, departmental philosophy, or clear statement of goals. It was further revealed that communication was very poor among the officers who did not work closely together, and that communication from the command staff was negligible. It was recognized by many that an improvement in structure and communication would be a necessary condition to clarifying their values and organizational identity.

There was also a concentration on the immediate, and a lack of institutional requirement to provide innovation either from the bottom up or the top down. One supervisor told us:

> ...the one frustrating thing about the job is it is crisis management. [Someone might say,] I just found out that I need this yesterday, so stop what you are doing. Yesterday I told you something was real important, but that's not important today. That gets on your nerves a little bit. As a working supervisor, we're not able to sit back and analyze.

94

Again, another aspect of this "crisis orientation" is illustrated by the comment:

> My biggest argument doesn't come from off the street,
> it comes from my supervisor. I'm stressing out for the
> wrong reasons, because of the administration not because
> of the streets.

The department was characterized by a diverse number of unconnected styles of policing and management. Interviews revealed a theme in which officers, unaided by institutional direction, worked out an approach acceptable to each. These varied from an attempt at a pro-active community based concept of policing to hard line "lock em up and throw away the key" reactions. Unfortunately, there was no common thread, singular identity or distinct set of values portrayed by the respondents. Individual officers reported a perception of their individual role, but failed to exhibit a collective opinion on what structure or strategy of communication would be useful or desirable to improve policing in the city as a whole.

This lack of harmony was viewed as developed easily and naturally. Traditionally, police departments look to training to provide an initial sense of purpose and institutional identity. New recruits are taught the traditions of the service, its mission and role in society and their place in the wider scheme of things, along with the specific skills and knowledge needed to perform their tasks.

In South Carolina, at least, there is effectively little provision for anything other than skills teaching, such is the treadmill of basic training at the Criminal Justice Academy. This centralized institution is uniquely placed to influence and shape new members of the profession, for all police officers must attend and qualify within twelve months of their appointment, but it is forced by the demands of a high turnover rate to cram sixty or seventy recruits into a class and force feed them full of law and procedure with precious little time left for reflection on mission or role.

The high turnover rate is itself a result of relatively poor salaries, and helps create a spiral of deficiency which feeds upon itself. Poor pay does not attract a wide array of applicants, so policing is unable to compete effectively with other employment opportunities. Our respondents informed us that their low pay encourages moonlighting. This is officially condoned, and inevitably leads to a confusion of the officers' role, and erosion of officer attachment to the department, not to mention the damage caused by winking at minor violations.

The in-service training attempted to address the short fall in attitudinal training was appropriate and the quality of the officers engaged in this area was high. Unfortunately, the opportunities were limited by the man-hours allocated to training. Typically, this training was limited to roll call situations and focused on legal updates. Some senior officers had attended the F.B.I. Academy or Southern Police Institute, and this was seen as an important and valuable qualification. However, some officers reported that to be sent to a course often took more than five years.

Career opportunities and promotions were limited by the small size of the department. It was reported that officers with ambition and capabilities often left law enforcement for more stable and predictable futures. This cost an enormous amount of money which had been invested in the individuals who left. It also created the situation where more recruits are introduced into the system to keep the numbers up. This burdens the training system, which responds by becoming efficient and dedicated to more, not better quality training. Again, this leads to a situation in which no time in the curriculum is dedicated for teaching mission, role and values.

There are unresolved conflicts as a result of this lack of continuity and security. One officer voiced a concern which was echoed by many others:

> There is too much messing around with city govern-
> ment even though they are in charge and sign our pay-
> checks. They still have too many political influences on
> how the department runs. If the city manager calls up and
> says "Chief, my friend's friend was robbed and I want
> something done about it now." These people jump through
> the ceiling.

Deficiencies that may exist in the basic training and supervision which fail to instill a sense of role are compounded by the almost total lack of provision for in-service training and the training of supervisory officers. An officer promoted through the ranks to Lieutenant will typically have received little or no management training. Officers are encouraged to study on their own time and receive an enhancement of pay for academic qualifications, but the number of officers who are able to take advantage of this opportunity is small, as shift patterns have not been designed to permit regular attendance at college. A supervisor is therefore thrown onto his or her own devices, and similar to those in the ranks below, will develop an approach which is his/hers alone, and does not bear the stamp of approval of the institution. A sergeant made the following comment about training illustrating this point:

> We are probably in the best position that we have ever
> been far as Academy training. My complaint in that area
> is that we have equipped the officer with the basic skills
> and knowledge when he comes out of the Academy [but]
> we have very little follow up. For example, you talk about

in-service training when the officer moves just one level
up, for example to squad leader, we have very little
management courses. Another, long serving officer expressed a view of the quality of the supervisory officers,
saying: I'm not knocking the supervisors here, they're
good people, you can't blame them. A lot of people have
been put in positions that they shouldn't be in, in my
opinion. They are the first ones to admit, hell, I was put
here, I don't know what I am doing. So you can't really go
to the supervisors anymore, because hell they don't know
what they are doing either.

Stagnation is an illusive condition. It is necessary to look beneath the
surface activity for signs of genuine change. Our data indicate that just such
a situation existed in the Columbia Police Department: there had been
change, but it was not always directed and planned with a mission, singular
identity or distinct set of values in mind. For example, supervisors were
moved around, ostensibly to provide them with experience and to prevent
stagnation and over familiarity between them and the officers they supervised. There were strong indications that this movement had adverse effects,
as supervisors were not all imbued with a common set of objectives and
policies. One officer told us:

Within the last couple of years we've had a lot of
instability in supervisors. Within two years I've had six.
You know what happens when you change supervisors
that much. Things tend not to get done, things tend to get
screwed up because everybody has their own way of doing
it.

Another officer reflected this view, and added an element of isolation,
when he commented about his office:

We are kind of in our own little world here. The only
time we get with a higher up is if one of their friends or
somebody who believes they have political influence
becomes a victim. The way I've always felt [however] it
doesn't matter if you are a rich man or a poor man, you get
treated the same.

Yet another referred to the lack of a sense of common purpose:

> I want to be a police officer but it is just that you take
> on everyone else's problems. I doesn't bother me because
> I've learned to block that out, but the problem that we are
> having at this time is not with people on the street, it's just
> administrative problems the police department is having.
> It is not ready for anything because they are not organizing,
> they lack the knowledge and they are discriminatory and
> everything else.

Although there were strong indications that serious morale and identity problems were related to the officers' system (or lack of system) of values, an effort was being made to restructure the department and to successfully achieve accreditation. This method of securing some standardization is the chief officers' means of providing a sense of direction and it helps inform his officers that their fellow officers in other departments of the same size are taking a similar approach to policing and its problems. The move is toward consistency, that will bring policing a basic structure of standards which will be familiar to all officers in the department.

Common Themes and Lessons Learned

The police officers who were the subject of these two research projects believe that there is a lack of common agreement concerning the officers' and departments' values and identity relating to the relationships among the officers, between the officers and command staff and between the officers and the public.

In Philadelphia the change process underway has been actively resisted by top commanders and those in the rank-and-file, partly because they did not want to change, and partly because the reasons and methods of change expected of them were unclear. The "play of power" in the organization effectively pitted competing values and identities against one another, such that no dominant value or identity could take hold. Furthermore, the communication of values through advanced and management training were under-developed and lacked credibility in what is a "tightly controlled" patriarchal management network.

In Columbia, the communication of values was also thwarted, partly because of bureaucratization within the department and partly because the mechanisms to effectively communicate values were under developed or non existent.

While the Columbia Police Department may have features similar to many like sized departments, it has neither the resources nor administrative history of a major metropolitan department. Nonetheless, it attempts to incorporate many characteristics of bureaucracy found in larger more complicated departments. By attempting to take on many traits of larger departments, it invites many of the same problems confronting those mega agencies, such as in Philadelphia.

In either city the conflict between bureaucracy and community raises the question "Do the police exist to serve the whole community "without fear or favor" or as the tool of the politically influential and rich?" Given the wide variation in style and individual philosophy driving police services in each of these cities, this disjunction between the image of policing that is issued for public consumption, and the realities of police practices is exposed for observers, critics, reformers and researchers (See Greene and Mastrofski, 1988; Mastrofski and Greene, forthcoming).

Our case studies also point to the centrality of the chief administrator (police chief or police commissioner) in the transmission and maintenance of values and identities throughout the organization. In each of these departments recruits are attracted by the promise of a place on the moral high ground, only to find that the very institution which advertised this advantage is expecting compromise. What then, is the officer's reaction to this? Our findings indicate that officers in Philadelphia and Columbia without the benefit of proper preparation often turn inward and rely on individual and subgroup interpretations of the situation in which they find themselves.

We see that individuals look to the immediate surroundings of their functional unit to provide values and identity, and often feel isolated from other members of their respective departments. Although there was a great deal of communication sideways in both organizations, little flowed up or down. The result of this was a loss of cohesion, a fragmentation of philosophy; a hive of industrious bees without a common purpose.

One question we believe which has not been addressed sufficiently is the relationship between departments of different sizes and their abilities to perform to the expectations of the community (Alpert and Dunham, 1988). In our two case studies we find quite different police departments behaving in similar way failing to define or transmit values, or worse letting sub-group and "political" values shape the perspectives of line level personnel, consequently affecting services to their respective communities.

Currently, it is not clear that creating a system of values and achieving a strong sense of agreement among officers regarding their relationships and those between the officers and the public will reduce crime or even make a department more efficient. However, the results of these two culture transmission studies suggest that the clarification and strengthening of values and the creation of a known value will make the difficult job of policing more appealing to both those within and outside of the police agency.

How then would King Arthur and his Knights have performed and how would they have been evaluated if a rank structure and bureaucratic model had been created? And what if King Arthur had held his roll call at three shifts at a rectangular table? Although King Arthur and his system of the Round Table is legend, it is a metaphor for a model of communication, purpose and identity, which as the Holy Grail remains more of a myth than reality.

About the Authors

Jack R. Greene is the Director of Temple University's Center for Public Policy. He is also a Professor of Criminal Justice and received his Ph.D. in Social Science from Michigan State University in 1977. His most recent book, an anthology of readings, Community Policing: Rhetoric and Reality (1988) examines a major institutional change occurring in American policing. In addition, Dr. Greene regularly consults with police officials in many countries. He serves as a consultant to the National Police College of Sweden, he writes regularly for police officials in India, and has most recently, served as a consultant to the Sao Paulo, Brazil Military Police.

Geoffrey P. Alpert, Ph.D., is Professor of Criminal Justice, University of South Carolina. He has been published widely in law reviews, criminology and sociology journals. His most recent book, Policing Urban America (1992) discusses policing which must incorporate value-driven directives and a community orientation. Dr. Alpert has worked extensively with various police departments including Dallas and Miami. He recently completed a year as Visiting Fellow at the Bureau of Justice Statistics.

Inspector Paul A. Styles has been employed by the Cambridgeshire Constabulary in England - a police force comprising some 1250 sworn officers and 800 civilian staff- for the last eighteen years. He has worked uniform patrol, C.I.D., training department and is a qualified police duty instructor . Currently, his role is in the H.Q. Community Affairs Department which involves responsibilities for developing inter-agency policies and cooperation on criminal justice matters, monitoring social trends, and encouraging pro-active policing initiatives.

References

Alpert, G. (1985). The American System of Criminal Justice. Beverly Hills, CA: Sage Publications.

Alpert, G., and R. Dunham. (1988). Policing Urban America. Prospect Heights, IL: Waveland Press.

Alpert, G., and R. Dunham. (1988b). Policing Multi Ethnic Neighborhoods. Westport, CT: Greenwood Press.

Black, D. (1980). The Manners and Customs of the Police. New York: Academic Press.

Bittner, E. (1967). "The Police on Skid Row: A Study of Peacekeeping", American Sociological Review, 32 (October): 699-715.

Brooks, L. (1989) "Police Discretionary Behavior: A Study in Style". In R. Dunham and G. Alpert (eds.). Critical Issues in Policing. Prospect Heights, IL: Waveland Press, pp. 121-145.

Brown, M. (1981). Working the Street. New York: Russell Sage Foundation.

Brown, S.,and R. Vogel. (1983) "Police Professionalism", Journal of Crime and Justice, 6:17-37.

Bureau of Justice Statistics. (1989). Profile of State and Local Law Enforcement Agencies, 1987. Washington, DC: Bureau of Justice Statistics.

Cordner, G. (1989). "Police Agency Size and Investigative Effectiveness", Journal of Criminal Justice 17: 145-156.

Crank, J. (1989). "Civilianization in Small and Medium Police Departments in Illinois, 1973-1986", Journal of Criminal Justice 17: 167-177.

Cronin, K. (1977). "Supervision in a Small Town Department", Police Law Quarterly, 6: 31-35.

Daviss, B. (1983). "From Urban Sprawl to Country Drawl Big City Cops Seek Satisfaction as Small Town Chiefs", Police Magazine, 6: 50-56.

Domonoske, C. (1978). "Administration of Small Municipal Police", Police Chief, 45: 62-67.

Department of Justice. (1988). Uniform Crime Report. Washington, DC: USGPO.

Eck, J., W. Spelman, D. Hill, D. Stephans, J. Stedman and G. Murphy. (1988) Problem Solving: Problem Oriented Policing in Newport News. Washington, DC: Police Executive Research Forum.

Etzioni, A. (1975). A Comparative Analysis of Complex Organizations. Rev. Ed. New York: Free Press.

Goldstein, H. (1990). Problem Oriented Policing. New York: McGraw Hill Book Company.

Goldstein, H. (1987). "Toward Community Oriented Policing: Potential, Basic Requirements, and Threshold Questions", Crime and Delinquency, 33: 6-30.

Gouldner, A. W. (1954). Patterns of Industrial Bureaucracy. Glencoe, IL: Free Press.

Greene, J.R. (1990a). "Assist Officer: The Role of the Consultant in Affecting Change in a Big City Police Department", Paper presented at the annual meetings of the Academy of Criminal Justice Sciences, Denver, CO, March.

Greene, J.R. (1990b) "Community Policing and Cultural Change in Law Enforcement: Prospects and Challenges", Paper prepared for the Southwestern Legal Foundation, Law Enforcement Institute, Advanced Management College, Richardson, TX, November, 1990.

Greene, J.R., and S.D. Mastrofski (eds.) (1988). Community Policing: Rhetoric or Reality. New York: Praeger.

Greene, J.R. and S. Decker (1989). "Police and Community Perceptions of the Community Role in Policing: The Philadelphia Experience", The Howard Journal of Criminal Justice, 22,8 (May): 105-123.

Greene, J.R. (1989). "Police Officer Job Satisfaction and Community Perceptions: Implications for Community Policing", Journal of Research in Crime and Delinquency, 26, 2 (May): 168-183.

Hoetmer, G. (1989). "Police, Fire and Refuse Collection, 1988", The Municipal Yearbook 1989. Washington, DC: International City Management Association, pp. 180-234.

Kelling, G.L., and M.H. Moore. (1988). "From Political to Reform to Community: The Evolving Strategy of Police", in J.R. Greene and S.D. Mastrofski (eds). Community Policing: Rhetoric or Reality. New York: Praeger.

Kelling, G.L., R. Wasserman and H. Williams (1988). "Police Accountability and Community Policing". Perspectives on Policing, No. 7, Washington, DC National Institute of Justice. November.

Kilmann, R.H., Saxton, M.J., and Serpa, R. (eds) (1985). Gaining Control of the Corporate Culture. San Francisco: Jossey Bass.

Manning, P.K. (1977). Police Work: The Social Organization of Policing. Cambridge, MA: The MIT Press.

Mastrofski, S.D., and J.R. Greene (forthcoming). "Community Policing and the Rule of Law", in C. Uchida and D. Wesiburd (eds). The Changing Focus of Police Innovation: Problems of Law, Order and Community. New York: Springer Verlag.

Morgan, G. (1986). Images of Organization. Beverly Hills, CA: Sage Publications.

Muir, W.K., Jr. (1977). Police: Streetcorner Politicians. Chicago: University of Chicago Press.

Neiderhoffer, A. (1967). Behind the Shield. New York: Doubleday.

Ostrom, E., Parks, R. and G. Whitaker. (1978). "Police Agency Size: Some Evidence on its Effects", Police Studies, 1:34-46.

Ostrom, E., Parks, R. and G. Whitaker. (1978b). Patterns of Metropolitan Policing. Cambridge, MA: Ballinger.

Ott, J. S. (1989). The Organizational Culture Perspective. Pacific Grove, CA: Brooks/Cole Publishing Co.

Peters, T.J., and R.H. Waterman, Jr. (1982). In Search of Excellence. New York: Harper and Row.

Police Task Force Study. (1987). Philadelphia and Its Police. Philadelphia: Philadelphia Police Department.

Pratt, C. (1979). "Small Department's Experience in Aggressively Pursuing Success", Police Chief, 45: 58-60, 79.

Reiss, A.J., Jr. (1971). The Police and the Public. New Haven: Yale University Press.

Reuss Ianni, E., and F.A. J. Ianni. (1983). "Street Cops and Management Cops: The Two Cultures of Policing", in M. Punch (ed). Control in the Police Organization. Cambridge, MA: The MIT Press, 251-274.

Sims, V. (1988). Small Town and Rural Police. Springfield, IL: Charles C. Thomas.

Skolnick, J., and D. Bayley. (1986). The New Blue Line. New York: Free Press.

Slovak, J. (1986). Styles of Urban Policing. New York: New York University Press.

Trojanowicz, R.C., and M.H. Moore (1988). "Corporate Strategies for Policing", Perspectives on Policing. No. 6, Washington, DC: National Institute of Justice, November.

Van Mannen, J. (1973). "Observations On the Making of Policemen", Human Organization, 32: 407-418.

Van Mannen, J. (1974). "Working the Street: A Developmental View of Police Behavior", in H. Jacob (ed). The Potential for Reform in Criminal Justice. Beverly Hills, CA: Sage Publications.

Van Mannen, J. (1983). "The Boss: First Line Supervision in an American Police Agency", in M. Punch (ed). Control in the Police Organization. Cambridge, MA: The MIT Press, 227-250.

Wasserman, R. and M. Moore. (1988). "Values in Policing", Perspectives on Policing, No. 8, Washington, DC: National Institute of Justice, November.

Watson, D. (1977). "Administering the 'Small' Department", Police Chief, 44: 20,22,86-87.

Westley, W.A. (1953). "Violence and the Police", American Journal of Sociology, 59 (August): 34-41.

Westley, W.A. (1970). Violence and the Police: A Study of Law, Custom, and Morality. Cambridge, MA: The MIT Press.

Wilson, J.Q. (1978). Varieties of Police Behavior. Cambridge, MA: Harvard University Press.

Wilson, J.Q. and G.L. Kelling. (1989). "Making Neighborhoods Safe", The Atlantic Monthly :46-52.

REVIEW ESSAY ON
THE LAW ENFORCEMENT RESPONSE
TO SPOUSE ABUSE: PAST, PRESENT,
AND FUTURE

J. DAVID HIRSCHEL
Department of Criminal Justice
University of North Carolina—Charlotte

IRA W. HUTCHISON
Department of Sociology, Anthropology and Social Work
University of North Carolina—Charlotte

CHARLES W. DEAN
Department of Criminal Justice
University of North Carolina—Charlotte

ANNE-MARIE MILLS
Department of Criminal Justice
University of North Carolina—Charlotte

In this review article the authors critically assess the role of law enforcement in spouse abuse. After discussing definitional issues and tracing the evolution of attitudes and treatment of the physical abuse of wives, they examine the extent to which spouse abuse occurs. The role of law enforcement then is examined from both a historical and a theoretical perspective, and research studies of the law enforcement response are evaluated. Particular attention is paid to current pro-arrest policies. The article concludes with a discussion of policy issues and suggestions for the future.

For many centuries husbands had the right to use force to coerce their wives to conform to their expectations. Until very recently, spouse abuse has been considered more a problem of public order than a criminal matter.

Societal acceptance of spouse abuse as criminal has been slow and inconsistent, and attitudes favoring nonintervention have been

Prepared in conjunction with grant 87-IJ-CX-K004 from the National Institute of Justice, Office of Justice Programs, U.S. Department of Justice. Points of view or opinions in this document are those of the authors and do not necessarily represent the official position or policies of the U.S. Department of Justice.

JUSTICE QUARTERLY, Vol. 9 No. 2, June 1992

slow to change. Competition for resources occurs when the criminal justice system is asked to assign higher priority to this problem. On the felony level the battle has been won; there is no dispute that felonious spouse abuse is considered a matter for the criminal justice system. This is not the case, however, on the misdemeanor level. Because domestic violence accounts for a significant proportion of all calls for police service, assigning a higher priority to such calls requires a major reallocation of police resources. Although many people do not question the morality of arresting a man for assaulting his wife or partner, the real question is whether to arrest and prosecute those who commit this crime at the expense of other governmental responsibilities or of law enforcement and judicial responses to other crimes.

This article examines the historical treatment of wives and the evolution of the law enforcement response to spouse abuse. We first address the issue of definition: some confusion exists between the generic concept of spouse abuse and other types of family disturbance that may or may not be similar. Both conceptual and practical problems are present in defining abuse. The definitional problem is particularly noteworthy in view of the fact that most domestic calls for police service involve situations which are either shouting matches or in which there are no victims with apparent injuries. Verbal abuse seldom qualifies as criminal behavior, so police can do little in this respect.

It is important to address current social attitudes towards spouse abuse and to discuss how we reached this point. An examination of the historical treatment of wives helps us to understand why hostile behavior, now viewed as spouse abuse, was acceptable for so long, why it is currently an unresolved public policy issue, and why both the public and the legal system resist in treating all spouse abusers as criminals.

In this article we also address different estimates of the prevalence of spouse abuse, and then focus on that segment of spouse abuse which is reported to police. We examine problems of definition, different data sources, and varying probabilities of calling the police in order to explain the difficulties in measuring the extent to which spouse abuse actually constitutes a law enforcement problem.

The basic question at the center of the current public debate is the proper role of law enforcement in spouse abuse. Significant research now has been conducted on the police response to spouse abuse, but the findings are not entirely consistent with each other or with the position of advocacy groups. Nationwide there has been considerable momentum toward the adoption of pro-arrest policies. We explore the rationale for such policies and examine the empirical studies that test the effectiveness of arrest in reducing subsequent recidivism by spouse abusers. We conclude by discussing the multiple issues involved in achieving a more comprehensive understanding of the place of law enforcement as only one possible societal response to spouse abuse.

DEFINITIONS

A preliminary issue involves an understanding of the key concepts that are the focus of this article: *spouse* and *abuse*. Although these words have apparent common sense meanings, each may be used in a variety of ways which makes effective comparisons more difficult.

The common, popular understanding of *spouse* is congruent with dictionary definitions, and focuses on married couples. The more common definition of spouse in research literature, however, pertains to persons in conjugal or conjugal-like relationships, including married, separated, and cohabiting couples (Berk and Loseke 1981; Buzawa and Buzawa 1990; Ford and Regoli forthcoming; Goolkasian 1986; Williams and Hawkins 1989). This difference is relatively important because a large proportion of abusive incidents reported to police involve cohabiting couples, an issue that we will examine later in greater detail.

The term *spouse* is gender-free and may erroneously imply a parity between men and women. As we will discuss later, husbands often are the targets of abuse, but their probability of being injured is much lower than that of wives. Morley and Mullender (1991) note that the gender-specific term *woman-battering* has given way to the androgynous terms *domestic, spouse, marital*, and *family* violence. It is unclear whether the broadening of this concept has had a positive or a harmful effect on family violence studies. The variation both in concepts and in their references (i.e., who is included) creates some confusion.

A second major issue is whether to define *abuse* as measured by aggressive actions or as measured by the outcome of such acts (i.e., injuries; Straus 1990). According to Berk et al. (1983), there is little consensus on the kinds of behavior to which the term *abuse* refers. Feld and Straus (1989:143) define violence as "an act carried out with the intention or perceived intention of causing physical pain or injury to another person." Schulman (1979), Straus (1979), and Straus, Gelles, and Steinmetz (1980) also use acts as a definition of abuse. On the other hand, Berk et al. (1983) emphasize the severity of injuries as the focus of their study.

This article defines spouse abuse to include married, separated, divorced, cohabiting, and formerly cohabiting couples, and focuses primarily on female victims unless noted otherwise. The literature we include here encompasses abuse as defined either by act or by outcome. In general we concentrate on physical aggression because of the paucity of data on verbal aggression such as threats. Although we recognize both the frequency and the seriousness of threats, this type of abuse is less likely to produce a law enforcement response.

EVOLVING ATTITUDES TOWARD SPOUSE ABUSE

Historical Overview

Wife abuse appears to be a cultural universal that has been approved implicitly or explicitly until very recently. From an anthropological perspective it may be observed that a large proportion of societies have given adult males authority to coerce the behavior of dependent females. This authority appears to be an integral part of a monogamous marriage relationship, which involves differential power between the partners in a setting culturally defined as private. When formal governments emerged and legal codes developed, the wife consistently was treated as legally subordinate to the husband; wife beating either was not considered criminal or was formally approved.

Roman law, which has been served as a basis for many legal systems in the Western world, originally gave a husband sovereign authority over his wife, who acquired the status of daughter at marriage. This authority, known as *patria potestas*, included the power of life and death and the right to unrestrained physical chastisement of the wife and other family members (Hecker 1914:13; Pleck 1987:9).

A modified form of *patria potestas* was incorporated into English common law (Oppenlander 1981:386) under the guise of family protection (Gamache, Edleson, and Schock 1988:194; Sigler 1989:2; Walker 1990:48). Although the male's authority in this system did not include the power of life and death, physical chastisement was both accepted and expected (Dobash and Dobash 1978: Hecker 1914:124-27; Smith 1989:3). In 1768 Blackstone described the husband's right to chastise his wife moderately in order to enforce obedience (1897:147). The criterion for "moderate" was the "rule of thumb," which allowed a husband to use any reasonable instrument, including a rod no thicker than his thumb, to correct his "wayward" wife.

The English heritage was brought to the American colonies; husbands in America, as in England, retained the power to chastise their wives. Although the Puritans enacted the first laws against wife beating in 1641 with the passage of the Massachusetts *Body of Laws and Liberties*, the integrity and privacy of the family still were considered more important that the protection of victims. This orientation contributed greatly to tolerance and indifference toward wife beating (Pleck 1987:21-2; 1989). Between 1633 and 1802, for example, only 12 cases involving wife beating are to found in the court records of Plymouth Colony (Pleck 1989:25).

Although it is debatable how accurately these cases represent the law in the United States in general (Pleck 1989:32-33), a number of appellate court decisions in this period upheld a husband's right to chastise his wife physically. In 1824 the Mississippi State Supreme Court declared in *Bradley v. State* that "the husband be permitted to exercise the right of moderate chastisement." The Court emphasized that "family broils and dissentions" were not proper matters to bring before a court of law, but were best left inside the walls of the home (158).

Other cases reinforced this position, holding that a wife was incompetent to testify against her husband in a case where "a lasting injury or great bodily harm" was not inflicted or threatened (*State v. Hussey* 1852:128); that "the law gives the husband power to use such a degree of force as is necessary to make the wife behave herself and know her place," and that bruises left by a horsewhip or switch may be justified by the circumstances so as not to give a wife a right to abandon her husband and "claim to be divorced" (*Joyner v. Joyner* 1862:252-53); that the effect, not the instrument, was the standard to be used in determining whether the husband had exceeded his authority (*State v. Black* 1864; *State v. Rhodes* 1865); and that a husband was permitted to use the force necessary to control an unruly wife, even if they were living apart by agreement. The court would "not invade the domestic forum unless some permanent injury be inflicted" except in cases of excessive violence to "gratify . . . bad passions" (*State v. Black* (1864:163)).

The Puritan attitude of indifference or outright approval was maintained until the late 1830s (Pleck 1989). Working initially through churches and later through the temperance societies, the women's rights movements gained momentum during the nineteenth century. Whereas the Puritans placed family preservation ahead of women's rights, the temperance movement reversed the order (Pleck 1989).

Women's growing activism evolved in the 1850s into a push for women's rights which helped to sponsor legislation regarding married women's property, conventions on women's rights, and recommendations on divorce (Pleck 1989). The interest in women's rights, however, did not peak until the 1870s. After the Civil War, state invention in the family was viewed as more acceptable than in the past because of the broader governmental control allowed by the war (Pleck 1987:89). As a consequence, state legislatures began to pass Married Women's Acts, which allowed married women to enter contracts, sue, and own property in their own right, and liberalized the divorce laws, thus eroding men's absolute dominance over women.

A focus on law and order and a humanitarian concern for the victims of spouse abuse led to attempts to enact legislation that expressed a more serious view of this problem (Pleck 1989:35). Between 1876 and 1906 bills were introduced in 12 states, and were passed in three, to punish wife beaters with a whipping (Pleck 1989:40). Passing a statute and enforcing it, however, are not the same. After Maryland enacted a law in 1882 to punish wife beaters with either a whip or a year in jail, no one was prosecuted under that statutory provision for a year and only two convictions occurred in three years. Although unused, the provision remained on the books until 1948 (Pleck 1989:41).

During this period dicta and holdings in court cases likewise became less supportive of a husband's right to exercise physical control over his wife. In the Alabama case of *Fulgham v. State* (1871) the court denied the right, declaring that wife whipping was "at best, but a low and barbarous custom" (147). Three years later, in *State v. Oliver* (1874), a lower court found guilty a husband who had whipped his wife with two thin switches, leaving bruises. The North Carolina Supreme Court affirmed this judgment, stating that the old "rule of thumb" no longer was the law in North Carolina. Yet despite the legal rejection of the right to chastise, the belief that spouse abuse belonged within the privacy of the home continued to be very much a part of American culture. Physical cruelty was disapproved, but it was not grounds for a woman to obtain a divorce especially because nagging women were regarded as having provoked their husbands (Pleck 1987:25).

The de facto decriminalization of spouse abuse was reinforced by the emergence of family courts in the second decade of the twentieth century. These courts tended to view family violence as a domestic problem rather than as a crime, and urged reconciliation whenever possible (Pleck 1987:136-37). From 1920 until the late 1970s, relatively little occurred, legislatively or judicially, in the area of spouse abuse.

Because law both reflects and shapes societal values, we can expect its development and enforcement to be inconsistent over time among jurisdictions and among agencies within a given jurisdiction. The legislation and court rulings discussed above trace the uneven evolution of law regarding spouse abuse. Generally the changes in legislation and in enforcement were roughly parallel. Yet in spousal relationships, moderate force that otherwise would be treated as criminal often went unpunished.

Past and Current Attitudes

A certain ambivalence toward spouse abuse always has existed and still persists today. A number of reasons are advanced for this attitude: the privacy of the home, the social approval of violence, the inequality of women in society, and noninvolvement by criminal justice officials (Gelles and Straus 1988:25; Oppenlander 1981:385; Pleck 1989:20-21).

Spouse abuse has been viewed differently from "ordinary" assault between other principals because spouse abuse has been regarded as less serious on the grounds that the wife belongs to the husband and the home is his castle; therefore what happens in the castle is not a concern for his neighbors or the criminal justice system (Belknap 1990:248; Dobash and Dobash 1991; Fyfe and Flavin 1991; Pleck 1989:21). Although the state can punish violators, it continues to give family members special immunity to protect family life and the marriage (Oppenlander 1981:385; Pleck 1989:20). Senator Jesse Helms argued against federal funding of domestic violence shelters because they constituted "social engineering," removing the husband as the "head of the family" (126 Cong. Rec. 24, 12058, 1980).

The cultural belief in the sanctity of family privacy prevents societal, legal, or personal intervention (Balos and Trotzky 1988:83; Berk and Loseke 1981:319; Buda and Butler 1984:366; Gelles and Straus 1988:27; Roy 1977:138; Sigler 1989:2; Waits 1985:299). Modern industrial societies—characterized by urbanization, anonymity, high residential mobility, neolocal monogamous family patterns, and religiously reinforced family privacy—seem to have difficulty in developing and enforcing effective community standards that would limit wife abuse.

Because "violence is as American as apple pie" (Gelles and Straus 1988:26), some researchers suggest that abuse in the family is a result of the approval given to other forms of violence (Breslin 1978:298; Gelles and Straus 1988:26; Oppenlander 1981:394; Sigler

1989:98). The family is less authoritarian and more egalitarian than in the past; spouse abuse continues, however (Pleck 1989).

Men receive implicit social permission to beat their wives when nothing is done to stop abuse (Buzawa and Buzawa 1985:143; Roy 1977:138, Walker 1990:48). The problem is convincing the police to arrest, the prosecutors to prosecute vigorously, and the court system to sanction (Balos and Trotzky 1988:106; Goolkasian 1986:3). The criminal justice system is reluctant to punish batterers (Waits 1985:271), thus giving the impression that the abuser faces very little risk (Gelles and Straus 1988:24). Although spouse abuse is condemned in theory, the law still allows it to continue (Waits 1985:299).

THE EXTENT OF THE PROBLEM

The empirical study of family violence is relatively recent; only since the 1970s has it been studied in depth and extensively. Accurate prevalence and incidence data remain beyond reach, however. Both official records, such as those based on calls to police, and self-report data are best regarded as rough estimates of the extent of actual abuse.

Scope and Probability of Abuse

Despite 20 years of empirical research, estimates of the number of women abused by their partners each year vary greatly, ranging from 2.1 million (Langan and Innes 1986) to more than 8 million (Straus 1989). It has been estimated that violence occurs each year in approximately one relationship in six (Straus et al. 1980). The probability estimate is that between 25 and 30 percent of couples will experience a violent incident in their lifetime (Gelles and Straus 1988; Nisonoff and Bitman 1979; Straus et al. 1980).

The widespread variation in numerical estimates is due to four factors. First, definitional differences are great; they range from any threat of unwanted touching to the infliction of serious injuries. Straus and Gelles (1990:96) estimate rates of any husband-to-wife violence at 116 per 1,000 couples per year (6,250,000 women), whereas they estimate any severe husband-to-wife violence at 34 per 1,000 couples per year (1,800,000 women). Second, estimates are based on different data sources: police data, shelter intakes, injuries reported to police or hospitals, and extrapolations from surveys. Even if there were no definitional differences, the different sources of data would produce widely varying parameters because they capture different segments of the abused population. Third, the time factor varies: published reports do not always make clear whether authors are using a data base to project estimates for a given year or for a lifetime probability of ever-abuse. In a given year, an estimate for that year will include those who entered the pool of abused women in a previous year, as well as those who are "new" to the pool. Fourth, although everyone agrees that abuse is underreported, nobody agrees about the extent of underreporting; this issue is discussed in greater detail below.

Predictors associated with spouse abuse. In review of characteristics associated with spouse abuse, Hotaling and Sugarman (1986) investigated more than 400 empirical studies of husband-to-wife violence. Their review produced a total of 97 potential risk markers; a risk marker is defined as "an attribute or characteristic that is associated with an increased probability to either the use of husband-to-wife violence, or the risk of being victimized by husband-to-wife violence" (1986:102). Because this review unquestionably is the most comprehensive available, we rely on it for our overview.

Of the 97 characteristics investigated, Hotaling and Sugarman found very few to be consistent risk markers. In particular, attributes of women associated with being abused by men were rare. Of the 42 female-related characteristics investigated, only one appeared as a consistent risk marker: witnessing violence between parents while growing up. All of the other female characteristics investigated were determined to be inconsistent or nonrisk markers: for example, experiencing violence as a child (although this trait almost qualified), age, race, educational level, income, traditional sex role expectations, alcohol use, and self-esteem.

Far more predictive of spouse abuse in Hotaling and Sugarman's (1986) review were the characteristics associated with men. Of the 38 potential risk markers attributed to men, nine appeared as consistent predictors of abuse: being sexually aggressive toward their wives, violence toward their children, witnessing violence as a child, witnessing violence as an adolescent, occupational status, alcohol use, income, assertiveness, and educational level. Hotaling and Sugarman (1986) also investigated risk markers associated with the couple, and found five variables associated with higher levels of spouse abuse: frequency of verbal arguments, religious incompatibility, family income/social class (primarily through the husband's income), marital adjustment, and marital status. In sum, it is far more difficult to predict victimization of women in spouse abuse situations on the basis of any characteristic of the woman than on the basis of her male partner's attributes. Hotaling and Sugarman (1986) conclude that the psychiatric model of spouse abuse receives strong support from their review.

113

As new research is conducted, other factors may emerge as consistent risk markers; perhaps some of those now identified as increasing the probability of abuse will emerge as less accurate predictors. One dilemma is that comparisons (both within and across studies) include men who have abused a woman only once as well as those who are chronic batterers. We should not expect to find a consistent set of predictors when the entire range of wife abuse is reduced to the threshold requirement of a single incident. Greater progress on the question of prediction would be made if more attention were given to developing typologies of abusers, victims, and relationships and then to determining predictor variables associated with particular types. For example, it may be that chronic abusers (of one or more female partners) are differentiated from occasional abusers by particular characteristics associated with both personality and situational variables.

Social class characteristics.   As documented by both police reports and numerous researchers, marital violence exists in every class and income group, regardless of race and social class (Finesmith 1983; Lockhart 1987; Schulman 1979; Straus et al. 1980). Years of research, however, have failed to produce clear-cut and convincing documentation on the degree to which spouse abuse is distributed *equally* across various demographic groups. The most accurate current conclusion is that spouse abuse is comparable across social class variables; that is, more similarity than difference exists between groups. Yet although intragroup differences are greater than intergroup differences, we simply cannot conclude that demographic differences are absent. Some studies have discovered an inverse relationship between income and violence: as income increases, violence decreases (Finesmith 1983; Yllo and Straus 1981).

Schulman (1979) found, however, that although abusive families tend to be urban, young, and nonwhite, these violent families are not differentiated easily from similar nonabusive families. In a study of 307 black and white women from various social classes, Lockhart (1987) found no significant intergroup difference in victimization by domestic violence.

We speculate that researchers and the interpreters of research sometimes may bend over backward in their efforts to avoid any bias, and thus may distort results unwittingly by down playing any intergroup differences. It is clear that spouse abuse is not characteristic of any particular group. It is less clear whether all groups are truly equal in both prevalence and incidence of abusive behavior.

114

Abusive incidents reported to the police. The proportion of spouse assaults reported to the police differs widely, depending on how the study was conducted (Bowker 1984). According to estimates, from one-tenth to two-thirds of abused women call the police to report an incident. In a survey of 1,793 Kentucky women, Schulman (1979) found that women called police in only 9 percent of the incidents. Compared to findings from other studies, this figure implies an extremely high proportion of unreported incidents. The generally accepted estimate (based in particular on national samples) is that approximately one-half of all incidents are reported to the police. Analysis of 1973-1976 National Crime Panel Survey data revealed that approximately 55 of every 100 incidents of intimate violence went unreported to law enforcement (U.S. Department of Justice 1980). Analysis of 1978-1982 data showed that 48 percent of the incidents were not reported to the police (Langan and Innes 1986). In a study of 420 women who sought treatment in a domestic abuse program in Washington State, Kuhl (1982) discovered that 66 percent of the women had not filed a report.

Characteristics of persons calling police. Much of the dilemma in understanding demographic material in abuse rates is due again to data sources; there is no way to reconcile somewhat disparate information. As in some other areas of the criminal justice system, citizens who call the police to report a particular criminal action are not representative of all who experience that particular crime. An inherent self-selection process is present in the use of police services. Thus no one concludes that abused women who call the police are a representative demographic sample of all women who experience abuse.

Although domestic disturbances cut across all demographic boundaries, police are involved most often in domestic disturbances among the poor and uneducated (Hamberger and Hastings 1988; Moore 1979; Parnas 1967). Bowker (1982, 1984) reports that the police are more likely to come into contact with couples of relatively low socioeconomic status, with low-quality marital relationships, and suffering or inflicting severe violence. Nonwhite and lower-income women (under $7,500) are more than twice as likely to report an incident to the police as are white, high-income women (over $15,000) (Schulman 1979). Underreporting occurs at all socioeconomic levels but is particularly likely among middle-and upper-income persons.

Reasons for underreporting. A clear relationship between selective perception and underreporting has emerged in various studies. An unknown number of victims do not consider their assault to be

115

a crime, or, if they do so, they do not report the incident or disclose to any official how they received their injuries (Breslin 1978).
Because spouse abuse is so common in society, many victims do not
view it as a crime and therefore do not report it to the police. As
Langley and Levy (1978:5) note, these are the missing persons of
official statistics.

Some women do not perceive a slap in the face as abuse, and
so do not report it; others perceive such an action as abusive, but
only a fraction of those women report it. The more severe the behavior, the more likely it is to be both perceived as abusive and reported often; often, however, even very severe abuse is never
reported to the police. Langan and Innes (1986) found that the primary reason offered by women for not reporting an abusive incident to the police was that they considered it a private or personal
matter (49 percent of respondents). A further 12 percent of the
victims did not report because they feared reprisal. Similar proportions failed to report because they thought the crime was not
important enough, or because they believed the police could not or
would not do anything.

Some women report most incidents of abuse, some report
some incidents, and some never report any incident that takes
place. Unfortunately, the accumulation of studies does not tell us
how many of each type are found in the reported and in the unreported incidents.

Abuse reported in surveys.   Other than police reports, surveys
provide the most comprehensive data on spouse abuse. Yet these,
too, must be interpreted with some caution for a number of reasons. First, the perception of what constitutes abuse remains a
problem. As Straus (1989:27) points out, victims and suspects may
not view abuse as a crime and therefore may not report it in a
crime survey. National Crime Surveys (NCS) estimates of the
crime of woman battering are one-fiftieth of the rate revealed in a
national survey produced by Straus (1990). Second, national
surveys face the problem of distilling spouse abuse from other
forms of domestic violence as well as from nonfamily violence.
National crime surveys find family offenses a difficult subject to
quantify: neither the Uniform Crime Reports (UCR) nor the NCS
are designed to measure family violence specifically (Rose and
Goss 1989). As a result, an assault on a spouse is counted among
the other nondomestic assaults (Miller 1979). Third, surveys such

as the NCS can be problematic because interviews may be conducted with both the victim and the offender present. It is reasonable to assume that many victims would not report violence because of fear of reprisal by the offender (Straus 1989).

Nonwife abuse. The common perception of spouse abuse involves a husband and a wife, with the latter as the victim. Although wife abuse is the modal adult domestic violence, there is a growing recognition of the abuse of husbands, cohabitants, and—to a lesser extent—gay or lesbian partners. Offenders are not always men, nor are victims always women; instead the problem is one of "spouse" abuse because men also are victims (Dobash and Dobash 1991:350).

The same elements in society that explain violence against wives cause women's violence towards men (Straus 1980). Violence against men, however, was and still is perceived as unusual in patriarchal societies, where men are expected to dominate and control the female (Dobash and Dobash 1991). Many women hit and beat their husbands, but the data have been "misreported, misinterpreted, and misunderstood" (Gelles and Straus 1988:90).

Steinmetz (1977) estimated that of 47 million married couples, more than a quarter-million husbands experience several beatings from their spouses. In Straus, Gelles, and Steinmetz's 1975 study (Gelles and Straus 1988), 2 million men were victims of violence inflicted by their wives. Straus and Gelles (1986, 1990) showed that the rate of wife-to-husband assault is slightly higher than that of husband-to-wife assault, but an attack by a woman is less severe and less likely to cause injury. In addition, men are much less likely to report an attack by a women (Dutton, 1988; Edleson and Brygger 1986; Jouriles and O'Leary 1985; Stets and Straus 1989; Straus 1989; Szinovacz 1983).

Gelles and Straus (1988) concluded that violence against women has received more publicity because men's greater strength causes more damage and because the women are acting in self-defense in about three-quarters of the cases. Some feminists, however, have tried to maintain a low profile on battered husbands so that battered women would receive funding (Gelles and Straus 1988:188).

Any discussion of spouse abuse must also include some attention to cohabitants. The number of cohabitants has increased almost fourfold in the past 20 years, and such individuals are primarily young: two-thirds of males and three-fourths of females are less than 35 years old (Spanier 1983). There is increasing evidence that cohabitants are particularly prone to abusive relationships. In their comparison of married, dating, and cohabiting couples, Stets and Straus (1989) report that the highest rates of assault and the most severe assaults are found among cohabiting couples. Hutchison, Hirschel, and Pesackis (1988) found that the number of calls for abusive situations to police by cohabitants equaled the number of similar calls by married couples, although the latter group made up a far greater proportion of the population. Stets concluded that cohabitants experience more aggression than married couples because of a combination of factors: youth, minority status, problems including depression and alcohol use, and the lack of "social control associated with participation in organizations and being tied to their relationships" (1991:678).

Family and Spouse Homicides

Murder data are more systematic, more extensive, and more reliable than abuse data. Because such data have been collected nationally for many years, it is possible to determine both patterns and changes with some degree of precision. Nonetheless, distilling spouse abuse data from national data sources, such as the uniform Crime Reports, presents possibilities of misinterpretation and confusion.

In 1984 the Attorney General's Task Force on Family Violence found that almost 20 percent of murders involve family members and that nearly one-third of female homicide victims are murdered by their husbands or boyfriends (U.S. Department of Justice 1984:11). A review of FBI Uniform Crime Reports data (1985-1990) shows that the percentage of all murder victims who were killed by a spouse or boyfriend/girlfriend has remained relatively constant over the past few years. In the five-year period 1986-1990, 28 to 30 percent of all female murder victims were killed by husbands or boyfriends; in the same period, 4 to 6 percent of all male victims were killed by wives or girlfriends. Despite the escalation of homicide rates, some consistency remains in homicide rates of offenders and victims. In the past few years, 75 percent of the murder victims have been male. In addition, just as males are killed primarily by other males, females also are killed by males: approximately 90 percent of female victims are murdered by men (U.S. Department of Justice 1986-1991).

FBI homicide data disclose that women make up only 14 percent of the homicide offenders; the relationship between offender and victim varies, however (Straus 1989). In contrast to women's low representation as offenders in stranger homicide, Straus (1989) found a much higher proportion in family homicide: women murder male partners 56 to 62 percent as often as men murder female partners. It appears that men kill "across the board," but women are more likely to kill husbands or boyfriends. Zahn and Sagi (1987:394-95) found that although males were the predominant offenders in family homicides, a much higher proportion of family homicides than of any other homicide type involved a female offender. Males were almost equally likely to offend against males and against females in the family. In contrast, female offenders' victims were almost exclusively male.

These data do not suggest any kind of murder "parity" between husbands and wives; the cold facts disguise the family dynamics. Wives are seven times more likely than husbands to have killed in self-defense (Jolin 1983) or in response to an assault initiated by the male partner (Straus 1989). In a study of 144 women who killed a mate in a domestic incident, Mann (1986:10) found that 58.6 percent stated self-defense as a reason for the killing. Recognition of the family dynamics involved in these killings is evidenced by the growing use of the "battered women's syndrome" defense by wives on trial for killing their husbands.

THE ROLE OF LAW ENFORCEMENT

Historical Background

In the past, domestic violence calls often were assigned low priority (Fleming 1979; Parnas 1971; U.S. Commission on Civil Rights 1982). Police responded reluctantly to abuse calls, attempted to restore peace and order between the disputants, and typically left without taking more formal action.

Explanations for the long-term avoidance of formal action are manifold. First, violence within the family had been considered to be essentially a private matter; this view allowed adults to use force to solve personal disputes (Breslin 1978; Martin 1976). Second, female victims had been perceived as uncooperative; this situation, it was claimed, made arresting and prosecuting abusers a waste of time (Parnas 1967:931; U.S. Commission on Civil Rights 1982). Third was a concern that taking action against abusers hurt their families, especially members financially dependent on the offenders (Parnas 1967:931; U.S. Department of Justice 1984). Fourth, intervening in family disputes was not regarded as "real police work" (Buzawa and Buzawa 1990:29; Fyfe and Flavin 1991:4; Parnas 1971:542). Finally, Martin (1976) and others argued that responding officers, who usually were male, typically sided with offenders. This taking of sides reinforced a cultural norm stressing male superiority; this norm was exemplified, as discussed in an earlier section, by laws in colonial and later times that allowed a man to chastise his wife.

The police response to spouse abuse changed little until the 1960s. Under the influence of social scientists, psychologists, and a developing women's movement, the order maintenance approach received a professional twist. Mediation and crisis intervention were promoted as the appropriate tools for dealing with family violence. This development led to police training in crisis intervention techniques (Bard 1970, 1973, 1975; Spitzner and McGee 1975), the establishment of police family crisis intervention units (Bard 1970, 1975), and mixed police crisis teams composed of police officers and social workers (Burnett et al. 1976).

Despite the added training and the use of specialized units, there is little evidence that crisis intervention and mediation have had much success in reducing abuse. Oppenlander (1982), for example, reported that police tended to make more arrests in abusive situations than in other cases, even though crisis intervention approaches often took precedence over arrest. Relatively few evaluations were made, however (see, e.g., Pearce and Snortum 1983; Wylie et al. 1976), to assess the effects of these changes; most of the innovations occurred before controlled experimental research on the effects of police policy was conducted.

In addition, many police officers did not welcome these changes. Mediation seemed more like social work than police work. Moreover, some commentators (e.g., Langley and Levy 1978) thought that the police were inadequately prepared to perform family crisis intervention. Others were concerned about applying crisis intervention techniques and mediation to abuse situations. Loving (1980), for example, wrote that techniques designed for situations involving verbal abuse were being applied inappropriately to situations involving physical assaults.

The Attorney General's Task Force on Family Violence (U.S. Department of Justice 1984) identified what may well be a fundamental flaw in the mediation approach. The process of mediation assumes some equality of culpability between the parties to a dispute. The assumption of equal culpability and the failure to hold the offender accountable for his actions give him no incentive to reform. Thus, "rather than stopping the violence and providing protection for the victim, mediation may inadvertently contribute to a dangerous escalation of violence" (U.S. Department of Justice 1984:23).

These concerns about crisis intervention and mediation, coupled with arguments that female victims' rights were violated by the failure of police enforcement, produced demands for the arrest of abusers as the appropriate police response (Langley and Levy 1978; U.S. Commission on Civil Rights 1982). In some jurisdictions, women's groups filed suits to effect this change in policy (see, e.g., *Bruno v. Codd* 1977; *Scott v. Hart* 1976; *Thurman v. City of Torrington* 1984). The rationale for advocating arrest was clear. As the Attorney General's Task Force on Family Violence stated unequivocally, *"The legal response to family violence must be guided primarily by the nature of the abusive act, not the relationship between the victim and the abuser"* (U.S. Department of Justice 1984:4).

Contemporary Preferred Arrest Policies

Many vexing issues are raised by the meaning, implementation, and effects of the preferred arrest movement, but the current trend toward preferred arrest policies is indisputable. In recent years we have seen a major increase in the number of police departments that apply such policies. It is uncertain to what extent this increase is attributable to changes that have taken place in state statutes. Lerman, Landis, and Goldzweig observed in 1983 that "twenty-seven of the recent state laws on domestic violence expand(ed) police power to arrest in domestic abuse cases" (1983:44). Ferraro notes that as of 1986, six states had passed laws requiring arrest with a positive determination of probable cause and the presence of the offender on the scene (1989:61). By 1988, 10 states had enacted such laws (Victim Services Agency 1988:3).

Often, however, the potential of such statutory provisions is limited by the existence of requirements that must be satisfied before the laws can be invoked. Some state laws, for example, require the existence of a visible injury and/or the elapsing of only a short time between the commission of the offense and the arrival of the police. In their survey of police departments with preferred arrest policies, Hirschel and Hutchison (1991) reported that although all of the departments applied such a policy in cases of visible injury or a threat with a deadly weapon, only in a minority of the departments was such a policy in effect for situations involving verbal threats or property damage. Moreover, there is evidence that (subject to jurisdictional variation) about half of all offenders leave the scene before the police arrive (Hirschel and Hutchison 1987:11), and thus would not be arrested unless the victims swore out arrest warrants. Finally, policy trends favoring either preferred or mandatory arrest decisions do not necessarily include all abuse victims. It is known, for example, that cohabiting women call police disproportionately more than married women for domestic assault (Hutchison et al. 1988:14). Nonetheless, in at least some states nonmarried couples are not included in preferred arrest policies (Ferraro 1989).

The police also are asked to take action against abusers who have violated provisions of protective orders granted to abused women by the courts. Such orders currently are available in 48 states and in Washington, DC (Finn and Colson 1990:1). Suspected violation of the provisions of these orders may (and in 10 states must; Victim Services Agency 1988:4) result in arrest of the offender.

Preferred arrest (also called pro-arrest or presumptive) policies are far more common than mandatory policies. A 1986 study by the Crime Control Institute ("Roughening Up" 1987; Sherman and Cohn 1989) investigated arrest policies and found that the number of departments with such policies had increased fourfold since 1984. The study, however, did not include police departments in cities with populations of less than 100,000, so we cannot determine the extent to which the trend in large cities is being replicated elsewhere.

In general, the literature does not examine whether police departments adopted these arrest policies on their own initiative or as a result of changes in state law. It is clear that a number of factors have prompted police departments to change their policies. The same forces that operated on state legislatures also have influenced police departments. Foremost among these are various women's groups, including the National Coalition Against Domestic Violence, state chapters of this organization, and local coalitions that formed to alter existing policy and practice.

Although it is difficult to unravel the various factors that have motivated police departments to move toward preferred arrest policies, it is important to gauge the extent to which departments have adopted these policies willingly. This point is important because the orientation of top administrators influences rank-and-file enforcement of the policies. Available information suggests that police departments generally have not played a leading role in adopting arrest policies, and occasionally have been very reluctant to do so. In 1980, for example, Arizona's legislature passed a law that expanded police arrest powers. The chief of the Phoenix Police Department, however, adopted a presumptive arrest policy for his department only when faced with the possibility of legislation *mandating* arrest (Ferraro 1989:63). Miller (1979:16) in Oregon, Bell (1985:532) in Ohio and Buzawa (1988:174-75) in New Hampshire have noted a similar reluctance on the part of police departments to change their policies to conform with new statutory provisions.

The success of formal policies depends upon the support of both command and line personnel. The impact of negative attitudes among chiefs of police regarding the use of arrest in abuse cases is demonstrated clearly by Buzawa's (1988) research in New Hampshire. She found that a lack of support by chiefs was associated with low enrollments in the voluntary state-administered training program, the absence of written departmental policies, low or nonexistent arrest rates for domestic violence incidents, and a feeling among officers that responding to abuse calls was usually a waste of time (Buzawa 1988:175-78). In one jurisdiction the chief even said that "he could not recall a 'genuine' call for domestic violence in his numerous years as an administrator," and consequently "did not highly value" (undoubtedly an understatement) "the role of police intervention in this area" (Buzawa 1988:175).

Whatever policy might be, police officers are accustomed to making their own decisions on the street and traditionally are antagonistic to policies that limit their discretion. In his survey of Minneapolis officers, conducted after the Sherman and Berk experiment, Steinman found a strong indication of independence: 99 percent of respondents voiced the belief that they "should make their own decisions about problems that arise on duty," 77 percent reported that they "usually do what they think necessary even if they expect supervisors to disagree," and 43 percent declared that "they should use their own standards of police work even when department procedures prohibit them from doing so" (1988:2).

In the only available in-depth study of police response to a new presumptive arrest policy, Ferraro (1989) provides a fascinating study of the Phoenix Police Department. Even though the State of Arizona passed such legislation in 1980, little actual change occurred until 1984, when the Phoenix Police Department finally adopted a presumptive arrest policy. On the basis of ride-along observational data, Ferraro reports that in spite of this policy, arrests were made in only 18 percent of the battering incidents to which her research team responded. One problem was that in interpreting probable cause, officers were employing "a level of evidence high enough for felony arrests" (1989:64). In the face of opportunity and discretion to interpret both policy and circumstance, there is no reason to expect that police in general suddenly will reverse their traditional reluctance to arrest.

Research shows that certain factors are associated with positive attitudes toward preferred arrest policies. Not surprisingly, an officer's general orientation toward domestic violence is likely to affect his or her attitude (Berk and Loseke 1981:320-21; Ferraro 1989:66-67; Homant and Kennedy 1985; Walter 1981). Female police officers tend to be more supportive of arrest policies than male police officers (see, e.g., Ferraro 1989; Homant and Kennedy 1985). Training also influences police attitudes; studies have found that training is associated positively with both officers' perception and citizens' evaluation of officers' handling of disturbance calls (Pearce and Snortum 1983), with improvement in officers' attitudes toward domestic situations (Buchanon and Perry 1985), and with officers' willingness to arrest domestic violence offenders (Buzawa 1982:421-22).

Two final issues that affect police officers' attitudes toward domestic violence calls arise from their perceptions of the danger posed by such calls and from their fear of being sued at civil law for false arrest of an alleged offender. First, there persists a common perception that domestic disturbances are unusually dangerous for police in regard to frequencies of both assaults and homicides (Buzawa and Buzawa 1990:29). This perception has been "transmitted largely through police folklore" (Konstantin 1984:32). Such a perception has been supported by the interpretation of FBI "disturbance calls" data. These data grouped family quarrels with other types of disturbances, such as bar fights and "man with gun" calls, and were easily misinterpreted by some individuals, who took all of the disturbance calls to be domestic disturbance calls (see, e.g., Bard 1974:foreword; Stephens 1977:164). In addition, it has been suggested that crisis intervention trainers projected this perception of danger deliberately to attract the attention of antagonistic recruits (Fyfe and Flavin 1991:8). It is clear, however, that only a small percentage of police officers killed in the line of duty died while responding to abuse calls (see, e.g., Konstantin 1984; Margarita 1980a). An in-depth analysis by Garner and Clemmer (1986) concluded that domestic disturbances are one of the least frequent contributors to police homicide. The danger of assault and injury likewise has been exaggerated (see, e.g., Geller and Karales 1981; Margarita 1980b). Recent studies, however, suggest that in some locations, domestic calls still may constitute the most dangerous category both in assault (see, e.g., Uchida, Brooks, and Kopers 1987) and in injury (see, e.g., Stanford and Mowry 1990; Uchida et al. 1987).

In addition, the fear of being sued (at least successfully) in civil court for wrongful arrest of an alleged offender has been exaggerated greatly. Although this concern is raised frequently by officers in police departments that adopt preferred arrest policies, in reality this is a rare occurrence. It is possible that officers and police departments in fact are as likely to be sued successfully for failure to arrest an alleged offender (see, e.g., *Nearing v. Weaver* 1983; *Thurman v. City of Torrington* 1984) as for wrongful arrest of an alleged offender. Such suits for failure to arrest have been based on allegations of denial of due process or equal protection of the law (see, e.g., *Balistreri v. Pacifica Police Department* 1990; *Dudosh v. City of Allentown* 1987; *Thurman v. City of Torrington* 1984) or infringement of rights granted victims by state statutes (see, e.g., *Nearing v. Weaver* 1983; *Turner v. City of North Charleston* 1987). Yet despite some large awards (e.g. $2.3 million in *Thurman*), not many suits have been successful. It has been suggested that recent Supreme Court case law (*Deshaney v. Winnebago County Department of Social Services* 1989) will make it more difficult for abused women to win civil suits in federal court against police departments that failed to protect them (Zalman forthcoming).

Deterrence and Preferred Arrest Policies

An argument that has been raised both for and against arresting spouse abusers arises from the findings of research studies designed to test the deterrent effect of arrest in such cases. Although the deterrence argument generally is not considered necessary to justify the arrest of the alleged perpetrators of other criminal offense, such as rape, robbery, burglary, and auto theft, it has played a central part in the debate about the role of arrest in the social measures adopted to combat spouse abuse.

The Minneapolis Study. The formulation of social policy involves at best an amalgam of competing interests, viewpoints, and resources. Maintenance of the status quo is likely except in the face of compelling evidence that seems to justify a change. Extant procedures are likely to remain in effect unless policy makers are convinced that an alternative is either essential or better. Experimental research offers both the scientific community and policy makers a plausible basis for policy recommendations. Experimental methodology, in brief, is the most convincing of methodologies. Perhaps the major contribution of the Minneapolis experiment lies not in its substantive findings but in its reception by those involved in spouse abuse policies. We speculate that neither police departments nor advocates of change would have paid so much attention if the Minneapolis study had not been a controlled scientific experiment.

The Minneapolis experiment, conducted by Sherman and Berk in 1981-1982, was the first study to test the deterrent effect of arrest in spouse abuse cases—more accurately domestic violence cases, because the research design also included same-sex and other familial relationships (Sherman and Berk 1984a, 1984b). In that study certain predefined misdemeanor domestic assault cases, in which both the offender and the victim were present when the police arrived on the scene, were assigned randomly to one of three treatment responses: 1) advising the couple (including informal mediation in some cases); 2) separating the couple by ordering the offender to leave for eight hours; and 3) arresting the offender, which meant that he stayed overnight in jail. The selected cases then were tracked for six months: official record checks were made on offenders, and interviews were conducted with victims every two weeks to determine whether subsequent abuse occurred. A "police recorded failure" occurred when the offender generated a written offense or arrest report for domestic violence. A "victim reported failure" occurred when a victim reported "a repeat incident with the same suspect, broadly defined to include an actual assault, threatened assault or property damage" (Sherman and Berk 1984b:266).

During the course of the study, the participating officers (about 52 in number) produced a total of 330 eligible cases; three officers turned in 28 percent of the cases (Sherman and Berk 1984b:263-64). Sixteen cases were excluded from analyses because no treatment was applied or because reports had been generated on cases with victim-offender relationships that were outside the ambit of the study.[1] Whereas 99 percent of the cases targeted for arrest received the "arrest" treatment, only 78 percent of the "advise" cases and 73 percent of the "separate" cases were treated as assigned. All 12 follow-up interviews were obtained from 161 victims, for an interview completion rate of 49 percent (Sherman and Berk 1984b).

Analysis of the data showed that arrest was more effective than the other two responses in deterring subsequent abuse. According to police data, the overall failure rate was 18.2 percent; the arrest treatment returned the lowest failure rate (13%), and the separate treatment the highest (26%; Sherman and Berk 1984b).[2] Only the difference between the arrest and the separate treatments, however, was significant at the .05 level. The victim data showed a failure rate of 19 percent for those assigned the arrest

---

[1] Later changed to 17 (see Berk, Smyth, and Sherman 1988; Berk and Sherman 1988:71).

[2] The failure rate for the advise treatment is not reported here, but is reported elsewhere as 19 percent (Sherman and Berk 1984a). This figure is slightly high in view of the overall failure rate reported in the publication cited in the text (Sherman and Berk 1984b). Furthermore, discrepancies exist between the failure rates reported in different publications. For example, Sherman and Berk (1984a) report official failure rates of 10 percent for cases in the arrest treatment, 19 percent for cases in the advise treatment, and 24 percent for cases in the separate treatment.

treatment, as compared to 33 percent for those assigned the separate treatment and 37 percent for those assigned the advise treatment. Here the only significant difference was between the advise and the arrest treatments (Sherman and Berk 1984a, 1984b).

Both the researchers themselves (e.g., Sherman and Berk 1984b:263-66, 269) and others (e.g., Binder and Meeker 1988; Elliot 1989:453-54; Lempert 1989:152-54) have pointed out problems with the study. These problems include inadequate sample size; the submission of a disproportionate number of cases by a few officers; inadequate controls over the treatments actually delivered; the possibility of surveillance effects caused by multiple follow-up interviews; and lack of generalizability of the findings due to attributes of the city in which the sample was obtained, and of the sample itself.

Despite these methodological problems, the Minneapolis study received unprecedented national attention and is credited with helping to promote the nationwide movement toward arrest as the preferred response in abuse cases ("Roughening Up" 1987; Sherman and Cohn 1989). Yet if fundamental policy changes were to be undertaken with a clear (i.e., generalizable) basis for estimating the effects of an arrest policy, additional field experiments based on random assignment were needed. Accordingly, in order to test the validity of the results obtained in the Minneapolis experiment, the National Institute of Justice funded additional experiments in Omaha, Atlanta, Colorado Springs, Dade County (Florida), Milwaukee, and Charlotte (North Carolina).

. *Subsequent studies.* Like the Minneapolis study, the six later studies examined whether arrest is the most effective law enforcement response for deterring spouse abusers from committing subsequent acts of abuse. Certain elements were common to the six projects: all employed an experimental design in which cases that met predefined eligibility requirements were assigned randomly to treatment responses; all used arrest as one of the treatment responses; all focused on the misdemeanor range of cases, in which the police were empowered but not required to make an arrest; and a six-month follow-up was conducted on all eligible cases through use of police records and interviews with victims.

The Omaha study, which was funded about two years before the others, employed a two-part research design that focused on whether the offender was present when the officers arrived on the scene. If the offender was present, the case was assigned randomly to one of the treatments employed in the Minneapolis study;

127

arrest, separate, or mediate. If the offender had gone when the police arrived, the case was assigned randomly either to receive or not to receive a warrant for the offender's arrest. Like the Minneapolis and the Milwaukee studies (but not the other four), the Omaha study extended beyond heterosexual couples who were or had been married or cohabiting. It also included same-sex couples as well as victims and offenders in other familial relationships.

Analysis of the 330 eligible cases in which the offender was present revealed no significant differences between the failure rates of the three treatments, whether official measures or victim-reported measures of recidivism were employed (Dunford, Huizinga, and Elliot 1990). Analysis of the 247 cases in the offender-absent part of the experiment, however, showed that cases in which warrants were issued were both less likely and slower to result in further abuse than cases in which no warrant was issued (Dunford et al. 1989; Dunford 1990).

The Charlotte Project was the only one to employ the entire patrol division in round-the-clock and citywide sampling for the full duration of the project. It used three treatment responses: 1) advising and possibly separating the couple; 2) arresting the offender; and 3) issuing a citation to the offender (an order requiring the offender to appear in court to answer specific charges). Analysis of the 650 eligible cases obtained by the project produced only two significant findings: the differences between the effects of the advise/separate and the citation treatments and between the effects of the informal (advise/separate) and the formal (arrest and citation) treatments on the official incidence (but not the prevalence) measures of arrest recidivism. In no case, whether official- or victim-reported measures of recidivism were employed, did the failure rate of the arrest treatment differ significantly from those of the other two treatments (Hirschel et al. 1991; Hirschel, Hutchison and Dean, 1992).

The Milwaukee Project also employed three treatment responses: 1) full arrest accompanied by a relatively long period of detention in jail (a mean of 11.1 hours); 2) short arrest, which resulted in the release of the offender within a few hours (a mean of 2.8 hours); and 3) no arrest (warning only). Analysis of the 1,200 eligible cases revealed, in general, no significant differences between the treatments. However, according to interviews and one official measure (the commission of subsequent violence against *any* victim), short arrest had a substantial initial (30-day) deterrent effect in relation to warning only, although this deterrent effect dissipated over a longer follow-up period. These data highlight the importance of both multiple measures of recidivism and an adequate follow-up period to determine treatment effects. On the basis of the official measure that the authors consider to be their most comprehensive indicator of official recidivism (police reports to the local shelter's hotline concerning all probable-cause domestic violence cases), the short-arrest group consistently showed significantly higher rates of long-term recidivism than the warning-only group (Sherman et al. 1991).

Comments. The results of these three studies (Omaha, Charlotte, and Milwaukee) present an unambiguous picture: arrest of misdemeanor spouse abusers is no more or less effective in preventing recurrence of abuse than the other responses examined. These results, coupled with the concerns that have been raised about the validity of the Minneapolis findings (e.g., Binder and Meeker 1988), suggest a lack of adequate support for a mandatory or presumptive arrest policy based on specific deterrence. Possibly this picture will be modified when the three other sites present their findings. At this point, the hope that arrest alone could contribute significantly to solving the problem of spouse abuse is unfulfilled.

We offer several possible explanations why arrest has not been found to deter subsequent abuse. First, the majority of offenders in these studies have previous criminal histories: 59 percent in Minneapolis (Sherman and Berk 1984b:266), 65 percent in Omaha (Dunford et al. 1990:194), 69 percent in Charlotte (Hirschel et al. 1991:37), and fifty percent in Milwaukee (Sherman et al. 1991:827). Thus in many cases, arrest is neither a new nor an unusual experience.

Second, for many of the couples in these studies, abuse is a common rather than an occasional occurrence. Indeed, for some, abuse is chronic. For offenders who have criminal histories or who have been offenders in chronically abusive relationships, it is unrealistic to imagine that arrest will have much impact.

Third, arrest alone, which was a focal point of the research projects, may not constitute as strong a societal response as commonly perceived. The popular conception is that the arrested person is put in jail and that that punitive action is sufficient to change behavior. The fact is that "time in jail" is often minimal beyond the booking time required: it is estimated to have averaged about 16 hours in Omaha (Dunford et al. 1990:191), nine hours in Charlotte (Hirschel et al. 1991:151), and three hours for short and 11 hours for long arrest in Milwaukee (Sherman et al. 1991). Thus arrest with immediate release simply may not mean much, particularly when the offenders have been arrested before.

Fourth, although not technically within the scope of the project, some information was gathered on the processing of offenders through the criminal justice system. The data support the conclusion that a spouse very rarely is found guilty and ordered to spend any significant time in jail. In Minneapolis "only 3 (2%) of the 136 arrested offenders were formally punished by fines or subsequent incarceration" (Sherman and Berk 1984b:270). In Charlotte only four (1%) of all the men who had been issued a citation or arrested spent time in jail beyond the initial arrest; another eight (2%) received credit for time served before going to trial (Hirschel et al. 1991:147). In Milwaukee initial charges were filed in 37 (5%) of the 802 arrest cases, and only 11 (1%) resulted in convictions (Sherman et al. 1991). In Omaha, however, 64 percent of those arrested were sentenced to jail, probation or fine (Dunford, Huizinga and Elliot 1989:31).

Fifth, these studies focus on whether arrest constitutes a deterrent for spouse abusers as a whole. For the most part they do not examine whether there is any particular subgroup of spouse abusers for whom arrest may serve as a deterrent. In a study in southern California, Berk and Newton (1985) generally confirm the deterrent value of arrest (on the basis of an ex post facto analysis of 783 wife-battering incidents) but argue carefully that a conditional effect is present. They note in particular, that arrest is most effective for batterers whom police ordinarily would be inclined to arrest. In subsequent analyses of the Milwaukee data, Sherman et al. (1992) found, however, that arrest exerted a deterrent effect on those with high stakes in social conformity (the employed, married, high school graduates and whites), but an escalation effect on those with the opposite attributes (the unemployed, etc.) as measured by reports of subsequent abuse to the domestic violence hotline.

Preferred Arrest Policies as Part of a Coordinated Community Response

In some jurisdictions, police departments have moved to a preferred arrest policy without the involvement of other agencies. In other jurisdictions the movement to such a policy has been part of a new, coordinated, community response to the problem of abuse. In general it is the latter departments that have reported positive results with their new policies. Gamache et al. (1988) report that after the introduction of community intervention projects in three Minnesota communities, rates of both arrests and successful prosecutions increased; similar results are recorded by Steinman (1988:2) in Lincoln, Nebraska, by Ferguson (1987:9) and Goolkasian

(1986:37-38) in Seattle, by Pence (1983:257-58) in Duluth, and by Burris and Jaffe (1983:312) in London, Ontario. After noting that police policies in Lincoln, Seattle, Duluth, and London are coordinated with community wide support, Steinman suggests that "this is probably not the case in most communities where departments have adopted arrest policies" (1988:2).

In addition, with the exception of Seattle, the cities that have been studied most closely are small, with relatively modest crime and domestic violence rates. In the three Minnesota communities studied by Gamache et al., the populations range from 15,000 to 36,000 inhabitants and recorded five or fewer domestic violence arrests a month per community during the research period (1988:195, 201). Duluth has received considerable national attention for its Domestic Abuse Intervention Project, which coordinates the efforts of nine law enforcement, criminal justice, and human service agencies; this city has a population under 100,000 and recorded only some 10 arrests a month during the research period reported by Pence (1983:258-59). These observations suggest that postarrest coordination can be achieved more easily in smaller communities with relatively modest crime and domestic violence rates. Yet even this type of coordinated community response, however commendable for other purposes, provides no evidence that abuse rates are affected.

SUMMARY AND DISCUSSION

Describing the law enforcement response to spouse abuse requires some understanding of the social and legal foundations. In this article we have presented a brief review of the historical attitudes toward wife abuse, the evolution of the response by the legal system to such abuse, the contemporary scope of the problem, the traditional law enforcement role of the past, and the current and sometimes controversial movement toward the arrest of spouse abusers. We have focused primarily on the abuse of women who are in marital or spouselike (e.g., cohabitant) relationships. Although we recognize that the abuse of men in both marital and cohabitant relationships falls clearly within the parameters of spouse abuse, both the research literature and social concern regarding abused men are quite limited.

As we have shown in this article, the United States has a long and inglorious tradition, inherited from our English origins, of ignoring and minimizing spouse abuse. Indeed, only recently has our society begun to consider such behavior as "abuse," much less as a social "problem." Males' rights to chastise and abuse females are rooted deeply in our social and legal traditions.

Although protective laws had been passed as long ago as the latter part of the seventeenth century, they hardly were enforced. The predominant patterns, lodged in the perceived rights of male power and primacy, reflected highly permissive attitudes toward spouse abusers. Legal intervention was minimal, at least as may be determined through extant court records; serious laws, with serious enforcement, were not initiated until the latter part of the twentieth century. We have identified some of the reasons for the traditional police reluctance to intervene in family disputes. As described above, we have traced such reluctance to a combination of factors including traditional values of family privacy, the perception that family disputes are inappropriate as police work, and the perception of danger in responding to domestic violence calls. In addition, many police simply do not believe that intervening in spouse abuse does much to address the problem—either for a particular couple or for the larger social issue. In this regard, such sentiments may be typical of much work that police do for a variety of criminal offenses.

Our review concludes with a significant focus on the current scene: perhaps it can be summarized adequately as a gradual strengthening of spouse abuse laws by state legislatures, but it is marked by a continued and pervasive reluctance of police to do more than is absolutely required by law. We also review the original movement toward pro-arrest policies, and discuss the nearly conclusive current evidence that arrest for misdemeanor spouse abuse has little unique deterrent effect in reducing further abuse.

A number of issues remain to be addressed, ranging from the interpretation of data to the design and implementation of effective social policies.

First, as made clear by this review and by comprehensive assessments of the scope of spouse abuse, there is much room for misinterpretation, distortion, and manipulation of data. Because spouse abuse itself (finally) raises social concern, if not anger, it almost begs for exaggeration. Estimates both of the number of people affected and of probabilities of abuse vary widely, depending on definitions, data sources, and the quality of work performed by the researchers, interpreters, and disseminators of results. One cannot dispute that spouse abuse is an immense social problem; the scope needs no exaggeration in order to warrant concerted, unrelenting action in search of solutions. We believe that carelessness or exaggeration in reporting estimates actually may contribute to less rather than more concern for the problem. There is no reason to expect policy makers, often already jaded by causes, to believe exaggerated claims or to act on them.

132

Second, some confusion exists about the true extent of popular support for taking significant action to combat spouse abuse. Like any cause for any social problem, this cause has ardent supporters who are in the forefront of change. Most communities know by now that spouse abuse is a major problem and that there is a great need for social support services such as shelters, victims' assistance agencies, treatment programs for men, and employment and relocation services for abused women. It is beyond the scope of this article to determine whether the generally inadequate level of social services represents weariness of community support or reflects the reality that limited resources must be allocated to multiple and therefore competing programs.

Third, the law enforcement role in spouse abuse is hinged inevitably to both state law and community pressures. In this review we have documented the gradual change in state laws, which have moved toward giving police more authority and more responsibility for intervening in abusive situations. Police authority always is defined and limited by state law; the fact is that such law, although stronger than 50 or even 20 years ago, still leaves much to be desired. Law is influenced in turn by pressure brought to bear on lawmakers; such pressure often has developed from women's groups within communities, with varying degrees of success at the state level. Thus, what police ultimately are empowered to do (or are prohibited from doing) derives from state laws, most of which were enacted originally by men and now are under attack primarily by women. It is an unequal battle, and real successes in changing state laws typically come only after much pressure. Ironically although not surprisingly, in this situation (as in others) it is primarily women who are battling for the rights of other women, to protect them against a social and personal problem inflicted largely by men (at least in cases of serious injury).

Fourth, one can make a case that the recent movement toward pro-arrest policies for police, although motivated nobly by the sincere (but perhaps futile) hope that arrest will make a difference, also reflects a "quick fix" mentality by both activists and sympathizers. Placing hopes on the success of arrest as a deterrent to spouse abuse removes pressure from other possible responses, such as the social support services mentioned above. It would be satisfying and simple if the fact of arrest had made a difference in the Minneapolis replication studies, but unfortunately, the hoped-for results have not yet materialized.

Fifth, study of the role of arrest of spouse abusers has been limited. All of the experiments funded by the National Institute of Justice focused on the misdemeanor range of spouse abuse, in

which police are empowered, but not required, to make warrant-
less arrests on the scene. Only the Omaha study examined situations in which police obtained warrants, located offenders, and
made arrests off-scene. A significant issue is the degree to which
police officers may interpret the facts of a situation (upon their arrival at the scene of a reported incident) so as to find that it does
not meet the criteria for an on-the-scene arrest for an offense committed in their absence. State law stipulates the general conditions
for a finding of the legal authority to make such an arrest, but interpretation always depends on the responding officers. When the
threshold requirements are high, it is virtually guaranteed that the
great majority of reported incidents will not be subject to official
police action beyond a simple response to the incident because
many police officers will decide subjectively that the minimum requirements have not been met.

If state laws were to cast a wider net so as to encompass a
broader range of abusive behavior, and if local police departments
stood solidly behind pro-arrest policies, far more abusers would be
arrested. In the Charlotte study, for example, only a minority (approximately 18%) of domestic calls to which police responded were
classified as misdemeanors and hence as subject to the discretionary power of police to make an arrest. A very small minority were
felony-type cases, in which police almost always make an arrest.
Thus in the great majority of calls to which police responded, the
incident was evaluated by responding officers as not meeting the
legal criteria for either a felony or a misdemeanor. Very simply,
officers decided that no crime had been committed.

Sixth, spouse abuse is probably the only area of criminal behavior in which it has been considered necessary to justify the
arrest of offenders on the grounds that such arrests will serve as a
deterrent. To our knowledge, it has never been suggested that
drug dealers, thieves, or rapists not be arrested because arrest had
failed to reduce subsequent recidivism for these crimes. Ironically,
the great hope placed in the arrest of spouse abusers as a deterrent
ultimately may be counterproductive if either police or lawmakers
react to the replication experiments with diminished concern for
making such arrests. As we argue elsewhere (Hirschel et al. 1991),
one can make a strong case that spouse abusers should be arrested
for a variety of other reasons beyond any deterrent value of arrest.
Even if arrest may not have much punitive value, it still may constitute a more conscionable choice than nonarrest. Not to arrest
may communicate to men the message that abuse is not serious
and to women the message that they are on their own. It may
communicate to children, who very often witness abuse of their

mothers, that the abuse of women is tolerated, if not legitimated. It may communicate to the public at large that a level of violence which is unacceptable when inflicted by a stranger is acceptable when inflicted by an intimate.

Seventh, the law enforcement role, on which this article has focused, inevitably is shaped by the response of the judicial system. It is a reasonably human response of police to question the efficacy of arresting spouse abusers when they already are reluctant to do so because of traditional beliefs, and when they know that little will happen to such abusers as they enter the judicial system. As we stated earlier, the popular perception is that arrest means time in jail, in this case time in jail for spouse abusers. In fact, as we pointed out, actual time in jail (beyond booking time) is extremely rare. For the many men who already have been in jail for other offenses, such nonaction hardly can be expected to be punitive. Indeed, the impotence of the criminal justice system in sentencing abusers to active time could even have a reinforcing effect on the norm held by some males, that abusing one's partner simply does not matter very much. We have received the impression, although it is well beyond the scope of this article, that creative sentencing for spouse abusers is an option used infrequently by the courts. Thus neither police nor offenders have reason to believe in either the deterrent or the punitive powers of arrest.

Finally, as jail space becomes even more crowded and as communities are hard pressed to confine offenders for other crimes viewed as more "serious," some hard decisions must be made and alternatives to jail (e.g., mandated treatment for offenders) must be imposed.

What, then might realistically be the most suitable law enforcement role in dealing with spouse abuse? A number of avenues seem both plausible and appropriate. The law enforcement role must be integrated more carefully with the social support systems within communities. Although we do not believe that such coordination provides a measurable deterrent to further abuse, it creates both real and symbolic support for abuse victims.

Although we do not suggest a return to the now-discarded crisis mediation approach, there is some evidence that police characteristics and the manner in which police manage incidents influence women's perceptions of the adequacy of the police response. In those departments which can afford to assign specialized teams to respond to abuse calls, it is likely that women will feel more strongly supported (even if they are not, in fact, protected any better) by the existence of such teams. There is some evidence that simply calling the police to report an abusive incident is an advantage in reducing subsequent incidents (Langan and Innes 1986). We speculate that if women felt that they were supported more strongly when reporting incidents to police, some change might occur in the long run for some couples. The problem of spouse abuse is so intractable that no single approach will have a major impact; the accumulation of small successes is the most that can be anticipated.

In addition, it is both incredible and quite baffling that neither social science researchers nor the police have developed more sophisticated ways of profiling and responding to spouse abusers. To our knowledge, the ordinary police policy in responding to a reported incident is to treat it as a new event and to respond (except for information that the responding officer may possess) only on the basis of that event. For many couples, such a response is perfectly appropriate. For many other couples, however, abuse is both serious and chronic. There is no logical reason why these couples should be treated as one would treat a new couple in the initial stages of abusiveness. It would seem that researchers and police could cooperate to identify "high-risk" couples, if for no other reason than that police receive the most virulent criticism when often-reported abuse terminates in a murder.

Finally, we are left with the question "What should be the law enforcement response to spouse abuse?" The only answer is quite simple, if unsatisfactory: to enforce the law. Police deserve some criticism for their laxity in enforcing the existing laws, but much of the criticism is undeserved because it disregards the reality that police are limited severely in what they can and cannot do. Responsible communities will look as critically at strengthening the prosecutorial, judicial, and social support systems as they have viewed the police for their apparent inability to solve this problem; it is a police problem only insofar as it is a law enforcement problem. Police do not possess the legal mandate, the credentials, or the resources to solve the problem by themselves. They have the responsibility to enforce the law, however. Beyond that, it is the responsibility of concerned citizens and lawmakers to address the multiple legal and social service issues encompassed by the problem of spouse abuse.

REFERENCES

Balos, Beverly and Katie Trotzky (1988) "Enforcement of the Domestic Abuse Act in Minnesota: A Preliminary Study." *Law & Inequality* 6:38-125.

Bard, Morton (1970) *Training Crisis Intervention: From Concept to Implementation*. Washington, DC: U.S. Department of Justice.

―――― (1973) *Family Crisis Intervention: From Concept to Implementation*. Washington, DC: U.S. Government Printing Office.

―――― (1975) "Role of Law Enforcement in the Helping System." In Alan R. Coffey and Vernon E. Renner (eds.) *Criminal Justice as a System: Readings* pp. 56-66. Englewood Cliffs, NJ: Prentice-Hall.

Belknap, Joanne (1990) "Police Training in Domestic Violence: Perceptions of Training and Knowledge of the Law." *American Criminal Justice Society* 14 (2):248-67.

Bell, Daniel (1985) "Domestic Violence: Victimization, Police Intervention, and Disposition." *Journal of Criminal Justice* 13:525-34.

Berk, Richard A., Sarah F. Berk, Donileen R. Loseke, and David Raume (1983) "Mutual Combat and Other Family Violence Myths." In David Finkelhor, Richard J. Gelles, Gerald Hotaling, and Murray V. Straus (eds.), *The Dark Side of Families: Current Family Violence Research* pp. 197-212. Beverly Hills: Sage.

Berk, Sarah and Donileen R. Loseke (1981) "Handling Family Violence: Situational Determinants of Police Arrest in Domestic Disturbances." *Law and Society Review* 15:317-46.

Berk, Richard and Phyllis Newton (1985) "Does Arrest Really Deter Wife Battery?" An Effort to Replicate the Findings of the Minneapolis Spouse Abuse Experiment." *American Sociological Review* 50:253-62.

Berk, Richard A., and Lawrence W. Sherman (1988) "Police Responses to Family Violence Incidents: An analysis of an Experimental Design with Incomplete Randomization." *Journal of the American Statistical Association* 83:70-76.

Berk, Richard, Gordon Smyth, and Lawrence Sherman (1988) "When Random Assignment Fails: Some Lessons from the Minneapolis Spouse Abuse Experiment." *Journal of Quantitative Criminology* 43:209-23.

Binder, Arnold and James W. Meeker (1988) "Experiments as Reforms." *Journal of Criminal Justice* 16:347-58.

Blackstone, William (1987) *Commentaries on the Laws of England*, edited by W. Hardcastle Browne. St. Paul: West.

Bowker, Lee (1982) "Police Services to Battered Women: Bad or Not So Bad?" *Criminal Justice and Behavior* 9:476-94.

―――― (1984) "Battered Wives and the Police: A National Study of Usage and Effectiveness." *Police Studies* 7:84-93.

Breslin, Warren J. (1978) "Police Intervention in Domestic Confrontations." *Journal of Police Science and Administration* 6:293-302.

Buchanon, Dale R. and Patricia A. Perry (1985) "Attitudes of Police Recruits towards Domestic Disturbances: An Evaluation of Family Crisis Intervention Training." *Journal of Criminal Justice* 13:561-72.

Buda, Michael A. and Teresa L. Butler (1984) "The Battered Wife Syndrome: A Backdoor Assault on Domestic Violence." *Journal of Family Law* 23:359-90.

Burnett, Bruce B., John J. Carr, John Sinapi, and Roy Taylor (1976) "Police and Social Workers in a Community Outreach Program." *Social Casework* 57:41-49.

Burris, Carole A. and Peter Jaffe (1983) "Wife Abuse as a Crime: The Impact of Police Laying Charges." *Canadian Journal of Criminology* 25:309-18.

Buzawa, Eve S. (1982) "Police Officer Response to Domestic Violence Legislation in Michigan." *Journal of Police Science and Administration* __-:415-24.

―――― (1988) "Explaining Variations in Police Response to Domestic Violence: A Case Study in Detroit and New England." In Gerald T. Hotaling, David Finkelhor, John T. Kirkpatrick, and Murray A. Straus (eds.), *Coping with Family Violence* pp. 169-82. Beverly Hills: Sage.

Buzawa, Eve S. and Carl. G. Buzawa (1985) "Legislative Trends in the Criminal Justice Response to Domestic Violence." In Alan J. Lincoln and Murray A. Straus (eds.), *Crime and the Family* pp. 134-47. Springfield, IL: Thomas.

―――― (1990) *Domestic Violence: The Criminal Justice Response*. Newbury Park, CA: Sage.

Dobash, Russell P. and R. Emerson Dobash (1978) "Wives: The 'Appropriate' Victims of Marital Violence." *Victimology* 3-4:426-42.

―――― (1991) "Gender, Methodology, and Methods in Criminological Research: The Case of Spousal Violence." Paper presented at the British Criminology Conference, York.

Dunford, Franklyn W. (1990). "System Initiated Warrants for Suspects of Misdemeanor Domestic Assault: A Pilot Study." *Justice Quarterly* 7:631-53.

Dunford, Franklyn W., David Huizinga and Delbert S. Elliot (1989). *The Omaha Domestic Violence Police Experiment: Final Report*, Washington DC: National Institute of Justice.

———— (1990) "The Role of Arrest in Domestic Assault: The Omaha Police Experiment." *Criminology* 28:183-206.

Dutton, Donald G. (1988) *The Domestic Assault of Women: The Psychological and Criminal Justice Perspectives*. Boston: Allyn & Bacon.

Edleson, Jeffrey L. and Mary P. Brygger (1986) "Gender Differences in Reporting of Battering Incidences." *Family Relations* 35:377-82.

Elliot, Delbert S. (1989) "Criminal Justice Procedures in Family Violence Crimes." In Lloyd Ohlin and Michael Tonry (eds.), *Family Violence* pp. 427-80. Chicago: University of Chicago Press.

Feld, Scott L. and Murray A. Straus (1989) "Escalation and Desistance of Wife Assault in Marriage." *Criminology* 27:141-61.

Ferguson, Harv (1987) "Mandating Arrests for Domestic Violence." *FBI Law Enforcement Bulletin* 56:6-11.

Ferraro, Kathleen J. (1989) "Policing Woman Battering." *Social Problems* 36:61-74.

Finesmith, Barbara K. (1983) "Police Response to Battered Women: A Critique and Proposals for Reform." *Seton Hall Law Review* 14:74-109.

Finn, Peter and Sarah Colson (1990) *Civil Protection Orders: Legislation, Current Court Practice, and Enforcement.* Washington, DC: U.S. Department of Justice.

Fleming, Jennifer B. (1979) *Stopping Wife Abuse: A Guide to the Psychological and Legal Implications for the Abused Woman and Those Helping Her.* Garden City, NY: Anchor.

Ford, David A. and Mary J. Regoli (forthcoming) "The Preventive Impacts of Policies for Prosecuting Wife Batterers." In Eve S. Buzawa and Carl G. Buzawa (eds.), *Domestic Violence: The Changing Criminal Justice Response to Domestic Violence.* Westport, CT: Greenwood.

Fyfe, James J. and Jeanne Flavin (1991) "Differential Police Processing of Domestic Assault Complaints." Paper presented at the annual meeting of the Academy of Criminal Justice Sciences, Nashville.

Gamache, Denise J., Jeffrey L. Edleson, and Michael D. Schock (1988) "Coordinated Police, Judicial, and Social Service Response to Woman Battering: A Multiple-Baseline Evaluation across Three Communities." In Gerald T. Hotaling, David Finkelhor, John T. Kirkpatrick, and Murray A. Straus (eds.), *Coping with Family Violence* pp. 193-209. Beverly Hills: Sage.

Garner, Joel and Elizabeth Clemmer (1986) *Danger to Police in Domestic Disturbances: A New Look.* Washington, DC: U.S. Department of Justice.

Geller, William A. and Kevin J. Karales (1981) Split-Second Decisions: Shoots of and by Chicago Police. Chicago: Chicago Law Enforcement.

Gelles, Richard J. and Murray A. Straus (1988) *Intimate Violence.* New York: Simon and Schuster.

Goolkasian, Gail A. (1986) *Confronting Domestic Violence: A Guide for Criminal Justice Agencies.* Washington, DC: U.S. Department of Justice.

Hamberger, L. Kevin and James Hastings (1988) "Characteristics of Male Spouse Abusers Consistent with Personality Disorders." *Hospital and Community Psychiatry* 39:763-70.

Hecker, Eugene A. (1914) *A Short History of Women's Rights.* Westport, CT: Greenwood.

Hirschel, J. David, Ira W. Hutchison, Charles W. Dean, Joseph J. Kelley and Carolyn E. Pesackis (1991) *Charlotte Spouse Assault Replication Project: Final Report.* Washington, DC: National Institute of Justice.

Hirschel, J. David and Ira W. Hutchison (1991) "Police-Preferred Arrest Policies." In Michael Steinman (ed.), *Wife Battering: Policy Responses* pp. 49-72. Cincinnati: Anderson.

Hirschel, J. David, Ira W. Hutchison and Charles W. Dean (1992). "The Failure of Arrest to Deter Spouse Abuse" (1992) *Journal of Research in Crime and Delinquency* 29:7-33.

Homant, Robert J. and Daniel B. Kennedy (1985) "Police Perceptions of Spouse Abuse: A Comparison of Male and Female Officers." *Journal of Criminal Justice* 13:29-47.

Hotaling, Gerald T. and David B. Sugarman (1986) "An Analysis of Risk Markers in Husband to Wife Violence: The Current State of Knowledge." *Violence and Victims* 1:101-24.

Hutchison, Ira W., J. David Hirschel, and Carolyn E. Pesackis (1988) "Domestic Variations in Domestic Violence Calls to Police." Paper presented at the annual meeting of the Southern Sociological Association, Nashville.

Jolin, Annette (1983) "Domestic Violence Legislation: An Impact Assessment." *Journal of Police Science and Administration* 11:451-56.

Jouriles, Ernest N. and K. Daniel O'Leary (1985) "Interspousal Reliability of Reports of Marital Violence." *Journal of Consulting and Clinical Psychology* 53:419-21.

Konstantin, David N. (1984) "Homicides of American Law Enforcement Officers 1978-1980." *Justice Quarterly* 1:29-45.

Kuhl, Anna F. (1982) "Community Responses to Battered Women." *Victimology* 7:49-59.

Langan, Patrick and Christopher Innes (1986) *Preventing Domestic Violence against Women.* Washington, DC: U.S. Department of Justice.

Langley, Roger and Richard G. Levy (1978) "Wife Abuse and the Police Response." *FBI Law Enforcement Bulletin* 47:4-9.

Lempert, Richard (1989) "Humility Is a Virtue: On the Publicization of Policy Relevant Research." *Law and Society Review* 23:145-61.

Lerman, Lisa G., Leslie Landis, and Sharon Goldzweig (1983) "State Legislation on Domestic Violence." In J. J. Costa (ed.), *Abuse of Women: Legislation, Reporting and Prevention* pp. 39-75. Lexington, MA: Heath.

Lockhart, Lettie L. (1987) "A Reexamination of the Effects of Race and Social Class on the Incidence of Marital Violence: A Search for Reliable Differences." *Journal of Marriage and the Family* 49:603-10.

Loving, N. (1980) *Responding to Spouse Abuse and Wife Beating.* Washington, DC: Police Executive Research Forum.

Mann, Coramae R. (1986). "Getting Even: Women Who Kill in Domestic Encounters." Paper presented at the Annual Meeting of the American Society of Criminology, Atlanta.

Margarita, Mona (1980a) "Killing the Police: Myths and Motives." *Annals of the American Association of Political and Social Science* 452:63-71.

———— (1980b) "Criminal Violence against Police." Doctoral dissertation, University of New York at Albany.

Martin, Del. (1976) *Battered Wives.* San Francisco: Glide.

Miller, Marilyn G. (1979) *Domestic Violence in Oregon.* Salem: Governor's Commission for Women, State of Oregon Executive Department.

Moore, Donna M. (1979) *Battered Women.* Beverly Hills: Sage.

Morley, Rebecca and Audrey Mullender (1991) "Preventing Violence against Women in the Home: Feminist Dilemmas Concerning Recent British Developments." Paper presented at the British Criminology Conference, York.

Nisonoff, Linda and Irving Bitman (1979) "Spouse Abuse: Incidence and Relationship to Selected Demographic Variables." *Victimology* 4:131-40.

Oppenlander, Nan (1981) "The Evolution of Law and Wife Abuse." *Law and Police Quarterly* 3:382-405.

———— (1982) "Coping or Copping Out: Police Service Delivery in Domestic Disputes." *Criminology* 20:449-65.

Parnas, Raymond I. (1967) "The Police Response to the Domestic Disturbance." *Wisconsin Law Review* (Fall):914-60.

———— (1971) "Police Discretion and Diversion of Incidents of Intra-Family Violence." *Law and Contemporary Problems* 36:539-65.

Pearce, Jack B. and John R. Snortum (1983) "Police Effectiveness in Handling Disturbance Calls: An Evaluation of Crisis Intervention Training." *Criminal Justice and Behavior* 10:71-92.

Pence, Ellen (1983) "The Duluth Domestic Abuse Intervention Project." *Hamline Law Review* 6:247-75.

Pleck, Elizabeth (1987) *Domestic Tyranny: The Making of Social Policy against Family Violence from Colonial Times to the Present.* New York: Oxford University Press.

———— (1989) "Criminal Approaches to Family Violence 1640-1980." In Lloyd Ohlin and Michael Tonry (eds.), *Crime and Justice: A Review of Research* pp. 19-58. Chicago: University of Chicago Press.

Rose, Kristina and Janet Goss (1989) *Domestic Violence Statistics*. Rockville, MD: Justice Statistics Clearinghouse.

"Roughening Up: Spouse Abuse Arrests Grow (1987) *Law Enforcement News* 13:1-13.

Roy, Maria (1977) "Some Thoughts Regarding the Criminal Justice System and Wife-Beating." In Maria Roy (ed.), *Battered Women: A Psychosociological Study of Domestic Violence* pp. 138-39. New York: Van Nostrand Reinhold.

Schulman, Mark A. (1979) *A Survey of Spousal Violence against Women in Kentucky*. Washington, DC: U.S. Department of Justice.

Sherman, Lawrence W. and Richard A. Berk (1984a) *The Minneapolis Domestic Violence Experiment*. Washington, DC: Police Foundation.

—— (1984b) "The Specific Deterrent Effects of Arrest for Domestic Assault." *American Sociological Review* 49:261-72.

Sherman, Lawrence W. and Ellen G. Cohn (1989) "The Impact of Research on Legal Policy: The Minneapolis Domestic Violence Experiment." *Law and Society Review* 23:117-44.

Sherman, Lawrence W., Janell D. Schmidt, Dennis P. Rogan, Patrick R. Gartin, Ellen G. Cohn, Dean Collins, and Anthony R. Bacich (1991) "From Initial Deterrence to Long Term Escalation: Short Custody Arrest for Poverty Ghetto Domestic Violence." *Criminology* 29:821-50.

Sherman, Lawrence W. Janell D. Schmidt, Dennis P. Rogan, Douglas A. Smith, Patrick R. Gartin, Ellen G. Cohn, Dean J. Collins and Anthony R. Bacich (1992) "The Variable Effects of Arrest on Criminal Careers: The Milwaukee Domestic Violence Experiment." *The Journal of Criminal Law and Criminology* 83:forthcoming.

Sherman, Lawrence W., Douglas A. Smith, Janell D. Schmidt, and Dennis P. Rogan (1991) *Ghetto Poverty, Crime and Punishment: Legal and Informal Control of Domestic Violence*. Washington, DC: Crime Control Institute.

Sigler, Robert T. (1989) *Domestic Violence in Context: An Assessment of Community Attitudes*. Lexington, MA: Heath.

Smith, Lorna J. F. (1989) *Domestic Violence: An Overview of the Literature*. London: Her Majesty's Stationery Office.

Spanier, Graham B. (1983) "Married and Unmarried Cohabitation in the United States: 1980." *Journal of Marriage and the Family* 45:277-88.

Spitzner, Joseph H. and Donald H. McGee (1975) "Family Crisis Intervention Training, Diversion, and the Prevention of Crimes of Violence." *Police Chief* 42:252-53.

Stanford, Rose M. and Bonney L. Mowry (1990) "Domestic Disturbance Danger Rate." *Journal of Police Science and Administration* 17(4):244-49.

Steinman, Michael (1988) "Anticipating Rank and File Police Reactions to Arrest Policies Regarding Spouse Abuse." *Criminal Justice Research Bulletin* 4:1-5.

Steinmetz, Suzanne K. (1977) *The Cycle of Violence: Assertive and Abusive Family Interaction*. New York: Praeger.

Stephens, Darrell V. (1977) "Domestic Assault: The Police Response." In Maria Roy (ed.), *Battered Women: A Psychosociological Study of Domestic Violence* pp. 164-72. New York: Van Nostrand Reinhold.

Stets, Jan E. (1991) "Cohabiting and Marital Aggression: The Role of Social Isolation." *Journal of Marriage and the Family* 53:669-80.

Stets, Jan E. and Murray A. Straus (1989) "The Marriage License as a Hitting License: A Comparison of Assaults in Dating, Cohabiting and Married Couples." *Journal of Family Violence* 41:33-52.

Straus, Murray A. (1979) "Measuring Intrafamily Conflict and Violence: The Conflict Tactics (CT) Scales." *Journal of Marriage and the Family* 41:75-88.

—— (1980) "Victims and Aggressors in Marital Violence." *American Behavioral Scientist* 23:681-704.

—— (1989) "Assaults by Wives on Husbands: Implications for Primary Prevention of Marital Violence." Paper presented at annual meetings of the American Society of Criminology, Reno.

—— (1990) "Conceptualization and Measurement of Battering: Implications for Public Policy." In Michael Steinman (ed.), *Woman Battering: Policy Responses* pp. 19-47. Cincinnati: Anderson.

Straus, Murray A. and Richard J. Gelles (1986) "Societal Change and Change in Family Violence from 1975 to 1985 as Revealed in Two National Surveys." *Journal of Marriage and the Family* 48:465-79.

―――― (1990) *Physical Violence in American Families.* New Brunswick, NJ: Transaction Books.

Straus, Murray, Richard Gelles, and Suzanne Steinmetz (1980) *Behind Closed Doors: Violence in the American Family.* Garden City, NY: Anchor.

Szinovacz, Maximiliane (1983) "Using Couple Data as a Methodological Tool: The Case of Marital Violence." *Journal of Marriage and the Family* 45:633-44.

Uchida, Craig D., Laure W. Brooks, and Christopher S. Kopers (1987) "Danger to Police during Domestic Encounters: Assaults on Baltimore County Police, 1984-1986." *Criminal Justice Policy Review* 2:357-71.

U.S. Commission on Civil Rights (1982) *Under the Rule of Thumb: Battered Women and the Administration of Justice.* Washington, DC: U.S. Government Printing Office.

U.S. Department of Justice (1980) *Intimate Victims: A Study of Violence among Friends and Relatives.* Washington, DC: U.S. Government Printing Office.

―――― (1984) *Attorney General's Task Force on Family Violence: Final Report.* Washington, DC: Author.

―――― (1986-1991) *Crime in the United States: 1985-1990.* Washington, DC: U.S. Government Printing Office.

Victim Services Agency (1988) *The Law Enforcement Response to Family Violence: A State by State Guide to Family Violence Legislation.* New York: Author.

Waits, Kathleen (1985) "The Criminal Justice System's Response to Battering: Understanding the Problem, Forging the Solutions." *Washington Law Review* 60:267-329.

Walker, Gillian A. (1990) *Family Violence and the Women's Movement: A Conceptual Politics of Struggle.* Toronto: University of Toronto Press.

Walter, James D. (1981) "Police in the Middle: A Study of Small City Police Intervention in Domestic Disputes." *Journal of Police Science Administration* 9:243-60.

Williams, Kirk R. and Richard Hawkins (1989) "The Meaning of Arrest for Wife Assault." *Criminology* 27:163-81.

Wylie, Peter B., Louis F. Basinger, Charlotte L. Heinecke and Jean A. Rueckert (1976) *An Approach to Evaluating a Police Program of Family Crisis Intervention in Six Demonstration Cities: Final Report.* Washington, DC: U.S. Government Printing Office.

Yllo, Kersti and Murray A. Straus (1981) "Interpersonal Violence among Married and Cohabiting Couples." *Family Relations* 30:339-47.

Zahn, Margaret A. and Philip C. Sagi (1987) "Stranger Homicides in Nine American Cities." *Journal of Criminal Law and Criminology* 78(2):377-97.

Zalman, Marvin (forthcoming) "The Court's Response to Police Intervention in Domestic Violence." In Eve S. Buzawa and Carl G. Buzawa (eds.), *Domestic Violence: The Changing Criminal Justice Response.* Westport, CT: Greenwood.

CASES CITED

Balistreri v. Pacifica Police Department 901 F.2d 696, 9th Cir. (1990)

Bradley v. State 2 Miss. 156 (1824)

Bruno v. Codd 396 N.Y.S. 974 (1977)

Deshaney v. Winnebago County Department of Social Services 489 U.S. 189 (1989)

Dudosh v. City of Allentown 665 F. Supp. 381, E.D. Pa. (1987)

Fulgham v. State 46 Ala. 143 (1871)

Joyner v. Joyner 59 N.C. 322 (1862)

Nearing v. Weaver 295 Or. 702 (1983)

Scott v. Hart No. 6-76-2395, N.D. Cal. (1976)

State v. Black 60 N.C. 262 (1864)

State v. Hussey 44 N.C. 124 (1852)

State v. Oliver 70 N.C. 44 (1874)

State v. Rhodes 61 N.C. 452 (1865)

Thurman v. City of Torrington 595 F. Supp. 1521, D. Conn. (1984)

Turner v. City of Charleston 675 F. Supp. 314, D.S.C. (1987)

olicing and Society, 1992, Vol 2, pp. 193–204
\teprints available directly from the publisher
*hotocopying available by license only

THE POLICE AND SOCIAL THREAT: URBAN TRANSITION, YOUTH GANGS, AND SOCIAL CONTROL

PAMELA IRVING JACKSON

Department of Sociology, Rhode Island College, Providence, Rhode Island 02908

(Received 19 February 1991)

3ased on a study of U.S. cities of 25,000 or more, this paper describes the impact of urban decline from 1970–1980 and the magnitude of youth gang problems on municipal fiscal commitment to policing. After statistical controls are imposed for the city's crime rate, revenues and demographic characteristics, the results indicate that urban transition and recognition of youth gang problems influence municipal police funding. Implications are drawn concerning the extent to which police are called upon to manage social threats that rise from the ashes of urban decay.

KEY WORDS: Police, gangs, threat, demographic characteristics, urban decline, crime

INTRODUCTION

During the past twenty years our understanding of the police as a social control mechanism responding to threats to the established order has sprouted and taken root. Social threats, other than crime, have been conceptualized in terms of the presence of threatening populations (measured as minority group size), the occurrence of threatening events (such as riots and non-violent civil disturbances), the degree of contact between heterogeneous populations (greater where there is less residential segregation), and the level of income inequality (reflected in the Gini index or the ratio of black to white median income) (cf. Jacobs, 1979; Liska, Lawrence, and Benson, 1981; Jackson, 1989).

There is reason to expect that two contemporary characteristics of U.S. cities, socioeconomic decline and youth gangs, both apparent early in the 1980s, are similarly viewed as threatening to the social order and that they contribute to municipal fiscal commitment to policing. In the mid-1970s and early 1980s, population losses and decreases in labor market opportunities in manufacturing and wholesale trades disrupted cities' social and economic foundations. They were inescapable manifestations of the nation's transition from a manufacturing to a service based economy. Consequent high levels of unemployment and poverty, coupled with the visibility of low income urban minority populations (cf. Kasarda, 1985) were viewed as harbingers of change for the worse in U.S. cities.

Such visible reminders of the demise of the city center could well spark support for law enforcement efforts to maintain order. Formal social control mechanisms become most important during times of transition, when informal normative structures and processes erode. As police chief Anthony Bouza (1990: 20) notes in his recent book, *The Police Mystique*, there is tremendous pressure on police to keep "'street conditions' under wraps;" to control conditions that "communicate a distressing sense of decline . . . troubling to citizens."

While the criminogenic influence of the urban transition and decline consequent to postindustrial economic change has received serious scrutiny in recent research, still relatively unexplored is the impact of these conditions on public fiscal commitment to policing, after the effect of crime on police resources is taken into consideration. This paper begins that exploration. It is expected that even after controls for municipal crime rates and other related community characteristics, urban socioeconomic decline will influence municipal expenditures for policing. When urban residents feel threatened by the changing economic and demographic circumstances around them, they may provide greater fiscal support for the police in a misguided attempt to restore the stability of the past.

As a recent U.S. Department of Justice Bulletin (Bryant, 1989: 1) indicates, fear that another urban problem, youth gangs, is out of control has led to intensive law enforcement and prosecution efforts. Bouza (1990: 235) points out that public fear of gangs provides "another invitation to roust black kids without examining the conditions of their lives." The Justice Department Bulletin cites testimony by Frank Radke of the Chicago Police Department to a national conference on youth gangs indicating that "we are arresting more gang members than ever before; we are getting more convictions than ever before; and we are getting longer sentences than ever before. But ironically, we have more gangs than ever before. Arrest and prosecution are not the deterrent that we expected them to be." The message of the bulletin is in its title which states that a "Communitywide Response [is] Crucial for Dealing With Youth Gangs." Nonetheless, it is clear that a "preoccupation with delinquency control, rather than its prevention" (Short, 1990: 1) has characterized this period of urban change. As a result, it is likely that perceived youth gang problems have an independent impact on municipal appropriations for policing, even after the crime rate is taken into consideration.

METHOD AND HYPOTHESES

Population and data

This study of the impact of urban transition on public fiscal commitment to policing is based on a multivariate analysis of quantitative data from all U.S. cities of 25,000 or more in 1970 and 1980. Additional analyses of the impact of perceived youth gang problems on police expenditures were conducted in a subset of these cities. The U.S. Census of Population (1970, 1980), the Uniform Crime Report (Federal Bureau of Investigation, 1980), the Law Enforcement Assistance Administration (1978, 1981), and the 1981 National Juvenile Assessment Center survey regarding youth gangs (Needle and Stapleton, 1983) were the sources of data.

Urban socioeconomic decline

Population decline in large urban centers in the 1970s heralded economic deterioration, as employment opportunities in manufacturing and wholesale operations moved to less densely settled sunbelt locations and to less developed nations. Urban centers have increasingly been left to unskilled minority individuals as better educated members of the work force have relocated to improve their employment and living conditions.

Several authors have elaborated on the extent to which informal social controls erode in the face of such population turnover. Taylor and Covington (1988: 533) quote McKenzie (1968 [1921]: 62) in citing the "striking instability of local life" under conditions of high mobility. Bursik (1988: 521, 527) refers to the work of Kornhauser (1978), Berry and Kasarda (1977), and Greenberg with others (1982a, 1982b, 1985) in describing several consequences of population turnover that together undermine the effectiveness of informal social controls in maintaining order and stability: deterioration of "institutions pertaining to internal control," reduction in the "development of primary relationships," erosion of informal surveillance and direct intervention. The focus of this paper is on the extent to which socioeconomic transitions known to destabilize the social order of city life also predict municipal commitment to the formal social control represented by policing even after their effect on the crime rate has been taken into account.

Percent city population change (1970–80), and percent of city residents born in the state where they are now residing (1980) are included in the analysis as measures of short and long term demographic change. Such measures have been viewed by others as a reflection of "a declining city syndrome" (Clark, 1985: 254; Muller, 1975; and Peterson, 1976) and of "urban distress" (Clark, 1985: 259; Nathan and Dommel, 1977). The percent change in civilian labor force opportunities in manufacturing between 1970 and 1980, and in wholesale and retail trades 1970–1980, also included in the analysis, represent economic instability.

The loss of such employment opportunities for unskilled laborers in central cities as a result of the national economic shift toward a service based economy requiring technologically sophisticated training for many new positions have created a mismatch between the skill levels of employees and the positions available in urban centers. (In fact, recent evidence indicates that growth in jobs with low educational requirements has been limited to the suburbs and exurbs (cf. Kasarda, 1985).) It is expected that in cities with the largest declines in population and in opportunities for unskilled labor, the level of fiscal support for policing will be greater even after the influence of these factors on the crime rate and the influence of other known determinants of municipal police expenditures have been controlled. This hypothesis will be investigated for all cities of 25,000 or more.

Reported youth gangs

Youth gangs represent another threat to urban dwellers. In a summary of their recent examination of youth gang program effectiveness in 45 cities, Spergel and Curry (1990: 299–300) note that suppression (arrest, incarceration, and supervision) is the most common primary strategy in response to the problem of youth gangs, while provision of opportunities (jobs, job training, and education) is the least frequently chosen tactic. Although they later indicate that "in cities or areas with chronic youth gang problems, agencies perceive there is a significant reduction in the problem mainly when the primary response strategy is the provision of social opportunities" (Spergel and Curry, 1990: 306), a law enforcement response is most often invoked when citizens feel threatened by youth gangs. Police chief Bouza (1990: 234–5) corroborates this proposition, pointing out that "summer jobs, dropout programs, recreational centers, and other costly projects" are generally avoided as solutions to

youth problems in favor of the "action" inherent to a law enforcement response.
To test the impact of the youth gang threat on collective fiscal support for policing, the National Juvenile Justice Assessment Center's data (Needle and Stapleton, 1983) on the existence of youth gangs in a random, representative sample of 60 U.S. cities of 100,000 or more is used. These cities constitute a subset of the larger population of cities on which this study is based. In each of the 60 cities police department gang control and youth personnel were interviewed concerning the existence, size, and activity of street gangs. On the basis of this information Center staff classified the magnitude of the gang problem as minor, moderate, or major (Needle and Stapleton, 1981: 20). This three-point index of reported youth gang activity is included in the present investigation. Using the 60 cities for which data are available, a multivariate analysis of the influence of the perceived gang problem on the proportion of city government expenditures spent on policing will be conducted controlling for other recognized determinants of police allocations.

Other city characteristics

Since crime fighting, traffic control, and emergency service calls are major police activities, several structural and budgetary characteristics of cities contribute to per capita levels of police spending. Many of these variables can also be expected to be related to the measures of demographic and economic decline, requiring the use of ordinary least squares regression to develop a multivariate model.

City revenue per capita (1980) is included in the model as a measure of a community's fiscal ability to pay for policing. The total index crime rate per capita (1980) (FBI), a measure of the level of the direct contact predatory crime (Cohen and Felson, 1979) that most occupies police crime fighting attention, represents to some degree the need for policing. Per cent poor is also included as an indicator of a city's fiscal situation, but could, in addition, be expected to increase the demand for policing since the poor are more likely than others to rely on the police for the provision of emergency services. City population size and density influence the need for policing through their effects on traffic control problems and service related demands. Per cent unemployed and the ratio of black to white median income have recently been included as police resource determinants because it is expected that unemployment and inequality make people more difficult to control by loosening the conventional bonds circumscribing individuals' behavior and by undermining the legitimacy of the established order (cf. Jacobs, 1979, 1982). Percent black is included directly, as is percent Hispanic since they have been found to influence the level of policing resources, even after the crime rate and other community characteristics are controlled (Jackson and Carroll, 1981; Jackson, 1985).

As suggested above, the indicators of demographic and economic decline included in the model may be related to the relative size of the black and Hispanic populations in a city, as well as to city revenue per capita, interracial inequality, population size, density, and the level of poverty. Use of the multivariate model will permit determination of the extent to which any observed impact of socioeconomic decline on police spending levels is spurious.

Dependent variables

In assessing the impact on public fiscal commitment to policing of the 1970s decade of transition in urban centers and of the early 1980s youth gang threat, two measures of police expenditures in U.S. cities are used: per capita police expenditures, and police expenditures as a proportion of total city government expenditures in 1981. The per capita total police expenditures indicator is used in determining the influence of demographic and economic decline on the level of municipal commitment to social control. The measure has been deployed many times before as an indicator of public fiscal commitment to policing (cf. Jackson, 1989). Since youth gang threat, to be studied in the 60 city subsample, is a phenomenon with newspaper headline potential, its influence on the proportion of total city government expenditures allocated to policing is investigated.

RESULTS

Bivariate associations between variables included in the analysis (in Table 1) indicate little cause for concern about problems associated with multicolinearity. The independent variables are not highly intercorrelated, but do appear to be related to police expenditures. Cities with a lower percentage of population born in the state, population decline between 1970–1980, and decline in the proportion of wholesale and retail positions have greater per capita police expenditures. Control variables in the analysis, including indicators of racial composition, unemployment, and population size and density are significantly related to both per capita police expenditures and to one of the measures of urban decline. Other control variables, such as interractial income inequality help to specify the model as direct or indirect influences on police expenditures.

For the 60–city subsample to be used in the investigation of the youth gang threat, it is evident that the measure of a perceived gang problem has a positive bivariate association with the proportion of city government expenditures allocated to policing in 1981 (r = .29), and with several other city characteristics. The multivariate results below help to determine whether or nor the associations of the police appropriations measures with socioeconomic decline and youth gang problems are spurious.

The ordinary least squares regression results (in Table 2) provide further support for the hypothesis that urban decline fosters greater public fiscal support for policing, even after controls for the municipal crime rate. As expected city revenue per capita and the overall crime rate have the greatest impact on end of the decade municipal police expenditures, with population density and the negative impact of per cent poor next in importance. Following them in order of statistically significant explanatory impact on total police expenditures per capita are decline in wholesale/retail positions, percent black, percent unemployed, lower proportions of city residents born in the state, and decline in the number of manufacturing positions in the city. This model including sociodemographic change and decline during the 1970s explains over 50% of the variance in per capita police expenditures at the end of the decade.

Decline in wholesale, retail and manufacturing position;, as well as long-term population transition (reflected in low proportions of city residents born in the state in which they are now residing), may disorganize communities to the point where informal mechanisms of social control no longer seem sufficient to maintain order. Despite the fact that their impact on the crime rate has been controlled in the multivariate equations, these indicators of demographic transition and economic decline exert a significant positive influence on collective fiscal commitment to the formal

Table 1 Zero Order Correlation Matrix with Means and Standard Deviations (All cities ≥ 25,000, N = 563) (Pearson's r)

	(1)	(2)	(3)	(4)	(5)	(6)	(7)	(8)	(9)	(10)	(11)	(12)	(13)	(14)	(15)	X	S.D.
1. Police Expenditures Per Capita	—	.33c	.35c	.00	.21c	-.20c	-.19c	.22c	.23c	-.06	-.27c	-.06	.49c	.50c	.29c	45.3	21.5
2. Percent Black		—	.13b	-.17c	.41c	.11b	-.23b	.12b	.69c	-.28c	-.20c	-.06	.43c	.21c	-.24c	15.5	17.0
3. Density			—	.26c	.13b	-.16c	-.23c	.28c	.17c	.11b	-.15c	-.13b	.05	.21c	.14c	4271.5	3488.9
4. Percent Hispanic				—	-.04	-.35c	.23c	.08	.20c	.21c	-.07	.25c	.07	-.14c	.46c	8.2	13.3
5. Percent Unemployed					—	.24c	-.30c	.05	.57c	-.03	.09	-.28c	.22c	.10a	-.04	7.0	3.0
6. Residents Born in State						—	-.37	-.06	.14c	-.04	.11b	-.28c	-.25c	.01	-.36c	60.4	16.0
7. Percent Population Change							—	-.03	-.18c	.07	.04	.22c	-.06	-.21c	.13b	6.8	21.8
8. Population Size								—	.13b	-.08	-.06	.00	.10	.32c	.26c	131.7	370.5
9. Percent Poor									—	-.25c	-.12b	.03	.44c	.19c	-.02	10.4	5.4
10. Black/White Income										—	-.04	-.07	-.23c	-.11b	.01	.7	.2
11. Wholesale/Retail Change											—	-.29c	-.17c	-.16c	-.02	-.1	2.2
12. Manufacturing Change												—	.12b	-.03	.31c	-2.7	4.0
13. Index Crime Rate													—	.26c	-.05	79.9	27.7
14. City Revenues Per Capita														—	-.08a	528.8	316.4
15. Perceived Gang Problem[d,e]															—	.9	1.1

[a]$p<.05$ [b]$p<.01$ [c]$p<.001$
[d]Perceived Gang Problem correlations based on 52 cases.
[e]Police Expenditures as a Percent of City Government Expenditures used in Gang Presence/Police Expenditures Correlation.

Table 2   Regression Equation for Per Capita Police Expenditures on 1970–80 Transition and Other Social Characteristics of Cities (All Cities ≥ 25,000, N = 563) (Standardized Regression Coefficients)

Constant	14.665
City Revenues Per Capita	.336[c]
Residents Born in State	−.137[c]
Black/White Income	.015
Wholesale/Retail Change	−.148[c]
Percent Unemployed	.139[c]
Population Size	.015
Density	.196[c]
Percent Hispanic	.005
Index Crime Rate	.333[c]
Manufacturing Change	−.086[b]
Percent Population Change	−.040
Percent Black	.145[c]
Percent Poor	−.191[c]
R^2	.51[c]

[a]p (for one-tailed test) <.05   [b]p<.01   [c]p<.001

social control that police provide.

In the subsample for which the youth gang data are available, the signficant bivariate association between reported gang presence and the proportion of city government spending devoted to policing holds in the multivariate regression equation despite controls for other variables expected to influence the impact of gangs on policing, including the crime rate, racial and ethnic heterogeneity, per capita city revenues, per cent poor and inequality. Per capita city revenues and percent poor both have a negative statistically significant impact on the percent of city revenues devoted to policing. After them, the positive significant impact of reported youth gang presence follows that of percent black and the crime rate in order of explanatory importance. Overall, this model including perceived youth gang problems explains 51% percent of the variance in the relative size of the 1981 budgetary law enforcement commitment for the subsample where the data on gangs is available.

IMPLICATIONS

These results have implications for three areas of concern: (1) the role of the police in responding to perceived societal threats; (2) the capacity of postindustrial societies to respond to urban dislocations triggered by the economic shift from a manufacturing to a service based economy; and (3) the effectiveness of the municipal response to youth gang problems.

Police and social threat

The fact that demographic and economic transition in cities influences public fiscal commitment to policing independently of its effect on crime and other relevant city characteristics underscores once again the public's reliance on police to stem change. This is a source of great concern, since police are not trained, equipped, or staffed sufficiently to successfully resolve or confront these strains. City governments had just begun to recognize this when the threats inherent to urban decline became apparent.

Table 3 Regression Equation for Police Expenditures as a Percent of City Government Expenditures on Perceived Gang Problem (1981) and Other Social Characteristics of Cities (N = 52) (Standardized Regression Coefficients)

Constant	12.449
Perceived Gang Problem	.212[a]
Black/White Income	.024
Index Crime Rate	.254[b]
Density	.206
Percent Black	.715[c]
Percent Hispanic	.226
Population Size	.220
City Revenue Per Capita	-.789[c]
Percent Poor	-.713[c]
R^2	.51[c]

[a]p (for one-tailed text) <.05   [b]p<.01   [c]p<.001

With the racially turbulent 1960s behind them, municipal police departments in the United States had set aside by the late 1970s their riot preparations and demonstration control strategies. In response to public demand they had begun to redefine themselves as community relations officers. Overnight, it seemed, police administrators sought to transform the force and its image. They moved away from the "tough" cop model described by Mayor Rizzo in his pre-election loss assertion that the Philadelphia Police Department could "invade Cuba and win" (*Evening Bulletin*, 8/14/79), favoring instead the "community relations officer" described by newly appointed Philadelphia Police Commissioner Solomon in his promise to start "building up a mutual respect between the people of Philadelphia and the police department" (*Philadelphia Inquirer*, 1/13/80) (cf. Jackson, 1989: 77, 118).

Times had changed. A decade of civil rights demands initially backed by the White House, and the increasingly minority composition of U.S. cities helped: (1) to usher out those members of the old guard who condoned police brutality as a regrettable, but necessary evil; (2) to rein in police use of deadly force; and (3) to diversify the police force, in terms of race, ethnicity, gender, and sexual preference. New demands for police accountability and responsiveness emerged, as did recognition of "their problems with the minorities they've been sent to police and their resentment toward an overclass that has issued the *sub rosa* marching orders" (Bouza, 1990: 6).

Unstated pressure to control the underclass has been recognized as dangerous, encouraging excessive and illegal behaviors. Police cannot solve the current problems of urban decline any more than they could resolve the riots and disturbances of the 1960s. Yet the results of this study indicate that the transitions associated with such decline trigger public fiscal commitment to policing.

Responding to urban dislocations

In a recent National Institute of Justice document, Williams and Murphy (1990: 12) point out the Commission on the Cities' finding that after a brief period of improvement, the conditions that led to the deterioration of ghetto communities are actually getting worse. "'Quiet riots,' the report concludes are occurring in America's central cities: unemployment, poverty, social disorganization, segregation, housing and school deterioration, and crime are worse now than ever . . . "

Wilson (1987) has also drawn attention to these conditions, suggesting their link to rising violent crime rates, increasing rates of out-of-wedlock births, and greater reliance on welfare in inner city communities. Citing the problems of black male joblessness, Wilson addresses the need for a full employment policy combined with a federally sponsored job training program geared toward retooling unskilled labor sufficiently to create a flexible workforce for a postindustrial economy.

Police chief Bouza (1990: 22), however, reminds those who argue for such policy solutions to these problems that "citizens want the cop back on the beat;" they want "action now." "The frightened and impatient citizen's eyes glaze over with frustration and ill-concealed hostility," he explains, "at the mention of cultural, social, or especially, economic forces channeling the underclass into lives of crime . . . Long-term strategies for the prevention of crime are lost in a desire for the prompt removal of undesirables."

Research has shown that within the currently feasible range of police resource levels cities cannot control their crime problem through law enforcement (cf. Greenberg et. al., 1983; Loftin and McDowall, 1982). Certainly police have an indispensable role in managing and processing those involved in crime, and in helping citizens to deal with its aftermath. However, their efforts in detecting and preventing crime simply cannot stem its tide. As we have known for almost half a decade, the causes of crime are considerably beyond the effectiveness of detection and prevention. Public reliance on policing to resolve the consequences of demographic change and economic decline in urban areas may prevent both inquiry into and implementation of more effective strategies for responding to the urban dislocations of postindustrial economic growth.

Municipal response to youth gang problems

In assessing "why the U.S. has failed to solve its youth gang problem," Miller (1990) cites lack of a coordinated national policy as a chief determinant, fuelled by "a pervasive reluctance to face squarely the issue of the social context of gang crime" (Miller, 1990: 277). However, Miller (1990: 281) goes on to label as "misdirected, inefficient, and uneconomical," the position that "the totality of lower-class life must be changed to affect gangs. However desirable such change might be . . . " He cites instead the need for "carefully targeted programs with specific specific objectives" and argues for further investigation of the effectiveness of specific programs along the lines of recent work by Spergel, Curry, Ross, and Chance (1989).

Sullivan's (1990) new study of Brooklyn gangs leads him, as Short (1990b: 666) points out, to argue that improvement of social control and enhancement of economic opportunity be seen as complementary, rather than alternative and opposed strategies for reducing youth crime. Another key element in Sullivan's perspective is that involvement of the poor in increasing community safety will have important effects on disadvantaged communities as well as on the individuals within them. Short (1990: 667) goes on to support this argument, noting that youth gangs "are more likely to be a factor in the reproduction of the underclass . . . when they become institutionalized in local communities . . . "

While work by Miller (1990), Short (1990b), Sullivan (1990), and Moore (1988) suggests the importance of law enforcement in preventing gang "ownership" of communities, these recent investigations also indicate that in the long term, resolution of conditions fostering gang development is critical in reducing the significance of youth gang problems in cities. Law enforcement in and of itself is insufficient "when young people cannot find good jobs in conventional society . . . " (Short, 1990b: 667).

Since the research presented in this paper suggests that municipal fiscal commitment to policing is greater in cities where youth gang problems are perceived, the centrality of police in the societal response to this issue cannot be ignored. In light of the public's reliance on the police as a first line of defense against gangs, integration of police sponsored gang control efforts with opportunity building and community empowerment strategies may be the most fruitful approach to long term repair of those community conditions that foster youth gangs.

SUMMARY AND CONCLUSIONS

Two central conclusions can be drawn from the data analysis in this study. The first involves the impact of demographic and economic decline on municipal support for policing. The results indicate that sociodemographic change and decline in U.S. urban centers in the 1970s contributed to municipal fiscal commitment to policing even after the city's crime rate, financial, and demographic characteristics are statistically controlled. Decline in wholesale/retail and manufacturing positions in the city from 1970–80 and long term population transition increase the collective financial commitment to the municipal police effort.

The second conclusion of the analysis has to do with the influence of recognized youth gangs on the level of the urban police effort. The magnitude of a city's youth gang problems as perceived by knowledgeable sources is related to the level of its public investment in policing. Cities with youth gang problems spend more per capita on policing.

Overall, these results suggest that transition and decline in the demographic and economic base of urban centers, as well as the spectre of youth gangs trigger funding for formal social control in the form of municipal police even when the crime rate, revenues and other city characteristics are held constant. Police are called upon to manage the social threats that rise from the ashes of urban decay. They are also the first to discern the gap between management and amelioration of such problems (cf. Bouza, 1990).

Recognition of the extent to which police efforts are city residents' first line of defense against the threats of urban decline will facilitate a more accurate assessment of the resources, training, and public support necessary to permit police and police related agencies to help lay the groundwork necessary to rebuild the city's infrastructure. It may be that successful strategies of urban revitalization can be constructed on an integrated set of social control, economic growth, and opportunity enhancement initiatives.

References

Berry, Brian J.L. and John D. Kasarda 1977 *Contemporary Urban Ecology*. New York: Macmillan.
Bouza, Anthony V. 1990 *The Police Mystique*. New York: Plenum.
Bryant, Dan 1989 *Communitywide Responses Crucial for Dealing with Youth Gangs*. Washington, D.C.: U.S. Department of Justice, Juvenile Justice Bulletin.
Bursik, Robert J., Jr. 1988 "Social Disorganization and Theories of Crime and Delinquency: Problems and Prospects." *Criminology* 26 (4): 519–551.
Clark, Terry Nichols 1985 "Fiscal Strain: How Different Are Snow Belt and Sun Belt Cities." Pp. 253–280

in *The New Urban Reality*, ed. P.E. Peterson. Washington, D.C.: Brookings.

Cohen, Lawrence E. and Marcus Felson 1979 "Social Change and Crime Rate Trends." *American Sociological Review* 44: 533–607.

Evening Bulletin (Philadelphia) 8/14/79 "Mayor is Eager to Battle Charges."

Federal Bureau of Investigation 1980 *Annual Report of the Federal Bureau of Investigation*. Washington, D.C.: U.S. Government Printing Office.

Greenberg, David F. Ronald C. Kessler, and Colin Loftin 1983 "The Effect of Police Employment on Crime." *Criminology* 21 (3) 375–394.

Greenberg, Stephanie, William M. Rohe, and Jay R. Williams 1982a "The Relationship Between Informal Social Control, Neighborhood Crime and Fear: A Synthesis and Assessment of the Research." Paper presented at the annual meetings of the American Society of Criminology, Toronto.

1982b "Safe and Secure Neighborhoods: Physical Characteristics and Informal Territorial Control" in *High and Low Crime Neighborhoods*. Washington, D.C.: National Institute of Justice.

1985 *Informal Citizen Action and Crime Prevention at the Neighborhood Level*. Washington, D.C.: National Institute of Justice.

Jacobs, David 1979 "Inequality and Police Strength: Conflict Theory and Coercive Control in Metropolitan Areas." *American Sociological Review* 44: 913–925.

1982 "Inequality and Economic Crime." *Sociology and Social Research* 66: 12–28.

Jackson, Pamela Irving 1989 *Minority Group Threat, Crime, and Policing*. New York: Praeger.

1985 "Ethnicity, Region, and Public Fiscal Commitment to Policing." *Justice Quarterly* 2 (2) 167–194.

Jackson, Pamela Irving and Leo Carroll 1981 "Race and the War on Crime: The Sociopolitical Determinants of Municipal Expenditures in 90 U.S. Cities." *American Sociological Review* 46: 290–305.

Kasarda, John D. 1985 "Urban Change and Minority Opportunities." Pp. 33–68 in P.E. Peterson (ed.), *The New Urban Reality*. Washington, D.C.: Brookings.

Kornhauser, Ruth R. 1978 *Social Sources of Delinquency*. Chicago: University of Chicago Press.

Law Enforcement Assistance Administration 1978 *Expenditures and Employment Data for the Criminal Justice System*. 1981 Washington, D.C.: U.S. Government Printing Office.

Liska, Allen E., Joseph J. Lawrence, and Michael Benson 1981 "Perspectives on the Legal Order: The Capacity for Social Control." *American Journal of Sociology* 87: 413–26.

Loftin, Colin and David McDowell 1982 "The Police, Crime, and Economic Theory: An Assessment." *American Sociological Review* 47: 393–401.

McKenzie, Roderick D. 1968 "The Neighborhood." (1921). In A.H. Hawley (ed.), *Roderick D. McKenzie on Human Ecology*. Chicago: University of Chicago Press.

Miller, Walter B. 1990 "Why the United States Has Failed to Solve Its Youth Gang Problem." Pp. 263–287 in C. Ronald Huff (ed.), *Gangs in America*. Newbury Park: Sage.

Moore, Joan 1988 "Gangs and the Underclass: A Comparative Perspective." Pp. 3–17 in John M. Hagedorn, *People and Folks: Gangs, Crime and the Underclass in a Rustbelt City*. Chicago: Lake View Press.

Muller, Thomas 1975 *Growing and Declining Urban Areas: A Fiscal Comparison*. Washington, D.C.: Urban Institute.

Nathan, Richard P. and Paul R. Dommel 1977 "The Cities." Pp. 283–316 in Joseph A. Peckman (ed.), *Setting National Priorities: The 1978 Budget*. Washington, D.C.: Brookings.

Needle, Jerome A. and Wm. Vaughn Stapleton 1983 *Report of the National Juvenile Justice Assessment Centers: Police Handling of Youth Gangs*. Washington, D.C.: U.S. Department of Justice.

Peterson, George E. 1976 "Finance." Pp. 35–118 in William Gorham and Nathan Glazer (eds.), *The Urban Predicament*. Washington, D.C.: Urban Institute.

Philadelphia Inquirer 1/13/80 "At the Police Department, A New Broom Sweeps Fast.

Short, James F. 1990a "Gangs, Neighborhoods, and Youth Crime." *Criminal Justice Research Bulletin*, Vol. 5 (4). Texas: Sam Houston State University.

Short, James F. 1990b "Cities, Gangs, and Delinquency." *Sociological Forum* 5 (4): 657–688.

Spergel, Irving A. and G. David Curry 1990 "Strategies and Perceived Agency Effectiveness in Dealing with the Youth Gang Problem." Pp. 288–309 in C. Ronald Huff (ed.), *Gangs in America*. Newbury Park: Sage.

Spergel, Irving A., G. David Curry, R.A. Ross, and R. Chance 1989 *Survey of Youth Gang Problems and Programs in 45 Cities and 6 sites*. (Technical Report No. 2, National Youth Gang Suppression and Intervention Project). Chicago: University of Chicago, School of Social Service Administration.

Sullivan, Mercer L. 1990 "Getting Paid". *Youth Crime and Work in the Inner City*. Ithaca: Cornell University Press.

Taylor, Ralph B. and Jeanette Covington 1988 "Neighborhood Changes in Ecology and Violence." *Criminology* 26 (4): 553–589.

U.S. Bureau of the Census 1970 *Characteristics of the Population. 1980 Washington, D.C.: U.S. Government Printing Office.*

Williams, Hubert and Patrick V. Murphy 1990 *"The Evolving Strategy of Police: A Minority View." Perspectives on Policing* 13 (January). Washington, D.C.: U.S. Department of Justice, National Institute of Justice.

Wilson, William Julius 1987 *The Truly Disadvantaged: the Inner City, the Underclass, and Public Policy.* Chicago: University of Chicago Press.

POLICE FORUM

Academy of Criminal Justice Sciences Police Section

VOLUME 3 NUMBER 1   JANUARY 1993

THE LEGACY OF CONSERVATIVE IDEOLOGY AND POLICE

Carl B. Klockars
University of Delaware

The topic of the legacy of the conservative ideology and police must be approached with the greatest caution. The fact is that both "conservatism" and "police" have meant, do mean, and can mean so many different things to so many different people that it is scarcely possible to speak of either of them without being seriously misunderstood. To avoid this problem I will adopt the pedantic academic custom of defining my terms in some detail. Please bear with me. The great problem in debate over any variety of politics is not in eliciting opinion about where anybody stands. Just ask them and they will tell you. It is rather to pose the questions of politics in a sufficiently provocative enough manner to make discussion of where one stands and why one does so a topic worthy of discussion.

Police

By "police" I have in mind the domestic institution and individuals in the direct and full-time employ of the state to whom the state gives the general right to use coercive force. It is their general right to use coercive force which defines police and distinguishes them from all other citizens. It is the special competence of police and what police and no one else make available to us in modern society.

Understanding "police" in this way has at least one immediate political virtue. It permits us to dispose of a major issue that is often understood and discussed in ideological terms, when, in fact, it is an ineluctable property of the role of police, a role that is largely immune to change in any free society. This problem I would like attempt to jettison at the outset is the charge that the focus of police effort is disproportionately on the activities of the poor and ignores for the most part the crimes and delicts of corporate and white collar criminals. The charge is absolutely true, the evidence for it is empirically overwhelming, and anyone with even passing familiarity with the routine activities of a patrol officer or detective in any contemporary American city would be obliged to agree with it. The work of the police consists largely of superintending the activities of poor people.

VIOLENCE AND SYMBOLIC VIOLENCE

Peter K. Manning
Michigan State University

This brief comment on Carl Klockars' essay contains two main points. I find his basic conception of the police mandate and its relationship to violence quite convincing. Certainly, violence is an ineluctable aspect of policing in Western Democratic societies, and perhaps in all developed societies. Furthermore, the police in Anglo-American societies are granted an almost exclusive legitimate right or mandate to use coercive force. Having made this point, Klockars overlooks the changing meaning and definition of "violence" and police adaptation to such changes. I believe he misconstrues the causes for the "poor-focus" of the police and the portent for policing that this carries for the future. To delineate the present police preoccupations does not serve to envision the contours and demands of policing in the next century.

Violence and the Police

What follows is a sketch of my own conception of modern policing. Policing as an institution is ubiquitous in developed societies. Yet, it takes many forms, performs a wide range of functions, has diverse political and historical origins, and possesses various levels of legitimacy (Bayley, 1985). Although policing is in part "law enforcement;" in practice, the common law in Anglo-American policing plays a symbolic role and acts as a resource when other control strategies fail. The law provides little guidance as to where, when, and in what quantity it should be applied. In the nation-state context, policing serves the state, but the state's interests are rarely directly served. The police, as the behavior of Chief Daryl Gates and the LAPD illustrates, also serve frequently their own political and moral interests in a rather complex fashion (This subtle concatenation of activities is something of a quandary for police scholars such as David Bayley who have sought a functional theory to account for patterns of police tasks, imagery and structure).

As Bittner and Kelsen (1961) have argued, the police mandate is constrained by two matters: the right to apply violence and the grounding norm of state authority. The police are an archaic occupation. The core role expectation is the situa-

© 1993 Academy of Criminal Justice Sciences   ISSN 1061-1517
Published by Alpha Enterprises, Post Office Box 326, Richmond, Kentucky 40476

The question, though, is whether this predominant focus of police activity is a reflection of discrimination and class bias and ought to be interpreted and understood in ideological terms. I do not believe it should for the same reason that I find no political message in the discovery that the clients of the welfare system are largely poor people, that those of stock brokers are mostly well to do, or that those of hospitals are predominantly the sick. The police, like other vendors of services, offer a service that tends to be of use to certain categories of persons on certain types of occasions. The service that police make available is, to use Egon Bittner's phrase, the "distribution of non-negotiably coercive force." And we should not be surprised that certain people should have need for this service more frequently than others. One reason that the cops attend predominantly to the lives of poor people is that poor people require and request their services far more frequently than anyone else. That police attend predominantly to the lives and activities of poor people, largely upon request of poor people is, though only half the story. The other half is that crimes poor people are likely to commit and the circumstances under which they are likely to commit them are radically different from those of corporate or white collar offenders. Three features of the crimes of the poor are of particular relevance to the police. First, the type of crimes that poor people tend to commit are more likely to involve interpersonal violence than those of white collar or corporate offenders. White collar and corporate offenders steal with paper, pens, contracts, and computers, poor people by breaking, entering, and threatening. Second, poor people are far more likely to resist their apprehension by forceful means. White collar and corporate offenders employ lawyers and accountants to offer resistance. And, third, poor people are more likely to flee to avoid arrest and prosecution than the white collar offender with a stable, valuable place of residence or a corporate address.

Each of these differences is critical because of the different demand it makes on the special competence of the police, the right to use coercive force, to deal with it. Consider an example: a NYPD officer is sitting in his patrol car on a Manhattan street. An agitated pedestrian approaches the vehicle and explains to the officer that he is convinced that insider trading is afoot on Wall Street. The officer, aware that such activity is a crime, and that millions may be involved, tells the complainant to hop in his patrol car. He slips the Crown Vic into gear, flips on his Twin Sonics and speeds to Wall Street. Upon arrival, he leaves his car, one hand on his new 9mm the other fingering his PR-24. Tall, broad shouldered, with an air of confidence he strides onto the floor of the stock exchange, the epiphany of New York's finest. He is, of course, received there as some kind of nut.

What make this imaginary officer's behavior preposterous is that he has no competence for the task he has undertaken because all the tools of the police trade are inappropriate and

tional application of force. They moderate strength and restraint. The police are linked symbolically with the Medieval Christian tradition of knighthood, honor and duty. They serve the state's higher espoused principles and stated mottos.

Their attachment to force and honor places them outside the sectarian stream of everyday events. They are watchers, standing above the moral fray until and unless they define their proximal role as once again plunging into the secular world to: right a balance (as they read it); seek the just (as they see it); and produce a good (as they define it). Police violence blends subtle avoidance of frequent application and an appreciation of its aberrant origins and quotidian character. For a patrol officer, the key to effectiveness is judgment and restraint, not applied violence.

Klockars' conception, also drawing on Bittner, is both sound and insightful. It avoids a functionalist argument that police must carry out particular named functions (Cf. the ABA listing circa 1972), and a class-repression model of police actions. In practice, Klockars claims, the police focus on the control of the poor. The police deliver "services" to the poor. The poor need corrective violence, or at least close supervision, he asserts, because they commit more violent crimes than other groups, resist apprehension by violent means, and more often flee to avoid prosecution.

This formulation rests on a slight misreading of the history of Anglo-American policing, and restricts the definition of violence to concretely applied force. It thus ignores the importance of symbolic violence, violations of the social space of a person or group in the name of the state. Ironically, while policing has focused previously on control of the poor, it is now expanding into the management of symbolic violence.

A Watchful, Questioning Pose

To claim that contemporary Anglo-American police employ violence against the poor because the poor behave in ways that demand such overlooks the historic use of the criminal law as a tool, or means of ordering and regulating often large and contentious marginal populations. Policing has attended primarily to the political control of the poor and the disorderly as these matters have been defined by the dominant societal coalition and the government of the nation state. Historically, it is not true that intrinsically the poor require ordering. Rather, the criminal law, with other legal sanctions and regulatory actions, is used by the police to restrict the movements and activities of the poor and marginal and to protect property. It has been used to control rising groups as in the case of the English Factories Act (Carson, 1970). Sometimes ironically, since it involves controlling population segments from similar class and ethnic origins, the police are actively

156

virtually useless in the environment he has entered. It is not because the officer himself is not outraged by insider trading. He may find it to be a more serious type of offense than he has ever been called upon to deal with, considering that the welfare of his pension fund, life insurance, and personal investments all depend on a fair market, not to mention the economy in general.

But despite his feelings, neither he nor any other NYPD officer will deal with a complaint of such a crime. They will advise the complainant to contact a regulatory agency with the special competence necessary to deal with this problem, probably the Securities and Exchange Commission. My point can now be stated very simply. What is often spoken of as the ideological bias of police, their unwillingness to focus on crimes of the rich and their disproportionate attention to the behavior of the poor is largely without a political dimension. Such behavior on the part of the police does not stem from ideology but from the special and defining competence of police. We should find no more political nor ideological information in the discovery that policing is disproportionately focused on poor people than the discovery that grammar school teachers focus their attentions primarily upon the behavior of young children. It is simply what they are competent to do.

Having said that much about the definition of police and having attempted to show that it permits us to dismiss as wrong headed what is often advanced as a major ideological critique of police practice, I would like now to turn to the problem of defining a concept of conservatism that will be helpful in adumbrating its legacy. There are at least three active strains of conservative ideology that bear directly on police and have shaped not only the institution but its practitioners and our societal response to them. I will refer to these three varieties of conservatism as libertarianism, traditionalism, and populism. Each is far more complex than I will be able to consider here and, within each, one can find advocates of rather different stripes. I thus confess that I will treat each of them crudely but, I trust, respectfully for their respective ideological contributions.

Traditionalism

First, *traditionalism*. Conservatism as a historical political philosophy is probably best understood as a reaction to both a philosophy and a historical event. The philosophy was that of the Enlightenment, probably best represented by Rousseau, and the event the French Revolution. Both reflected an abhorrence for all received institutions and a confidence in the capacity of enlightened individual reason to solve all human problems.

In contrast to this faith, conservatives held that society and social order were the product of an infinitely rich and complex historical evolution, one that was not reducible to a set

engaged in dramatic marking and arranging of the vertical and horizontal order, and in defending, in a variety of ways, the status quo.

This drama of policing, maintaining the vertical order and the symbolic hierarchy of worth, has been played out in several ways in Anglo-American societies.

(1) As activities either slip away from popularity, or drift downward to the lower classes, they are defined as criminal and subject to arrest and prosecution. This can be seen in a close analysis of changes in the English sports of hunting, and bull and bear baiting, various forms of gambling, drug use and sex.

(2) Certain "deviant" life styles are stigmatized and defined as "criminal." Activities publicly associated with lower class, native peoples', or immigrant pastimes and lifestyles, such as cock- fighting, dog fights, and peyote use, are subject to criminal sanction.

(3) Space is regulated to maintain control of symbolically valued property and places. Changes in the uses and control of space marginalize certain powerless groups and place them at risk from public and private policing.

(4) Shared activities are differentially sanctioned. When leisure patterns are shared by middle and lower middle classes, such as sport gambling, the middle class form is legalized while the lower class form(s) are made subject to the criminal sanction and police-initiated control.

(5) As newly respectable activities gain respectability they are de-criminalized and are diffused widely e.g., marijuana and alcohol use.

(6) Life style conflicts or "cultural wars" between cultural segments such as the fundamentalist Catholics and Protestants and more liberal or agnostic groups, e.g. alcohol use and legal abortion, may lead to a movement to redefine some behavior or lifestyles as criminal. The targets of control shift from providers to those demanding the goods or services. In effect, a market is controlled with the aim of eradication rather than symbolic regulation.

(7) Dissent such as flag burning, public demonstrations and draft evasion, when carried out by members of the dominant coalition, is treated sub rosa, and with discretion within the criminal justice system, while marginal groups are given the full benefit and force of the law.

Change arises from the dialectic between class interests and control processes. Suffice it to note that the content of the "threat" and "disorder" shifts while the form (criminal sanctioning) and direction of governmental social control (down)

[Klockars Continued]
of political principles or formulae, one whose ecology was, on the whole, so intricate that the best minds could not comprehend it. For the conservatives tradition was the guide and when it ran afoul of some set of abstract principles, rational argument, or political theory that challenged it, the inclination of conservatives, from Edmund Burke to William Buckley, is to doubt the wisdom of the principle, the argument, or the theory and to side with tradition.

Police and Traditionalism

Because police are the agents of the government in power, because police often changes slowly and in response to challenge, criticism, or complaint, much of the work of police is in defense of the *status quo*. This is particularly so under conditions in which efforts to change law take the form of protest, defiance, and civil disobedience. It does not matter whether the issue is the right of the Ku Klux Klan to march through a black neighborhood; an anti-abortion group to block the entrance to a clinic; a union to block scabs from crossing a picket line, or; students shutting down a university to protest a tuition increase or an immoral war. In each of these cases police find themselves defenders of the *status quo* and bound by law to use their coercive capacities against those who would disturb it.

Structurally, as an institution, police are committed to such a position irrespective of their personal preferences. We should not be surprised, however, to find that those whose work calls upon them so often to defend the *status quo* should develop occupational ideologies that reconcile them to it. Although attempts to establish the "authoritarian personality" of police have not survived methodological scrutiny, attitudes of police are probably more traditional than those of the general population, not only because the work they are called upon to do inclines them to adopt a personal political philosophy that comports with it, but because those who are attracted to police work are reasonably likely to begin with a traditional political orientation. Police are, in this sense, traditionalist conservatives. It is a political position they are structurally obliged to assume and whose ideology they are occupationally inclined to embrace.

Populism

The second strain of conservatism I should like to consider is *populism*. In identifying it as a strain of conservative thinking I do so in the knowledge that many conservatives intentionally distance themselves from it and find its terms offensive. It is the conservatism of Archie Bunker, David Duke, and Morton Downey, Jr. not that of George Will, Irving Kristol, or Norman Podhoretz, who regard it not as a strain but as a perversion of conservatism. While traditionalist conservatives find suspect abstractions that purport to challenge it, populists convert these sentiments to anti-intellectualism and crude intolerance of difference. Populism celebrates the ignorance and prejudices of the common man.

[Manning Continued]
remains. The background aim is class control and political ordering. Only definitions of phenomena in need of control change. Both rising groups and the powerless are potential targets for control and regulation. Since adherence to a rule, any rule, is itself the source of rewards and status, the indirect value of compliance is that one does not lose symbolic capital. Those on the political edges of society are denied not only access to the material resources of the society, but the symbolic resources as well. By constant changes in control strategies, misrecognition of the powerless of their interests and the interests of the police remains.

Having noted this about the relationships between "poor" and violence historically, the "service" notion used by Klockars is problematic. The implicit idea in "service" is that it is requested. While this is true for some police activities, some of the "service" applied to the poor is unwanted, deserved or not. The application of coercive force, stop and frisk and street sweeps, serving search warrants, especially in poor areas for drugs violations, are police-initiated activities, not reactive. The residents of Central Los Angeles did not request a war on the Afro-American poor (Davis, 1992). It is misleading to attribute essential qualities to groups when these are typically a product of historic developments and patterns of social domination.

New Forms of Violence and Control

The Klockars essay does not address the growing significance of new forms of violence. Some violence is perpetrated by the police against middle class citizens under various ideological covers. By "symbolic violence," I mean the ideological acceptance of directly deleterious costs and social patterns by those experiencing them even as they support the dominant order (Bourdieu, 1977: 190-197). The concrete notion of violence used colors and limits the scope of Klockars' essay.

Anglo-American democratic societies are in many ways less violent than they were one hundred and certainly two hundred years ago, but the public preoccupation with violence remains. The "new violence" is symbolic, and it at least in part derives from actions of the state's agents against it's citizens. This is not a novel idea, but the capacity of the agents to carry out their fantasies of control has vastly increased in the last ten years. To say this is not to minimize the high incidence and prevalence of violence in American society. Contemporary violence arises from the violation of public trust, the renting asunder of civil ties and moral obligations, especially of those in positions of trust in government and amongst what C. Wright Mills called the "Higher Circles of Power," as well as against and amongst the poor.

A New Focal Concern

The focus of control of the police is changing. They are sensitive to and part of creating new forms of symbolic

[Klockars Continued]

Populism is an occupational hazard of police work and one to which an unknown but probably substantial number of officers succumb. The best analysis I know of this problem is offered by William Ker Muir, Jr. in his extraordinary book, *Police: Streetcorner Politicians*. To understand Muir's analysis one must begin by accepting the fact that policing is a profoundly *moral occupation*. By "moral occupation" I mean an occupation in which its practitioners must come to a personal moral and intellectual reconciliation with the requirements of their job. What makes policing a moral occupation is the police officer's obligation to coerce, to threaten to hurt, and on occasion, to actually do so. To be a competent police officer one must become both morally and intellectually comfortable with doing so. One way to do so is to come to embrace a whole set of popular prejudices and crude characterizations that reduce the people on whom coercive means may have to be employed to something less than human beings - assholes, scumbags, skells, scrotes, shads, and groids - the litany is endless, replete with local variations, and need not be repeated here.

We should expect that police, as a product of dealing routinely in crises, will develop a certain hardness and insensitivity to suffering. However, it is important to understand exactly why a populist resolution to the moral obligation to coerce and hurt is unacceptable. It is not that such terms are offensive in polite society. Rather, it is that in effecting such a reconciliation with the obligation to coerce and hurt, the police officer so distorts the reality in which he works that it compromises his ability to work there competently. A world divided into good and evil, black and white, scrotes and honest folks is a cartoon world. It is a view of the world which makes Archie Bunker a buffoon, and any policeman who tries to work in such a world incompetent.

It is probably the case that public figures like David Duke and other crude populists tend to give support to such defective resolutions of the policeman's moral mandate. It is the obvious obligation of police leaders to stand against such sentiments and inexcusable, as in the case of Darryl Gates, when they fail to do so.

Libertarianism

The third strain of modern conservatism I should like to consider is *libertarianism*. Like populism it is a strain of conservatism over which there is, among conservatives, sharp division. Historically, the mark of both liberals and radicals of the left has been a faith that the state, through central planning, social engineering, and enlightened regulation of both social and economic life would produce the good society. Conservatives, by contrast, have stood for the minimization of the role of the state and resisted the expansion of the role of the state, distrusting profoundly its professed beneficence.

[Manning Continued]

violence. The focus of symbolic control for Anglo-American urban police is changing from the visible street disorder and crimes that shaped the mandate, strategy and style of the 19th century police. An emerging police focus is "risk prevention" through "proactive," "community," "problem-solving," and window-sensitive (Wilson and Kelling, 1982) policing and new forms of technologically-assisted surveillance. The police are almost unintentionally becoming "information workers" (Ericson, 1992), becoming experts in gathering, storing and retrieving information from an assemblage of strategic data bases. The focal interest of the police is shifting from "crime" in the sense of street crime, to control of matters that involve trust violations, risk prevention and management. They are actively devising and commodifying new modes of "security." As the legally granted permission for police monitoring and synthesizing gathered information increases, their ability to do so surreptitiously, and even illegally, has escalated.

A number of trends suggest the growth in patterns of use of symbolic violence by the police against citizens. Some are subtle expansions in the police mandate, while others are technologically-driven.

(1) Police variously penetrate private relations using quasi-legal powers. They sometimes employ the vehicle of high politics and national security, such as a declining public order, a needed "War on Drugs" and new threats of foreign espionage industrial to secrets, to justify their security measures.

(2) Increased penetration of the family and private relations, the result of increased police powers, reduced legal controls on police interventions in private relations, and the punishment of domestic violence by arrest.

(3) Police, with the cooperation of A. T.& T., have developed new forms of surveillance that allow sophisticated tracking of vehicles, and invisible monitoring of telephone calls (especially of cellular phones), e-mail, and faxes.

(4) Police use forensic-genetic evidence to eliminate or include suspects in criminal cases.

(5) Police encourage and use on themselves random drug testing. It is used also in government, many critical occupations, and schools without permission. Information so gathered can be used by the police as a basis for further investigation.

(6) The police in many cities mobilize DARE programs that place uniformed officers in third and fifth grade classrooms. They preach often incorrect information about

[Klockars Continued]
The irony in the liberal and radical positions on the one hand and in the conservative on the other is that both appear to reverse themselves on the issue of police. Typically critics of police, both liberals and radicals, by pressing for extensions of the state role, enlarge the police role at the same moment they despise the police. Conservatives, by contrast, typically resist and distrust the extension of the state in virtually every area of social and economic life, but generally support efforts that expand the police role and tend to resist those that limit or restrain it. In short, liberals and radicals ought to love the police and conservatives ought to find them suspect, but at least historically neither has behaved in this way.

They have not, I suspect, because both traditionalist and populist sympathies for police have overwhelmed the libertarian sentiments that ought to incline against them. The extent to which this domination will continue would seem to depend upon the degree to which police continue to appear to serve traditionalist and populist interests. They may well continue to do so. But if there is a single lesson to be learned from contemporary politics, it is how quickly yesterday's enemies can become friends - and vice versa.

Carl B. Klockars is Professor of Criminal Justice, University of Delaware. He is the author of The Idea of Police (Sage 1985) and co-editor (with Stephen Mastrofski) of Thinking about Police (McGraw Hill, 1991). This essay is based on a speech given at the Academy of Criminal Justice Sciences national meeting in Pittsburgh, PA on March 12, 1992.

[Manning Continued]
drugs and urge total abstinence without differentiating critically amongst the costs and benefits of currently legal and illegal drugs.

(7) Policing is characterized by a growing integration of public and private policing, mutual cooperation and data-sharing.

(8) Police, as they move away from a sanctioning mode to a restitutive and preventive mode, seek to control the conditions or circumstances under which crime occurs. They refine "preventive" and "risk management" strategies.

These trends appear to increase the potential for policing to evolve beyond current preoccupations into more subtle forms of control and security assurance.

Comment

The police are not the servants of the government of the day, the poor, or the rich. They apply violence, and as the definition of violence changes, they can be counted upon to apply it to classes marginal to the dominant order. The work of policing is changing and entails new forms of state-created monitoring and surveillance. In this sense, they may well use their authority in innovative ways, including policing violations of trust by other information workers. These issues are neither liberal nor conservative in character.

Peter K. Manning is a Professor in the School of Criminal Justice, Michigan State University. He is the author of numerous books and scholarly journal articles on policing. Prepared 26 Oct. 1992 as a comment on Carl Klockars, "The Legacy of Conservative Ideology and the Police" for the Police Forum, Newsletter of the Police Section of the ACJS.

References

Bayley, D. (1985). *Patterns of Policing*. Rutgers: Rutgers University Press.

Bourdieu, P. (1977). *Outline of a Theory of Practice*. Cambridge: Cambridge Univerity Press.

Carson, W.G.O. (1970). White collar crime and the enforcement of factory legislation. *British Journal of Criminology*,10: 383-398.

Davis, M. (1992). *City of Quartz*. New York: Random House.

Ericson, R. (1992). The division of labour and the concept of security. Unpublished paper, University of Toronto, Centre of Criminology, Fall, 1992.

Kelsen, H. (1961). *A General Theory of Law and the State*. New York: Russell and Russell.

Wilson, J.Q. and G. Kelling (1982). The police and neighborhood safety: Broken windows. *Atlantic*, 127 (March): 29-38.

Standards of Professionalization:
Do The American Police Measure Up?

Richard C. Lumb

University of North Carolina/Charlotte

ABSTRACT

Professional recognition is the ultimate goal of police throughout the world. Professionalism consists of occupational requirements including selection, education, training, and development of an individual's skills, knowledge, and abilities in a particular field of practice. Emphasis is on high standards of practice and provision of quality service to the occupation's clientele. Professional organizations periodically evaluate member standards of practice and their skills and knowledge as part of the occupation's certification requirement. Professional recognition generally emerges from the occupation's compliance to five standards of professionalization. This study compares current information from each of the fifty states' Education and Training Standards Commissions to police compliance with the five standards of professionalization.

INTRODUCTION

Achievement of professional status and recognition is a high priority among police. However, declarations claiming professionalism are meaningless unless the group is able to withstand scrutiny and evaluation of how closely they match existing standards and requirements. Acceptance by peers and the public is not given freely nor can it be purchased or assumed. Acquiring the rights and privileges that accompany professional status must be earned by following a prescription born of tradition, steeped in experience and modified by practice. Whereas other occupations (e.g., physicians, attorneys, dentists, psychologists, etc.) must be certified to provide services under the umbrella of that group, police point to their certification requirements as proof of professional status.

Perhaps it is unimportant for the occupation of policing to aspire to professional status. Professionalization, while desired, may not make any significant difference in methods of policing or actual practice. The desire for professional status may simply appease a longing for citizen respect that officers feel is lacking. The diversity of demands and citizen expectations are massive obstacles to overcome if police practices are to become standardized (Small, 1991). A major task is the definitive assignment of responsibility between the multiple levels of federal, state, county, and local law enforcement agencies. The multiplicity of duties and responsibility of each would be difficult to sort out, assuming commitment could be obtained to undertake such a project. One can speculate that there would be scant interest in this process given the legal mandates, established practices, allocation of resources, and depth of role protectionism occurring in each agency.

Furthermore, it may not be possible for the police to achieve professionalization. Hand-in-hand with considering oneself a professional is the demand for self-regulation and autonomy from external regulation or scrutiny. Within our democratic society and system of government neither of these two conditions is possible for the police. External review of the police is jealously protected by citizens and governmental figures. As a branch of the executive arm of government, police autonomy is not allowed, even though distancing from political control is the desire of all police. Accountability to citizens should not be diminished or eliminated. Regardless of these concerns, efforts are taking place to achieve professionalism.

The purpose of this study is to compare general standards of occupational professionalization to standards of police certification as they currently exist in the United States to determine whether or not the police have achieved professional status.

In this study "standards" refers to statements of how the organization views itself in terms of its ethics, ideals, morals, and principles of doing business. Established on the basis of some authority or by general consensus, standards are used as a model to compare actual practice or behavior against acceptable and approved criteria. Unable to meet every demand or satisfy multiple expectations, the police are expected to perform their duties based on established standards of practice (Roberg & Kuykendal, 1993). These standards are a collection of policy, rules, regulations, and minimum requirements which officers must follow. They are guidelines that provide the underlying basis of the organization's commitment to public service.

Occupational professionalization includes an individual's education and training preparing him or her for entry into a field of practice (Block, 1991; Little, 1991). For example, the President's Commission on Law Enforcement and Administration of Justice (1967) recommended possession of a bachelors degree by all police officers. As a determining factor of a profession, this recommendation sought to move the police toward higher standards of knowledge and resulting practice (Sheehan, 1989). Examination of an occupation's conformity to accepted procedures and doctrines, consistent with professional practice, aids in determining status. The major impetus for creating standards for police was the Commission of Accreditation for Law Enforcement Agencies (CALEA). Established in 1979 as a result of the combined efforts of the four major police administrative organizations,[1] the Commission established accreditation standards for police (Peak, 1993). The success of CALEA in promoting professionalism is not known. However, it represents an organized attempt to measure agencies against established criteria, an important undertaking with potential benefit to the police and citizens. While claiming to be professionals in their field, the police must subject themselves to scrutiny and evaluation against the defining characteristics of a profession.

Components of Professionalization

Education and Training Standards. As early as 1908, August Vollmer called for the assistance of university educators to help develop job-related police training programs (Christian & Edwards, 1985). The result of his effort was the initiation of a course on evidence collection for police officers (Carte, 1975; Caiden, 1977). The Kefauver Committee (1951) sought mandatory minimum standards of basic training for police officers. In 1952 the American Bar Association Committee on Organized Crime, House of Delegates, adopted recommendations calling for each state to establish a Police Council (Boolsen, 1959). Because of their recommendation, the proposed Model Police Council Act included a statement seeking more effective selection and training of police personnel. As they became known, Police Officer Standards and Training (POST) Commissions sprang up across the United States. The Law Enforcement Assistance Administration Act of 1965 authorized the Office of Law Enforcement Assistance to help finance state and local law enforcement training and demonstration projects (Christian & Edwards, 1985). Funds available through the Omnibus Crime Control and Safe Streets Act of 1968 assisted in establishing POST Councils in thirty-nine states (The President's Commission, 1967). The National Advisory Commission on Criminal Justice Standards and Goals (1973) recommended every state should enact legislation establishing a State Standards Commission. The purpose was to develop and administer standards of training for police personnel (Christian & Edwards, 1985).

Control over police agencies varies from state to state, dependent on legislative willingness to centralize power with POSTs, rather than with individual police and sheriff departments. All fifty states now have a POST Commission, and state statutory training requirements serve as minimum prerequisites for purposes of certification and licensing police officers (Cox and Moore, 1992:237). Today POSTs are involved in a variety of endeavors. They include establishing minimum employment standards, developing content and minimum hours of basic, advanced, and in-service training, conducting job task analyses, and certification and decertification of police officers (Blumberg, 1985; Stratton, 1992).

Selection and Recruitment. Professionalization also includes elements of selection and recruitment of qualified individuals into an occupation that is perceived as professional. The purpose of recruitment is to provide qualified candidates for employment who have potential for practice within the tenets of the occupation (Holt, 1993). In professional organizations the candidate for certification must meet basic minimum standards of education, training, and development within the confines of established criteria. Therefore, standards of practice should establish the criteria required for admission leading to certification and permission to practice.

Mission and Goals. A mission statement comprehensively delineates an agency's purpose and distinguishes it from other organizations that may be similar in nature (Roberg & Kuykendall, 1993; Swanson et al., 1993; Holt, 1987). Contrasting differences between what professionals should be doing and what they actually do relates to the mission and goals of the occupation. The organization's mission statement usually includes its strategic purpose, objectives, goals, and service philosophy. Organizational goals distinguish the organization's purpose and provide a broad framework for defining role and responsibility (Roberg & Kuykendall, 1990).

Police Certification

Police certification is granting the right to practice as a law enforcement officer, to investigate crimes and arrest suspects, testify in court, and carry out a variety of other duties proscribed by law and regulation. Certification is licensure of the individual as a police officer. Minimum criteria of age, education, no criminal record, good moral character, physical attributes of eyesight and strength, and successful completion of prescribed training are some of the essential aspects required.

Police certification is a requirement across this nation. The problem is a lack of standardization among the states, varying pre-service requirements and post-certification expectations. The variance is so great it becomes difficult to detect commonalities.

An important post-certification expectation is the maintenance of certification which requires providing opportunities for the individual to remain current with the knowledge and technology of his or her occupation. A standardized method for periodic assessment of an individual's skills, knowledge, and abilities, within occupational parameters, is also essential (Phillips, 1991; Poole & Gill, 1991; Cotter, 1985). Assessment suggests that a formal means should exist to test the ability of practitioners to perform their duties at an acceptable level (Houle, 1980; Merriam & Caffarella, 1991; Sork, 1988).

METHODOLOGY

Houle's (1980:35-75) *Conceptual Characteristics of a Profession* provides the standards of professionalization used in this study. These standards include:

1. Clarification of central mission, roles and Responsibilities.
2. Commonalities of recruitment and selection.
3. Education and training including continuing professional development (mastery of theoretical and practical knowledge, skills, practices, and problem-solving ability particular to the occupation).
4. Criteria required for Credentialing of a person who meets the existing standards.
5. The legality of Credentialing agencies to control granting officer certification and decertification for violations of rules and policy.
6. Periodic evaluation of competence and skill maintenance needed for recertification.

Data for the study are from the International Association of Directors of Law Enforcement Standards and Training (IADLEST) survey which provides information on the current state of education, training, and professional development of criminal justice personnel. IADLEST is an association of standards and training managers and leaders from each of the fifty states (Lumb, 1993). The IADLEST survey provides information on five of the six standards of police certification as they relate to professionalization.

This study compares the IADLEST data against the six standards of professionalization to decide how closely state standards are in compliance. In doing so, the study shows how selected police officer standards of certification compare to generalized standards of professionalization.

The survey questionnaire which consisted of 740 items, was sent to each state's Law Enforcement Standards and Training Commission Director. Questionnaire items addressed many aspects of criminal justice, including administrative and legal authority, selection and certification standards, basic, in-service, refresher training requirements, and miscellaneous items concerning the authority invested in each state's commission. Additionally, the questionnaire elicited information about each state's authority to oversee the general certification and decertification of police officers. Questionnaire items were answered by selecting a provided option or by writing in the desired information. Directors in all fifty states returned their questionnaires for a 100 percent return rate. However, some directors did not respond to all items, resulting in missing data for those items.

ANALYSIS AND RESULTS

Standards of Professionalization #1:
Clarification of Mission, Roles, and Responsibilities.

None of the Commissions provides or mandates collection of this information. Police standards of certification are dependent on each jurisdiction to decide the scope and depth of any mission statement, delineation of roles, and the existence, if any, of written instructions of police responsibility.

Standards of Professionalization #2:
Commonalities of Recruitment and Selection.

The states of Indiana, Louisiana, Maine, Massachusetts, Nebraska, Vermont, and West Virginia do *not* mandate minimum hiring standards for hiring criminal justice personnel; minimum standards may be waived in twelve states and six states indicated there are *no* penalties for noncompliance of minimum selection standards. Perrier (1978) recommends use of structured entrance requirements as characteristics of professionalization.

Other indicators showing an inattention to mandating standards for entrance to the field include required fingerprinting of the candidate (not required in the six states of Connecticut, Massachusetts, North Dakota, Ohio, Oklahoma, and Washington); *not* requiring a background investigation (nine states); and, *not* requiring psychological examinations (twenty-seven states). Finally, only twenty-one states require minimum physical standards prior to hiring.

If minimum selection standards are indicators of professional status, then the police, on a national basis, do not meet requirements. Globally, the police should not be considered as professionals within the categories discussed thus far. See Table 1.

Table 1
Standards of Professionalization #2:
Commonalities of Recruitment and Selection in the States

Minimum Hiring Standards	Number	Percent
Yes	43	86
No	7	14
Waiver of Minimum Standards	Number	Percent
Yes	12	27.9
No	31	72.1
Noncompliance with Standards Penalties	Number	Percent
Yes	35	85.4
No	6	14.6
Fingerprints Required	Number	Percent
Yes	42	84
No	6	12
Background Investigation	Number	Percent
Yes	39	78
No	9	18
Psychological Examination Required	Number	Percent
Yes	18	40
No	27	60.0
Minimum Physical Standards Prior to Hiring	Number	Percent
Yes	21	42
No	22	44

167

Standards of Professionalization #3: Education & Training Requirements.

Formal education and training are prerequisites for individuals entering an occupation considered as professional (Cox, 1992). As early as 1967, the President's Commission on Law Enforcement and Administration of Justice recommended that all police officers be required to obtain a bachelor's degree. Forty-nine state directors responded to the item about requiring a bachelor's degree for entry as a police officer. Twenty-six years after this recommendation was made by the President's Commission, only Minnesota requires an associates degree prior to appointment as a criminal justice officer. Forty-three states require a high school diploma or GED for entry, while five of the states (Massachusetts, New Jersey, Ohio, Pennsylvania, and West Virginia) indicated they do not have an educational requirement.

A variety of training delivery systems are available across the country. Most of the delivery systems are through state, local, and county facilities. Eighteen states award college credit for successful completion of Academy basic training. Additionally, one might assume that success of Academy training is partially dependent on the individual's reading comprehension ability. A total of twenty-four states do not test a recruit's reading level before beginning basic training. Seventeen test prior to basic training and eight states test during training. One state (Texas) did not respond to this question. Finally, for those Academies and/or instructors who fail to achieve minimum standards with basic training, most of the states can initiate some type of punitive action. Statewide uniform mandated performance objectives for basic training have been established in thirty states. There are thirty-nine states that require a minimum academic passing grade of 70 or better, eight have a pass/fail requirement, and three indicated they use other unspecified standards. Assumptions regarding the reliability of a standardized certification examination that measures professional competence cannot be inferred from this data. See Table 2.

Standards of Professionalization #4:
Credentialing - Qualification of Academies and Instructors.

Many states have standard educational requirements for pre-service entry into a professional field of practice. In the case of the police, a high school diploma or equivalency is the minimum educational requirement in 49 states. Thus, the focus of training academy curricula in the preparation of police officers is directed at the high school level of education. This minimum requirement does not qualify as a difficult standard when compared to other occupations that are more demanding in their educational mandates.

Table 2
Standards of Professionalization #3:
Education and Training Requirements

Minimum Education Requirements	Number	Percent
None	5	10.0
High School	43	86.0
Associates degree	1	2.0
College Credits for Basic Training	**Number**	**Percent**
Yes	17	34.7
In some cases	27	55.1
No	5	10.2
Recruit Reading Level Tested	**Number**	**Percent**
No	28	56.0
Prior to training	14	28.0
During training	6	12.0
Training Delivery Systems Available[a]	**Number**	**Percent**
College	15	
Regional Academy	10	
State, County, Local Academy	29	
Central Academy only	6	
Central Academy & Regional Training	7	

[a] More than one system available in some states.

States control police training academies and instructors by exercising their right to levy sanctions against those who violate rules and policy. Commissions can bring sanctions against academies in forty states and against instructors in forty-four. A total of thirty-nine states can waive basic training requirements, while eleven states do not have standardized performance measurement criteria of any kind. Uniform statewide basic training curriculum for law enforcement exists in forty-five of the states, while the states of Hawaii, Maryland, Minnesota, North Dakota, and Rhode island indicated they do not have this requirement. However, all states but Minnesota and New Jersey indicated the establishment of minimum hours of basic training. These hours range from a low of 120 in Missouri to a high if 650 in Connecticut. It can be concluded that while five states do not have a uniform statewide curriculum, all but Minnesota and New Jersey do require minimum hours of training. Customary standards of professionalization include control of an individual's performance using internalized standards as a mechanism (Smith, 1976). DeCotiis (1978) notes that professionalism consists in part on the existence of a unique, codified body of occupational knowledge that is subject to investigation and verification. Without standards for training, there can be no professionalism.

Instructor formal standard criteria for certification is a requirement in forty-four states. The states of Hawaii, Oregon, and Rhode Island indicated no formal standard criteria for instructor certification. Three states did not answer. A variety of criteria measures instructor compliance with certification. These include experience, education, completion of a standardized course, evaluated teaching, and sometimes an apprenticeship. However, even with the existence of formal standards criteria, thirteen of the states do not require instructor recertification. Thirty-eight states have authority to bring sanctions against instructors for noncompliance with recertification. See Table 3.

Standards of professionalization #5:
Legality of Certification Control.

State Criminal Justice Education and Training Standards Commissions establish minimum standards using a variety of authorities that include mandating rules by executive order and legislation. Enforcing established standards and rules demands that police officer appointments are registered with the Commission. Without this knowledge, Commissions are not able to maintain control of who is and is not employed as a police officer. However, thirteen of the states do not require Commission notification of officer appointment. In addition, the authority to conduct investigations may require Commission subpoena power. Twenty-eight states do not have investigative subpoena power. Commissions are hampered by a lack of knowledge of who is appointed coupled with the inability to conduct investigations and subpoena people to testify. This greatly hampers any authority's ability to establish meaningful controls.

Table 3
Standards of Professionalization #4:
Credentialing Qualification of Academics and Instructors

Commission Authority to Sanction Academies	Number	Percent
Yes	38	76.0
No	7	14.0
Can Basic Training Requirements Be Waived	**Number**	**Percent**
Yes	26	52.0
No	24	48.0
Standardized Criteria for Performance Measurement	**Number**	**Percent**
Yes	39	78.0
No	11	22.0
Uniform Statewide Basic Training Curriculum Developed for Law Enforcement	**Number**	**Percent**
Yes	45	90.0
No	5	10.0
Formal Standard Certification Criteria	**Number**	**Percent**
Yes	44	88.0
No	3	6.0
Recertification Required for Instructors	**Number**	**Percent**
Yes	36	72.0
No	13	26.0
Authority to Bring Sanctions Against Instructor for Noncompliance with Recertification	**Number**	**Percent**
Yes	38	76.0
No	3	6.0

A telling measure is the authority of the state to impose sanctions against certified officers. Sanctions include the right to revoke a person's license (certification), decertify, suspend, and/or put the officer on probation. Twelve of the responding states do not have this authority.

Standards of Professionalization #6:
Evaluation for Continued Learning and Recertification.

Continued learning and development are essential to sustaining efficient and competent practice. Persons who hold a professional position should continuously strive to enhance their skills, knowledge, and abilities (SKAs) in a variety of ways (Block, 1991; Greenberg, 1989; Houle, 1980). A measure of continued development is through in-service refresher training. Thirty of the states have mandatory in-service refresher training rules, nineteen do not, and one did not respond. If officer in-service refresher training is not mandated, an obvious conclusion is that some officers never experience upgrading of their SKA's. Of the thirty states with them, in-service refresher training ranges from eight to eighty hours.

Twenty states require annual in-service refresher training, while the other ten states require training every from 24 to 36 months. Twenty-five states do not have a uniform statewide curriculum for in-service refresher training. In-service refresher training is prescribed by the Commission alone in twenty-one states, by law in three, seventeen do not mandate standards, and the others have a combination of sources. Uniform statewide standards of in-service training curriculum do not exist in thirty states. The states of Connecticut, Kentucky, Louisiana, Massachusetts, New Mexico, North Carolina, Pennsylvania, South Carolina, and Texas indicated they do have statewide curriculum, while eleven did not reply. This raises questions about what types of in-service training are provided, who makes that determination, what criteria are used in the decision-making, and whether officer needs are being considered.

Successful completion of in-service refresher training must meet a variety of criteria that include: (a) complete all phases of training; (b) maintain an overall passing grade; (c) meet each performance objective; and, (d) pass or demonstrate proficiency in other established areas.

A variety of in-service refresher training delivery systems exist in the states. These include: (a) an approved academy (N=18); local departments (N=20); college or technical schools (N=12); and other methods (N=8). Obviously more than one method of in-service refresher training is available in some of the states. In thirty of the states, penalties exist for noncompliance of in-service refresher training. These penalties/sanctions consist of: (a) removal or

172

suspension; (b) civil or criminal penalties; (c) decertification; (d) suspension of funding; and other sanctions. More than one sanction alternative is available in some states. Of the thirty-two states directors responding to the question: "Are commission certified instructors required to deliver in-service training?" twenty-six answered yes. See Table 4.

DISCUSSION AND CONCLUSIONS

In an effort to determine whether or not police in the United States are achieving professional status, this study compared selected items from a national study of state education and training standards commissions with six standards or indicators of general occupational professionalization. Findings from this study suggest that police, at least in some states, are some distance from accepted general standards of occupational professionalization. For example, none of the states require mission statements that define police role and responsibility. When considering the diversity of police in the United States, the multiple levels of federal, state, county, and local agencies, the range of departmental sizes, the political influences and variations of role expectations, it is little wonder any similarity exists. Finding commonality of purpose is not to difficult; however, establishing one all-encompassing mission statement among police agencies is, at this time, an unreasonable expectation. If mission statements exist, they are the products of individual departments and are not globally applicable to other agencies. Many states do not mandate minimum selection standards; others waive them. The President's Commission (1967) recommended a minimum requirement of a bachelor's degree for police officers. Now, more twenty-five years later, this minimum standard is not a requirement in any state, although the State of Minnesota does mandate an associates degree.

There is no consistency across states in education and training standards for police personnel. Waiver of basic training requirements are allowed in many states. In eleven states, standardized training performance criteria do not exist. This lack of internalized control seriously undermines the perception that training is monitored using rigid standards of practice. Instructor certification for those individuals who teach other police officers in basic training is inconsistent. Not all state Standards Commissions can bring action against an instructor who is incompetent. Commission control of police officer certification and/or decertification is nonexistent in several states. Challenge of officer practices, judged incorrect or harmful, is not allowed in over one-quarter of the states responding. The lack of sanction power precludes state Commissions from taking action against incompetent officers, effectively putting "policing the

Table 4
Standards of Professionalization #6:
Evaluatiou for continuing Learning and Recertification

Mandatory In-Service Refresher Training	Number	Percent
Yes	30	60.0
No	19	38.0
Frequency of In-Service Training	Number	Percent
Annually	21	
Every Other Calendar Year	1	
Within 24 Months	4	
Every 36 Months	4	
Other or No Answer	20	
Uniform Statewide Curriculum for In-Service Training	Number	Percent
Yes	9	18.0
No	30	60.0
No answer	11	22.0
Uniform Standards Statewide In-Service Training Curriculum	Number	Percent
Yes	8	16.0
No	30	60.0
Penalties for Noncompliance In-Service Training Required	Number	Percent
Yes	27	
No	4	

police" into the domain of the officer's agency. Many agencies are conscientious and thorough in their control of police officer behavior and treatment of the public, resolving problems and maintaining high standards of practice. Yet, many inconsistencies exist in supporting the role of States Commissions for determining police officer competence and right to practice.

Many states cannot exercise control over the recertification of officers based on continuing professional development and training. Mandatory in-service training does not exist in 17 states. States with mandatory in-service training rules require a range of between eight and eighty hours of training. To compound the problem, 25 states do not have uniform statewide curricula. As an indication of state inability to impose sanctions for noncompliance with in-service training requirements, eighteen states do not have penalties or sanctions available to them.

Suggesting that the police are professionals in their field has great appeal given the specialized and unique duties they perform. However, at this time in their history, the police do not meet acceptable standards of practice warranting entitlement to professional status. The police fall instead into the lesser category of semi-professional. Professional status can only occur if substantial changes take place. Necessary changes include selection, training, continuing professional development, recertification criteria, tight controls of training providers, curriculum, and in-service training improvements.

However difficult the path toward professionalization, there are immediate needs currently being unmet. State Criminal Justice Education and Training Standards Commissions should undertake the difficult task of developing a basic mission statement reflecting police duties and obligations to citizens. When a police officer is given the right to deprive a person of his or her liberty, bring charges, and in an extreme circumstance take someone's life, basic responsibilities and specific roles should be stipulated. Furthermore, these mission statements should be similar in all states so as to provide the basis for discussion and debate in the quest toward national police standardization.

Minimum standards of structured entrance requirements for police is a reasonable goal. Police training and certification requirements emerge from the mission of the police, the quality and caliber of personnel hired, and the tasks and duties required of officers. As such, states should establish performance-based training taught by certified instructors at approved training facilities. Instructors should be subjected to periodic recertification based on stringent criteria that measures their skills and knowledge of the subject matter taught. Teaching methods, style, and classroom pedagogy are also important. Instructors should be subject to recertification criteria.

The issue of in-service training is a hotly debated concern. Whereas some departments refuse or discourage officer training beyond the initial basic school, many officers go for months or years without the benefit of updated information. Atrophy is the unwanted outcome of a policy that does not mandate and enforce stringent officer in-service training and continuing professional development. Many agencies only respond to mandated requirements, electing otherwise to ignore the issue.

Finally, State Commissions should have the power to investigate, subpoena witnesses, and conduct hearings into officer misconduct and alleged illegal practices. Officer misconduct and the failure to follow or maintain training standards must be addressed uniformly. Jurisdiction over established violations belongs at the state level with supporting legislation to guide the process. Obviously, failure to address identified problems with officer behavior and practices has serious consequences throughout the law enforcement community.

Summarizing state responses with selected questions from the IADLEST survey, which was used in comparison with Houle's (1980) six standards of professionalization. The following compliance outcomes were revealed by. Thirteen states (26%) did not comply with between six and eleven measures as shown in Category III, Table 5. Another thirteen states (26%) were not in compliance with five measures (Category II, Table 5), and the remaining twenty-four states (48%) did not meet compliance with four or less measures (Category I, Table 5).

Those states in compliance with most of the measures used in determining professionalization 12.5 percent are from the northeast, 16.7 percent from the Midwest, 33.3 percent from the west, with the majority, 37.5 percent from the south. Overall, forty-eight percent of the states are in Category I which represents high compliance with the measures examined. Categories II and III are equally distributed with twenty-six percent in each. It seems that almost half of the states meet most of the criteria used to measure compliance with measures selected for this study. Another twenty-six percent meet at least half of the criteria. Those states represented in Category III are the furthest from compliance. Given the wide distribution across the categories there can be no consensus that the majority of police across the nation are meeting those criteria selected consistent with measures of professionalization.

Placing states in regions we find nine are located in the northeast, fourteen in the south, twelve in the Midwest, and fifteen in the west. Results of comparing state compliance with measures of standardization shows the state of Georgia meets 95.5 percent of the standards measured in this study and ranks highest among the states. There are six states in Category I meeting 91 percent of the standard measured, eight states meeting 86 percent of the standards in Category II, and the remainder of the states range between 50 and 81 percent of the standards.

Table 5
Categories Representing How States, By Region, Meet
Compliance with Measures of Professionalization

	Category I[a]	Category II[b]	Category III[c]
Northeast	3 (12.5%)	2 (15.4%)	4 (30.8%)
South	9 (37.5%)	3 (23.1%)	2 (15.3%)
Midwest	4 (16.7%)	5 (38.4%)	3 (23.1%)
West	8 (33.3%)	3 (23.1%)	4 (30.8%)
Column Totals	24 (48.0%)	13 (26.0%)	13 (26.0%)

Note: A total of 22 measures of professionalization were used in this study.

[a] Category I represents non-compliance with 1-4 measures.
[b] Category II represents non-compliance with 5 measures.
[c] Category III represents non-compliance with between 6 and 11 measures.

The department's role in issues of education, selection, training, and certification versus the role of the state in these matters is a moot point as we approach the 21st Century.   There is no substitute for a well-prepared police force that can bring solutions to problems facing society.   This process of standardization will require planning and guidance from state commissions whose responsibilities are to provide quality education and training standards.   The transformation has been evolving for over twenty years -- a good beginning but with much left to do.

As a final comment to the professionalization of police, acknowledgment of the diversity and variety of police organizations existing in the United States is in order.   Obviously, there are variations in how departments measure up to established standards of professionalization.   The shear number of police agencies, variations of size, demands for service, and the availability of resources all impact on the ability to professionalize.   An obvious assumption of this study is that departments appear to be spread along a continuum of professional development that ranges from minimal to high acquisition.   As such, it is difficult to arrive at definite conclusions about the state of police professionalization as a whole.

ENDNOTE

1. Consisting of the International Association of Chiefs of Police, the National Organization of Black Law Enforcement Executives, the National Sheriff's Association, and the Police Executive Research Forum.

REFERENCES

Block, S. (1991). *California Law Enforcement Training in the 1990's...A Vision of Excellence.* Sacramento: California Commission on Peace Officer Standards and Training.

Blumberg, A.S. and E. Niederhoffer (1985). *The Ambivalent Force: Perspectives on the Police.* (3rd ed.). New York: Hot, Rinehart & Winston.

Boolsen, F.M. (1959). Law Enforcement Training in California. California State Department of Education. In Kenneth Christian and Steven Edwards, Law enforcement standards and training councils: A human resource planning force in the future. *Journal of Police Science and Administration,* (1985) 13(1):1-9.

Caiden, G.E. (1977). *Police Revitalization.* Lexington, M.A.: D.C. Health and Co.

Carte, G.E. and E.H. Carte (1975). *Police Reform in the United* States. Berkeley, CA: University of California Press.

Christian, K.E. and S.M. Edwards (1985). Law Enforcement Standards and Training Councils: A Human Resource Planning Force in the Future. *Journal of Police Science and Administration* 13(1):March, 1-9.

Cotter, J. (1985). Law Enforcement Agency Accreditation to 1985. Fairfax, VA: Commission on Accreditation for law Enforcement Agencies, Inc.

Cox, B.G. and R.H. Moore (1992). Toward the Twenty-first Century: Law Enforcement Training Now and Them. *Journal of Contemporary Criminal Justice* 8(3):235-255.

DeCotiis, T.A. and T.A. Kochan (1978). Professionalization and Unions in Law Enforcement. From *Police-Community Relations - Selected Readings* - 2nd ED, by Paul Cromwall, Jr. & George Keefer. West Publishing.

Greenberg, S. (1989). Police Accreditation. In D. Kenney (Ed.). *Police and Policing* (pp.247-256). New York: Praeger.

Holt, D. (1993). *Management Principles and Practices.* Englewood Cliffs: Prentice-Hall.

Houle, C.O. (1980). *Continuing Learning in the Professions.* San Francisco: Jossey-Bass.

Kefauver, E. (1951). *Third Interim Report of the Special Senate Committee to Investigate Organized Crime in Interstate Commerce.* May. Washington, D.C.: U.S. GPO.

178

Little, R.E. (1990). Toward a Typology of Modes of Anticipatory Occupational Socialization Among a Sample of Police Recruits. *Police Journal,* 63(2):159-167.

Lumb, R. (1993). *Sourcebook.* Charlotte, N.C.: University of North Carolina.

Merriam, S.B. and R.S. Caffarella (1991). *Learning in Adulthood.* San Francisco: Jossey-Bass.

Peak, K.J. (1993). *Policing American.* Englewood Cliffs: Prentice Hall.

Perrier, D.C. (1978). "Police Professionalism." *Canadian Police College Journal,* 2(2):209-214.

Phillips, J.D. (1991). "Professionalism." *Police Journal,* 64(2):April-June, 124-133.

Pooler, L. and L. Gill (1991). Evaluation of Police Training. *Police Journal,* 64(1):47-57.

Roberg, R. and J. Kuykendall (1993). *Police and Society.* Belmont, CA: Wadsworth.

Roberg, R. and J. Kuykendall (1990). *Police Organization and Management.* Pacific Grove, CA: Brooks/Cole.

Sheehan, R. and G. Cordner (1989). *Introduction to Police Administration.* Cincinnati: Anderson.

Small, M.W. (1991). Police Professionalism: Problems and Issues in Upgrading an Occupation. *Police Journal,* 64(4):314-320.

Smith, D.C. (1976). "Police Professionalization and Performance: An Analysis of Public Policy from the Perspective of Police as Producers and Citizens as Consumers of a Public Service." Indiana University - Dissertation.

Sork, T.J. (1988). "Ethical Issues in Program Planning." In R.G. Brackett (ed.), *Ethical Issues in Adult Education.* New York: Teachers College Press.

Stratton, D. (1992). Improving Police Professionalism. *Police Times,* 32(6):1, 6, 22.

Swanson, C., L. Territo, and R. Taylor (1993). *Police Administration.* New York: MacMillan.

U.S. Department of Justice, The National Advisory Commission on Criminal Justice Standards and Goals. (1973). *Police.* Washington, DC: US GPO.

U.S. Department of Justice, The President's Commission on Law Enforcement and Administration of Justice, 1967 Task Force Report: *Challenge of Crime in a Free Society.* Washington, D.C.: U.S. Government Printing Office.

U.S. Department of Justice, The President's Commission on Law Enforcement and Administration of Justice, 1967, *Task Force Report: The Police.* Washington, D.C.: U.S. Government Printing Office.

THE EFFECTIVENESS OF AFFIRMATIVE ACTION: THE CASE OF WOMEN IN POLICING*

SUSAN E. MARTIN
National Institute on Alcohol Abuse and Alcoholism

Although the legal bases of affirmative action plans have been debated widely, empirical examination of their effectiveness has been limited. This paper examines the impact of affirmative action on the hiring and promotion of women in policing. A survey of municipal departments serving populations of more than 50,000 found that women still constitute less than 10 percent of all police officers. Nevertheless, multivariate analyses show that both court-ordered and voluntary affirmative action policies have had a statistically significant impact on the hiring but not the promotion of female officers. In addition, case study data from five agencies show that affirmative action policies have widened women's opportunities to receive specialized assignments. These findings suggest the importance of continuing affirmative action policies despite recent legal setbacks.

The 1972 amendments to the 1964 Civil Rights Act extended to public employers the prohibition against employment discrimination and made them responsible for taking "affirmative action" to assure equal employment opportunities. Since that time there has been heated debate about the legality of various mechanisms for achieving affirmative action, but only limited examination of its effectiveness in reducing employment discrimination. This paper examines the effects of efforts to eliminate discriminatory employment practices through affirmative action plans and related policy changes in policing. It suggests that substantial change has occurred, although women continue to be greatly underrepresented in policing, and that affirmative action policies have had a significant impact on the hiring and the assignment mobility of women in urban police departments.

* This research was conducted while the author was on the staff at the Police Foundation. It was supported in part by funding from the Ford Foundation. The paper is a revision of a paper presented at the meetings of the American Sociological Association held in San Francisco in August 1989.

BACKGROUND: THE DEVELOPMENT AND EFFECTS OF AFFIRMATIVE ACTION

In the past 25 years, many employers have adopted affirmative action policies to bring about equal employment opportunity in the workplace. This process often has involved implementing "goals and timetables" to overcome the effects of past discrimination, whether intentional or not, in order to comply with federal law and EEOC implementation guidelines.

The principles of equal employment opportunity law were established in *Griggs v. Duke Power Co.* (1971). In that case the Supreme Court held that employment criteria whose effect was to exclude minorities disproportionately were illegal, regardless of the employer's intent, unless the employer could show that such selection standards were job-related.

Since *Griggs*, several Supreme Court decisions have narrowed the grounds on which plaintiffs can prevail in employment discrimination cases, while upholding governmental and private organizations' efforts to eliminate employment discrimination through affirmative action plans.[1] In 1989, however, in *Wards Cove Packing Co. Inc. v. Atonio* (1989), the Court effectively eliminated the *Griggs* rule, shifting the burden of proof of alleged job discrimination back to workers. The future of affirmative action still is uncertain despite passage of the Civil Rights Act of 1991 because of vague language regarding quotas and its likely interpretation by the conservative majority on the Supreme Court. Therefore, at this critical political juncture, it is useful to examine empirical evidence regarding the actual impact of affirmative action efforts. I do this by focusing on one occupation, namely policing.

Throughout the 1970s, municipal police departments, like many other employers, faced lawsuits alleging discrimination on the basis of both race and sex. Litigation challenged departments' entrance requirements related to education, age, height, weight, and arrest records; their selection criteria, including written examinations, agility tests, and veterans' preference; and their promotion procedures (Potts 1983; Sulton and Townsey 1981). Frequently these suits were initiated separately by blacks and by women but were consolidated by the courts (Sullivan 1989).

---

[1] These cases include Bakke v. Regents of the University of California (1978), in which the Court ruled that public organizations' affirmative action plans may take race into account as long as the preferential programs do not use quotas, and United Steelworkers v. Weber (1979), which upheld the right of a private employer to adopt a voluntary affirmative action hiring plan under Title VII. Nearly a decade later, in United States v. Paradise (1987) and Johnson v. Transportation Agency (1987), the Court continued to allow affirmative action plans based on individual circumstances when the impact of the plan did not "unnecessarily trammel" the rights of white male employees.

Many of these cases resulted in court orders or consent decrees that established affirmative action programs, including quotas and timetables for hiring and promoting minorities and women. Other departments, to avoid the expense of litigation and the restrictions of court-imposed remedies, modified their recruitment practices, eligibility requirements, and selection criteria. To comply with emerging case law, most agencies eliminated or altered height and weight requirements and physical agility tests that disqualified women disproportionately. By 1986, for example, fewer than 4 percent of municipal departments retained minimum standards for height (mean = 5'4") and weight (mean = 135.3 pounds) as entry criteria (Fyfe 1986). Agencies also rewrote and validated the written entrance examinations that adversely affected blacks, and standardized their oral screening procedures for both selection and promotion.

In addition, affirmative action plans were in effect in most departments. By the end of 1986, 15 percent of the departments in cities serving populations of more than 50,000 (and 40% of the 53 agencies in jurisdictions with populations of more than 250,000) were operating under court orders or consent decrees, 42 percent had adopted voluntary affirmative action plans, and 43 percent had no affirmative action policy (Martin 1990).

Assessing the impact of affirmative action policies is difficult because of the problems involved in separating the effects of those policies from other factors influencing employment practices, such as compliance with other legal decisions and workers' mobility.[2] Nonetheless, in one recent study focused on race and policing, W.G. Lewis (1989) found that affirmative action has significantly increased the representation of black officers.

RESEARCH DESIGN AND METHODOLOGY

The data reported here are part of a larger study designed to assess the status of women in policing, which draws on a national survey and on case studies in five agencies. The findings are based on responses to questionnaires sent to 446 municipal departments serving populations of more than 50,000 in 1986 (Martin 1990) and on a similar survey conducted in 1978 by the Police Foundation

---

[2] For a discussion of the development and rationale of affirmative action, see U.S. Commission on Civil Rights (1981). For analyses of the effectiveness of affirmative action programs see Benokraitis and Feagin (1978), Cayer (1980), Feinberg (1984), Harriman (1982), Leonard (1985), G.B. Lewis (1988), and Vernon-Gerstenfeld (1985). For studies focused specifically on women, see Clynch and Gaudin (1982), Huckle (1983), Leonard (1988), Marlin (1977), Sigelman (1976), and Steel and Lovrich (1987).

and using the same sample (Sulton and Townsey 1981). The response rates to these surveys were 72 and 74 percent respectively. Analyses of the survey data included descriptive statistics and multivariate techniques to explore the relative importance of the presence of affirmative action policies in several outcomes.

The case studies conducted in the five large municipal agencies explored departmental policies and procedures for integrating women into policing and probed officers' perspectives on changes in the status of women over the past two decades. The agencies were diverse with regard to the proportions of female officers and supervisors, region, and affirmative action status. Two were under court order or consent decree with respect to both selection and promotion of women and minorities; three had voluntary affirmative action plans in effect (although one of these plans involved court-approved race- and sex-based promotion quotas).

In each agency in the case study, approximately 25 randomly selected officers and mid-level supervisors of both sexes were interviewed during on-duty time. Interviews were semistructured, lasted about 2½ hours, and explored respondents' experience of discrimination, views on affirmative action, and perception of departmental policies regarding the integration of women. Interviews also were conducted with about eight high-ranking policy makers in each department, including command staff members and those administrators responsible for recruitment, selection, training, EEO matters, and the promotion process. The interviews focused on departmental policies and procedures for integrating women into policing. (For details of the research methodology see Martin 1990.)

FINDINGS

Affirmative Action Policies and Changes in the Representation of Women and Minorities: 1978-1986

Between 1978 and 1986, the proportion of women in policing increased from 4.2 to 8.8 percent of municipal officers, as shown in Table 1. During the same period the representation of minority officers in large and moderate-sized urban departments rose from 13.8 to 22.5 percent of the sworn personnel. Thus the representation of minorities in policing now approaches their representation in the urban population (Sullivan 1989), but women continue to be vastly underrepresented in policing.[3] The table also suggests that

---

[3] In 1985, blacks made up 12.1 percent of the American population, Hispanics 6.4 percent. Because both minority groups tend to live in cities rather than in suburban or rural areas, however, they probably remain somewhat underrepresented

although minority women made up only 3.5 percent of all officers in 1986, they constituted 40 percent of all female officers. Minority males, in contrast, made up 14 percent of the urban police personnel but only 21 percent of the male officers. About 75 percent of those minority female officers and 62 percent of the minority males were black. Thus black women made up a much larger fraction of the female officers (31%) than did black men of the male officers (12.5%).

Table 1. Mean Percentages of Police in Municipal Departments in 1978 and 1986, by Ethnicity and Sex

	1978			1986		
Ethnicity	Male	Female	Total (N=290)	Male	Female	Total (N=316)
White	83.6	2.6	86.2	72.2	5.3	77.5
Nonwhite	12.2	1.6	13.8	19.0	3.5	22.5
Total	95.8	4.2	100%	91.2	8.8	100%

Women have made more modest gains in obtaining promotions to supervisory ranks. In 1978 they constituted only 1 percent of all supervisory personnel. By the end of 1986, their representation had increased to 3.3 percent of those with the rank of sergeant or higher. The proportion of minority women increased from 20 percent to nearly 33 percent of the female supervisors.

How have affirmative action policies affected these increases? As shown in Table 2, at the end of 1986 women made up 10.1 percent of the sworn personnel in agencies under court order to increase the representation of women and minorities, 8.3 percent of the sworn officers in agencies with voluntary affirmative action plans, and only 6.1 percent of personnel in agencies without any affirmative action plans. The relationship of affirmative action to the representation of minority women was even clearer.

Affirmative action also was associated with the proportion of female supervisors. In departments with court-ordered affirmative action, women made up 3.5 percent of all supervisors. In those with voluntary affirmative action programs and without affirmative action plans, they accounted respectively for 2.4 percent and 2.2 percent of all supervisors.

A variety of other factors, including region, city size, and minority representation, also were found to be associated with the

in urban police agencies. In contrast, women represent 52 percent of the population and 44 percent of the labor force.

Table 2.   Weighted Proportions of Female Officers and Supervisors, by Type of Affirmative Action Policy

Type of Policy	White Officers	Minority Officers	Total Officers	Total Supervisors
Court-Ordered (N=45)	5.7	4.4	10.1	3.5
Voluntary (N=126)	5.5	2.8	8.3	2.4
None (N=126)	4.1	2.0	6.1	2.2
Total	5.3	3.5	8.8	3.3

representation of women. To control for the effects of these variables, we used multivariate analyses to determine whether the presence of either a court-ordered or a voluntary affirmative action policy had an independent effect. We did this in two ways. First we included affirmative action and several other variables in a full regression model. As shown in Table 3, both court-ordered and voluntary affirmative action were associated significantly with the proportion of women in a department in the presence of other variables. Next we restricted the model by including all but the two affirmative action variables to test the significance of the difference between the two models (Namboodiri, Carter, and Blalock 1975). This test showed that the restricted model explained nearly 3 percent less of the variance than the full regression model. The difference between the two models was statistically significant (t = 5.78; df = 12,279; p < .01).

In an additional regression model we explored the factors associated with changes in the proportion of female officers from 1978 to 1986, in those departments for which data were available for both years. With this model we found that the presence of an affirmative action policy in 1986 was significantly associated with an increase in the representation of female officers, after we controlled for other variables.

Affirmative Action and Officer Selection Procedures

In the long run, the proportion of female officers is likely to be no greater than their representation among new recruits. Application and selection rates, in turn, are shaped by the eligibility criteria and the mechanisms used to recruit, screen, and select candidate officers. For many years, minimum height and weight standards, as well as educational standards that were higher for women than for men, greatly limited the pool of female applicants (Milton 1972; Sulton and Townsey 1981). In the past 15 years,

Table 3.   Regression of Percentage of Female Officers

	Full Model			Restricted Model		
Variable	b	seb	t	b	seb	t
Large Department	.016	.005	3.08**	.018	.005	3.47***
Small Department	−.002	.004	−.70	−.006	.004	−1.53
Percent Female						
Turnover	−.009	.013	−.71	−.005	.013	−.34
Percent Hispanic	−.012	.017	−.69	−.018	.017	−1.04
Percent Black	.101	.020	4.99***	.107	.021	5.21***
Females on Patrol						
before 1974	.003	.003	1.12	.004	.004	1.04
North Central	.011	.005	2.28*	.012	.005	2.52*
West	.018	.005	3.30***	.020	.005	3.74***
South	.030	.005	5.73***	.030	.005	5.79***
Increased in Size						
since 1982	.006	.003	1.64	.006	.003	1.85
Voluntary						
Affirmative Action	.012	.004	5.02***			
Court-Ordered						
Affirmative Action	.017	.005	3.22**			
Constant	.028	.006	5.02***	.034	.005	6.38***
	$R^2 = .395$			$R^2 = .367$		
	df = 12,279			df = 10,281		
	F = 16.86***			F = 17.89**		

*   = significant $< .05$
** = significant $< .01$
*** = significant $< .001$

however, the eligibility criteria for policing positions have been altered dramatically, often because of litigation and the adoption of federal regulations (Fyfe 1986; Sulton and Townsey 1981). Consequently the pool of eligible candidates for policing now includes virtually all healthy high school graduates.

The types of selection mechanisms used by municipal agencies are quite similar: most include written, oral, and medical examinations, a psychological screening test, and a pretraining physical fitness or agility test.[4] The content and the administration of those tests, however, appear to vary widely.

Departments provided data on the number of male and female officers of each ethnic group who, during 1986, 1) filed an application, 2) were offered employment by the department, 3) entered the training academy, and 4) completed training. This information permitted us to examine broad patterns in selection.[5] We found

---

[4] Fyfe (1986) reports that such tests now are used in 76 percent of municipal agencies.

[5] Because in many jurisdictions, county or municipal personnel boards administer the initial entry test and "certify" qualified applicants from a list ranked

that women made up 20 percent of the applicants for police positions in 1986, 20.6 percent of the persons accepted, and 19.2 percent of those who completed academy training. Because the actual qualifications of the male and female applicants are unknown, we could not determine whether discrimination was present in the selection process. Nevertheless, the data suggest that women overall, once in the eligible pool, are not excluded at disproportionate rates. At the same time, the large standard deviations suggest that some departments may favor women by recruiting them actively and selecting them disproportionately, while others seem to attract few women and to reject them at a higher rate than men.

Minority women made up 45 percent of the female applicants and 44 percent of the females who completed academy training. In contrast, minority males made up 40 percent of all male applicants but only 32 percent of those completing the academy. Minority men were both more likely than white men to decline the offer of employment in policing and less likely to complete the academy.

Several factors appear to contribute to the high proportion of minority women (75% of whom are black) in policing. First, minority women may regard policing as an attractive alternative among the narrow range of occupational options traditionally open to them. For high school-educated minority women, policing offers a step up in prestige and pay from factory and domestic work, and it pays more than a clerical job. Second, municipal departments appear to focus affirmative action recruiting efforts on the black community. The recruitment message, emphasizing a good career and service to the community, reaches both men and women but may be more convincing to the latter. Black adolescent males and young men have long been, and continue to be, objects of police suspicion. They are more likely than black women or other men to be stopped and questioned and to be arrested. Therefore, a higher proportion are likely to view the police in a negative light and to be disqualified from police work by their criminal record. Third, a dynamic may exist whereby minority officers in a department recruit their friends and associates so that departments

---

by written examination scores, only 60 percent of the departments were able to provide data on the number of applicants; 72 percent supplied data on the number of acceptances, and 77 percent on academy entrances and completions. Some agencies that did not provide the latter information stated that no officers had been hired and/or had completed training in 1986.

with minority members find it easier to recruit more such officers.[6] Finally, departments may recruit and select minority women to meet affirmative action goals simultaneously for women and for racial minorities.

Predictors of the Proportions of Female Applicants and Female Rookies

The presence of an affirmative action policy also was related significantly to both the proportion of women among all applicants and the proportion of female applicants accepted as recruits. As Table 4 shows, 21 percent of the applicants were female in agencies with court-ordered affirmative action plans, in contrast to 17 percent in agencies with voluntary affirmative action plans and 13 percent in agencies with no such plans ($F=9.46$; $p<.001$). Women made up a significantly larger proportion of the applicants accepted in agencies with court-ordered affirmative action plans (21%) than in those with voluntary plans (18%) or no plans (14%) ($F=4.09$; $p<.02$).

Table 4. Impact of Affirmative Action on Unweighted Representation of Female Applicants and Persons Selected by Departments

Type of Affirmative Action Plan	% of Applicants Who Are Female	% of Accepted Applicants Who Are Female
Court-Ordered	20.5	21.3
	(6.7)	(13.2)
Voluntary	16.7	17.6
	(8.7)	(12.8)
None	12.9	14.1
	(7.8)	(12.6)
Total	15.7	16.7
	N=181	N=220
	F=9.46	F=4.09
	p < .001	p < .02

Standard deviations given in parentheses.

Again we developed two models, using multivariate analysis to examine the effect of affirmative action after controlling for the effects of other variables. The full model included the following as independent variables: percent black, percent Hispanic, percent female, total percentage of applicants accepted in 1986, agency size, region, whether the agency had increased its authorized sworn personnel since 1982, whether women had been assigned to patrol

---

[6] Several of the case study agencies even pay an incentive bonus to officers for recruiting a minority candidate who is accepted for training.

before 1974, the total percentage of applicants accepted in 1986, whether candidates had to pass a pretraining agility test, whether department policy required a female or minority representative on the oral screening panel, and whether the department had a court-ordered or voluntary affirmative action policy. The restricted model excluded the two affirmative action variables.

We found four factors to be significant predictors of females' application rates. The percentages of blacks and of females already in the department were associated positively with the proportion of female applicants. The presence of a pretraining physical agility test and the location of the department in a small city (between 50,000 and 100,000 population) were associated negatively with that dependent variable. Neither affirmative action variable was statistically significant.

Next we ran the restricted model, which excluded the affirmative action variables, to test the significance of the difference between the full and the restricted regression models. This test revealed that both affirmative action variables made a difference in the proportion of women among applicants for police jobs, after the effects of the other variables were controlled ($F=2.31$; $df=16$, 150; $p < .05$).

We used the same procedures to examine the effect of affirmative action on the proportion of female recruits accepted for training and the proportion that completed training. The affirmative action variables were not significant in either of the full regression models or in the tests of difference between the full and the restricted models.

These findings suggest that the principal impact of affirmative action policies on the selection process is on candidate recruitment, primarily in widening the applicant pool. Once that pool is enlarged, women are selected roughly in proportion to their presence there. Therefore, to increase female representation in policing, agencies must enlarge their female applicant pool, initially by active recruitment of women. Without additional recruiting efforts or a change in women's application rates, women are not likely to make up more than 20 percent of sworn police personnel.

Affirmative Action and Promotions to Sergeant

We also examined the effect of affirmative action on promotions. Overall, 6.8 percent of all persons eligible for promotion to the rank of sergeant were female, but 8.8 percent of those actually promoted were female. As with selection, promotion eligibility and actual promotions were affected by a variety of factors, including the presence of an affirmative action policy. Women were significantly more likely to be eligible for promotion to sergeant in departments with court-ordered affirmative action (8.3% of the eligibles) than in departments with voluntary (6.0%) or no affirmative action plans (4.5%). Using multivariate techniques to control statistically for other factors, however, we found that affirmative action was not associated significantly with the rate of women's promotion to sergeant, either in the full regression model or in the test of the significance of differences between the full and the restricted models. Irrespective of affirmative action policy, women were promoted at rates marginally higher than their representation in the eligible pool.

The Effects of Affirmative Action on Case Study Agencies

Data from the case studies suggest that affirmative action policies have contributed to the integration of female officers, particularly in the departments in which management has made a clear commitment to implement those policies. In the five case study agencies the proportion of women among all the applicants for entry-level positions ranged from 21 to 34 percent. Females' application rates in those agencies were related more closely to the proportion of women already on the job than to actual recruitment efforts. In two agencies in which female and minority representation was above the mean for agencies of that size, females constituted about one-third of the applicants, a voluntary affirmative action program was in effect, and only passive recruitment efforts were made. In contrast, in the case study department with the lowest proportion of women (8%), women made up only 21 percent of the applicants despite an aggressive voluntary affirmative action effort.

This finding suggests that as women come to perceive real job opportunities in policing, the proportion of qualified female applicants increases and the need for active recruitment decreases. An aggressive recruitment program is required initially in a community to increase women's representation. Once recruitment is routinized, however, it is likely to become self-sustaining. Women in that community observe other women on patrol, see them on TV, and are more likely to have had personal contact with a female officer; thus they view police work as a viable option for themselves.

In the past, female officers not only faced discriminatory hiring and selection standards, but also received different assignments from male officers. Data provided by three of the departments regarding the assignment histories of matched male

191

and female officer samples showed that women had a greater number and wider variety of different assignments than the men who had been officers for the same length of time.

Several factors shape opportunities to obtain specialized assignments. These include administrative regulations regarding transfers (including seniority rules and selection procedures), the degree of civilianization, turnover rates, availability of training, and an agency's affirmative action policies. In the case study agencies each factor affected women's assignment mobility, but the most important was implementation of policies to achieve sex integration in all units.

The interviews suggest that women sometimes changed their assignment to escape particularly hostile work environments. More often, however, they seized opportunities when departments required the integration of many specialized units. Because of their small numbers, women who were regarded as effective officers or who had political connections with unit commanders were able to obtain desirable positions ahead of men with more seniority, experience, and informal "old boy" ties. They also obtained many clerical, administrative, and dispatching positions that males regard as less desirable "inside" assignments, a situation which increases the perception that women are moving out of patrol. Indeed, one patrol supervisor noted ruefully that the patrol division in his agency cannot retain female sergeants because they are constantly recruited to more prestigious specialized units.

Departmental leaders used various strategies to integrate women into diverse units. In some instances, these strategies placed extraordinary stress on the "advantaged" women. One agency developed general orders that established clear selection criteria for specific assignments and made success in implementing affirmative action policies a criterion in supervisors' evaluations. Another department found a way to circumvent seniority rules that often hindered its affirmative action efforts. In that agency, seniority governs transfers but not initial assignments. Therefore, to integrate several elite units, the agency assigned women to those units directly from the academy rather than assigning them to serve on patrol.[7] In a third agency, a precinct commander explained:

---

7 This policy placed the rookie women, who had neither street patrol experience nor the specialized skills required of others in this unit, in a very difficult situation. They faced the isolation, stereotyped expectations, and performance pressures to which "tokens" are subjected (Kanter 1977), hostility from male co-workers who had "paid their dues," and, for these reasons, an increased likelihood that they would fail to become effective officers.

This city is very affirmative action oriented and "complexion aware". . . . If there are four specialized squad sergeants, they can't all be one race or sex. . . . It's important to demonstrate to everyone they have an opportunity to advance and I may . . . give a position to someone who has less ability or expertise who is of the appropriate group . . . to show that I've done a visible job of being equitable.

Implementation of EEO policies and of affirmative action plans appears to have sent a clear message that organized discrimination and harassment, which were tolerated widely when women first went onto patrol (Bloch and Anderson 1974; Martin 1980), no longer are permissible. These actions, coupled with the effectiveness of many women on patrol and the presence of some women in supervisory positions, seem to have resulted in a reduction in "rational bias" discrimination by mid-level personnel (Larwood, Szwajkowski, and Rose, 1988). Such discrimination occurs when mid-level supervisors perceive cues from superiors suggesting that a show of bias would be rewarded by them, or, in the absence of such cues, when they believe they are acting on their bosses' preferences. When the bosses make clear that discriminatory treatment will not be tolerated regardless of an individual's attitudes toward female officers, subordinates have tended to alter their behavior.

This study and several others (Bremer and Howe 1988; Vernon-Gerstenfeld 1985) have found that the commitment of management to achieving affirmative action goals is a key factor. In several of the case study agencies, the mayor and the chief were dedicated to increasing the number of women and assuring them equal opportunities throughout the agency through voluntary affirmative action programs. Police of all ranks in those departments (including men opposed to the integration of women) were more likely to assert that women were not limited by a "glass ceiling" and to predict that women would be appointed to the command staff sooner than officers in departments with court-ordered policies. In the former agencies, management's commitment to overcoming the barriers to equality has gone beyond pro forma adoption of an affirmative action policy to making equal opportunity not only a matter of policy but of practice.

DISCUSSION

The entry of women into patrol work, the backbone of policing, was met with strong resistance by high-ranking administrators and individual officers in many departments. Both court-ordered and voluntary affirmative action policies have contributed significantly to the steady increase in the proportion of female officers and supervisors.

Interpreting the magnitude of the increase in women's representation is a matter of perspective. On the one hand, the proportion of female officers grew by more than 100 percent between 1971 and 1978 (from about 2% to 4.2% to all officers) and more than doubled again between 1978 and 1986 (to 8.8% of sworn personnel). On the other hand, the net increase was less than 7 percent. In contrast to several other traditionally male occupations, such as law, medicine, and management, the change in women's representation in police work is small; when compared with growth in such blue-collar occupations as carpentry and firefighting, however, women's gains in policing seem quite impressive. (For additional comparative data see Reskin and Roos 1990: Tables 1.6 and 1.7.) Alternatively, if one compares the effects of affirmative action on the representation of minorities in policing with its effects on the representation of women, the net growth of the former is greater. Minority representation increased by more than 15 percent, from about 7 percent of sworn personnel in 1971 (Sullivan 1989:335) to 13.8 percent in large and medium-sized municipal agencies in 1978 and to 22.5 percent at the end of 1986.

Although women continue to be greatly underrepresented in policing as both officers and supervisors, affirmative action has made a major contribution to the change that has occurred. We found a statistically significant difference in women's representation between departments that have adopted and have not adopted affirmative action policies.

Increased representation and career opportunities for women in policing are not due to affirmative action alone. First it was necessary to widen the pool of female applicants and rookies by eliminating discriminatory eligibility criteria and selection procedures, and by more active recruitment. Because police supervisors are drawn from the pool of officers, the increase in the pool of women eligible for promotion, coupled with changes in promotion procedures and with affirmative action policies, also has resulted in gains in the representation of women above the entry rank.

Yet, the continuation of even the current rate of growth in female representation in policing is uncertain. Without an increase in current application rates, women are likely to constitute less than 20 percent of the police officers as we enter the twenty-first century. Questions about the future of affirmative action also cloud the picture. In the late 1980s, several decisions of the new conservative majority on the Supreme Court overturned long-established rules on proof and procedure. As a result, plaintiffs find it more costly and more difficult to win discrimination cases and opponents of change find it easier to challenge voluntary affirmative action programs and long-standing consent decrees. These decisions led Congress to pass the Civil Rights Act of 1991, which restored the language of the *Griggs* decision but was vague regarding affirmative action.

The data presented here suggest that during the 1980s, despite several court restrictions and the Reagan administration's withdrawal of federal government support, affirmative action did not end, as some people had predicted. In part it survived because many features of affirmative action plans have been institutionalized over the past two decades (Nalbandian 1989). Many administrators now are sensitive to and accept as legitimate the value of social equity in employment practices such as targeted recruitment, job-related tests, and performance appraisals. We do not know, however, to what extent these practices will continue without legal pressures and a decreased federal presence.

Policing also has undergone important changes in the past two decades. Increased heterogeneity among police personnel has strengthened the recognition that all kinds of officers can contribute to police work. The growing emphasis on community policing demands personnel with problem-solving and communication skills that enable them to deal effectively with the citizens they are to employed to serve and protect. Perhaps these changes will sustain the commitment of municipalities and police agencies to assuring all individuals an equal employment opportunity. Indeed it would be unfortunate if police organizations, which are dedicated to protecting the rights and liberties of all citizens, were to do any less for their officers.

REFERENCES

Benokraitis, N. and J. Feagin (1978) *Affirmative Action and Equal Opportunity: Action, Reaction, Inaction.* Boulder: Westview.

Bloch, P. and D. Anderson (1974) *Policewomen on Patrol.* Washington, DC: Police Foundation.

Block, W.E. and M.A. Walker, eds. (1982) *Discrimination, Affirmative Action, and Equal Opportunity.* Vancouver: Frazier Institute.

Bremer, K. and D.A. Howe (1988) "Strategies Used to Advance Women's Careers in the Public Service: Examples from Oregon." *Public Administration Review* 48:957-61.

Cayer, N.J. (1980) "Minorities and Women in State and Local Governments: 1973-1975." *Public Administration Review* 40:439-72.

Clynch, E.J. and C.A. Gaudin (1982) "Sex in the Shipyards: An Assessment of Affirmative Action Policy." *Public Administration Review* 42:114-20.

Feinberg, W.E. (1984) "At a Snail's Pace: Time to Equality in Simple Models of Affirmative Action Programs." *American Journal of Sociology* 90:168-81.

Fyfe, J. (1986) *Police Personnel Practices, 1986.* Washington, DC: International City Management Association.

Harriman, A. (1982) *Women/Men/Management.* New York: Praeger.

Huckle, P. (1983) "A Decade's Difference: Mid Level Managers and Affirmative Action." *Public Personnel Management* 12:249-57.

Kanter, R.M. (1977) *Men and Women of the Corporation.* New York: Basic.

Larwood, L. E. Szwajkowski, and S. Rose (1988) "Sex and Race Discrimination Resulting from Manager-Client Relationships: Applying the Rational Bias Theory of Managerial Discrimination." *Sex Roles* 18:9-29.

Leonard, J.S. (1985) "What Promises Are Worth: The Impact of Affirmative Action Goals." *Journal of Human Resources* 20:3-14.

—— (1988) "Women and Affirmative Action in the 1980s." Paper presented at the annual meetings of the American Economic Association, in New York

Lewis, G.B. (1988) "Race, Sex, and Supervisory Authority in Federal White-Collar Employment." *Public Administration Review* 46:25-30.

Lewis, W.G. (1989) "Toward Representative Bureaucracy: Blacks in City Police Organizations, 1975-1985." *Public Administration Review* 47:257-67.

Marlin, J.T. (1977) "City Affirmative Action Efforts." *Public Administration Review* 37:508-10.

Martin, S.E. (1980) *"Breaking and Entering": Policewomen on Patrol.* Berkeley: University of California Press.

—— (1990) *On the Move: The Status of Women in Policing.* Washington, DC: Police Foundation.

Nalbandian, G. (1989) "The U.S. Supreme Court's 'Consensus' on Affirmative Action." *Public Administration Review* 49:38-45.

Namboordiri, H.K., L.F. Carter, and H.M. Blalock (1975) *Applied Multivariate Analysis and Experimental Designs.* New York: McGraw-Hill.

Potts, L.W. (1983) "Equal Employment Opportunity and Female Employment in Police Agencies." *Journal of Criminal Justice* 11:505-23.

Reskin, B.F. and P.A. Roos (1990) *Job Queues, Gender Queues: Explaining Women's Inroads into Male Occupations.* Philadelphia: Temple University Press.

Sigelman, L. (1976) "The Curious Case of Women in State and Local Government." *Social Science Quarterly* 56:591-604.

Steel, B.S. and N.P. Lovrich (1987) "Equality and Efficiency Tradeoffs in Affirmative Action—Real or Imagined? The Case of Women in Policing." *Social Science Journal* 24:53-70.

Sullivan, F.A. (1989) "Minority Officers: Current Issues." In R. Dunham and G. Alpert (eds.), *Critical Issues in Policing: Contemporary Readings,* pp. 331-46. Prospect Heights, IL: Waveland.

Sulton, C. and R. Townsey (1981) *A Progress Report on Women in Policing.* Washington, DC: Police Foundation.

U.S. Commission on Civil Rights (1981) *Affirmative Action in the 1980s: Dismantling the Process of Discrimination.* Washington, DC: Commission on Civil Rights.

Vernon-Gerstenfeld, S. (1985) "Affirmative Action in Nine Large Companies: A Field Study." *Personnel* 62:54-60.

CASES CITED

Bakke v. Regents of the University of California, 438 U.S. 265 (1978).

Griggs v. Duke Power Co., 401 U.S. 424 (1971).

Johnson v. Transportation Agency, 94 L. Ed. 615 (1987).

United States v. Paradise, 94 L. Ed. 203 (1987).

United Steelworkers v. Weber, 443 U.S. 193 (1979).

Wards Cove Packing Co. Inc. v. Atonio, 109 S. Ct. 2115 (1989).

Policing and Society, 1992, Vol 2, pp. 197–211
Reprints available directly from the publisher
Photocopying available by license only

WHEN THE GUARDS GUARD THEMSELVES: UNDERCOVER TACTICS TURNED INWARD

GARY T. MARX

Department of Urban Studies and Planning, Cambridge, Mass. 02139, U.S.A

(Received 22 April 1991)

You must first enable the government to control the governed; and in the next place, oblige it to control itself.

James Madison

The perennial issue of "who guards the guards?" has taken a new turn in the U.S. with the increased use of covert means to ferret out corruption among police, prison guards, prosecutors, defense attorneys and judges. This specialized use is located within the recent general expansion of undercover policing in the United States. Theoretical issues involved in controlling the controllers, empirical examples, intended and unintended consequences and the policy issues this raises are discussed.

KEY WORDS: Guarding the guards, undercover means, internal control, social control, police, democracy

Covert means have recently become much more important as criminal justice tools – whether directed externally or internally. For example consider the following:

In Los Angeles nine officers from an elite narcotics unit were arrested for the large scale theft of seized funds. The Los Angeles Sheriff's Department and the FBI staged a phoney drug operation and videotaped the deputies stealing money. (L.A. Times, Sept. 2, 1989)

In Cleveland FBI undercover agents set up and ran two gambling operations as part of a two year sting directed at local police. Thirty officers were arrested as a result and charged with extortion, obstruction of justice and narcotics and gambling violations. (Law Enforcement News, June 15, 1990)

A New York prosecutor was arrested after taking money for arranging the dismissal of gun charges against a person he thought was an organized crime figure, but who was actually a federal agent. (Blecker 1984).

As part of an FBI undercover operation, a Federal district judge in Florida was arrested on charges of obstructing justice and conspiring to collect bribes from a defendant posing as a racketeer. (N.Y.T. Nov. 29, 1987).

In 1986 the New York City Corrections Department began placing undercover corrections officers in the city's jails to investigate drug offences, excessive use of force and theft of weapons. (N.T.Y. Nov. 6, 1986).

These efforts at internal control are illustrative of a broader problem faced by any complex society: controlling those with the authority to control others.

In the first century the Roman poet Juvenal asked "quis custodiet ipsos custodes"

– who guards the guards? There are few questions of greater practical or theoretical import. All organizations of course must devote some attention to matters of internal control. (Katz 1977) But the issue has special poignancy and symbolism, when it involves organizations whose primary goal is creating, interpretating or enforcing law. The answer to Juvenal's question for despotic regimes may be "no one". The guards are a law unto themselves, and with respect to the public are relatively uncontrolled. (1) But in the United States with its pluralistic system, the executive, legislative and judical bodies watch and constrain each other. Outside institutions such as the mass media and professional associations (American Bar Association and International Association of Chiefs of Police) and public interest groups concerned with democracy and civil liberties also play a role.

However the guards are also expected to guard themselves. Self-regulation is a central tenet of professionalization. In the case of law enforcement, by careful selection, training, policy, and supervision the guards are expected to keep their own house in order. Day-to-day responsibility lies with self-control on the part of individual agents and bureaucratically defined supervisory roles, internal affairs units and inspectors general.

This paper focuses on one means of self-regulation which has recently become much more important: undercover tactics.(2) The topic of undercover work is rich in complexity and paradox. If we wish to see the guards guarded using these means, how is this best done? What are the risks and costs to other important values? If an undercover policy works and is legal, is it therefore necessarily good public policy? Should those in positions of authority be subject to greater restrictions on their liberty because of the greater temptations they face? Can we be sure that the evidence discovered is not itself simply an artefact of the investigation? How should we balance the access to evidence that may be otherwise unavailable, with the invasions of privacy and other unintended consequences that may be present? Will the internal use of covert means lower morale and productivity and mean less risk taking and innovation? With multiple agencies with overlapping jurisdictions, can authorities avoid ensnaring each other in their traps? Is it appropriate to do good by doing bad? When the state uses deception does it set a bad example, modelling and legitimating the use of deception for its citizens? Given the power of the tactic to tempt and entrap, can political targeting be avoided? These issues run throughout the examples we consider and are discussed in the concluding section.

I. THE NEW POLICE UNDERCOVER WORK

This section describes and attempts to account for the recent changes in the use of undercover means. New uses within criminal justice are part of something broader. Undercover work has changed significantly in the United States in the past decade, expanding in scale and appearing in new forms.(3) Covert tactics have been adopted by new users and directed at new targets and new offenses. Applying ingenuity previously associated with fictional accounts, law enforcement agents have penetrated criminal and sometimes noncriminal milieus to an extraordinary degree. Even organized crime, long thought to be immune, has been infiltrated. The lone undercover worker making an isolated arrest has been supplemented by highly coordinated team activities involving complex technology, organizational fronts, and multiple arrests. What was traditionally viewed as a relatively marginal and insignificant weapon used only by vice and "red squads" has become a cutting-edge tactic.

The agency with the greatest change in its application of undercover operations is the Federal Bureau of Investigation. It has moved from viewing them as too risky and costly for routine use to viewing them as important tools. The FBI has come a long way from the description offered by leading agent Melvin Purvis in 1936: "No government operative may enter into illegal compacts or pursue illegal courses of action; it does not matter what desirable ends might be served." (Purvis 1936) Four decades later, an FBI agent wrote: "Undercover operations have become the cutting edge of the FBI's effort to ferret out concealed criminal activity. (Riley 1982)

The Bureau of Alcohol, Tobacco and Firearms (BATF) foreshadowed this expansion by significantly increasing its use of undercover methods after the passage of the 1968 Gun Control Act. In 1982 the Internal Revenue Service (IRS), vastly expanded its intelligence and undercover activities. A special unit was created with unprecedented powers to collect and analyse data on taxpayers including the increased use of undercover agents and sting operations. United States marshals have made extensive use of covert tactics to facilitate the location and apprehension of fugitives through Operation FIST (Fugitive Investigative Strike Team). (Select Committee 1982).

Federal agencies whose primary goal is not criminal law enforcement, such as the Departments of Agriculture, Interior, and Housing and Urban Development; the Customs Service; the Government Services Administration; the Nuclear Regulatory Commission; the Commodity Futures Trading Commission and the Securities and Exchange Commission; and congressional committees, have also made increased use of undercover tactics, as have consumer, health, environmental protection, and motor vehicle agencies, and departments of investigation at the state and local levels. Even Smokey the Bear has gone undercover. In 1985, the U.S. Forest Service revealed a plan to combat marijuana growing in national forests involving the use of 500 special agents and the expenditure of up to $20 million a year. Under President Reagan, the Central Intelligence Agency was given new authority to conduct domestic undercover operations. The tactic is being used for civil and administrative, as well as for criminal violations.

Following the recommendations of several national commissions, covert means have also become more sophisticated and significant at the local level since the late 1960s. (President's Commission 1967 and President's National Advisory Commission 1968) The past decade has seen state attorneys general, county district attorneys, and special prosecutors taking greater independent initiatives against crime, often using their own investigators and conducting their own undercover operations. In addition, undercover operations have brought what were often relatively uncooperative federal, local, or regional police agencies together in joint ventures via the task force approach. (Marx 1988)

The variety of targets has increased. Traditionally, undercover operations were targeted against consensual crimes (a crime between consenting individuals, such as a buyer and a seller of drugs), and they tended to focus on petty operators, street criminals, and lower-status persons. This has changed.

Anticrime decoys, fencing stings (police posing as purchasers of stolen goods), and infiltration have brought the tactic to relatively unorganized street crime and burglary, thus including crimes where there is a clearly identifiable victim. Undercover agents have adopted a new role – that of victim rather than co-conspirator. For example, a police officer may pose as a derelict with an exposed wallet in order to foster a crime.

New targets have also emerged within traditional vice operations. In what is termed the "sell-bust" strategy, customers (whether consumers or distributors) have joined "suppliers" as targets. Undercover officers may offer to sell drugs and other contraband instead of buying it. The expansion of covert operations into white-collar crime means that corporate executives, bankers, persons in retail and service businesses, labor leaders, and elected and other government officials have all become targets. This represents a shift in emphasis to crimes involving corruption, labor racketeering, industrial espionage, and export trade law violations.

Other new targets include foreign businesses suspected of trade violations, exporters of high technology and military equipment, dumpers of hazardous waste, promoters of tax shelters, landlords, building inspectors, automobile salesmen and mechanics, fixers of horse races, poachers of cacti, elk, bighorn sheep, and bear, and traffickers in endangered or protected plants and wildlife, such as Jamaican boa constrictors and great horned owls. Even baseball fans are facing increased covert surveillance. Thus, in 1982, the New York Yankees began an ambitious program of placing plainclothes police in the stands pretending to be fans.

Rather than being directed at specific crime categories, investigations may start with suspect groups or individuals to find out what offenses they might be committing. In other words, authorities now actively seek out violators. With this focus on potential offenders and offenses, targeting has become more fluid and based more on probabilities. Investigations, for example, may be directed at various white-collar groups (business people, labor leaders, government officials) where a variety of offenses may be occurring.

The scope of most traditional undercover investigations (excluding those against political groups) has been relatively limited. Their goal has been to apprehend either a specific person or persons believed likely to commit a limited range of previously identified offenses. The investigations are reactive in that they occur in response to a particular crime, a crime pattern, or to specific factors that arouse police suspicion. This investigative model has been supplemented by one that is more proactive, diffuse, and open-ended. The new model involves a radar-like discovery sweep. Many investigations have become uncoupled from specific complaints, suspects, or offenses and (at least initially) less focused. Deterrence and intelligence gathering have become important objectives, along with the traditional goal of apprehending those responsible for specific offenses.

Secret testing on a random basis is a well-established aspect of private policing, for example, the testing of cashiers, and it has become more common in the public sector as well. Some investigations have taken as their implicit goal the determination of whether or not a person can be induced to break the law, rather than whether the person is in fact breaking the law.

The question "Is he corrupt?" may be replaced by the question "Is he corruptible?" Some operations amount to random integrity testing. Rather than intervention into ongoing criminal activities, there is an effort to create them apart from specific grounds for suspicion. Using the tactic for general intelligence purposes, or to test at random, represents a significant extension of law enforcement discretion.

Undercover means have become a prominent and sophisticated part of the arsenal of American law enforcement. This represents a marked departure from the police activities envisioned by the founders of the country and from the Anglo-American police ideal that eventually evolved. More sophisticated covert practices are one part of an extension and redefinition of social control, which, together with other practices, constitute what can be called the "new surveillance." (Marx, 1988)

The new surveillance is related to broad changes in both technology and social organization. The rationalization of crime control that began in the nineteenth century has crossed a critical threshold as a result of these changes. Technology has enhanced the power of social control. The information-gathering powers of the state and of private organizations have torn asunder many of our conventional notions of privacy. Traditional lines between private and public and between the rights of the individual and the state are being redrawn.

Changes in crime patterns, public attitudes and law enforcement priorities, in conjunction with organizational, legislative, judicial and technical changes, supported the general expansion of the undercover technique. These are treated at length in Marx (1988). But brief mention can be made of several judicial, legislative, and resource factors that are particularly relevant to the increased internal use of the tactic.

The civil rights movement helped call attention to the inequality in law enforcement that exists when government focuses only on the violations of the poor, while ignoring those of the rich and powerful. In addition, public indignation over Watergate and related abuses both reflected and contributed to the declining tolerance for white collar violations. The struggle against the corruption of authority is one strand of that. The diffuse, often victimless quality of corruption lends itself well to discovery via covert means.

Federal legislation such as The Hobbs Act and the 1961 Travel Act have come to be applied to anyone who obstructs interstate commerce – including those who offer bribes, as we well as local and state officials (not just to federal officials). Interstate commerce can be obstructed because of a threat of violence and direct extortion, or merely by obtaining government benefits passively "under color of official right." This "federalization" of local offences has reduced the burden of proof for prosecutors and helped open the way to the vast increase in federal corruption prosecutions at the local and state level.

The 1970 RICO Act (Racketeer Influence and Corrupt Organizations Act) permits convictions on the basis of a "pattern" of activities comprising a criminal enterprise. Such a pattern of "racketeering" is very broadly interpreted to include a variety of offences that are repeated several times. In a 1981 decision the Supreme Court held that prosecution need not be restricted to criminal organizations that infiltrate or take over legitimate business, but instead could be applied to any group which demonstrated a pattern of racketeering activity. This law and subsequent interpretations, vastly increased white collar prosecutions of those not usually thought of as involved in organized crime.(4)

New federal resources such as a public integrity unit in the Justice Department, the Federal Witness Relocation Program, the Federal Law Enforcement Training Center and the creation of offices of Inspectors General made internal investigations easier. In the case of the first, in 1976 the Justice Department created a public integrity section within it criminal division. This now has more than 25 attorneys who specialize in the supervision and oversight of under cover operations for serious corruption cases. This unit offers training, seminars, lectures, and consultation to prosecutors and investigators for the prosecution of corruption cases. (Marx 1988)

This paper focuses on an area where the changes in covert means are particularly clear and dramatic – the use of undercover means by government against itself. The vast expansion of drug enforcement has greatly increased corruption temptations. Among those arrested in recent police stings have been Drug Enforcement Agency and FBI agents, as well as many local police. Concern over drugs and violence, has sent still other agents to prison – although posing as prisoners, in a trick used by the renowned French detective Vidocq. (Stead 1953 and Gerson 1977) It is no longer uncommon to hear of police, legislators and even judges and prosecutors as the targets of undercover investigations.

Let us move from consideration of the broad expansion of undercover tactics in the last two decades (of which uses within government is one strand), to some of the difficulties involved in seeking to control those with the authority to control others. Then in Section III we consider examples involving police, courts and other elected officials. Section IV discusses some broader implications for public policy.

II. THE PROBLEM OF GUARDING THE GUARDS

If there are forces operating to expand the internal use of covert means there are also powerful forces opposing this. To the social analyst, as against the social reformer, what might seem remarkable is that there is as much internal social control among law enforcement agencies and government as there is, rather than how far from ideal the situation is. As with dancing bears, the point may be not that they dance badly, but that they dance at all.

Many factors work against the guards guarding themselves as aggressively as they guard others. The separation of powers doctrine may inhibit enforcement agencies from actively investigating judicial and legislative bodies. Judges control the issuance of warrants and may be hesitant to judge their peers. The rule making, budgetary, and approval power of the legislature over executive and administrative agencies may subtly (or not so subtly) inhibit the latter's enforcement actions.(5) Judges may owe their appointments to the very politicians they could be asked to judge.

Within the same enforcement organization simple self-interest and reciprocity work against aggressive action. Those within the same organization have a strong interest in getting along. Reaching organizational goals requires cooperation, and loyalty is valued. Boat rockers and whistle blowers are not usually rewarded. Violations may be tolerated as resources and rewards. There may even be a kind of implied black-mail in which those with the power to sanction rarely use it in order to keep the peace and assure the organization's functioning.

American police, lacking the lateral entry of European police are thought to have a higher degree of inner solidarity and weakened supervision. Since leaders rise from the ranks, they may find it more difficult to act decisively. Also unlike the situation in Europe, being a prosecutor or a local judge is rarely a life-long career insulated from political pressures, or assessments of future career moves. Rather such positions are often stepping stones to other public offices or jobs in the private sector (e.g. as defense attorneys). This may mean lesser professionalism and greater receptivity to political pressures.

District attorneys for example are usually elected and very much a part of their communities. They are generally not inclined to make cases against the political establishment that nurtures them and is likely to hold the key to their futures. Federal or state agents are freer to do this, on the other hand they may not know the local scene as well, and they must often work together with local officials on other matters.

Local prosecutors who wish actively to enforce corruption laws need to obtain a critical mass of evidence, such that an investigation creates its own momentum and can proceed in spite of the political pressures that may be brought against it.

As a result of the above factors, the ecology of internal enforcement generally flows downward from federal to state and local levels (and from state to local) rather than the reverse. As noted, for political reasons it is often easier for outsiders to act. The federal government of course also has greater resources, and broader laws and jurisdiction.(6)

A related issue arises from the special skills of control agents. Even when the will is present, it is more difficult to catch those in criminal justice because of their knowledge of the system and contacts within it. They are likely to know how to protect themselves and to identify investigative efforts.

Given resource inequality within organizations, internal enforcement, when present, is more likely to be directed at those lower in the organizational heirarchy. Those higher up usually have more information and are in a better position to defuse an investigation, or to retaliate, not to mention their formal and informal control over those carrying out an investigation. They are likely to have legitimate discretion which permits starting or stopping an investigation, this may mask cover ups. The issue of when (in the words of one agent) "to pull out the plug" as against when "to run out the string" is rarely formally reviewed. The folklore of some police and radicals is in agreement that investigations are likely to be stopped before they get to the really big fish in government.

Maurice Nadjari for example was appointed Special Prosecutor with responsibility for investigating corruption throughout the criminal justice system by Governor Rockefeller in 1972. (Nadjari 1977) He successfully prosecuted police and minor public officials. However his major cases involving high level politicians and the judiciary were dismissed (as was Nadjari).

Investigations may be subtly derailed in many ways and sometimes with competing moral justifications. The damage against letting an investigation continue once evidence against a corrupt official has been gathered may not be balanced by the lure of getting higher-ups. For example, in a controversial action at the end of his term, Mayor Ed Koch of New York refused to reappoint a corrupt city official as way of continuing an investigation. Koch viewed the reappointment of a known corrupt official as very damaging to the workings of government. The moral ambiguity is clear. Should a corrupt official be allowed to continue to profit from his position and to do harm, in the hope of building the strongest possible case and widening the net of those charged?

But among other less noble factors that may lead to the premature closing of an investigation of elites are fear of reprisals, the richness of the reward or favor that may be forthcoming as a result of cessation or a subtle warning, and concern over damaging legitimacy. The complexity of many such investigations and the fact that they may be of lengthy duration also increases the chance of leaks or accidental discovery. Also because of the sensitive circumstances a stronger predicate may be required to begin an investigation than is the case for those not in government.

Agressive actions are more likely to be taken by outsiders – whether organizationally or socially. To be effective internal authority must to some degree be insulated from the pressures that would corrupt it. In New York city once an officer works in Internal Affairs he or she can rarely go elsewhere in the department. The building is isolated and so are its members (even to the point of having to be promoted in secret so other members of the department won't know their identity). The absence of camaraderie from, and rejection by one's colleagues and their view of you as a rat, may take an enormous stress toll on those assigned to such units. This is compounded by a sense that higher authorities, regardless of their public pronouncement are ambivalent about your activities.

Cultural and psychological factors may work against the active pursuit of official rule breaking. As an embodiment of a society's values, leaders may be held in reverence and surrounded by an aura of the sacred (although this may be less true for the United States than for more traditional societies). There may be psychologically rooted inhibitions about challenging those in authority and suspecting ill of them; although that may be more true of Europe where there is a tradition of the strong state and greater fear of what would happen if it is weakened.

There is probably a cultural tilt toward wanting to believe that officials are good. If not 100% pure, they are seen to have a very hard job to do and to need all the support they can get. Everrett Hughes (1962) in an important article on "good people and dirty work" develops this argument. Some official violations are seen to be "necessary", or at least unavoidable in the pursuit of important social goals. The expression "its a tough job, but somebody's got to do it" captures this. Moderate rule breaking and rule bending can also be seen as rewards or perks for those in high status positions.

Even when the above factors are absent, the collusive nature of many official violations operates against discovery and prosecution. For example with political corruption there is usually no complainant and the damage is diffused. Such cases tend to lack a "smoking gun".

With respect to bribes three important situations can be identified. The first and most common ("back-scratching") involves a willing, even joyful exchange among a bribe offerer and receiver. Both wear black hats (although given the official power of the person in government, a hint of extortion hangs over many such relationships).(7) In return for compensation, the bribed person agrees to deliver a contract, provide inside information, withhold information, fix a case, introduce legislation, vote a particular way or otherwise act to advance the payee's interests. While the public may be victimized, both parties get what they want and neither is likely to come forward to complain. This is the quintessential economic relationship, it just happens that the currency is corruption. This serves the interests of the involved parties, but has costs for the public at large.

The symmetry in the above contrasts with the asymmetry in situations where a bribe is requested or offered. In the latter ("citizens bearing gifts") bribes are offered to those with authority. They may accept for obvious reasons. Again the mutually enriched parties enter into a conspiracy of silence.

But even when the bribe is refused, the appropriate authorities are unlikely to be informed. The bribe refuser may conclude that since the offer was rejected, no real harm was done. Norms of reciprocity also work against reporting such crimes (i.e. turning in someone who offers you a gift and who defines it as a token of appreciation, "here's a little something for you, a show of good faith and support").

In the third form, "the coercive power of office", the source is a demand for payment from the office-holder, rather than a citizen-initiated offer. Yet this too, is usually unreported. The target of the briber or extorter may be offended, but none-the-less go along because the latter's cooperation is needed, or out of intimidation. Even if the individual refuses to pay, the fear of retaliation may be great enough to prevent reporting. A further constraint on reporting is that many of those victimized by this type of corruption are themselves involved in illegal and/or morally discrediting activities. They do not want to call attention to themselves and, with their potentially impugnable reputations are unlikely to be believed, relative to the claims of a government official.

Finally, even rejected asymmetrical corrupt proposals may not be reported for some of the same reasons that other violations are under reported – a belief that reporting will do no good, fear of retaliation, and a desire to avoid unwanted publicity and entanglements.

Yet as we noted in Section I there are also factors encouraging efforts at internal control. Organizations differ in the amount and kind of resources they devote to internal control. However lacking government may be in some ideal sense, it appears to devote relatively greater resources to internal control when compared to many other institutions (e.g. universities). More abstractly we can hypothesize that the extent of resources devoted to inner control is dependent on factors such as:

1) The internal and external costs of rule violation.
2) The extent of opportunities for rule violation.
3) The visibility of the violation after-the-fact.
4) The extent to which organizational goals can be obtained by following the rules.
5) The degree of professionalization.
6) The relative size and power of external organizations charged with enforcement with respect to the organization.
7) The relative heterogeneity and extent of stratification within the organization.
8) The type of organization.

However, precisely because of the hidden quality of such violations and the incentives and fears of the involved parties, if police are actively to enforce anti-corruption laws other means such as informers, infiltration, undercover traps and wiretaps are used. As Special Prosecutor Nadjari (1977) notes "the prosecutor who waits for clearly defined [corruption] cases to be brought before him will spend long days in mental repose." Let us consider the diversity of uses in recent cases within government.

SOME EXAMPLES

The secrecy associated with undercover investigations means that they can ensnarle unlikely persons. Serendipity sometimes means that police, (along with judges, legislators and college professors) unaware of who and what they are dealing with, are swept up in stings. Thus in New York a police officer was arrested in a fake insurance scheme when he paid to have his car stolen and an Atlantic City policeman was arrested when he sold his badge and motorcycle to a property sting run by the New Jersey State Police. (Marx, 1988) But our concern here is with undercover means directed against those in criminal justice.

There is an important distinction between using covert means in a targeted fashion in response to intelligence (predicated use) which suggests that a crime is occurring and routinely using them absent specific suspicions (open-ended use). Predicated uses are a traditional tactic, even if police are often reluctant to apply them internally. What is new is the willingness of some departments to now use undercover tactics as a routine part of the inspection process.

Targeted uses are common during the periodic reform periods that police departments experience. Thus O.W. Wilson in Chicago, in response to claims that police were stealing welfare checks and shaking down motorists had internal affairs agents secretly watch suspects and his agents posed as motorists to see if they would be

G.T. MARX

shaken down. William Parker, the reform chief in Los Angeles, came to his position after serving as head of internal affairs. It was widely believed that he used his information from secret investigations as a way to have informal and formal leverage over the department. (Woods 1973)

The Knapp Commission and Patrick Murphy in New York City also made effective use of the tactic. (The Knapp Commission 1972) The Knapp Commission was appointed in 1970 to investigate police corruption, officers facing corruption charges agreed to work undercover against their former colleagues. Police corruption was found to be systematic and widespread. The Commission rejected the "bad apple" theory of corruption in which the problem is seen to be one of a few bad individuals who somehow managed to slip through, in favor of an approach which looked at police organization and culture as factors which supported corruption.

In response, under Police Commissioner Patrick Murphy the department instituted a variety of reforms aimed at *preventing,* as well as investigating corruption. The extra ordinary enforcement challenge posed by police who are criminals was seen to require innovative approaches. The department routineized complex sting operations. An undercover capability (previously available only to narcotics and organized crime units) was added to the Internal Affairs Division.

"Field internal affairs units" within borough headquarters subjecting officers to random integrity tests were created. A "field associates" program, designed to break the "code of silence" was also set up in which hundreds of officers assigned to regular duty secretly agree to report on corruption among their colleagues. The goal is prevention, as well as general intelligence to assess a problem.

Integrity tests are used absent specific suspicions. Police are warned they may be subjected to various tests at any time. The warning is intended to deter violations by creating fear that any corrupt offer might be other than what it appears to be. The tests carried out by members of internal affairs may take a number of forms – an interacial couple asking a police officer for information, a person turning over cash they claim they found, or a confused drunk with a fat wallet.

The largest New York city corruption investigation since the Knapp Commission in the early 1970s (Commission 1972) was in 1986 in Brooklyn's 77th Precinct. Thirteen officers were suspended following an investigation. The officers are alleged to have taken cash and drugs from addicts and dealers. A drug dealer who complained was wired and he gathered evidence against two officers. In the "domino" process common to undercover investigations, under threat of prison the two officers were then wired and gathered evidence against their colleagues. (McAlary 1988)

In Los Angeles a tip from an FBI informer passed on to the police department led to the setting of a trap that caught two members of a special burglary unit.(8) After an initial investigation, a fake burglary situation was created and the suspects took the bait and were arrested. The arrested officers had an ideal situation for continually committing crime. They were part of a special burglar alarm response unit. After responding to the alarms, the officers would then pilfer the store themselves. They were believed to trip the alarms of stores specializing in expensive electronic equipment and then respond to the alarms. Investigators turned the tables and set off an alarm at one such store. They then watched as the two officers made several trips carrying out cash and expensive goods which had been treated to leave an indelible, invisible mark on anyone who touched them. In later searches of their homes and those of several other suspects, authorities seized almost a truckload worth of electronic equipment.

Some departments use stings as part of a procedural audit to be sure that rules are being followed. The idea is to create a secret test to see if policies are correctly carried out. Thus after civil rights groups complained that Long Beach, California police supervisors were ignoring complaints of police misconduct which were phoned in, agents secretly called in complaints, and monitored their treatment. The rationale is clearly expressed by police commander Billy Thomas, "it did get the attention of the personnel here, in that they never know who is on the other end of the phone." (Law Enforcement News June 15, 1990).

The potential for corruption is particularly rich in agencies charged with licensing, inspection and regulation. A significant amount of discretion, a heavy workload, lack of resources for full enforcement and lack of public visibility are conducive to influence purchasing and peddling and compromised enforcement. The value of discretion to the corrupt official is greatly enhanced when delays can cost vast sums, as with construction. Bribes may be used to obtain expedited treatement. They may also of course be used to more directly hurt the public.

New York City's Commission of Investigation has pioneered in using covert techniques in this area. In its "Operation Ampscam" for example more than half of the 26 employees of the New York City Bureau of Electrical Control, the agency that inspects electrical installations, were arrested after a 14-month investigation. (N.Y.T. June 8, 1984) Two bogus electrical companies were set up and investigators pretended to have done work at buildings supposedly being rehabilitated, yet the buildings had dangling wires, water deposits, and lack of grounding. Payoffs were accepted in return for licenses. In another part of the operation, agents posed as inspectors and arrested contractors who paid bribes.

In "Operation Undertow" eight undercover investigators – six pretending to be car owners who owed unpaid fines and two posing as employees, gathered evidence that workers at a New York City car pound solicited and accepted cash from persons who wished to retrieve their vehicles without paying outstanding traffic tickets. (N.Y.T. Mar. 15, 1985)

In an audit example an investigator filed a fraudulent disability claim which demonstrated how easy it was to cheat the city's pension fund. He faked a back injury and used the X-rays of another person with an actual injury. He was then filmed lifting heavy boxes and playing paddleball. Doctors on the pension medical board were told about the films, but they none-the-less granted the disability claim. A report based on this case did not charge the doctors with wrongdoing and noted that they did not have time to adequately review the many cases they handled at their weekly meetings. The report recommended a number of policy changes. (Boston Globe, April 15, 1982)

A related topic is citizens' and private groups use of covert means against police. Publicity around the tactic and the availability of powerful, easily hidden audio and video recording devices evens up the odds in a sense. They can offer evidence of official misconduct that might not be believed were it just the citizen's word against an official. In this sense there is a democratization of surveillance.

In a controversial Long Beach, California case a black police sergeant, Don Jackson in conjunction with the Los Angeles Police Misconduct Lawyers Referral Service, ran a private sting which was videotaped and nationally televised. In the incident he and a colleague were stopped by two white officers, unaware of his identity. One of the officers used profanity when the sergeant at first refused an order to raise his hands above his head. After he finally did so, the officer rammed his head through a store front window. In their police report the officers said that the sergeant cursed at them and made threatening gestures. After the video tape was shown, one of the officers acknowledged that the report contained inaccuracies. Charges were dismissed, to the dismay of the Long Beach Police Department who felt that they were set up. The arresting officers were themselves arrested. The sergeant hopes to "export [his] activities nationwide" and he reports he will consult "with various civil rights leaders as to which are the worst areas and I'm going to set these things up anywhere and everywhere I can." (Law Enforcement News, Feb. 14, 1989)

The Grand Jury system offers a powerful tool for conviction, although not always for the initial offence of interest. Thus Paul Rao, a Chief Judge of the Federal Customs Court in New York was indicted for perjury in a simulated robbery case. An acquaintance, acting in an undercover capacity, asked him to help the son of a friend who was supposedly in trouble. The judge suggested that the agent see "a lawyer [who] knew the judge." He recommended his own son as the lawyer. Rao was called before a grand jury a year later and denied making that statement. A special grand jury indicted him for perjury. (Marx 1988 and Gershman 1981)

Operation Corkscrew an investigation into alleged municipal judicial corruption in Cleveland is a classic example of how not to carry out an investigation. (Report of the Subcommittee 1984) The story is one of incompetence and exploitation by an unwitting and then a witting informer. Marvin Bray, a court bailiff, did not know that two men hanging around the court who expressed an interest in bribing judges to fix cases were really FBI agents. Bray bragged that he had two judges in his pocket and agreed to set up payoff meetings. Over an 8-month period he held a series of tape-recorded meetings between the two "judges" and the agents. The FBI paid out $85,000. The "judges" did not know that the fixers were really FBI agents and the FBI agents did not know that the judges were really imposters. Bray has persuaded two friends to pose as judges. They were told that *they* were part of an undercover investigation to protect the judges and to combat corruption. One of the imposters, a man in his thirties, impersonated a judge who was 68.

Once Bray realized that they had been dealing with government agents he fled. The FBI located him and he convinced them that there really was corruption in the court and that he could help them gather evidence by directly approaching judges. He did not document any corruption, but the case demonstrates how a tape can be misused to make it appear that a target has committed a crime. With the hidden tape recorder on Marvin Bray asked a judge to revoke an arrest order for a friend who had missed a scheduled court appearance. The judge agreed to this routine request. Bray then left the judge's quarters and later said into the tape: "that envelope on the table is for you, judge." He then presented the tape as evidence that the judge had accepted a bribe in return for revoking the order. The investigation was closed. Bray was indicted but no judges were, although they were stigmatized by the publicity the case received.

Operation Greylord in Chicago which targeted judges and lawyers in Cook County's judicial system was a much more professional investigation. (N.Y.T. Aug. 12, 1983 and Tuohy and Warden 1987) Greylord is a reference to the wigs used by British judges. FBI agents posed as arrested criminals and as lawyers, and a state judge cooperated by wearing a tape recorder hidden in his cowboy boot. The investigation focused on payoffs between lawyers, police officers and judges suspected of having fixed cases in the past.

Finally let us briefly consider two undercover corruption investigations outside the criminal justice system, which raise some common issues. We will compare the use of undercover tactics against elected officials in the Abscam (Abdullah Scam) and Corcom (Corrupt Commissioners) investigations. Abscam involved FBI agent Anthony Amoroso posing as a sheik with immigration problems who sought to purchase political influence. (Select Committee 1983)

Abscam begain on Long Island in 1978 and went on for two years. It began as an inquiry into stolen art and securities and ended as an investigation of political corruption. When a subject spoke of his ability to influence politicians, the focus of the investigation changed. As a Senate Committee of inquiry observed: "Abscam was virtually unlimited in geographic scope, persons to be investigated and criminal activity to be investigated . . . [it] was in practical effect, a license for several agents to assume false identities, to create a false business front, and to see what criminal activities could be detected or developed throughout the country. (Select Committee 1983)

Abscam stands out because it was not in response to allegations about particular individuals, or in response to known offences. It used Mel Weinberg who had been involved in the use of stolen credit cards, income tax evasion and fraud as the principle informant. It also made extensive use of unwitting informers who had a strong financial incentive to draw in subjects who there was no prior reason to suspect were corrupt. This contrasts with prior corruption investigations that usually involved either a person from whom a bribe is demanded, playing along under police supervision, or a "turned" suspect who agrees to cooperate. The subjects attended secretly videotaped meetings believing they were coming to discuss campaign contributions. A script was followed in which in return for help with his problems the sheik would make various "gifts".

There were a number of Abscam cases and these raised somewhat different issues. One involves how persistent agents should be after a subject initially refuses. In the case of Senator Harrison Williams agents persisted until he finally accepted money, after twice rejecting their suggestions. He was led to believe that he would not have to take any illegal action. The main informant coached him in what to say, practically putting words in his mouth: "you gotta tell him how important you are, and you gotta tell him in no uncertain terms without me, there is no deal. I'm the man who's gonna open the doors. I'm the man who's gonna do this and use my influence, and I guarantee this." The senator was then assured that nothing wrong was happening: "it goes no further. It's all talk, all bullshit. It's a walk-through. You gotta just play and blow your horn."

In the case of two city councilmen in Philadelphia, George Schwartz and Harry Jannotti, the bribe was presented as necessary to a much broader plan to help rebuild their financially troubled city. They were told that in accordance with the "Arab mind" and "Arab way of doing business" that they had to convince the investors that they had friends in high places. In order to do this, money had to be accepted from the investors. The defendants were not asked to offer any commitments or to do anything improper, contingent on accepting the payment. The situation was structured so that acceptance of the money would be seen as payment for consulting services. Neither of the defendants asked for money, and both indicated that no payment was necessary. They were simply told that the project would not come to the city if they did not accept the sheik's "gift. While in Abscam all those arrested were convinced, other standards must be considered beyond strict legality.

In contrast CorCom which resulted in guilty findings against more than 200 county commissioners in Oklahoma in 1981 for taking kickbacks was more focused. A lumber-mill owner agreed to cooperate and secretly recorded 110 taped conversations with vendor colleagues, many of who admitted their complicity. A building materials salesman who testified that he had made 8,400 payoffs worth over $1 million to county officials secretly videotaped his dealings with commissioners in an Oklahoma City Hotel room. In contrast to Abscam, a U.S. attorney observes "we simply had Moore do business like he had for 28 years." (Newsweek, Sept. 21, 1981) There was a clear predicate for the corrupt temptations presented to targets – they were known to have previously had corrupt dealings. It would be difficult to claim that the crime was an artifact of the investigation nor that the corrupt nature was not clear. The investigation was carried out in a "natural" environment rather than an artificially created one.

IV. CONSEQUENCES COSTS AND CHOICES

In this section we consider the difficulty of evaluating the use of covert means in corruption cases, some preventive measures that would lessen the need to rely on them and some broad policy issues faced by a democratic society in its efforts to guard the guards.

There have been no efforts to systematically evaluate the government's use of undercover tactics against itself.(9) Unlike a fencing sting which involves many roughly similar cases over a period of time and for which before, during and after measures of reported crime are available, the corruption cases vary greatly among themselves. Since corruption is rarely reported, there are no easy measures of deterrence or prevention.

Evaluation measures for corruption cases have a type of face-validity. If clear evidence of serious wrongdoing is found and guilty verdicts are returned then they are presumed to have worked (assuming the violations are not simply an artifact of the investigation). This of course does not tell us whether they are more effective than some other measures, or have a deterrent impact. The impact may be significant at first and later diminish. The "wise" may learn to negate the controls – through special tests and language, indirect payments, payments abroad, or when an official retires etc. Knowledge that undercover tactics are in use may keep some from breaking the law, but it may simply make others more clever and careful. There is likely significant variation in outcomes. For example most observers agree that following the reforms and publicity of the Knapp Commission systematic widespread corruption in New York City stopped, even though pockets resurfaced. In contrast in Philadelphia reforms seem to have had less impact. There is a clear need for research here.

Even if the tactic "works" in a particular case in the sense that offenders are identified and prosecuted, such control can be seen as merely a bandaid or tourniquet, stopping the bleeding by external pressure, but having no impact on the source of the problem. Apprehension of an offender whether through undercover, or other means suggests a failure of social control – the damage has likely already been done. In most of the cases considered here government is simply picking up the pieces after-the-fact.

The U.S. attorney in the Corcom cases observes, "we can win all these cases, but if the system isn't changed, we've lost the war. It would be business as usual unless the legislature adopted new laws." (N.Y.T. Oct. 12, 1981) Actions taken to lessen the likelihood of corruption include: limits on campaign contributions and spending; public financing of election campaigns; disclosure laws; restrictions on political party leaders, legislators, and former officials going into a related private business immediately upon leaving government; higher salaries; stricter rules for competitive bidding; centralized purchasing; better accounting and audit procedures; a requirement that bribe offers be reported; and independent ethics committees with enforcement powers.

Disclosure rules are important because they may deter, or if not followed, offer a means for pursuing an investigation. In cases where prosecutors have other grounds for suspicion, but are unable to prove a bribe, they may still pursue a suspect for not disclosing questionable contributions or sources of income. One way to overcome the difficulty in discovering violations is to have laws, or internal policies requiring that bribe offers be reported.

On the other hand such rules can create a new resource to threaten people with – claiming a bribe offer was made when it wasn't. Such a requirement might create perjury on the part of the agent who ignores a bribe offer and later, if challenged, defends himself by denying the offer was ever made. Such requirements can also result in integrity tests being taken to a new extreme: targets may face double testing – initially to see if they will accept a corrupt offer and, then to see if they will report the offer. Individuals may become targets of an undercover trap not because they are suspected of wrongdoing, but to see if bribes are reported and other procedural rules are followed. This may offer a means to get rid of an employee whose performance is satisfactory, but who is disliked by a supervisor.

With respect to police, careful selection, adequate pay, anti-corruption training, more intensive field supervision and having sergeants present when arrests are made, a de facto policy of non-enforcement for minor offences likely to give rise to problems; a policy of requiring two people to be present during situations that are most likely to give rise to allegations of corruption (meetings with an informant, counting money, male-female encounters). Paper audit trails, audio and video recording, polygraphs and drug-tests are also used. Some departments have a rule which requires employees to immediately report any misconduct they are personally aware of, or any allegations of misconduct that they hear of. Failure to make such notification constitutes misconduct.

More effective prosecution (and less need for it) might follow from local equivalents of the federal Special Prosecutor, appointed by legislatures or attorney generals and from the establishment of inspector general's offices at the municipal and state levels.

Tougher criminal and civil penalties, increased provision, protection and rewards for whistle-blowers and informers might have some preventive effect. The law might be changed to make it easier to offer proof of corruption. If public officials were prohibited from taking anything of value from those they have regulatory jurisdiction over, it would be unnecessary to prove the often elusive concept of "corrupt motive" for purposes of prosecution. Specific legal presumptions could be written into the criminal law to indicate prima facie evidence of corrupt intent, e.g., any transaction of public business in a covert fashion, as with Abscam. A well publicized policy of prosecuting citizens who pay bribes, or fail to report such requests (rather than only officials who demand them) might have preventive impact. Laws that made it easy for citizens to recover damages from officials whose false reports or perjurious testimony contributes to detention, imprisonment, or prosecution could be adopted.

Given the special issues that are present, should investigations of official rule breaking, whether in the criminal justice system or among elected officials, involve a different standard than for investigations of citizens? If so, should the standard be more or less restrictive than is the case for general investigations?

Should the special advantages, powers and temptations that come with official positions subject their occupants to a voluntary waiving of privacy expectations? As a condition of office and a form of *noblis oblige*, should they agree to things such as periodic random integrity tests and public filing of income tax statements?(10) Boxers' fists are considered to be lethal weapons and lobbyists must register and report certain actions. Should there also be restrictions and special conditions on those in government such as elected officials and judges?

On the other hand, one might argue that because the risks of misuse are greater, undercover policy should go in the other direction when it is used in government (or against certain persons such as judges or elected officials). More stringent standards involving special internal review and a warrant could be required before undercover means are used against those in government.(11)

Some additional consequences

Apart from direct impact, using covert tactics internally may have other mixed and paradoxical consequences. Just because a policy may work and is legal, it does not follow that it is a wise policy. Covert anticipatory means have a price tag not found with conventional overt tactics, such as interviews and forensic analysis carried out after a violation has occurred.

Undercover tactics, regardless of the context in which they are used, raise troubling issues such as the possible creation of crimes that are an artifact of the investigation, the direction of resources from known to possible offences, police becoming criminals, the tangled web of interaction that can follow deception, the setting of bad examples by the state, the invasion of privacy and the creation of climates of suspicion and fear. When the state uses the tactic against itself the danger of political targeting is clear and there may be unintended threats to legitimacy.

The undercover tactic offers a resource which the unscrupulous can use against their rivals and taken to an extreme, can involve a kind of civil war between the branches of government.(12) Secrecy and the ability to tempt and manipulate may make it possible to present evidence of seeming violation. Even when there are fair grounds for an investigation, political issues may arise with respect to the timing of the inquiry and arrests. If done too close to an election, charges of partisanship may arise.(13)

Relative to offences such as theft and homicide, corruption is not only harder to discover, it is also generally harder to define, and easier to justify. The norms of a free enterprise, democratic society encourage wheeling and dealing and give and take. They support negotiation and persuasion. This can mean some persons back into committing technical violations without the intent to commit a crime. It can also mean greater ease in manipulating an individual into committing an offence than is the case for most other violations. For elected officials, the line between political contributions and buying favors and extortion can be thin. It is often not clear just what money buys – access or influence. This of course also offers protection for those wishing to commit crimes under color of serving constituents and responsive leadership. The language used may mask the essence of the transaction. It also makes it easier to justify. The accused often testify that they gave money as a gift, or a political contribution, not as a bribe and sometimes they are telling the truth. Yet those in office must be sensitive to the appearance of misconduct, as well as the reality.

The routine discretion in the enforcement role, the breadth of criminal laws such as conspiracy and the legitimate imperative to follow up on suggestions of illegality (which can be secretly contrived by agents wishing to carry out an injury) can mask the political motivation that may lie behind an investigation.

These dangers can be minimized by appropriate policies for targeting and carrying out an investigation. The FBI for example requires a special high level review of all "sensitive" cases, a category which includes any investigation of an important political figure. There are restrictions on how tempting an offer can be (it shouldn't exceed what would be found in the real world) and on how many times a target can be approached. Some investigations can be structured so that those drawn in self-select, rather than their being directly targeted.

Even absent political targeting, the expanded use of the tactic to deal with corruption has led to unintended consequences and conflict among agencies with similar goals. The tables may get turned and the original police targets seek to arrest those trying to arrest them. For example in a case in Bridgeport, Connecticut, as part of an FBI corruption investigation, an informer offered a $5,000 bribe to the superintendent of police, who at first pretended to be interested. However as the bribe was to be passed, the superintendent rejected it and arrested the informer. He latter sought to have the FBI agents involved arrested for bribery. The FBI in turn threatened to have him arrested on obstruction-of-justice charges. The FBI demanded its money and bugging equipment back, while Bridgeport officials wanted to give the $5,000 to charity. (N.Y.T. Aug. 21, 1981)

In what the sheriff of Galveston County, Texas, called "the sting that got stung," a man approached sheriff's deputies with an offer to "buy protection" for a cocaine-smuggling operation. He offered to pay $75,000 in bribes to three county officials. The sheriff's department in response set up its own undercover operation for what it thought was a major drug-smuggling operation. After several meetings, the bearer of the bribe was arrested and spent the night in jail. The sheriff's department sought to prosecute the agent, but the district attorney was unwilling. County officials gave the FBI a $7,000 bill for expenses incurred in their part of the investigation. (Marx 1988) Such keystone cop fiascos generate bad publicity and may harm cooperation between agencies. There is also the risk that competing agencies will make illegitimate use of covert means as part of interagency struggles. Even if it doesn't come to that, inter-organizational strains may be created and cooperation among agencies that need each other may be reduced.

Do such investigations help or hurt legitimacy? Law enforcement leaders publicly proclaim that internal investigations show that the agency is vigilant and can control itself. Aggressive internal uses can send a message to the public that the agency is honest and will not tolerate abuses. As such they may increase confidence in government and law abiding behavior.

Public images of the honesty of social control agents is likely to affect the public's behavior. Internal enforcement has symbolic communications consequences. It may increase public confidence in government. Elected officials, judges and police are role models and parental figures. When they are viewed as moral exemplars and beyond rapproach, there is probably less violation of the rules they are charged with enforcing and public cooperation is greater. There are both moral and practical reasons for this.

Practically, citizens may not report violations if police are seen as corrupt. They may believe that to do so would do no good, or that they would be subject to retaliation. That belief may encourage law breaking.

Morally, the belief that authority is corrupt can be a powerful "neutralization technique". Sykes and Matza (1957) note that cultural restraints against violations are weakened by beliefs such as "everyone is doing it", – when that belief extends to authorities, it becomes even easier to justify rule breaking. How serious could the rule be, if even those charged with enforcing it don't honor it? While dynamic and democratic societies need a degree of skepticism and cynicism, they don't need that kind.

Yet corruption patterns are complex. They reflect citizen attitudes and expectations, as well as those of police. There are likely limits on what administrative reforms can accomplish in the short run, when public attitudes are indifferent to or supportive of traditional corruption. Without an aroused citizenry exerting pressure on political leaders and unwilling to tolerate corruption, change will be modest.

Ironically corruption investigations may serve to decrease legitimacy as well. This involves the mythology around the sacred. Some citizens may conclude that if a few in government are revealed as corrupt, that many more are as well. They may see an investigation as only the visible part of the iceberg and see the revealed evidence as a sign of how bad things really are. Those arrested may be viewed as scapegoats and the investigation a kind of periodic window dressing. Anything that creates negative publicity for the regime may be seen to harm the public. The example of the government using devious means can also serve to legitimate lying among the public.

With respect to internal morale, the tactic is again likely to have contradictory consequences. For the honest it may be welcomed as way to clean up a problem and to improve the image of the department or institution. Knowledge that undercover investigations are common could help keep people honest and can help them resist peer pressure to participate.

On the other hand it can also lower internal morale, if targeting is done on a basis perceived to be unfair (e.g. directed against political opponents or those a supervisor doesn't like, rather than the worst offenders). It can further the gap between employees and management. The view that "they are out to get us and they don't trust, appreciate or understand us" is not conducive to the best performance. Aggressive efforts at internal control may even create challenges in which employees in effect say "if by your actions you imply that you don't trust me and treat me like a potential criminal when I work hard and risk my life, then I'll show you." An expression found in some police departments is "you got the name, play the game." Given the complexity of the law enforcement situation and pressures on police to produce, some internal enforcement efforts may seem from the police perspective (as put by a Los Angeles sheriff's deputy) to be "like hiring a guy to be a mechanic, and then they don't want you to be greasy." Police unions have attacked field associate programs as being "unAmerican".

Even police leaders of unimpeachable personal integrity tend to prefer to approach such problems piecemeal and to see corrupt officers simply dismissed, rather than to have extensive investigations and drawn-out trials. The desire to avoid bad publicity is one factor and the protection of higher level colleagues is another. An experienced undercover officer in New York who spent his career investigating his colleagues eventually concludes "I wasn't cop hunter; I was a public relations man." He states "we would never come close to eliminating police corruption unless we busted through two walls. The Blue Wall that surrounded the entire department was formidable enough, but there was a much stronger Brass Wall protecting the inner enclave, guarding the reputations and careers and pensions of the members of a very exclusive club." (Murano 1990, p. 239)

It is an American truism that effective government requires free and open exchange. Yet diplomacy and secrecy have a place as well, particularly in the early stages of policy. These would be damaged if undercover tactics were used on a much wider and more indiscriminate scale. When individuals believe that they are constantly being watched and may be tested at any point, conformity may increase as candor, spontaneity, innovation, and risk-taking decline. Organizations need to encourage flexibility and a confident encountering of their environment. But the fear that any colleague might be an informer, that any conversation recorded, or that secret integrity tests are rampant may encourage a pulling inward and passivity. While it is understandable, the sentiment expressed by former Special Prosecutor Maurice Nadjari "if we cannot have absolutely honest public officials, then let's have frightened public officials" must give one pause.

The case of Washington D.C. Mayor Marion Barry nicely illustrates some of the above issues. (N.Y.T. June 27, 1990 and Marx, 1991) Barry was lured to a police arranged meeting with a former girl friend. After he purchased and used drugs she provided, he was arrested on a misdemeanor possession charge.

Barry was widely believed to be a user of illegal drugs and many of those close to him had been indicted on corruption charges. An official who is thought to flagrantly violate the standards he is charged with enforcing communicates cynicism and hypocrisy. The behavior of leaders is not only instrumental, it is also educational and symbolic. Were law enforcement authorities to apply a more restrictive standard before a political figure became the target of an undercover investigation, they might be accused of favoritism and corruption themselves. It would be wrong for authorities not to pursue allegations of wrong doing, regardless of whom they implicate. The issue is in how those are pursued. The Barry case illustrates a number of questions about the uses of undercover tactics in political cases.

Some questions apply regardless of whether or not the target is in government: is it wise to focus scarce resources on occasional users rather than dealers? Shouldn't authorities try to prevent crime rather than to facilitate it? Or if the latter, shouldn't they seek to minimize it (in this case intervening after cocaine was purchased, but before it was used)? If a case for indictment can not be made before a grand jury, or before a judge for permission to search, wiretap or bug, is it appropriate to move to an undercover temptation for which there is no legal minimum threshold, particularly when a political figure from a minority group is involved?

Some observers perceive a discriminatory pattern in which scarce federal resources have been disproportionately focused on minority government officials. The Barry case appeared to some observers to be a witch hunt in which the government went to great lengths to find evidence against Barry. It was unable to find sufficient evidence to obtain a warrant or to indict. It then turned to the undercover tactic, for which there is no legal requirement, and it further traded in, what is to some observers the cheap currency of intimate relations.

The prosecutor who directed the case announced the highly publicized arrest three days before he himself announced that he was running for office. It also appears that the criminal law was being used not for prosecution, but as a resource to negotiate a political end. The prosecutor hinted he would exchange leniency in return for the Mayor's resignation.

215

The case also has symbolic aspects, with Barry being from a minority group and most of the enforcers from the dominant group. When law enforcement resorts to trickery and exploits intimate relations to make a misdemeanor arrest it communicates something. In the well honored words of Justice Holmes "for my part I think it less evil that some criminals should escape than that the government should play an ignoble part."(14) In publicly using deception the government sets an example which may serve to increase the use of deception by citizens against each other.

The future enters silently and with small, scattered, almost invisible steps. But these are cumulative and gradually forge a path. It is important that we anticipate and direct that path, rather than being at the mercy of an unseen accretive process. In the search for violations and more equitable enforcement, authorities are covering fresh ground. Certain institutions and activities have a sacred and/or private quality and should not be trifled with, absent extreme cause. Yet in the past decade we have seen incidents of police posing as priests, newspaper reporters, lawyers, psychologists, lovers and students; of their selling drugs, distributing pornography, and running casinos and houses of prostitution. Covert operations have been carried out in our most allowed institutions – churches, elections, courts and legislatures. False affidavits have been filed, sworn agents of the state have lied under oath and judge's chambers have been bugged. The significance of most of the above does not lie in their frequency, but in their break with the past. It is important to be aware of the precedents that may be created.

A story is told of a young rural couple who are taking the train for the first time. They ask the conductor if it will be on time. He looks up and down the track, pauses and finally answers "that depends." They ask "what does it depend on?" He again looks up and down the track and waits an even longer period of time and then responds "that depends too." It is the same with the use of covert means. Whether or not they are appropriate depends.

Among factors that this should depend on are the seriousness of the offence, the strength of the predicate for initiating the investigation, the availability of alternative means, the degree of intrusion and the nature of the betrayal, the extent to which use of the tactic casts government in a bad moral light, the cost of taking no action, the skill of the operatives and the liklihood that the deception will be publicly judged in court. In general covert means (whether used by government internally or externally) should be tactics of last resort, used with great caution after careful review and by agencies with the requisite skills, resources and controls.

Even then, there are times when it is better to do nothing. The choice between anarchy and repression is not a happy one. An important characteristic of our society is that means, as well as ends, have a moral component. In the *Merchant of Venice* Shakespeare advises that "to do a great right, do a little wrong." Were the government to direct a widespread campaign of deception and temptation against white-collar offenders, great things could undoubtedly be accomplished. But when intrusive and secret tactics are at hand, more is at stake than the immediate goal. There is no guarantee that the ratio would not quickly be reversed – to great wrong yielding little right. Covert practices involve short and long run risks that are not found with more conventional tactics. Their significance goes far beyond any given case. Secret behavior and surveillance go to the heart of the kind of society we are or might become.

Notes

1. Of course in a strict sense it is self-regulation only if done within the same organizational structure. However law enforcement is a relatively homogeneous world in which feelings of solidarity commonly transcend organizational boundaries and operational interdependence often occurs.
2. Ironically, corrupt regimes often have very strong means of internal control, since the ruler's power rests so clearly on the guards whose loyalty is essential. However the goal is not to see that the rule of law is enforced, but to look for disloyalty and even the failure to share ill gotten gains.
3. This section draws from Marx (1988).
4. U.S. v. Turkette, 101 S. CT. 2524 (1981).
5. An impetus to the creation of the FBI was congressional anger over a Justice Department investigation of corruption in Congress. In an effort to prevent such investigations the congress prohibited the Justice Department (which had no agents of its own at the turn of the century) from borrowing agents from other federal agencies. That led the Justice Department to create its own detective force – the FBI, against the wishes of congress. (Cummings and McFarland, 1937, Whitehead, 1956, Ungar, 1975) Following Abscam there were congressional calls for restricting the FBI. One FBI agent believes that "the congressional probes which followed Abscam were aimed more at the investigators than at the corrupt officials under investigation, and the guidelines which resulted really amount to an implicit OFF button." (Welch and Marston, 1984, p. 278).
6. In general it is easier for federal prosecutors to make such cases. Federal laws and evidentiary rules have greatly aided this. Prosecutors can gather evidence from grand jury witnesses without granting them total immunity, as local prosecutors are required to do. Indictments and convictions can be obtained on conspiracy charges with less proof than is required in a state court. The witness protection program which permits federal informants to begin a new life elsewhere is also a factor, as is the broad geographical and social network federal investigators have.
7. As a Boston prosecutor put it "if the person taking the money is wearing a uniform and carrying a gun, I am unwilling to believe that doesn't influence the state of mind of the person paying the money – you have a built-in element of extortion."
8. This investigation was carried out by the Los Angeles Police Department. In other cases, partly as a result of a lack of faith in a department's ability to investigate itself, the FBI may choose not to pass on a tip and carry out the investigation itself.
9. For a useful typology based on an analysis of cases prosecuted under the Federal Ethics Act that identifies variables likely relevant to different outcomes see Harriger (1989).
10. Sherman (1983) for example advocates random testing under controlled circumstances. Even if the principle of randomness is accepted, its use might depend on an assessment of how wide spread the problem is believed to be and the specific information available. Randomness (as a tactic for apprehension) would make the most sense if it is believed that corruption is rampant, but there are no specific suspects. In contrast if the problem is thought to be focused and there are suspects it makes less sense. Other than for a vague faith in its deterrent power, it makes the least sense when there is no reason to suspect corruption and no specific suspects.
11. Wilson (1980) suggests such a warrant procedure. Yet introducing a restrictive standard such as probable cause means that the investigation must follow the contours of what authorities can obtain probable cause for. There is no reason to think that the probable cause available to authorities will conform to the degree of social harm from an offense, nor that it will contain less biases than those found with the traditional system of mobilizing the law in a reactive fashion. This defeats one of the main advantages of undercover means which is to find out if wrong doing is going on, in order to justify obtaining a warrant for searchs or electronic eavesdropping.
12. This contrasts with a checks and balances view, in which the prospect of occasional secret investigations by other branches or units is thought to create honesty. It can prevent cover-ups, oversights and lazyness. Italy with rival national police forces is cited as an example of the guards keeping each other honest, if at some overlap of function and increased expense. The same argument holds for competition among federal and local prosecutors.
13. In an interesting commentary some Congressmen have even been elected after having been arrested and found guilty.
14. In Olmstead v. U.S., 277 U.S. 438 (1928)

References

Cummings, H. and McFarland, C. 1937. *Federal Justice*. New York: Macmillan.

Gerson, N. 1977. *The Vidocq Dossier*. Boston: Houghton Mifflin.

Gershman, B. "The Perjury Trap" *Univ. of Pa. Law Review* Vol. 129: 624–700.

Hughes, E. 1962. "Good People and Dirty Work" *Social Problems* 10:3–10.

Commission to Investigate Allegations of Police Corruption and the City's Anti-Corruption Procedures, 1972. *The Knapp Commission Report on Police Corruption*. New York: G. Braziller.

Lardner, J. "How Prosecutor's Are Nabbed". *New Republic*. Jan. 29, 1977. pp. 22–25.

Law Enforcement News, June 15, 1990

Marx, G. 1988. *Undercover Police Surveillance in America*. Berkeley, California: Univ. of California Press.

McAlary, M. 1988. *Buddy Boys* New York Charter Books.

Murano, V. 1990 *Cop Hunter* (New York: Pocket Books).

Nadjari, M. "I have No Regrets". *New York Times Magazine*. Mar. 27, 1977.

President's Commission on Law Enforcement and Administration of Justice 1967. *The Challenge of Crime in a Free Society*. Washington D.C.: GPO.

President's National Advisory Commission on Civil Disorders. 1968. *Report of the National Advisory Commission on Civil Disorders*. Washington D.C.:. G.P.O.

Purvis, M. 1936. *American Agent*. New York: Garden City Publishing Report of the Subcommittee on Civil and Constitutional Rights 1984. *FBI Undercover Operations*. Washington: U.S. Gov. Printing Office.

Riley, W. 1982 "Confessions of a Harvard Trained G-Man," *Harvard Business School Bulletin (Oct.)*.

Select Committee to Study Law Enforcement Undercover Activities of Components of the Department of Justice 1983. Hearings, Law Enforcement Undercover Activities. Washington D.C.: GPO.

Sherman, L. 1980. "From Whodunit to Who Does It: Fairness and Target Selection in Deceptive Investigations." in *Abscam Ethics*. edited by G. Caplan, Cambridge, Ma.: Ballinger.

Stead, P. 1953. *Vidocq: Picaron of Crime*. London: Staples.

Sykes, G. and D. Matza. 1957. "Techniques of Neutralization: A Theory of Delinquency." *American Sociological Review* 22: 664–670.

Ungar, S. 1975. *The FBI*. Boston: Little, Brown.

Welch, N. and Marston, D.W. 1984. *Inside Hoover's FBI*. Garden City, N.Y.: Doubelday.

Whitehead, D. 1956. *The FBI Story*. New York: Random House.

Wilson, J. 1980. "The Changing FBI – The Road to Abscam," *The Public Interest*. (Spring) pp. 3–14.

J. Woods. 1973 *The Progressutralization: A Theory of Delinquency."* American Sociological Review 22: 664–670.

LOCAL GOVERNMENT FISCAL SCARCITY: ITS CONTEXT AND AN EXAMINATION OF THE PRODUCTIVITY ISSUE AMONG MUNICIPAL POLICE DEPARTMENTS

Robert D. Pursley

SUNY- College at Buffalo

ABSTRACT

The article reviews the fiscal crisis facing many units of local government. Using this as a focus, attention is then turned to the results of a limited national study of productivity-enhancement efforts among medium-size municipal police departments. The survey results indicate that these police agencies while acknowledging resource scarcity are not pursuing meaningful productivity efforts; they are merely adopting a variety of cost-containment strategies. The article discusses the nature of managerial and organizational impediments to productivity efforts among local police agencies.

INTRODUCTION: THE PROBLEM AND ITS CONTEXT

To many observers of the state and local government scene, the major problem government managers of the 1990s face are two interrelated issues: cost-containment and productivity (Ott et al., 1991). The concern is framed in the context of the existing fiscal crisis which faces many state and local governments. How can public services hold the line and productivity, especially worker productivity, be increased among public agencies? While the search for effective strategies is becoming a critical agenda item among policymakers and public managers, satisfactory answers are proving elusive. Associated with this concern is the need to restore some measure of citizen confidence in governmental operations and administration. Public opinion polls show that three-fourths of all Americans consider government services both wastefulful and unsatisfactory and public employees less productive than their private sector counterparts (Hyde, 1985).

While cost-containment and productivity concerns are found among all levels of government, attention to the problem seems more pronounced among local governments (Downs & Larkey, 1986). There are probably several reasons for this. Local taxes (and services) are proximate to the taxpaying public. In this way, taxpayers are almost daily reminded of the local tax burden and the services these provide. Such proximity also allows for closer and more frequent citizen-recipient oversight of the provision of public services. Associated with these factors one also encounters the coupling effect of local financing initiatives: the relative lack of alternatives other than the already overgenerated traditional revenue sources that local governments can tap to support their services and operations (Weir, 1987).

City governments are a good example. Municipalities find themselves increasingly caught between the dilemma of public expectations, rising costs for government programs and operations, and the lack of available resources to underwrite these costs (Reid, 1988). Even a service such as public safety, which because of its nature has traditionally avoided scruitiny, is coming in for a fair share of attention. There is justification for this. In many municipal budgets, public safety services ranks as one of the most costly outlays that communities have to support out of their own tax base.

In spite of concerns over government cost-containment and increased productivity there are some not so obvious impediments to these efforts by local governments. Some states have adopted statutes which serve to thwart efforts to reduce costs and/or increase public service output which are unrecognized by the general public. Often generated out of protective self-interest by powerful local political interest groups these are meaningful impediments to reform. Barriers to reform are also found in the expression of self-interests among groups of organized labor in those states with strong public sector unions.

The finacially strapped State of New York is illustrative. That state has no state law permitting local governments to merge or consolidate services. Existing legislation even prohibits counties in that state from providing basic services which state law says must be provided by towns. State legislation also mandates overtime compensation for many local government workers rather than allowing employers to award compensatory time. Under the provisions of that state's Taylor Law regulating collective bargaining among state and local government workers, local governments are prohibited from contracting with private service providers unless the affected unions agree. Any legislative initiative to overturn such laws are vigorously opposed by strong interests representing local public officials or public employee unions (Zremski & Simon, 1992). While most states do not face obstacles as drastic as New York, there still exists in many states an array of legal hurdles and self-interest opposition to reform efforts that serve to thwart local consolidation, intergovernmental cooperation efforts, service and cost-sharing undertakings, or generally increased govenment efficiency/productivity and cost-containment strategies.

STATE AND LOCAL GOVERNMENT SPENDING AND REVENUE PATTERNS

The root cause of the problem is the push-pull of citizen expectations, federally mandated social assistance programs and increased outlays in these areas, rising costs for general services, and the shrinking tax base. These have combined as critical factors affecting local financing. To understand the dilemma of local governments, one must look at the coupling effect of state and local government spending and revenue. The problems of local governments cannot be understood without simultaneously looking at what is happening among the states and how this affects local financing.

States' spending from their own tax resources for Medicaid and prisons have risen twice as fast as personal income since the mid-1970s (Joyce & Mullins, 1991). States are also incurring rising costs in such areas as capital infrastructure needs, the growth in federal mandates for the provision and funding of social assistance programs, and rising costs for unemployment compensation benefits. Many cash-starved states are also feeling the effects of public payrolls that have swollen over the years. Local governments are also simultaneously feeling the strain. Many communities are facing rising costs for education and local services which are also growing faster than the growth in disposable personal income and property tax-pegged real property appreciation. This explains why the focus in state and local tax analysis these days is focused on reforms that broaden the tax base and insulate vital services from the anticipated effects of lagging revenue growth.

Of major concern in this situation is the realization by local governments that they can no longer rely upon state governments for the kinds of assistance to which they have grown accustomed. There is a bit of irony here. In the late 1970s, state governments were being heralded as the leaders of the "new federalism": A situation in which states by virtue of their then healthy economic vitality would assume a leadership role in intergovernmental relations, including fiscal support. In this role, they could share their revenue largesse with local governments. Today, this situation is only a hollow memory. States are faced with increased service and program costs of their own. This coupled with the fact that there has been less state-directed help from Washington to support spiraling costs in such areas as Medicaid, AFDC and welfare costs is causing serious problems for state governments. States have had no choice under such circumstances, but to cut-back on aid to local governments. Also taking its toll is the fact that direct federal assistance in "pass-through" expenditures to local communities has also been sharply curtailed (Watson & Vocino, 1990).

This is just one side of the revenue generating problem. Much of the problem facing states and local communities today is brought about by their inability to generate taxpayer support for increased taxes coupled with traditional local government revenue and cost-of-services inelasticity. While costs continue upward, revenues are failing to keep apace (Roberts, 1992). We can see this tax opposition in the adoption and spread among local governments of local tax and expenditure limitations (Joyce & Mullins, 1991). As a result, many local governments are finding themselves "capped-out" at statutory tax limits. As a result of the economic downturn, there has also been, in many areas, the stagnation or erosion of real property values. Thus, local government's primary tax base, the property tax, has become stagnant or declining as a revenue source. This stagnation or actual decline in real property evaluation is proving to be a major problem for local governments' efforts to "capture" additional tax revenues through "indexed" tax increases; those increases are automatically pegged to real property appreciation without requiring voter approval for additional millage levies. There is also the issue of tax abatements on commercial properties that local governments have been forced to make to keep or attract firms. And as urban economists have pointed out, the widespread economic downturn in our nation's economy has also resulted in the stagnation or diminishment of other irreplaceable revenue sources: local sales, business, licensing, and corporate taxes (Rymarowicz & Zimmerman, 1988).

Faced with these problems, public officials have turned to "creative" efforts to impose new taxes and devise sources of additional revenue generation. What has been noticeable among students of local finance initiatives has been the "hidden incidence" of this trend. These have taken many forms: Drastic boosts in payroll taxes borne by both the wage earner and the employer, another penny or two in state (or often local-option sales taxes), increases in sumptuary taxes, the adoption of real estate transfer taxes, aggressive traffic enforcement policies as a revenue raiser, surcharges on litigation and court costs, a constantly upward creep in gasoline taxes, and the growing imposition of user-fees for public services. While such revenue generating mechanisms are less obvious to the taxpaying public than sharp increases in property or income taxes, it is increasingly being recognized among the public that they are paying more and getting less from government. The American public is correct.

By 1990, the combined tax effort of all levels of government would account for slightly in excess of one-third of our nations total GNP (Advisory Commission on Intergovernmental Relations, 1991). Taxpayers feel driven to the wall and with some justification. Today the overall tax burden upon Americans has climbed back to it's all-time post WWII high. And unlike earlier periods, it is occurring when serious problems are wreaking havoc on our nation's economy and affecting taxpayers' ability to shoulder this burden. Only during the massive military buildup of WWII has government spending as a percentage of GNP been higher. In 1980, taxes (partly due to the inflationary spiral), had crept-up to the highest level in the postwar years. At the time, the federal government collected slightly over 20 percent of the GNP in taxes and fees. This fell slightly due to the massive tax cuts of 1981 as the Reagan Administration and Congress reduced the take from the personal and corporate income taxes by about a percentage point and a half. Slight reductions in the federal excise taxes chipped a bit more off the overall tax burden. But this was more than offset by increases in Social Security taxes and other marginal tax efforts. By 1990, the federal tax burden on the American taxpayer had climbed back to the all-time high of 1980 in spite of the much publicized efforts of the Republicans to slash taxes.

It is a similar story among state and local units of government. By the mid-1970s their combined revenues accounted for nearly 15% of the GNP. Then came the rollbacks such as proposition 13 in California and similar attempts by state and local anti-tax forces to curb runaway taxes especially property tax burdens. This would seem to signal a special victory for the grassroots tax foes and drive taxes down even further. Although such efforts did reduce temporarily the burden of state and local taxes as a percentage of GNP, it proved to be a temporary blip on an chart that seemed to point incessantly upward. Beginning in the 1980s with decreased assistance from Washington, state and local units of government were forced to raise the effective tax burden on their residents through increased and, as pointed out, often innovative tax schemes. Such efforts have had a homologous effect: the overall incidence of taxes are now back to the levels before the anti-tax initiatives (Passell, 1991).

State and local governments seem to be especially ripe for taxpayer concerns; they certainly are the levels of government most likely to be influenced by citizen anti-tax initiatives. While the public may attribute the disproportionate growth of state and local spending to waste, this is too facile an explanation for the problem. State and local services are the most resistant to productivity improvement by their very characteristics. Many of these services such as education, health care and police services are what some economists call "handicraft industries" (Passell, 1991). Their very nature combined with government-specific characteristics inhibts cost-saving and productivity applications. While a private sector firm may automate its production lines, institute cost-containment strategies, transfer resources to productivity-enhancement efforts, gains for public services are much harder won (Hatry et al., 1973). The quality of education, for example, may be measured by the teacher-pupil ratio. As a result, the costs of such services inevitably rise faster than overall inflation in the long run.

Still, ways must be found to deal with the dilemma. Special attention must focus on improving the service-level outputs— both qualitatively and quantitatively— of those public service areas proving so costly to local governments. The issue can only grow more critical as states and local communities, especially those in economically distressed areas of the country, struggle to match expenditures with existing revenues. The inability to generate sufficient operating revenues leaves few alternatives. Services must be cut or means must be found to provide existing service levels at lower costs. This latter recourse argues for the implementation of cost-containment strategies and simultaneous productivity improvement efforts.

EXAMINING A LIMITED SAMPLE OF MUNICIPAL POLICE PRODUCTIVITY EFFORTS

Acknowledging the fiscal plight that faces many local governments, a limited exploratory survey of medium-size municipal police departments was conducted to provide a framework for analysis. The answers sought were simple and twofold in nature: (1) Whether there is any evidence that these communities included in the survey and their representative police departments were facing fiscal constraints; and, if so, (2) what were these individual police agencies doing to increase effectiveness and efficiency, improve agency productivity, or to decrease or stabilize costs?

The survey was originally composed of a national sample of 100 randomly selected cities in the range of 75,000 to 150,000 population. Efforts were made to include cities that represented all geographical regions. This would ensure that different areas of the country would be represented. Although not a representative sample of all such cities, it would provide an exploratory survey of police productivity efforts from which some insights might be gathered and initial conclusions drawn.

Medium size communities were chosen for several reasons. First, this would provide a better picture of the efforts to develop police productivity undertakings than concentrating merely on large departments. It is small to medium-size communities and their police agencies that provide the vast bulk of police services to the public. An associated issue was the question whether concerns about productivity had "filtered-down" to these communities? It was also thought that it would be more difficult for medium-size departments to indicate that true productivity efforts had taken place which had not. While large departments might indicate that they had implemented questionable productivity improvement efforts through computerization or the adoption of "new" operational strategies, this would, it seemed, be more difficult for smaller agencies to contend unless such efforts actually occurred. And unlike the problems associated with uncovering true productivity efforts among larger departments, if medium-size departments indicated such productivity efforts, this could be more easily ascertained in future research efforts as to their nature and effect.

This survey would also serve as a follow-up on a similar productivity survey conducted in the early 1980s that examined this same issue (Levine, 1985). There was also the recognition that important precedent-setting steps had been taken in the 1970s by such organizations as the National Commission on Productivity (1973), Hatry, Winnie and Fisk

(1973), Wolfe and Heaphy (1975), and the National Center for Productivity and Quality of Working Life (1976), to foster and encourage productivity improvement applications among local public services including police operations. Have such earlier efforts provided any impetus or guidelines for dealing with today's crisis?

The survey was a two-stage effort. The initial open-ended questionnaire inquired whether the department was experiencing resource constraints brought about by local economic conditions and, if so, whether it had undertaken any specific effort to contain costs and/or improve productivity in the period 1989-1991. Although the focus of the survey was on productivity efforts, it asked respondents to provide information on cost-containment efforts generally so that a more complete picture of what was occurring would be reported. Of the original 100 communities, 54 returned the preliminary questionnaire. Thirty-seven of the respondents indicated they had experienced a period of "belt-tightening" and had initiated some form of cost-containment or productivity effort in the three preceeding years. A follow-up questionnaire was then mailed to each of the 37 municipal police departments. Thirty-two of the communities responded with information complete enough for analysis. In some cases, additional follow-up contacts were made with individual agencies for puposes of clarification.

THE ABSENCE OF PRODUCTIVITY-IMPROVEMENT EFFORTS

The police agencies in the survey showed little evidence of having adopted meaningful productivity improvement efforts. This was not unexpected. Like previous studies examining local government response to fiscal crisis, the major emphasis was on cost-containment strategies rather than improving the service provided through identifiable productivity-enhancement undertakings (Wolman, 1983). It was obvious that most agencies focused almost exclusively on containing costs instead of true productivity-enhancement efforts or a combination of the two. There are important distinctions to be made between these two concepts and their measurable outcomes that often escape public managers. Most police administrators in the survey generally thought of reducing costs or maintaining pre-existing budget levels rather than utilizing existing resources more effectively or efficiently. What seemed to be guiding these agencies is a policy of decrementalism in which the departments have been essentially pursuing small, short-term adjustments in their operating arrangements while trying to minimize at least the appearance of any visible loss in operating effectiveness (Levine, 1985). Although it may be considered to be a "productivity-enhancing" effort to maintain pre-existing levels of service in spite of diminished resources, there is little evidence that most of what is occurring during a period of austerity for these departments can be directly translated into that kind of outcome.

The results indicated that cost-containment or "productivity-improvement" efforts among the respondents took various forms. These included, hiring freezes involving "new hires" as well as not replacing personnel who resign or retire, reduction/curtailment of overtime, postponed replacement of police vehicles and deferred maintenance schedules for vehicles and equipment, improved court scheduling efforts, termination of programs, adoption of sick-time incentives, use of college interns, cutbacks on specialized and in-service training programs, reduction in recruiting efforts and associated personnel costs such as abbrieviated field training efforts for new recruits, the adoption of wellness programs, the limited adoption or purchase of such equipment as personal computers, car-mounted digital terminals and personal dictating units, some evidence of increased civilianization, "participative management" efforts, increased use of summonses in lieu of arrests, early retirement incentives, and one reported effort at reduction in force through lay-offs.

Other than three possible areas: the reduction or curtailment of overtime, hiring freezes, and deferred or reduced replacement and maintenance of police vehicles or equipment, there seemed to be no general similarity in efforts taken among the departments. Nor were there any discernible differences by department sizes among the respondents or the areas of the country they represented. While all the administrators answering the questionnaire acknowledged that they were constrained by operating resources and professed that "productivity-improvement" efforts were of importance to them and their departments, it is obvious that this has not been translated into major productivity-enhancing efforts.

It was also thought-provoking to find that some of the respondents reported that supposed cost-containment strategies may have actually heightened costs. Freezes on hiring, for example, were instrumental in some cases in incurring additional overtime costs for departments which found themselves understaffed. While communities may have escaped the costs of providing fringe benefits to "new hires" by utilizing existing personnel on an overtime basis, savings were at least partially offset by incurred overtime expenditures.

Table 1

Distribution of "Productivity" Efforts by a Sample of Medium Size Municipal Police Departments (N=32)

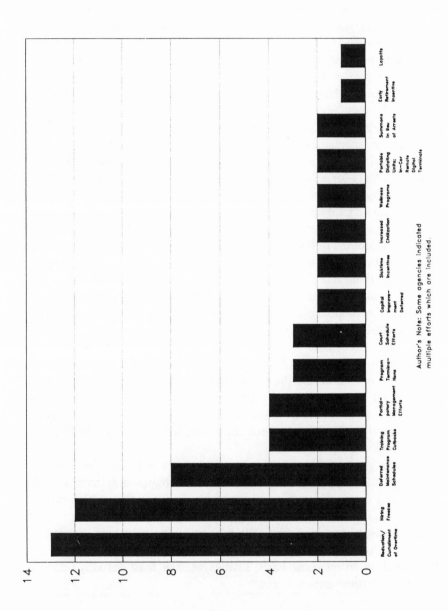

The implications are obvious. Although caution is warranted with such a small sample, it would seem that productivity-improvement does not seem to have made much of an impact notwithstanding the expressed concern that the provision of police services must be met in ever-tightening budgets. Like earlier expressions of concern (Heaphy, 1978) this raises issues about the viability of police productivity efforts aside from mere efforts to contain costs. It warrants what the Urban Institute and the National Commission on Productivity as long ago as the early 1970s called an "immediate priority" among local law enforcement agencies (Urban Institute, 1972; National Commission on Productivity, 1973). Apparently, nearly two decades has seen little progress or attention to this need.

It also raises fundamental questions about the possibility of organizational consequences. Mere cost-containment strategies in the absence of true productivity improvement efforts can have consequences for an organization and the services it provides. There is the issue of organizational/human resource erosion. This is represented by a decline in the aggregate skill level of an agency's work force brought about by physical, personnel and personnel-improvement resource cut-backs. There is also imposed the constraint of overcentralization in which increased control is placed over smaller and smaller expenditures which can discourage initiative and stifle innovation throughout the organization. A consequence of such an austerity strategy also ends-up causing important and consequential allocation shifts. Resources move to the more powerful service-delivering units in the department. In the case of police work, this means to basic patrol services and away from the less powerful staff units (e.g., planning and research, personnel or training). This may have important implications for both the short-term and long-term effectiveness of the department and, ironically, its possible ability to better cope with the existing problem. There is also the imposition of decisional paralysis. As the difficulty and consequences of austerity-imposed decision-making increase, greater reluctance to make decisions occurs. Managers (and policymakers) may find it increasingly difficult to make hard decisions about the long-term mission and priorities of the agency because of their concern about confronting police employees, unions, citizens, and interest groups with new work rules, service cutbacks or organizational arrangements (Levine, 1985, p. 24).

ANALYZING THE INGREDIENTS OF PRODUCTIVITY IMPROVEMENT: IT'S APPLICATION TO LOCAL LAW ENFORCEMENT

The analysis of productivity growth indicate that there are five basic sources that are commonly recommended to improve productivity (Kuper, 1975). We can apply each of these to police work. One is the application of new technology. This is the introduction of cost-reducing and productivity-enhancing technology. Common examples are computer-based applications, dispatch monitoring systems, and field unit remote dictating units. This makes three critical assumptions: (1) that true cost-reducing and productivity-improvement technology is available and/or can be adapted to police work; (2) that police managers have the resources and the know-how to maximize the utilization of available productivity-enhancing technology; and (3) its adoption will not be resisted, or at least, the available technology will be properly utilized by police personnel. To date, there is little evidence that assures one that any of these conditions have been met in the checkerboard world of local policing.

Another suggested method is the investment of more capital per worker. The premise is a simple one: increased capital investment in workers permits individual workers to be more productive. This has taken such forms as the use by some departments of in-car digital remote terminals, efforts at report simplification, or dictated reports. It can also include specialized training which suggests that such efforts result in improving job-related performance among police personnel. Still, there is a surprising lack of research that substantiates that any of these efforts are meaningfully linked to making police officers or police departments any more productive. Empirically-derived cost-benefit ratios such as cost accounting measures that are employed in the private sector for such investment strategies are simply non-existent in the world of local law enforcement. While some departments might make cost-benefit claims, very few could weather close scrutiny.

A third proposition calls for a higher quality of labor. This is related to better selection of police personnel, more effective training, better evaluation programs and associated remediation efforts for under-productive officers (Robinette, 1985). It suggests what America's private sector managers are learning: there must be concerted managerial efforts to develop a climate that fosters a greater commitment on the part of employees to perform well (National Center for Productivity and Quality of Working Life, 1978; Brown, 1983). Again, however, such assumptions are largely untested. Although they are commonly accepted as appropriate managerial goals, they rest on the shifting sand of still unknown cause and effect relationships.

Productivity experts also point to the need for the improved allocation of labor and the removal of jobs and labor from less productive jobs and moving them to more productive assignments. Examples in the police literature include better patrol force analysis and distribution, greater involvement of patrol personnel in preliminary investigations, analysis of criminal investigations case management, variations on neighborhood policing, directed patrol strategies and other adaptive and innovative patrol techinques, differential police response programs, and increased civilianization. Although such efforts have provided some preliminary evidence that they might be useful strategies to employ, they too, have not been meaningfully or widely adopted (or unfortunately, carefully evaluated) by the police establishment.

There is also the issue of operating economies of scale. This principle suggests that a relationship exists between area-level of service and associated costs. In the operating world of balkanized American police services such efforts as consolidation, resource sharing, forms of contractual policing arrangements, and interjurisdictional agreements are often recommended (Ostrom, 1973; Advisory Commission on Intergovernmental Relations, 1979; Langworthy, 1983). While there are some intuitive feelings that this may be a means to reduce or at least maintain costs while improving service (a definite productivity-enhancing outcome), local law enforcement agencies and communities are not exactly pursuing these options with vigor. Even among economically pressed communities in the same metropolitan areas, local governments are rarely actively examining such alternatives. Their usual strategy is to wring their hands and threaten reductions or cut-backs in police services unless citizens ante-up more tax revenues.

PROBLEMS ASSOCIATED WITH IMPROVING POLICE PRODUCTIVITY

So what are the problems confronting the American police in their efforts to improve their productivity? When we analyze the nature of police work and the existing operational environment among police managers and police personnel, some formidable problems exist. This does not suggest that productivity improvement is impossible or unwarranted; it merely points out that any efforts at productivity improvement must consider a number of impediments and understand their interactive implications.

The police, like other service sectors of the government, present almost insurmountable hurdles. They have come in too many cases to represent what one observer many years ago (when looking at what was occurring in government employment), warned was becoming a system devolving into "a triumph of technique over purpose" (Sayre, 1948). The years have, if anything, seen the situation worsen. Public employment (which certainly must include the police), in terms of its hiring, promotion and incentive systems has come to be recognized as increasingly devoid of "merit" (Savas & Ginsberg, 1973). Public managers find themselves choked with cumbersome and rigid civil service procedural rules that prevent management from reallocating and reorganizing work; a public personnel management approach that has created endless, cumbersome, inflexible systems of position descriptions, job classifications, testing, management-inhibiting and time-consuming grievance procedures, negotiated union work rules in many locales, and Equal Employment Opportunity and affirmative action requirements. Add to this situation of procedural and structural restrictions, political meddling and intransigent unionism, and a situation exists that has all but eliminated management's ability to restructure work organizations or to reward and punish workers for performance or lack thereof (Ott et al., 1991).

Particularly instructive has been the effect of strong police unions in some departments. It has grown more commonplace for police unions to be able to thwart productivity or cost-containment efforts by local officials. Unions have had some notable success in arbitration rulings over productivity-impeding negotiated work rules which have crept into labor contracts over the years. Sometimes the courts have also proven to be allies. In a number of cases, courts have issued injunctions against public officials' efforts at cutting back on public safety services which cities feel no longer justified or supportable. They have also legally restrained efforts to re-organize departments (Lyman, 1990).

In many ways such an operating environment has created a situation conducive to the formation of attitudes that express little interest in cooperating with management's efforts to improve police productivity. As a minimum, it certainly fails to provide much in the way of an incentive for such efforts. Here such limiting circumstances merge with the "publicness" of the police service. Unlike many private sector employees, police personnel realize that few meaningful sanctions can be imposed on them. In addition to the protection provided by civil service and strong unionism, there is little threat to job security posed to most police personnel. Experience indicates that officers will almost never lose their jobs regardless of mediocre work-related performance. Even transfer to less desirable jobs or shifts as a form of punishment for poor performance, is often inhibited by seniority-rights in negotiated contracts. And should a situation become so grave that personnel personnel cutbacks do occur, they will almost invariably take place in the form of natural attrition through retirement or resignations, or in the most critical of circumstances, among employees with the least seniority. There is also the knowledge that unlike the situation that exists in today's competitive private sector, police agencies do not confront the imposing threat of bankruptcy, the cessation of operations, or the spectre of organizational relocation to induce such outcomes as worker cooperation, renegotiation of workrule constraints, greater productivity efforts or cost-containment. Nor is the loss of competitive market share with its organizational implications a threat. By escaping these possible organizational consequences, the police service can largely escape any attempt at imposing accountability.

Associated with this set of circumstances are developed career-related attitudes that too often exist among police personnel; attitudes that militate against efforts to get them to cooperate with major organizational change (Tuttle & Sink, 1984). Here several issues present themselves: (1) Police personnel feel threatened by change and very skeptical of change-inducing efforts; (2) They view change as an effort by management to make them more accountable which they abhor; (3) Many experienced officers often develop attitudes that are generally contemptuous of police management and public officials and their efforts; (4) Police personnel, in some cities at least, see efforts at improvement and reform as mere efforts of "political appeasement" to vocal and critical minority interests— demands which they too often view as neither practical or legitimate; (5) department members feel no direct payoff to them if productivity is improved which provides them with no vested interest in the improvement of operations; and (6) the police believe there is no way to develop a quantitative expression of productivity which is truly meaningful. Cynicaly, they point to the writing of more tickets or increased arrests as examples of the questionableness of productivity efforts.

A recent element has been introduced into the equation which may prove to be a major impediment to reform efforts. It strangely comes at a time when the police are coming under increased criticism and it threatens to become a major obstacle to needed change and efforts at increased agency productivity and accountability. Police administrators who seek reform and change are finding that they do so at their own peril. Increasing crime rates, minority group criticisms and associated external demands for change together with microscopic inspection of police operations and leadership coupled with resistance by organizational members, has felled the police chiefs of eight of the nation's 15 largest cities in the past year alone (Witkin, 1992). A message is being sent to police chief executives. In such a situation, police managers in our largest urban areas at least, must sense the need for deliberate and cautionary restraint. Buffeted by increasing external criticism, few career-conscious police administrators want to simultaneously create internal dissension within the department by taking on the rank-and-file and the police union over issues of needed change. Torn by these opposing forces, their strategy may well be one of token marginality in change efforts. The immediate need is to ameliorate the external criticism while not making wide-ranging changes in departmental operations or attempting to bring about productivity-improving workrules or operational modifications. To do otherwise, runs the real risk of causing the administrator to also lose rank-and-file support which can, in a strange alliance of circumstances, join forces with the external criticisms to quickly turn into career-threatening opposition.

The nature of the police occupation itself poses a significant problem for productivity improvement through accountability. The nature of the job requires that police personnel be given a great deal of discretion. Although management experts point out that a broad scope of discretion among employees, especially if it involves very sensitive outcomes for the organization, requires more careful supervisory oversight and accountability standards, this management principle is conspicuously violated in police work. Much policing effort takes place within the context of little supervisory evaluation or really meaningful control as to what officers actually do on the street. If the nature of the job inhibits meaningful analysis and valid measurement of outcomes, the process of evaluation employed by many police agencies to assess meaningful performance is also equally devoid of standards and measurement criteria as to assignment of responsibility, accountability, analyis of outcome measures, and attention to corrective managerial action. The total range of effective assessment mechanisms for police personnel in most departments is simply non-existent.

There is also the waiting trap of applying productivity measures when used, to measuring crime-related services when in fact these services consume a relatively small percentage of police time. They are also the most difficult to measure with any degree of validity. Although any empirical conclusion of a relationship between law enforcement efforts and crime remains elusive, it is generally well-established that in most circumstances, the deterrent impact of the police on crime is very questionable (Wilson & Boland, 1979; Skogan & Antunes, 1979; Martin, 1986). There are, for example, questions raised about the relationship of arrest (and conviction outcomes) and crime rates and the mutual impact they actually have (Forst et al., 1977; Forst, 1984; Greenburg, 1975). In the final anaysis, what the police seem to generally provide is largely a symbolic presence and an order-maintenance function.

An example of the questionable application of crime-related evaluation criteria has recently been exposed in the Chicago Police Department. Police in that city are reportedly promoted or disciplined according to the number of people they arrest for criminal offenses. According to a performance evaluation system established many years ago police officers are given points for arrests regardless of whether they result in convictions. A weighted monthly numerical evaluation system based on a "head count" of felony and misdemeanor arrests awards varible points. A homicide arrest, for example, awards 35 points, 25 points are given for a gun recovered from a vehicle, 5 points for a felony narcotics arrest, and 3 points for a disorderly conduct arrest. In many units, police officers with the fewest points are counseled by their superiors and face the threat of transfer to less desirable assignments, are less likely to be promoted, and their requests for time off are given a lower priority (Martol, 1992). Obviously, such a system is seriously flawed.

In this way there remains neither in practice nor experience a practical or theoretical means of deriving a quantitative expression or theoretical means of deriving a qualitative indicator or series of indicators which expresses the individual or unit productivity of police officers. Many police managers are rightfully concerned that the pressure to measure the return on resources may cause this fact to be obscured, and that police priorities will be distorted by a mindless attempt to maximize some sterile number (e.g., the arrest rate) regardless of operational consequences. Others worry that the introduction of quantitative output measures will encourage the already widespread tendency to relate police performance to some universal measure of final ouput (e.g., a reduced crime rate) which is affected by so many other social phenomena that the most creative and professional police work may produce no measurable improvement whatsoever (Hamilton, 1975, p. 29).

Associated with successful productivity improvement efforts and the issue of motivation is also the issue of gainsharing. In order to provide an incentive for increased productivity, motivational rewards must be available (Wholey, 1983). Little or no attention has been given this factor by most police agencies. Except for an ill-fated police productivity gainsharing effort tied to police salary increases by Orange County, California in the 1970s (Grimes, 1975), which was anchored to the questionable measure of reduction in Part I Index crime rates, there has been a noticeable lack of other efforts or attempts to tie police productivity measures to an acceptable criterion (San Diego, 1979; Charlotte, 1976). The several issues are: How do we reward police personnel for productivity improvements? What specific measures do we apply? And how do we relate any such developed measures specifically to identifiable police efforts in an attributable cause-effect context?

It must be recognized that police services are by their nature highly labor intensive and the non-labor segment of the budget is quite small befitting an intensive service enterprise. On the average, about 75-80% of a municipal police department's budget is consumed by salary and fringe benefit costs. Several consequences are suggested by this fact. This requires focusing the utilization of productivity-enhancing technology, resources and efforts most directly on labor and labor costs; an area which is typically the most non-adaptive segment of capital substitution costs. It is also this fixed cost area— at least among the law enforcement enterprise— where labor-enhancing technology is least developed and available. We simply cannot, for example, develop machine-like robocop technoids to replace police officers. What it does suggest, however, is the need for increasing efforts to apply productivity-enhancing technology to this fixed labor resource. Productivity improvement in any other area other than direct labor costs as measured by associated (and apprpriate) cost/output ratios will provide only a marginal return on investment. This is true no matter how effective the applied technology resource may be.

There are also recognizably important constraints placed upon improving productivity in police work by the ideology of "due process" which governs the crime control efforts of the police. Appropriate legal limitations naturally make the police more ineffective in their efforts to deal with criminal events. We are not willing, for instance, to permit the police to make arrests based upon mere suspicion or to engage in massive dragnet operations to round-up suspects. The "rules-of-the-game" must be followed even though the police are less productive and effective in controlling crime as a consequence. And given this formidable impediment, it would again seem that technology-enhancing resources can only be of marginal utility in enhancing their "crime-fighting" capabilities.

Another impediment is the impossibility to measure with any degree of precision the broad role of the police. Neither the law enforcement establishment nor society have been able to clearly articulate the police role beyond such broad generalizations as "protecting the public," "maintenance of law and order," or "dealing with crime and criminals." In such a situation, there are real problems of operationalizing and prioritizing these goals and working to develop measures of more productive police practices. Yet, productivity practices require thorough analysis based on just such an operationalization. This must be followed with an operant rank-ordering of goals. This is currently absent. Such a requirement also assumes a commonality of acceptance of these productivity-enhancing goals across a broad spectrum of interests both internal to the department and from the community. Such consensual goal sharing is conspicuously absent.

Productivity improvement also assumes a relative degree of stable consensual agreement that identified and existing priorities remain relatively fixed over time to justify the cost of analysis, policy-making development, implementation, monitoring and measurement. These requirements are impeded by several considerations. One is the short-term budget cycle of local governments and how this affects long-range planning and establishing and maintaining priorities over any extended period (Halachmi, 1986). This fact is coupled with the twin phenomena of "lost-opportunity costs" and "zero-sum" outcomes: Resources and efforts devoted to a certain strategy or strategies reduces available resources for other efforts. A city may want to institute a variation of neighborhood or community-based policing with officers assigned to foot patrols in neighborhoods. There are attendant "costs" (e.g., resource allocations, possible public criticism, organizational resistance, etc.) associated with such an effort. While it may be beneficial in the particular neighborhoods effected (but this is yet to be demonstrated with empirical precision and reliability), it may likely result in reduced service levels and availability of police personnel for other tasks and in other areas. A commitment in one identified area to increase productivity— especially if it is associated with a shift in required resources— may limit the availability of efforts in other areas requiring attention.

Although police managers are likely to support productivity improvement in the abstract, they are very cautious to implement them. As frequently pointed out in the public management literature, an all too common characteristic among public sector managers generally is the aversion to risk-taking (Curtis, 1980). Police executives, like public managers, are noticeably not rewarded nor encouraged to be creative and innovative. And as has been mentioned, there are also internal and external "political costs"; a system that gives rise to many disencentives and few incentives, especially in an area of such sensitivity as public safety. In such an environment, police executives remain very cautious in trying to implement innovative efforts. And like other public managers, they are aware that they may possibly run the risk of having budgets cut if they can show a reduction in costs and a savings to the public.

In this context, the police world is also an action-oriented not a research-oriented enterprise. The worlds of the politician, the career police bureaucrat, and the operating police culture are similarly opposed to systematic collection and analysis of operational data as required by productivity efforts. Especially in these troubled times for the police, it is often perceived that such data could be employed against organizational and individual self-interest. Under these circumstances, they end-up eschewing such efforts especially by "outsiders", whom they see as anyone outside their own police enterprise. This may very well limit the application of greater objectivity and insight into operational strategies and overall organizational effectiveness. It is certainly true that without such data collection and analysis effort, problems cannot be identified, strategies developed, programs implemented, or results evaluated.

This leads us into another consideration. There is the common and faulty assumption that private sector organizations use productivity measurement and improvement in the same way that public sector organizations do. They do not. Most private sector organizations use productivity measurement systems to assign more work, more responsibility, more financial reward, more capital resources, and more power to the units that demonstrate the highest levels of productivity. They do not cut the most productive units, they give them more resources or rewards. This also affects the investment strategy that goes into a productivity improvement effort. Most public sector organizations commission productivity improvement efforts by assignment without up-front investment; workers are merely reassigned or reprogrammed to take on productivity responsibilities and in this way, productivity improvement endeavors must be financed by the agency internally. Contrast this to the private sector whose organizations expect to pay up-front costs to start a productivity-enhancement effort and then evaluate the results against total costs (Ott et al., 1991, p. 370).

There is also the issue of how budgetary mechanisms affect the planning process among local units of government and how this in turn affects the kind of planning that must go into productivity-improvement efforts. Any number of students of the public budget process point out that the traditional line-item (object of expenditure) budget employed by local governments is merely one of "incremental adjustment" (Schick, 1987; Ott et al., 1991; Sackton, 1989). Incremental changes are made to existing and established categories of base expenditures on an item-by-item basis. When revenue surpluses are available these may be adjusted upward; when revenue shortfalls occur, they are decrementally adjusted downward. No attention is focused on their relationship to program outcomes, nor importantly, do they foster the necessary and all-important planning development. Such budget formats are deliberately designed as short-term control-focused mechanisms that do not lend themselves to innovative strategies (or resource acquisition) that might be used for long-range programmed productivity improvement and measurement efforts.

It is also true that police managers have neither the training nor the know-how to analyze the question of police productivity. Nor have they been provided with much help in this area by research efforts and demonstrable examples of success that they can adopt. This should be a concern of no small consequence and an area needing immediate attention through demonstration projects and careful evaluation. In this situation there is no universal measure of comparative applicability such as a profit and loss statement. There is also the issue of existing differences between jurisdictions which make comparisons suspect. At least they can be argued as being such. These readily provide the basis for both real and contived excuses for not being more productivity conscious.

To some extent, the public must also be blamed for the situation. While some urban minorities have demanded changes in police operations, this is not the case among many non-minority community members. While the latter population segment has strangely joined the former in an increasing cynicism about their ability to influence government, this is not usually accompanied by commonly shared demands for police change or improvement— especially along the lines perceived by minority residents. This has stifled efforts directed at reform and permits elements internal to the police organization who are opposed to change to escape efforts to impose greater accountability or improved standards of service. It also creates opportunities for members of the organization to impose possible sanctions on police administrators who foolishly think otherwise.

Part of the public apathy in this area arises from the growing feeling that the government is an enterprise dedicated not to the welfare of the public, but to the self-interests of elected officials, special interests, and government employees. This may explain much of today's expressed hostility toward the public sector and its policymakers. It also is exhibited by the American public's collective psyche today of scornful ridicule and general apathy toward government. Feeling powerless, much of the public slinks away into a posture of seething hostility aroused only by the threat of additional tax increases.

It is also true that in spite of sensationalistic media exposure, the public still remains largely ignorant about the specific job responsibilities of the police and how to hold them accountable. Americans have always adopted a half patronizing and half suspicious attitude toward government agencies. In the eyes of much of the public, they are not expected to be productive. In the case of the police there is also the concern, that in some instances at least, we may not want law enforcement to be too effective.

CONCLUSION

Although there is a great deal of expressed concern over public service and public safety costs, little evidence exists that we are beginning to make strides in reducing or maintaining police service costs while improving service levels. Nearly twenty years of effort devoted to examining this problem have provided little in the way of tangible results or even guarded optimism that this situation is beginning or will change. For the most part, the scarcity of resources facing local governments is, at least among the segment of the police service examined in this survey, not forcing police departments to move much beyond beyond mere organizational cutbacks or questionably reliable efforts to maintain existing service levels. The inescapable fact is that these surveyed departments are not that unusual from the broader municipal police establishment; similar results might be expected if a larger sample were studied.

As discussed, much of the problem lies in the very nature of police work and the "publicness" of the police enterprise. There are also important and formidable problems present in the police occupation itself and among police personnel that show little sign of being easily overcome. While the factors giving rise to growing concerns are likely to grow unabated in the years ahead, there is little hope that important and innovative breakthroughs will be made in dealing with police service level costs or improvements in the provision of basic police service. Although there is a great deal of discussion about a new model of policing formulated on a community-based approach— at least in large cities— it remains questionable what overall impact this proposal will have. There still remain many questions about what this proposal can really expect to accomplish and whether it will in fact, improve service levels, reduce crime, generate proactive citizen-police anti-crime strategies, and improve police-community relations. There is an additional concern: What will it accomplish in relation to its cost? In these troubled times, this may well prove to be the most decisive question.

ENDNOTES

1. Although local communities also incur significant costs for education, this is somewhat alleviated by state aid to city school districts. The same is true of many major capital development expenses. Although a city may incur such capital expenses there exists the possibility to shift such costs to revenue bonds in which the incurred costs are amortized over the period of the bond costs by the revenues directly generated from the project. Even where this is not possible, municipal bonds can often be sold to finance a capital development or improvement project, and in this way, also amortized over successive budget cycles. No such mechanisms exist for the costs of public safety services which must be paid out of current operating revenues.

2. Much of the problem states are having is attributed to federal legislation which mandates service costs without providing states with the funds to pay for these services. Federal laws expanding Medicaid are a prime example as are increased welfare rolls. For example, in 1991, a record 13 million Americans are receiving checks from the AFDC program— A stunning 1 in 7 American children are now on relief (General Accounting Office, 1991).

3. The effects of the hidden "tax creep" has been most pronounced on the middle and working classes. Buffeted by a prolonged economic downturn and the loss of well paying jobs to low paying service jobs has left them both uneasy and fearful. Americans now grumble about a slipping standard of living made more difficult by the fact that spendable income has also been cut by creeping inflation. The facts support this. Median family household income adjusted for inflation was less in 1990 than it was in 1970 in constant dollar terms.

4. Some of this may be due in part— but only in part— to what some of the new taxation is earmarked for. The Congressional Budget Office, for example, estimates that two-thirds of all families pay more today in Social Security taxes than in federal income taxes. Only the top one percent of earners who benefitted from lower maximum tax rates and the bottom 20 percent who gained from cuts in the personal tax and more generous earned income tax credits have come out ahead on federal taxes. But such revelations are little consolation for many struugling wage earners who relaize only one thing: their disposable income is shrinking.

5. For example, a Princeton Survey Research study in early 1992 indicated that "payment of taxes" was second only to saving for retirement as the most difficult financial obligation faced by the respondents. See: Roberts (1992).

6. The issue between government spending and government-generated tax revenues is clouded by the fact that spending and tax revenues have become incongruent. Massive federal deficits have allowed spending to continue unabated while taxes to support government services have lagged. Thus, the spending picture for government services cannot be equally equated with taxation effort. Even so, taxes remain at an all-time high.

7. Part of this decrease in state and local taxes as a percentage of GNP is also due to the rapid inflation of the late 1970s and how this contributed to inflating the nation's GNP. In periods of rapidly rising inflation most tax revenues necessarily lag behind any inflationary spiral unless they are specifically designed to "capture" the impact of inflation. Most state and local taxes are not so designed. It may, for example, require legislative enactment to increase sales taxes or

impose higher service, users fees or licensing revenues, a public referendum to increase property taxes, periodic and frequent reassessments to capture appreciation in home values as a source of increased revenue etc. This automatically institutes a lag-effect in general economic trends (either upward or downward) and the incidence of taxes and the revenues they generate. See: Margoulis (1989).

8. These were grouped into 7 regions: The northeast, the middle-Atlantic states, the southeast, the midwest, the Rocky Mountain states, the southwest, and the Pacific coast.

9. The issue of effectiveness and efficiency in a work organization as a productivity measure recognizes that there is a contextual continuum to the issue of organizational productivity as measured by resource input. For example, along the continuum a number of outcomes are possible. In a period of declining budgetary resources, the agency may cut-back in service levels correspondingly. That is one common response. It may also cut-back in service levels less than its actual resource cutback. Another response is that in such a period of declining budgetary resources, the agency may try to maintain pre-existing levels of service output in spite of less resources. Another organizational response would be to increase service level output in a period of stable resources. There is also the situation where service level outputs might be made to increase beyond the growth of input resources in the form of budgetary increases. The latter four examples would all be instances of increased organizational productivity. Respondents were not apprised of this and the issue was not discussed with the surveyed police agencies.

REFERENCES

Advisory Commission on Intergovernmental Relations (1979) *Strategies for Improving Service Delivery Among Local Governments.* Washington, DC: author.

____ (1991) *Tax Burdens on Americans.* Washington, DC: author.

Blumberg, D.A. (1980) "Higher Productivity: The Only Answer to Spiraling Inflation." *Financial Planning Today* 4:159-165.

Brown, D.S. (1983) "The Managerial Ethic and Productivity Improve ment." *Public Productivity Review* 36:223-250.

Charlotte, North Carolina (1976) *Police Field Patrol Activities— An Evaluation.* Charlotte, NC: Budget and Evaluation Department.

Curtis, D.A. (1980) "Management in the Public Sector— It Really is Harder." *Management Review* 69:63-71.

Downs, G. and P. Larkey (1986) *The Search for Government Efficiency.* New York: Random House.

Forst, B. (1984) "Selective Incapacitation: A Sheep in Wolf's Clothing?" *Judicature* 68:23-31.

___, J. Lucianovic and S.J. Cox (1977) *What Happens After Arrest?* Washington, DC: Inslaw.

General Accounting Office (1991) *The Family Support Act of 1988: Analyzing Its Impact.* Washington, DC: GAO.

Greenburg, M. (1975) "The Incapacitative Effect of Imprisonment: Some Estimates." *Law and Society Review* 541:53-69.

Grimes, J.A. (1975) "The Police, the Union, and the Productivity Imperative." In J.L. Wolfe and J.F. Heaphy (eds.), *Readings in Productivity on Policing.* Washington, DC: The Police Foundation.

Halachmi, A. (1986) "Strategic Planning and Management? Not Necessary." *Public Productivity Review* 20: 21-29.

Hamilton, E.K. (1975) "Police Productivity the View from City Hall." In J.L. Wolfe and J.F. Heaphy (eds.), *Readings on Productivity in Policing.* Washington, DC: The Police Foundation.

Hatry, H.P., R.E. Winnie and D.M. Fisk (1973) *Practical Program Evaluation for State and Local Government Officials.* Washington, DC: Urban Institute.

Heaphy, J.F. (1978) "The Future of Police Improvement." In A.W. Cohn (ed.), *The Future of Policing.* Beverly Hills, CA: Sage.

Hyde, A.C. (1985) "Productivity Management for Public Sector Organizations." *Public Personnel Management* 14:319-332.

Joyce, P.G. and D.R. Mullins (1991) "The Changing Fiscal Structure of the State and Local Public Sector: The Impact of Tax and Expenditure Limitations." *Public Administration Review* 51:240-253.

Kuper, G.H. (1975) "Productivity: A National Concern." In J.L. Wolfe and J.F. Heaphy (eds.), *Readings on Productivity in Policing.* Washington, DC: The Police Foundation.

Langworthy, R.H. (1983) "Effects of Police Agency Size on the Use of Police Employees: A Reexamination of Ostrom, Parks and Whitaker." *Police Studies* 5:11-19.

Levine, C.H. (1985) *Fiscal Stress and Police Services: A Strategic Perspective.* Washington, DC: NIJ-U.S. Department of Justice.

Lyman, W.E. (1990) "Union Scuttles Police Cut-backs." *Law Enforcement News* April 12:4.

Margoulis, E.A. (1989) "State and Local Taxes: The Economic Lag-Effect." *Regional Economics* 14:13-22.

Martin, S.E. (1986) "Policing Career Criminals: An Examination of an Innovative Crime Control Program." *Journal of Criminal Law and Criminology* 77:1159-1182.

Martol, B. (1992) "Chicago Police Scoff at Arrest Measures." *Chicago Sun-Times* June 7, p.A-3.

National Center for Productivity and Quality of Working Life (1978) *Total Performance Management: Some Pointers for Action.* Washington, DC: U.S. Government Printing Office.

___ (1976) *Guide to Productivity Projects,* 3rd ed. Washington, DC: U.S. Government Printing Office.

National Commission on Productivity (1973) *Report of the Advisory Group on Productivity in Law Enforcement on Opportunities for Improving Productivity in Police Services.* Washington, DC: U.S. Government Printing Office.

Ostrom, E. (1973) "On the Meaning and Measurement of Output and Efficiency in the Provision of Urban Police Services." *Journal of Criminal Justice* 2:17-29.

Ott, J.S., A.C. Hyde and J.M. Shafritz (eds.) (1991) *Public Management— The Essential Readings.* Chicago, IL: Nelson-Hall.

Passell, P. (1991) "Despite All the Talks of Tax Cuts, People Can Expect to Pay More." *New York Times* November 7:A-1,A-32.

Reid, G.J. (1980) "How Cities in California Have Responded to Fiscal Pressures Since Proposition 13." *Public Budgeting and Finance* 8:23-37.

Roberts, S.B. (1992) "A Time of Fury and Despair." *U.S. News and World Report*, 112(February 17):22-24.

Robinette, H.M. (1985) "The Police Problem Employee." In J. Fyfe (ed.), *Police Management Today.* Washington, DC: International City Management Association.

Rymarowicz, L. and D. Zimmerman (1988) "Federal Budget and Tax Policy and the State-Local Sector: Retrenchment in the 1980s." *Congressional Research Service Report for Congress.* Washington, DC: The Library of Congress.

Sackton, F. (1989) "Financing Public Programs Under Fiscal Constraint." In R.E. Cleary and N.L. Henry (eds.), *Managing Public Programs.* San Francisco, CA: Jossey-Bass.

San Diego, California (1979) *Productivity Improvement Program— Police Investigations Bureau.* San Diego, CA: Financial Management Department.

Savas, E.S. and S.G. Ginsburg (1973) "The Civil Service: A Meritless System?" *Public Interest* 32:70-85.

Sayre, W. (1948) "The Triumph of Technique Over Purpose." *Public Administration Review* 8:134-137.

Schick, A. (1987) *Perspectives on Budgeting,* 2nd. ed. Washington, DC: American Society for Public Administration.

Skogan, W. and G. Antunes (1979) "Information, Apprehension and Deterrence: Exploring the Limits of Police Productivity." *Journal of Criminal Justice* 7:217-241.

Tuttle, T.C. and D.S. Sink (1991) "Taking the Threat Out of Productivity Measurement." In J.S. Ott, A.C. Hyde and J.M. Shafritz (eds.), *Public Management: The Essential Readings.* Chicago, IL: Nelson-Hall.

Urban Institute (1972) *The Challenge of Productivity Diversity: Improving Local Government Productivity Measurement and Evaluation, Part III. Measuring Police-Crime Control Productivity.* Washington, DC: author.

Watson, D.J. and T. Vocino (1990) "Changing Intergovernmental Fiscal Relations: Impact of the 1986 Tax Reform Act on State and Local Governments." *Public Administration Review* 50:427-434.

Weir, M.L. (1987) "Local Tax Burdens: Consensus Versus Conflict." *Journal of Urban Economics* 12:23-34.

Wilson, J.Q. and B. Boland (1979) *The Effect of the Police on Crime.* Washington, DC: U.S. Government Printing Office.

Witkin, G. (1992) "Police Chiefs at War." *U.S. News and World Report* (June 8):33-34.

Wholey, J.S. (1983) *Evaluation and Effective Public Management.* Chicago, IL: Scott, Foresman and Co.

Wolfe, J.L. and J.F. Heaphy (1975) *Readings in Productivity on Policing.* Washington, DC: The Police Foundation.

Wolman, H. (1983) "Understanding Local Government Responses to Fiscal Pressure: A Cross National Analysis." *Journal of Public Policy* 3:245-263.

Zremski, J. and P. Simon (1992) "Politics Termed Major Factor in State Budget Storm." *The Buffalo News* (February 7): A1-A-7.

POLICE ABUSE: CAN THE VIOLENCE BE CONTAINED?

*David Rudovsky**

I. Introduction

Thirty years ago, in *Monroe v. Pape*,[1] the United States Supreme Court first addressed the question of whether or not abuses committed by state police officers were subject to suit under the Ku Klux Klan Act of 1871, popularly known as Section 1983.[2] *Monroe* presented allegations of police abuse in a quintessential form: several heavily armed police officers broke into the plaintiffs' home without a judicial warrant, ransacked the house and terrorized the occupants, making racial and other derogatory slurs as they proceeded in their search. No contraband was found and no arrests were made.[3]

The Supreme Court ruled that these allegations stated a cause of action under Section 1983 for the violation of the plaintiffs' Fourth Amendment rights. The Court held that the phrase "under color of state law" in Section 1983 was intended to include actions undertaken by government officials without state approval or authorization.[4] Most incidents of police abuse involve the actions of officers who act contrary to state law, and, in determining that Section 1983 was intended to counter these violations, the Court held out the promise of an effective federal remedy for police abuse.

Unfortunately, the expectations engendered by *Monroe* have not been fully realized. After three decades and much constitu-

---

* Partner, Kairys & Rudovsky; Senior Fellow, University of Pennsylvania School of Law; B.A. Queens College (CUNY); LL.B. 1967, New York University School of Law. I am proud to contribute to an issue of the *Harvard Civil Rights-Civil Liberties Law Review* honoring Norman Dorsen, whose contributions to civil liberties over the past three decades are legion. Starting with my fellowship in the Arthur Garfield Hays Civil Liberties Program at NYU in 1966–67, I, like many of my colleagues, have greatly benefited from Norman Dorsen's unmatched skills as a teacher, lawyer and civil libertarian.
    [1] 365 U.S. 167 (1961), *overruled in part*, Monell v. New York Dep't of Social Servs., 436 U.S. 658 (1978).
    [2] 42 U.S.C. § 1983 (1988), originally enacted as § 1 of the Ku Klux Klan Act of 1871, ch. 22, § 1, 17 Stat. 13.
    [3] 365 U.S. at 169.
    [4] *Id.* at 183–85.

tional litigation,[5] the abuses continue, in many ways unabated. The beating of Rodney King by Los Angeles police in 1991 and the highly controversial acquittal of the officers involved focused attention once again on the problem of police abuse and demonstrated the continuing existence of the practices and policies that cause it.

Almost everyone who viewed the tape of the King beating was appalled by the display of senseless brutality. While some attempted to explain or defend the police actions, the evidence of brutality and abuse was so strong that a defense was rendered implausible.[6] The incident had the earmarks of classic police abuse: extremely excessive force used by white officers against a black suspect, an event infused with racism, and carried out with an attitude of impunity. For some, the event echoed numerous similar events in the past. Responding to the King incident, New York City Police Commissioner Lee P. Brown declared that "the problem of excessive force in American policing is real."[7] For many others, it was a first-time eyeopener, a window into a world of official violence that could not be squared with our cultural and political norms.[8]

The bookends of *Monroe v. Pape* and Rodney King embrace volumes of law and politics. An essential question that emerges

---

[5] *See, e.g.*, Estelle v. Gamble, 429 U.S. 97 (1976) (Eighth Amendment); Graham v. Connor, 490 U.S. 386 (1989) (Fourth Amendment); Katz v. United States, 389 U.S. 347 (1967) (Fourth Amendment); Tennessee v. Garner, 471 U.S. 1 (1985) (Fourth Amendment). *See also* Harry A. Blackmun, *Section 1983 and Federal Protection of Individual Rights—Will the Statute Remain Alive or Fade Away?*, 60 N.Y.U. L. REV. 1, 19–20 (1985).

[6] *See generally* Report of the Independent Commission on the Los Angeles Police Department (1991) (on file with the *Harvard Civil Rights-Civil Liberties Law Review*) [hereinafter LAIC].

[7] George James, *Police Chiefs Call for U.S. to Study Use of Force*, N.Y. TIMES, Apr. 17, 1991, at B3.

[8] Judge Alex Kozinski of the United States Court of Appeals for the Ninth Circuit has stated:

> [F]or a lot of naive people, including me, [the King case] puts a real doubt on the posture of prosecutors that police are disinterested civil servants just "telling it as it is."
>
> We should have known all along what this incident points out: that police get involved in what they do and that they are participants in the process just like anyone else. They are subject to bias and they do have a stake in the outcome.

Darlene Ricker, *Behind the Silence*, 77 A.B.A. J. 45, 48 (1991). This observation was foreshadowed by Justice Jackson's important insight, made over forty years earlier, that, in considering Fourth Amendment claims, we should be fully aware that the police are involved in the "often competitive enterprise of ferreting out crime." Johnson v. United States, 333 U.S. 10, 14 (1948).

from this thirty-year period is whether the institutions, programs and principles we have developed to empower the police are also adequate to the task of controlling the police. We must also ask whether in our society, which relies substantially on the courts to regulate and control governmental behavior, the legal response to police abuse is sufficiently sensitive to the institutional nature of the problem.

Enforcing the proper restraints on police power is a difficult problem in any society. In the United States there is both a fear of governmental abuse and a tolerance of repressive measures, the latter reflecting a belief that police excesses are necessary to combat crime.[9] The pervasiveness of violence, the lack of social cohesiveness, racial and ethnic discrimination, and sharp disparities in privilege, wealth and power supply a fertile ground for crime and social unrest. Frustration with disorder and crime in turn leads to a public acceptance of extra-constitutional police practices. Because police abuse is most often directed against those without political power or social status, their complaints are often dismissed or ignored.

Acceptance of a certain level of police abuse is a predictable majoritarian response to crime, upheaval and threats to the status quo. The true test of our society's commitment to constitutional constraints is how government and the courts respond to these systemic deviations from constitutional norms. If we examine current police conduct in light of this test, it is clear the response of government and the courts has been insufficient. We have manifested an indifference to documented abuses, and we have fostered official violence through social, political and legal structures that

---

[9] While most commentators condemn proven cases of police abuse, excuses are still made. For example, in the aftermath of the highly publicized beating of Rodney King, syndicated columnist Patrick Buchanan wrote:

> In our polarized and violent society, most Americans have come to look upon the cops as "us," and upon King, a convicted felon, as "them." He is the enemy in a war we are losing, badly; and we have come to believe the cops are our last line of defense.

Patrick J. Buchanan, *The Police Are the Last Line of Defense*, L.A. TIMES, Mar. 10, 1991, at M5.

Also writing after the King beating, another commentator wrote: "[T]he tape of some Los Angeles-area cops giving the what-for to an ex-con . . . is not a pleasant sight, of course; neither is cancer surgery. Did they hit him too many times? Sure, but that's not the issue: it's safe streets versus urban terror." Llewellyn H. Rockwell, *It's Safe Streets Versus Urban Terror*, L.A. TIMES, Mar. 10, 1991, at M5.

reinforce patterns of unlawfulness. We know much about the principles of accountability and organizational control, yet we often fail to apply these basic precepts to law enforcement officials.[10]

In order to explore the sharply differing perceptions of the nature of police abuse and analyze the contemporary legal and political disputes over this profoundly difficult problem, it is helpful to consider an updated version of *Monroe v. Pape.*

II. Metropolis, U.S.A., 1992

Metropolis, a large urban area, like many of its sister cities across the country, has over the past fifteen years experienced an increase in crime and has suffered the pernicious effects of drugs, unemployment and poverty. The police department is structured and operated along the lines of most large city departments. It has devoted an increasing amount of resources to training and supervision, and has recruited and hired additional minority members. The training program is well in line with professional standards, setting forth the appropriate constitutional standards for the use of police powers.[11]

The police are under substantial pressure to control and deter violent crime and illicit drug transactions. A special narcotics squad with city-wide jurisdiction has been established to combat drug activity. Members of this squad report only to the Unit Commander. The squad is responsible for building intelligence with respect to drug activity, conducting raids of suspected drug locations, recruiting informants and targeting areas that have significant drug and drug-related problems.

---

[10] *See, e.g.,* JEROME H. SKOLNICK & JAMES J. FYFE, ABOVE THE LAW: POLICE AND EXCESSIVE USE OF FORCE (forthcoming from Free Press 1992) (on file with the author); KENNETH CULP DAVIS, POLICE DISCRETION (1975). *See also* Susan Sturm, *Resolving the Remedial Dilemma: Strategies of Judicial Intervention in Prisons,* 138 U. PA. L. REV. 805 (1990).

[11] There are no binding national standards for police officer training. Each jurisdiction sets its own requirements, but all require a course of instruction in constitutional law. Metropolitan police forces typically exceed their state's minimum requirements. For example, the Boston Police Academy, while required to offer 420 training hours to recruits, provides over 800 hours of training, which includes approximately thirty hours of constitutional law. Instruction primarily consists of lectures conducted by the Constitutional Law Instructor, who is both a lawyer and a police officer. Police officers also receive annual updates. Telephone Interview with Lt. James Moore, Constitutional Law Instructor, Boston Police Academy (Apr. 17, 1992).

The nation is involved in a "war on drugs."[12] Congress and state legislatures have given the police and prosecution a powerful array of new law enforcement measures.[13] At the same time, the Supreme Court has drastically limited the substantive protections of the Fourth Amendment[14] and has significantly narrowed the exclusionary rule,[15] thus authorizing increasingly invasive police searches, seizures and other investigative practices.

Enormous sums of money have been expended on the drug war, primarily on the law enforcement side of the equation.[16] Between 1975 and 1990, there has been a three-fold increase in the number of prisoners in the United States; in 1992 we hold well over a million people behind bars, the largest prison population per capita of any industrialized country.[17] The war on drugs is

---

[12] The "war on drugs" was officially declared by President Ronald Reagan on October 14, 1982 in a speech to the United States Department of Justice. Leslie Maitland, *President Gives Plan to Combat Drug Networks*, N.Y. TIMES, Oct. 15, 1982, at A1. *See also* THE WHITE HOUSE, NATIONAL DRUG CONTROL STRATEGY (1989).

[13] *See generally* MARC MAUER, THE SENTENCING PROJECT, AMERICANS BEHIND BARS: A COMPARISON OF INTERNATIONAL RATES OF INCARCERATION 7–11 (1991); Paul Finkelman, *The War on Defense Lawyers*, in NEW FRONTIERS IN DRUG POLICY 113 (A.S. Trebach & K.B. Zeese eds., 1991); Max D. Stern & David Hoffman, *Privileged Informers: The Attorney Subpoena Problem and a Proposal for Reform*, 136 U. PA. L. REV. 1783 (1988); David Rudovsky, *The Right to Counsel Under Attack*, 136 U. PA. L. REV. 1965 (1988); United States v. Monsanto, 491 U.S. 600 (1989).

[14] *See, e.g.*, Florida v. Bostick, 111 S. Ct. 2382 (1991) (holding that searches of consenting bus passenger's luggage without articulable suspicion not per se unconstitutional); California v. Hodari D., 111 S. Ct. 1547 (1991); Michigan Dep't of State Police v. Sitz, 110 S. Ct. 2481 (1990); National Treasury Employees Union v. Von Raab, 489 U.S. 656 (1989).

[15] *See, e.g.*, United States v. Leon, 468 U.S. 897 (1984) (holding that exclusionary rule should not apply to evidence obtained by officers reasonably relying on a search warrant ultimately found to be invalid); Stone v. Powell, 428 U.S. 465 (1976); United States v. Calandra, 414 U.S. 338 (1974).

[16] At the federal level, total funding for drug enforcement was $4.6 billion in 1985, $6.6 billion in 1989 and $8.2 billion in 1992. The proposed budget for 1993 has earmarked $8.6 billion for drug enforcement efforts. OFFICE OF MANAGEMENT AND BUDGET, BUDGET OF THE UNITED STATES GOVERNMENT FISCAL YEAR 1993, 190 (1992). There are substantial additional costs for the courts, prosecutors, appointed counsel and the prisons. On the state and local level, a 1987 study by Wharton Econometric Forecasting Associates estimated state and local police expenditures (not including outlays for courts and prisons) at $5 billion for 1985. Ethan A. Nadelmann, *Drug Prohibition in the United States: Costs, Consequences, and Alternatives*, 245 SCIENCE 939, 940 (1989). State spending on prisons today is twelve times what it was just twenty years ago. Neal Pierce, *Filling Our Prisons Isn't Deterring Crimes*, PHILA. INQUIRER, Jan. 13, 1992, at 7A. Far less money is spent on drug rehabilitation and education programs. *See* Larry Gostin, *The Interconnected Epidemics of Drug Dependency and AIDS*, 26 HARV. C.R.-C.L. L. REV. 113 (1991); MAUER, *supra* note 11, at 13; MARC MAUER, THE SENTENCING PROJECT, AMERICANS BEHIND BARS: ONE YEAR LATER 9 (Feb. 1992) [hereinafter MAUER 1992 UPDATE]. *See also* BUDGET OF THE UNITED STATES GOVERNMENT FISCAL YEAR 1993, *supra*, at 190.

[17] MAUER, *supra* note 11, at 4, 6; Pierce, *supra* note 16, at 7A.

largely accountable for this development, due to greater numbers of arrests and significantly increased sentences caused by mandatory minimum sentences and guideline sentencing schemes.[18] Whatever the merits of this heavy-on-enforcement approach (and the results certainly justify acute skepticism),[19] the directives to police forces around the country have been unambiguous: it is a war, and virtually any means will be tolerated on the battlefield.

The Metropolis narcotics squad has for the past six months investigated drug selling in the Circle Park section, a predominantly African-American, lower-income neighborhood. Complaints by community residents and articles in the city newspaper have led to heightened police concern over the drug problem in this area. Rumors have associated Charles and Linda Raft with known drug sellers. To secure further information about these individuals, the police decide to arrest Robert Castle, a convicted drug abuser, who they believe is a friend of the Rafts. The police arrest Castle on false charges and tell him that things will go much better for him if he cooperates in the investigation of the Rafts. Castle agrees to cooperate and tells the police that cocaine is stored in the Raft residence and that he has seen them sell the drug as recently as two weeks before. Based on these assertions, the police obtain a warrant to search the Rafts' home.[20]

---

[18] See Marc Mauer, Americans Behind Bars, 6 CRIMINAL JUSTICE 12, 16–17, 38 (1992); MAUER 1992 UPDATE, supra note 16, at 7–9.

[19] See generally Michael Levine, The Drug "War": Fight It At Home, N.Y. TIMES, Feb. 16, 1992, at E15; Nadelmann, supra note 16; John Kaplan, Taking Drugs Seriously, THE PUBLIC INTEREST, Summer 1988, at 32; Milton Friedman, A War We're Losing, WALL ST. J., Mar. 7, 1991, at A14; STEVEN WISOTSKY, BEYOND THE WAR ON DRUGS (Prometheus Books 1990) (1986). See also Gostin, supra note 16 (arguing that this "penal" approach to controlling drug abuse has greatly contributed to other social ills, such as the needle-borne spread of AIDS).

[20] The affidavit of probable cause in the search warrant application states:

The undersigned affiant is a member of the Narcotics Unit of the Metropolis Police Department and has been involved in the investigation of drug and drug-related crime for the past three years. On [date] a confidential informant told the affiant that cocaine is stored in the residence of Charles and Linda Raft [address]. The informant has provided reliable information in the past. On three occasions, information provided by the informant resulted in the arrest of drug suspects or in the seizure of controlled substances. The confidential informant saw drugs in the Rafts' house two weeks ago. The Rafts sell the drug from their home to other persons. Based on the informant's contacts and sources, he believes that the Rafts will have a large amount of cocaine in their house on this date, in preparation for a large sale tomorrow.

At 7:30 p.m., ten heavily armed officers arrive to execute the warrant. They sledgehammer the front door and gain entry to the living room. To immobilize the occupants of the house, they order the Rafts and their twelve-year-old son to lie on the floor, guns trained at their heads; they are warned that if they move they will be shot. Police fan out through the house searching for drugs. They do not find any cocaine, but in the process of the search they do discover a small amount of marijuana. During the search, the police empty closets, overturn tables, take apart household equipment and tools and dismantle several pieces of furniture. Two of the officers direct racial epithets at the family; Mr. Raft is called a "black-ass drug dealer."

Frustrated by their lack of success, the police take Mr. Raft into the basement and threaten him with arrest for possession of marijuana unless he supplies them with information about drug dealers in the neighborhood. Raft tells the police that he knows nothing about drug transactions, and that the marijuana is left over from a party they gave several months before. The police inform Raft that their informant had been in the house and had observed narcotics transactions; Raft again states that he has no information and that he does not deal in drugs. Raft does add that he had recently been involved in a dispute with a person in the neighborhood who is known to be involved in drugs, Robert Castle. Raft asks the police if Castle was the informant, but the police decline to answer.

Believing that Raft is lying about his involvement in drug activity, the police decide to arrest him for possession of marijuana, even though they know that the amount involved is below the level established by the District Attorney as a minimum threshold for criminal charges. At the narcotics division, Raft is again questioned about drug activity; upon his denials, he is struck several times by one of the officers. He suffers injuries to the face and arms. He is then charged with assaulting a police officer and resisting arrest.

At the preliminary hearing on the criminal charges, an assistant district attorney offers to drop the criminal charges against Raft if he will agree to waive his right to sue the police. Raft agrees to these conditions, and the criminal charges are dismissed.

This version of *Monroe v. Pape*, updated to the 1990s, provides a point of departure for examining the key elements and dynamics of police misconduct.[21] The next section analyzes the hypothetical in terms of the legal response, the institutional causes of the conduct and the culture of police abuse. In the concluding section of this Article, I explore a possible agenda for reform.

III. Judicial and Administrative Remedies for Police Misconduct: The Failure of the Courts and the Political Process

As a matter of public policy and constitutional law, one would expect that the conduct of the police in our hypothetical would be subject to strong condemnation. Indeed, a video portrayal of these events would probably inspire reactions similar to those generated by the Rodney King video. Yet, in the real world of civil rights litigation and police administration, we can expect to find just the opposite: a good deal of the misconduct will not be remediable in the courts and, as an internal administrative matter, little if any evaluative or disciplinary action would be taken against the officers. In fact, as we will see, their actions were a predictable result of police policies and legal doctrine that subordinate individual rights to police power.

The hypothetical raises distinct issues of legal and administrative process, as well as social policy. To elucidate these systemic problems, it is helpful to examine each aspect of the Metropolis police officers' conduct.

A. The Search Warrant

The process by which the police obtained the warrant is highly problematic. The officers used an illegal arrest to put pressure on an informant, withheld this information from the judge who issued the warrant, and submitted an affidavit that arguably fell short of probable cause. In a civil suit, the warrant could be attacked for its failure to provide a sufficient factual basis for believing the informer's tip.[22] However, even if a reviewing court found there was no probable cause to justify the warrant, the doctrine of

---

[21] The facts in this hypothetical present events that occur on a far too regular basis. *See* HOUSE COMM. ON THE JUDICIARY, REPORT ON THE OMNIBUS CRIME CONTROL ACT OF 1991, H.R. REP. No. 242, 102d Cong., 1st Sess., pt. 1, at 135–39 (1991).

[22] *See* Illinois v. Gates, 462 U.S. 213, 239 (1983); Aguilar v. Texas, 378 U.S. 108 (1964).

qualified immunity would preclude a damage award against the officer who secured it unless no reasonably well-trained officer would have believed that probable cause existed.[23] Thus, even if a constitutional violation could be proven, the officer would be protected from liability in damages.[24]

The facts suggest that the informant acted out of a personal grudge against the Rafts and may have provided false information. However, unless this fact was known to the police, it would not provide an adequate basis for challenging the warrant.[25] Indeed, the warrant could still be upheld even if the police deliberately withheld the fact that they had illegally arrested Castle and pressured him to talk.[26] Suing Castle would not be a real option for the Rafts either, given the informant's privilege and the difficulty of establishing the level of state action necessary to bring his conduct within the purview of Section 1983.[27]

Finally, the Rafts could not assert a violation of their own Fourth Amendment rights based on Castle's unlawful pretext arrest. Even if the police deliberately violated Castle's rights to

---

[23] Malley v. Briggs, 475 U.S. 335, 345 (1986). In *United States v. Leon*, 468 U.S. 897, 922 n.23 (1984), the Supreme Court adopted the same standard for a "good-faith" exception to the exclusionary rule. *Leon* has been the subject of extensive discussion. *See* Abraham Goldstein, *The Search Warrant, the Magistrate, and Judicial Review*, 62 N.Y.U. L. Rev. 1173 (1987); Craig Uchida et al., *Acting in Good Faith: The Effects of* United States v. Leon *on the Police and Courts*, 30 Ariz. L. Rev. 467 (1988); Donald Dripps, *Living with* Leon, 95 Yale L.J. 906 (1986); Steven D. Duke, *Making* Leon *Worse*, 95 Yale L.J. 1405 (1986).

[24] The doctrine of qualified immunity shields government officials from damage awards in civil rights cases where their conduct "does not violate clearly established statutory or constitutional rights of which a reasonable person would have known." Harlow v. Fitzgerald, 457 U.S. 800, 818 (1982). For further discussion of this doctrine, *see infra* notes 35–37, 42–43 and accompanying text.

[25] Where an officer has a reasonable basis to credit the assertions of an informant, the fact that the informant knowingly provided false information is not a basis for attacking the warrant. Franks v. Delaware, 438 U.S. 154 (1978). *See also* Commonwealth v. Bradshaw, 434 A.2d 181 (Pa. Super. 1981).

[26] In *Franks*, 438 U.S. 154, the Court ruled that a search warrant will be deemed invalid for reasons of an affiant's misrepresentations only where the false information was given deliberately or in reckless disregard of the truth, and where probable cause would not have existed without that information. *See also Leon*, 468 U.S. at 923.

[27] On the informant's privilege, see McCray v. Illinois, 386 U.S. 300 (1967) (as a general rule, government need not reveal identity of informant at suppression hearing; disclosure only required where defendant makes a substantial showing that informant may not exist or that affiant has deliberately misstated information received). *See also Franks*, 438 U.S. at 167. In civil suits, the courts generally have not found informants to be acting "under color of state law" and therefore not subject to suit under § 1983. *See, e.g.*, Ghandi v. Police Dep't of City of Detroit, 823 F.2d 959 (6th Cir. 1987).

enable them to obtain information to be used against the Rafts, the Rafts would lack standing to challenge such unconstitutional conduct.[28]

There is a direct link between the legal standards regarding the search warrant process and the tactics used by the Metropolis police. Warrants can issue on little more than hearsay allegations of informants,[29] and the Court has erected virtually insurmountable barriers to requiring further judicial inquiry into the informant's credibility, motives or even her very existence.[30] Thus, the police have been told that barring the most unusual circumstances there will be no inquiry into the truthfulness of what the informant alleged or the truthfulness of the officer's assertions.

If Metropolis is true to contemporary police administration, it will have no standards for informant control.[31] Each detective or officer is relatively free to develop her own network of informants, and there is little overall supervision of individual informants' credibility, reliability or usefulness.[32] Moreover, in cases where a court actually strikes down a warrant and suppresses evidence in a criminal case, or awards a plaintiff damages in a civil matter, the adjudication is not likely to be reported to the department.[33]

The police and prosecutor also know that under the "good faith exception" to the exclusionary rule, even if the warrant does not state probable cause, it will be upheld if a reasonable officer

---

[28] Wong Sun v. United States, 371 U.S. 471 (1963). Indeed, even where the police commit a criminal act to obtain information about a third-party suspect, the Supreme Court has denied the third party standing to challenge the illegality, ruling that the federal courts should not invoke their supervisory powers to exclude the evidence obtained. See United States v. Payner, 447 U.S. 727 (1980).

[29] See, e.g., Illinois v. Gates, 462 U.S. 213 (1983); McCray, 386 U.S. 300 (1967).

[30] Absent extraordinary circumstances, the identity of the informant will not be disclosed. See Franks, 438 U.S. 154; McCray, 386 U.S. 300. See also Irving Younger, The Perjury Routine, THE NATION, May 8, 1967, at 596.

[31] The general practice among police departments is that informants are treated as the "property" of individual investigators; interactions between informants and investigators are most often informal and go undocumented. However, a more centralized and professionalized system has recently been proposed by groups such as the International Association of Chiefs of Police National Law Enforcement Policy Center. See INTERNATIONAL ASSOC. OF CHIEFS OF POLICE NATIONAL LAW ENFORCEMENT POLICY CENTER, MODEL POLICY: CONFIDENTIAL INFORMANTS—CONCEPTS AND ISSUES PAPER (June 1990). These standards have yet to be adopted on a national scale.

[32] See Selwyn Raab, Chief Warns of Corruption in Drug Unit, N.Y. TIMES, Jan. 9, 1992, at B1 (revelations that NYC narcotics investigators lied to strengthen cases and obtain arrest warrants demonstrates need for tighter internal controls and supervision).

[33] Response of Defendant City of Philadelphia to Interrogatories in Campbell v. City of Philadelphia, C.A. No. 91-4512 (E.D. Pa. 1991) (copy on file with author).

would have believed that it did, a standard that has sustained the most questionable of warrants.[34] The qualified immunity doctrine would then preclude recovery against the Metropolis officers where the conduct, though adjudged unconstitutional, had not been previously clearly proscribed.[35] The defense would be available even where the officers acted with malice or with an intent to violate the citizen's rights.[36] The policy considerations supporting some form of immunity—such as the desire to protect officials from suit where they were not reasonably on notice of the legal standards governing their conduct—could be satisfied with a far narrower defense.[37]

Whatever the theoretical and policy merits of qualified immunity, we must recognize that broader immunity creates greater incentives to cut constitutional corners. Where more surveillance or investigation might be indicated prior to seeking a warrant, an officer could decide to forego this work, knowing that she only has to approximate probable cause. Furthermore, an officer might be tempted to falsely assert than an informant has a strong record of reliability. Even worse, an officer could entirely fabricate an informant with minimal fear of negative repercussions. In the Rafts' case, there was a distinct possibility that the informant acted out of personal malice in providing the information, yet the officers had no incentive to examine his truthfulness.

B. Execution of the Search Warrant

Similar incentives to cut constitutional corners exist in executing the warrant. The officers' entry into the Raft house appears to have been a violation of the Fourth Amendment, as there was no "knock and announce" before the police used a sledgehammer

---

[34] See United States v. Leon, 468 U.S. 897, 920 (1984); United States v. Bishop, 890 F.2d 212, 216–18 (10th Cir. 1989).

[35] Anderson v. Creighton, 483 U.S. 635 (1987); Harlow v. Fitzgerald, 457 U.S. 800, 818 (1982).

[36] Harlow, 457 U.S. at 815–19.

[37] See David Rudovsky, The Qualified Immunity Doctrine in the Supreme Court: Judicial Activism and the Restriction of Constitutional Rights, 138 U. PA. L. REV. 23 (1989); Richard H. Fallon, Jr. & Daniel J. Meltzer, New Law, Non-Retroactivity, and Constitutional Remedies, 104 HARV. L. REV. 1731, 1822–23 (1991).

to invade the premises.[38] Of course, the police might dispute whether or not there was any prior announcement of purpose, presenting a factual issue at trial.

Moreover, it is possible that the officers would testify that they dispensed with the knock and announce procedure based on their belief that violence or destruction of the drugs would have resulted if they had identified themselves. While it seems to be settled law that an announcement of purpose is generally not forgiven in these circumstances, and that permission to dispense with these requirements must by granted by the judge who issues the warrant,[39] the police could still raise a qualified immunity defense to this claim.[40]

Several institutional factors also encourage police entry without announcement. The Metropolis police know that if drugs are found during the search, their testimony that they did in fact knock and announce—or that some exigent circumstances justified their entry without identification—would almost always be credited. The police also know that if nothing is found, legal action will be highly unlikely, and therefore the illegality of their entry will be rendered purely academic.

The manner in which the police searched the Raft house raises serious problems under the Fourth and Fourteenth Amendments. The occupants were terrorized; the police pointed guns at them and forced them to lie on the floor during the search. The destruction of personal property during the search may have constituted a Fourth Amendment violation.[41] The police would likely respond with a potent defense: in narcotics raids they often face violent opposition, and their tactic is to scare and immobilize the occupants to prevent anyone from getting hurt. The destruction of

---

[38] State and federal statutes typically require the police to knock and announce their purpose unless there are exigent circumstances that justify immediate entry. *See, e.g.,* CAL. PENAL CODE § 844 (West 1982); 18 U.S.C. § 3109 (1988). The Fourth Amendment also appears to require the "knock and announce," absent exigent circumstances. *See* Ker v. California, 374 U.S. 23 (1963).

[39] *See, e.g.,* Commonwealth v. Grubb, 595 A.2d 133 (Pa. Super. 1991); State v. Cleveland, 348 N.W.2d 512, 519 (Wis. 1984).

[40] The issue under the qualified immunity doctrine would be whether it was clearly established that an unannounced entry based on the generalized exigencies inherent in a drug search must be reviewed by the judge or magistrate reviewing the search warrant and not by the police officer. *See, e.g.,* Mitchell v. Forsyth, 472 U.S. 511 (1985).

[41] *See* Tarpley v. Greene, 684 F.2d 1, 9 (D.C. Cir. 1982) ("[D]estruction of property that is not reasonably necessary to effectively execute a search warrant may violate the Fourth Amendment.").

property would be justified by asserting that drugs are often hidden in these areas and that a close and intrusive search is permissible under the circumstances.

While a good case could be made that the search techniques were excessive, it is not at all clear that the Rafts would prevail as to all aspects of the search. Again, under the qualified immunity doctrine, there could be no recovery in damages against the officers unless the law was previously clearly established that the challenged conduct was unconstitutional.[42] Moreover, because a court can decide the immunity question without reaching the merits of the issue, it is possible that no clearly established principles would ever be articulated in this area, thus leaving the police free to engage in similar conduct in the future.[43]

It is unlikely that Metropolis police command officials would critically review these search practices.[44] It is also unlikely that the department would take remedial action. The failure to evaluate practices such as the "use of intimidation" during drug raids undermines individual officer accountability by providing implicit departmental approval of these questionable practices.

Even if a court found the officers' conduct to be unconstitutional, supervising officials would rightly consider it unfair to discipline them since the officers involved were not responsible for the adoption of the search techniques employed at the Raft house. It would be appropriate for the department to reconsider its search policy at this point, but unless the courts seem inclined to suppress evidence or to assess damages, the department's belief that these practices are essential to drug enforcement would almost certainly preempt any reform.

Municipal liability would be a potential source for relief. Qualified immunity would not be a defense here.[45] However, under the remedial scheme of Section 1983, municipalities are liable for unconstitutional police conduct only where a municipal policy, law

---

[42] *See supra* notes 24, 35–37 and accompanying text.

[43] *See* Rudovsky, *supra* note 37, at 53–55. *See also* Borucki v. Ryan, 827 F.2d 836 (1st Cir. 1987); Ramirez v. Webb, 835 F.2d 1153 (6th Cir. 1987); Walentas v. Lipper, 862 F.2d 414 (2d Cir. 1988), *cert. denied*, 490 U.S. 1021 (1989).

[44] Even if the unit command had reviewed plans for the search, since no command officials were present during its execution, review would be unlikely unless the Rafts initiated court proceedings. The average metropolitan police department has no device in place to evaluate the performance of specific officers and teams. *See* Raab, *supra* note 32.

[45] *See* Owen v. City of Independence, 445 U.S. 622 (1980).

or custom demonstrably caused it.[46] Because these search practices are unlikely to be "official" departmental policy, the Rafts would have the heavy burden of demonstrating a pattern of such excessive searches sufficient to prove a settled practice or custom.[47] The failure of the department to train or properly supervise its officers in this area is a basis for liability, but only where the plaintiff can show that policy makers were "deliberately indifferent" to the rights of the public.[48]

Given the problematic nature of a remedy in damages, the Rafts would probably seek equitable relief. But the Supreme Court has imposed substantial obstacles to such an action. In *City of Los Angeles v. Lyons*,[49] the Court refused to grant injunctive relief to a plaintiff who had suffered permanent physical injuries when a police officer administered a "chokehold" in effecting an arrest. Relief was denied even though the record demonstrated that this police practice was commonly used in circumstances not justifying such force and had resulted in sixteen deaths in recent years.[50] The Court determined that the past injury had no continuing effects sufficient to provide standing for prospective relief and that the plaintiff was unable to show that he, as opposed to any other citizen, would again be subject to the same unconstitutional conduct.[51] The Court has been disinclined to enjoin most local police procedures,[52] and it is highly unlikely that the Rafts would be granted equitable relief.

---

[46] In *Monell v. New York Dep't of Social Servs.*, 436 U.S. 658 (1978), the Court ruled that a municipality was liable under § 1983 only where "the action that is alleged to be unconstitutional implements or executes a policy statement, ordinance, regulation, or decision officially adopted and promulgated by [the municipality]." *Id.* at 690–91. The *Monell* doctrine has been further refined in more recent case law. *See, e.g.*, City of Canton v. Harris, 489 U.S. 378, 388–89 (1989) (holding that unsatisfactory training of police officers constitutes insufficient grounds for holding city liable unless city exhibited deliberate indifference); City of St. Louis v. Praprotnik, 485 U.S. 112, 122 (1988) (stating that a municipality is liable only if the challenged action was pursuant to official policy); Pembaur v. City of Cincinnati, 475 U.S. 469, 483–84 (1986) (recovery from a municipality can be based upon acts sanctioned by officials responsible for establishing municipal policy).

[47] *See* cases cited *supra* note 46. *See also* City of Oklahoma City v. Tuttle, 471 U.S. 808, 820–22 (1985); Languirand v. Hayden, 717 F.2d 220, 227–30 (5th Cir. 1983).

[48] *City of Canton*, 489 U.S. at 389. For application of this standard in the lower federal courts, see, e.g., Davis v. Mason County, 927 F.2d 1473, 1481–82 (9th Cir. 1991); Gentile v. County of Suffolk, 926 F.2d 142, 152–53 (2d Cir. 1991); Kerr v. City of West Palm Beach, 875 F.2d 1546, 1555–57 (11th Cir. 1989).

[49] 461 U.S. 95 (1983).

[50] *Id.* at 100, 110–13.

[51] *Id.* at 101–05.

[52] *See, e.g.*, Rizzo v. Goode, 423 U.S. 362 (1976).

C. Pretextual Arrests

The Metropolis police executed two pretextual arrests to accomplish their goals. They arrested Castle without probable cause; then they arrested Mr. Raft on charges for which they knew he would not be prosecuted. But Castle's arrest, regardless of its illegality, would not provide the Rafts with a constitutional claim.[53] Mr. Raft's own arrest for drug possession was constitutionally permissible since it was supported by objective probable cause.[54] Accordingly, unless the police department restricts the power of its officers to make pretext arrests or searches, this conduct is likely to be repeated.

The Raft case demonstrates how the Court's jurisprudence on pretext arrests provides incentives to the police to violate or avoid basic constitutional guarantees. The police knew in advance that their illegal arrest of Castle would be a moot legal issue in any resulting investigation or arrest of the Rafts. Castle was unlikely to complain since he was the beneficiary of a deal to drop all charges against him. Raft's arrest on drug charges would never have been made in the normal course of events, but the police used it in this case to gain leverage against Raft. This leverage was used both in the investigation and later to obtain the release of the officers from civil liability in exchange for the dismissal of the criminal charges. Surely, if deterring police misconduct is a principal purpose of the Court's Fourth Amendment doctrine, the pretextual arrests made in Metropolis should be classic candidates for strong remedial action.

---

[53] See United States v. Payner, 447 U.S. 727 (1980); Rakas v. Illinois, 439 U.S. 128 (1978). See also supra note 28 and accompanying text.

[54] Most federal courts have ruled that where a reasonable police officer could have taken the action in question consistent with the Fourth Amendment, the fact that she did it for improper purposes is irrelevant. See, e.g., United States v. Causey, 834 F.2d 1179, 1184–85 (5th Cir. 1987) (en banc); United States v. Hawkins, 811 F.2d 210, 213–15 (3d Cir. 1987). Other courts have ruled that where no reasonable officer would have made the pretextual stop, even though technically allowed under the Fourth Amendment, the evidence should be suppressed. See, e.g., United States v. Guzman, 864 F.2d 1512, 1515–18 (10th Cir. 1988); United States v. Smith, 799 F.2d 704, 708 (11th Cir. 1986). The Supreme Court recently denied certiorari, over Justice White's dissent, in three cases that presented this issue: Cummins v. United States, 90-1628, 60 U.S.L.W. 3358 (Nov. 12, 1991); Trigg v. United States, 91-5013, 60 U.S.L.W. 3358 (Nov. 12, 1991); Enriquez-Nevarez v. United States, 91-5087, 60 U.S.L.W. 3358 (Nov. 12, 1991).

See generally Daniel S. Jonas, Pretext Searches and the Fourth Amendment: Unconstitutional Abuses of Power, 137 U. PA. L. REV. 1791 (1989); John M. Burkoff, The Pretext Search Doctrine Returns After Never Leaving, 66 U. DET. L. REV. 363 (1989).

There is substantial evidence that police are quite sophisticated in exploiting the many loopholes created by the Court's constitutional remedies jurisprudence. For example, in *Cooper v. Dupnik*,[55] the police deliberately refused to honor the suspect's request for counsel during interrogation. The police knew that any statement given by the defendant would be suppressed at trial, but they also knew that the Supreme Court had ruled that such statements could be used to impeach the defendant if he testified at trial.[56] The defendant was in fact innocent and was exonerated of all charges. In an ensuing lawsuit under Section 1983, the police admitted that they had hoped their illegal questioning would result in a statement that would deter the defendant from testifying. The court nonetheless ruled that *Miranda* is not a constitutionally mandated rule, and that the plaintiff was not harmed by lack of counsel since no fruits of the questioning were introduced against him.[57] *Cooper* reveals a troubling judicial complacency and rigidity in the face of a police practice that consciously manipulated and ignored basic constitutional guarantees. If the courts do not address deliberate misconduct, it is unrealistic to believe that other institutions will respond.

In a world where most police officers and administrators continue to believe that ends justify means, few departments will forego pretextual police practices in the absence of judicial pressures to reform. This is particularly true of a narcotics unit operating under few, if any, meaningful constraints with respect to policies involving informants and undercover activity.

D. Excessive Force

The Metropolis officers' conduct back at the Narcotics Division probably violated the Fourth and Fourteenth Amendments.[58]

---

[55] 924 F.2d 1520 (9th Cir. 1991), *reh'g granted en banc*, 933 F.2d 798 (1991).
[56] *See* Harris v. New York, 401 U.S. 222 (1971).
[57] *Cooper*, 924 F.2d at 1528.
[58] In *Graham v. Connor*, 490 U.S. 386 (1989), the Court ruled that the use of excessive force by the police during an arrest or other seizure of a person violates the reasonableness standard of the Fourth Amendment. The Court rejected the state's assertion that such claims should be decided under a substantive due process test. Two issues have been contested in the wake of *Graham*. The first is the issue of what standard applies after the suspect has been arrested and taken to the police district. The Court has ruled that the Eighth Amendment applies to post-conviction claims of excessive force. *See* Hudson v. McMillian, 112 S. Ct. 995 (1992) (use of excessive physical force against a prisoner may violate Eighth Amendment although no serious injury resulted); Whitley v. Albers, 475

Raft would argue that the police used excessive force by striking him while they were questioning him, and that his arrest for the false cover charges constituted malicious prosecution and false imprisonment.[59] However, proving these allegations would not be easy. The police would undoubtedly testify that Raft became unruly and assaulted an officer, and that reasonable force was used to subdue him. Because of the police code of silence,[60] the officers who witnessed the assault would testify either that they did not observe the incident or, if they did, that the police acted properly in self-defense. The incident, unlike the Rodney King beating, would not have been videotaped.

Excessive force is a product of a police culture that rationalizes physical abuse as appropriate punishment for persons who are viewed as trouble-makers or deviants. Studies of excessive use of force point out that a predictable catalyst to abuse is the officers' perception that their authority is being questioned or defied.[61] Even verbal questioning of authority leads many police officers to believe that their power and position have been threat-

---

U.S. 312 (1986). The lower federal courts have divided on the question of how to evaluate claims by persons held between arrest and detention. See Wilkins v. May, 872 F.2d 190, 192–93 (7th Cir. 1989), cert. denied, 493 U.S. 1026 (1990) (applying substantive due process test); Titran v. Ackman, 893 F.2d 145, 147 (7th Cir. 1990) (applying due process standard which court describes as similar to the Fourth Amendment test); Austin v. Hamilton, 945 F.2d 1155 (10th Cir. 1991) (applying Fourth Amendment test).

The second question that has arisen is whether the plaintiff must demonstrate a certain level of injury to establish an excessive force claim. Compare Johnson v. Morel, 876 F.2d 477, 479–80 (5th Cir. 1989) (per curiam) with Gray v. Spillman, 925 F.2d 90, 93–94 (4th Cir. 1991). The Court's recent ruling in Hudson, 112 S. Ct. 995, makes clear that the nature of the physical injury suffered is not a controlling factor for Eighth Amendment purposes.

[59] A police defendant accused of using excessive force should not be able to prevail using the qualified immunity doctrine. Assuming the use of force was unjustified, the defendant cannot claim that a reasonable officer would have believed his actions to be lawful simply because it was not clear to him what legal standard applied. See Dixon v. Richer, 922 F.2d 1456, 1460–62 (10th Cir. 1991) (rejecting qualified immunity defense because legal standard for unreasonable force during seizure was clearly established at time of incident).

[60] The "police code of silence" is an unwritten rule and custom that police will not testify against a fellow officer and that police are expected to help in any cover-up of illegal actions. The code of silence has been recognized and documented in litigation and studies of police culture. See, e.g., Brandon v. Holt, 469 U.S. 464, 467 n.6 (1985) (quoting Brandon v. Allen, 516 F. Supp. 1355, 1361 (W.D. Tenn. 1981)); Bonsignore v. City of New York, 521 F. Supp. 394, 398–99 (S.D.N.Y. 1981), aff'd, 683 F.2d 635 (2d Cir. 1982); ALBERT J. REISS, THE POLICE AND THE PUBLIC 213–14 (1971); JEROME H. SKOLNICK, JUSTICE WITHOUT TRIAL: LAW ENFORCEMENT IN DEMOCRATIC SOCIETY 58, 249 (2d ed. 1975). The code of silence is discussed in greater detail below. See infra notes 83–89 and accompanying text.

[61] See PAUL CHEVIGNY, POLICE POWER: POLICE ABUSES IN NEW YORK 51–83 (1969); SKOLNICK, supra note 60.

ened. In these situations, the police will demand immediate compliance and acquiescence. If obedience is not forthcoming, the incident escalates and an arrest and use of force is likely to follow.[62]

Physical abuse is a constant threat and will occur most frequently in departments that do not take this conduct seriously.[63] The potential for illegal use of force is so great that the experienced administrator knows that without a meaningful system of accountability, officers will act illegally more frequently. Even those officers who normally would not use illegal force will be more likely to do so if they know it will be tolerated.[64]

The Rodney King incident is a paradigmatic event demonstrating the serious consequences of the failure to impose accountability. Rodney King underwent a beating that was both protracted and public. The officers involved had to be fully confident of their colleagues' silence and of their department's dismissal of any complaints made by the numerous witnesses to this incident. Indeed, so sure were these officers of their immunity from punishment that they bragged about their abuses on the official police computer system and to medical personnel at the hospital where King was belatedly taken for treatment. Only officers assured by prior experience and knowledge of departmental attitudes that the department would not investigate or punish this type of abuse (regardless of the credibility of the witnesses or of their own incriminating statements) could have rationally taken the risk of engaging in this type of behavior.[65]

---

[62] See CHEVIGNY, supra note 61, at 51–83, 88–98.

[63] LAIC, supra note 6, at 151–79; Recommendations of the Task Force on the Use of Force by the Kansas City, Missouri Police Department 45–49 (January 1991) (on file with the author) [hereinafter Kansas City Task Force]; Report of the Boston Police Department Management Review Committee 99–136 (January 1992) (on file with the Harvard Civil Rights-Civil Liberties Law Review) [hereinafter Boston Police Report].

[64] See supra notes 61 and 63. See also SKOLNICK & FYFE, supra note 10.

[65] The LAIC described the radio transmissions as follows:

> Computer and radio messages transmitted among officers immediately after the beating raised additional concerns that the King beating was part of a larger pattern of police abuse. Shortly before the King beating, Powell's and Wind's patrol unit transmitted the computer message that an earlier domestic dispute between an African-American couple was "right out of 'Gorillas in the Mist'", a reference to a motion picture about the study of gorillas in Africa.
> The initial report of the beating came at 12:56 a.m., when Koon's unit reported to the Watch Commander's desk at Foothill Station, "You just had a big time use

Examples from adjudicated cases and from independent investigations provide hard documentation of the systemic flaws in the complaint processes in many police departments.[66] It is not uncommon to find that officers who have been the subject of numerous citizen complaints of brutality are rarely disciplined and continue to serve on the force.[67] In Los Angeles, for example, the Independent Commission investigating the Rodney King incident determined that several officers who had been found responsible for the illegal use of force on civilians had at the same time received performance reviews that made no mention of these findings and which praised the officers' attitude toward civilians.[68]

---

of force . . . tased and beat the suspect of CHP pursuit, Big Time." The station responded at 12:57 a.m., "Oh well . . . I'm sure the lizard didn't deserve it . . . ."

. . . . In response to a request from the scene for assistance for a "victim of a beating," the LAPD dispatcher called the Los Angeles Fire Department for a rescue ambulance:

P.D.: . . . Foothill & Osborne. In the valley dude (Fire Department dispatcher laughs) and like he got beat up.
F.D.: (laugh) wait (laugh).
P.D.: We are on scene.
F.D.: Hold, hold on, give me the address again.
P.D.: Foothill & Osborne, he pissed us off, so I guess he needs an ambulance now.
F.D.: Oh, Osborne. Little attitude adjustment?
P.D.: Yeah, we had to chase him.
F.D.: OH!
P.D.: CHP and us, I think that kind of irritated us a little.
F.D.: Why would you want to do that for?
P.D.: (laughter) should know better than run, they are going to pay a price when they do that.
F.D.: What type of incident would you say this is?
P.D.: It's a . . . it's a . . . battery, he got beat up.

At Pacifica Hospital, where King was taken for initial treatment, nurses reported the officers who accompanied King (who included Wind) openly joked and bragged about the number of times King had been hit.

LAIC, *supra* note 6, at 14–15. *See also* Paul L. Hoffman, Legal Director, ACLU Foundation of Southern California, Prepared Remarks Submitted to the House Subcommmittee on Civil and Constitutional Rights of the House Committee on the Judiciary, Mar. 20, 1991, 3–6 (on file with the author) [hereinafter Hoffman].

[66] *See, e.g.*, Gutierrez-Rodriguez v. Cartagena, 882 F.2d 553, 562–66 (1st Cir. 1989); Spell v. McDaniel, 824 F.2d 1380, 1391–95 (4th Cir. 1987), *cert. denied*, 484 U.S. 1027 (1988); Harris v. City of Pagedale, 821 F.2d 499, 508 (8th Cir. 1987). For commentary on this issue, see LAIC, *supra* note 6, at 151–79; Kansas City Task Force, *supra* note 63, at 45–49; Boston Police Report, *supra* note 63, at 99–119 (The Boston Police Department, rather than responding to citizen complaints of abuse, "tries to outlast the [complaining] victim, to continue it and continue it until the victim gets fed up and no longer comes to the hearings.").

[67] *See* LAIC, *supra* note 6, at 37–48; Kansas City Task Force, *supra* note 63, at 45–46; Boston Police Report, *supra* note 63, at 113–14.

[68] LAIC, *supra* note 6, at 137–48.

It is quite likely that our hypothetical Metropolis has similar infirmities in its review and adjudication of civilian complaints. Not so hypothetically, assume that a study of the civilian complaints lodged against members of the Metropolis police department discloses that for a two-year period preceding this incident "a total of 756 individual officers were named as subjects of civilian complaints . . . . The names of 29 officers appeared collectively 303 times, each being named nine or more times . . . ."[69] If the officer who assaulted Raft was one of the officers with nine or more complaints, his conduct on this occasion should not be surprising.

The department's failure to investigate allegations of abuse, or to impose appropriate punishment, would lead the reasonable police officer to assume that even repeated violations of citizens' rights would be condoned within the department.[70] The failure to hold these officers accountable for their prior misconduct is a direct link to the abuse of Raft. The deleterious consequences of the department's failure to monitor and discipline these officers run far wider than the encouragement it might give them to continue to abuse civilians. The message that violence and abusive conduct will be ignored is also sent to every other officer on the force.[71]

For its part, the Supreme Court either does not grasp the institutional causes of abuse or, as a matter of ideology, is using the doctrines of federalism and judicial restraint to allow these conditions to persist. There is a striking disjunction between the widely recognized causes of abuse and the Court's response. The Supreme Court's rulings reflect a belief that abuse occurs in isolated instances and is caused by an occasional aberrant abusive officer. Faced with records that reflect institutional causes, the Court recoils at the argument that the Constitution requires intervention on that level.

In several key cases the Court has deliberately passed up the opportunity to craft an approach that would take into account systemic patterns of abuse. In *Rizzo v. Goode*,[72] a federal district

---

[69] Kansas City Task Force, *supra* note 63, at 45.

[70] LAIC, *supra* note 6, at 153–79. *See also* Boston Police Report, *supra* note 63, at 113–20.

[71] *See* LAIC, *supra* note 6, at 153–79; Boston Police Report, *supra*, note 63, at 113–20; Kansas City Task Force, *supra* note 63, at 45–49.

[72] 357 F. Supp. 1289 (E.D. Pa. 1973), *rev'd*, 423 U.S. 362 (1976).

court had ruled that there was a pattern of police abuse in Philadelphia. In response, the court ordered the implementation of an internal police department mechanism for the review and adjudication of civilian complaints against officers. The district court made the fairly obvious and well-supported finding that the failure of the police department to investigate these complaints and to discipline officers led to the high level of abuse. The district court's order was focused and limited. It did not, for example, create a civilian review or oversight board.[73]

The Supreme Court reversed, stating that principles of federalism and comity prohibited this kind of relief as an impermissible intervention in the affairs of local government.[74] As a matter of local governmental policy and police administration, the fact that the nation's fourth largest city (one with a well-earned reputation for police abuse) did not have a functioning internal review system is a cause for serious concern. The refusal of the Supreme Court to permit such a remedy demonstrates a studied ignorance of the political and social realities of police misconduct. In addressing the tension between the protection of constitutional rights and local governmental prerogatives, the Court adopted a judicial calculus that reinforces the systemic aspects of police abuse by abdicating any judicial responsibility for the proven structural causes of misconduct.

The Court followed a similar doctrinal approach in *City of Los Angeles v. Lyons*,[75] in which it refused to enjoin the Los Angeles Police Department's use of the deadly "chokehold." The Court found, *inter alia*, that the improper and illegal application of the chokehold was not a routine City policy, and therefore had been unauthorized.[76] Equitable relief was justified only if "the City ordered or authorized police officers to act [illegally]."[77]

---

[73] 423 U.S. at 366–70.

[74] *Id.* at 377–78.

[75] 461 U.S. 95 (1983). *See also supra* notes 49–51 and accompanying text.

[76] *Lyons*, 461 U.S. at 107–08.

[77] *Id.* at 106. *Lyons* has been the subject of severe criticism. *See, e.g.*, David Cole, *Obtaining Standing to Seek Equitable Relief: Taming* Lyons, *in* CIVIL RIGHTS LITIGATION AND ATTORNEY FEES ANNUAL HANDBOOK 101, 102 (J. Lobel ed., 1980) (arguing that *Lyons* should be construed narrowly to limit its potentially illegitimate reach); Richard H. Fallon, Jr., *Of Justiciability, Remedies, and Public Law Litigation: Notes on the Jurisprudence of* Lyons, 59 N.Y.U. L. REV. 1 (1984) (arguing that the Court's use of the doctrines of standing and equitable restraint to restrict public law litigation is flawed). The doctrinal flaws discussed in these articles are not the only problems with *Lyons*; the opinion reflects a startling lack of sensitivity to the fatal consequences of the police practice.

The formalism of *Lyons* is disturbing both as a matter of constitutional adjudication and as a matter of social policy. *Lyons* sent a chilling message to the Los Angeles Police Department: as long as abuses like the chokehold do not become city "policy," the Court would not interfere. It should come as no surprise that the Rodney King incident occurred in Los Angeles. There is a direct line from *Lyons* to Rodney King, and the Supreme Court bears some responsibility for the pattern of brutality in the Los Angeles Police Department that claimed King as one of its victims.

In a more recent case, the Court did finally understand the link between internal police policies and abuse. In *City of Canton v. Harris*,[78] the Court ruled that in some circumstances the failure of a police department to properly train or discipline its officers may give rise to municipal liability under Section 1983.[79] The causal connection between training and discipline and the incidence of abuse are well established and the Court's ruling should prompt further moves toward increased accountability. In this regard, *City of Canton* represents a short step towards correcting the ostrich-like approach in *Rizzo v. Goode*.[80] It is only a short step, however, because the Court limited the potential reach of its decision by insisting that the failure to train or discipline be the result of "deliberate indifference" of city officials. This is a level of culpability that approaches intentionality and that poses significant problems of proof.[81] The decision is further limited by the fact that the remedy for the failure to train is simply to extract damages from the municipality. This is significant in ensuring compensation for the victim, but unless the damages are substantial, they will probably have little or no affect on policymakers. Whether the judgment will be considered a cost of doing business or will operate as an incentive to reform is an open question in most jurisdictions.[82]

Investigation and adjudication of claims of excessive force (as well as other forms of police abuse) are often frustrated by the

---

[78] 489 U.S. 378 (1989).

[79] *Id.* at 388.

[80] *See* discussion *supra* at notes 72–74 and accompanying text.

[81] *City of Canton*, 489 U.S. at 388–92. Decisions in the lower federal courts demonstrate the difficulties involved in satisfying this burden of proof. *See, e.g.*, Colburn v. Upper Darby Township, 946 F.2d 1017 (3d Cir. 1991); Santiago v. Fenton, 891 F.2d 373 (1st Cir. 1989).

[82] *See* LAIC, *supra* note 6, at 55–61. *See also* SKOLNICK & FYFE, *supra* note 10.

police "code of silence."[83] In our hypothetical, several officers witnessed the attack on Mr. Raft. It is a virtual certainty that none of these officers would provide any evidence in an internal proceeding or court case against the offending officers. A former United States Attorney for the Eastern District of Pennsylvania, in recommending leniency for a police officer who testified in a police corruption trial, stated:

> [T]here is a custom that has developed within the Philadelphia Police Department that Philadelphia police officers will acquiesce in the illegal and improper conduct of their fellow officers and that when called to tell the truth, as is the duty of every other citizen in this nation when called before a grand jury or questioned by lawful authorities, that the Philadelphia police officer will remain silent.[84]

The code of silence does more than prevent testimony. It mandates that no officer report another for misconduct, that supervisors not discipline officers for abuse, that wrongdoing be covered up, and that any investigation or legal action into police misconduct be deflected and discouraged.[85] In Boston, for example, experienced investigators will not volunteer for the Internal Affairs Division unless they are promised the ability to choose their next assignment "because they fear retribution once they [go back on the street]."[86] Officers shun temporary promotions to "acting sergeant," despite higher pay and prestige, because they do not want to have to be in the position of disciplining a fellow officer when they "might be back riding with that officer sometime in the future."[87]

---

[83] The "code of silence" has been openly recognized by law enforcement officials. *See, e.g.,* Selwyn Raab, *Five Police Officers Indicted by Jury in Torture Case,* N.Y. TIMES, May 3, 1985, at A1 (Police Commissioner urges prison sentences for police officers to help shatter "the blue wall of silence"); Athelia Knight & Benjamin Weiser, *D.C. Police Chief Praises Officer Who Broke Police Code of Silence,* WASH. POST, Dec. 16, 1983, at B1; LAIC, *supra* note 6, at 168–71; Boston Police Report, *supra* note 63, at 59, 116, 124. *See also supra* note 60.

[84] Tim Weiner, *Ex-Officer Who Broke Code of Silence Given Probation,* PHILA. INQUIRER, Feb. 13, 1985, at 1 (Statement of U.S. Attorney Edward S. G. Dennis, Jr.).

[85] *See supra* notes 60, 83.

[86] Boston Police Report, *supra* note 63, at 124.

[87] *Id.* at 59.

Other participants in the criminal justice system abet this policy: prosecutors are highly reluctant to indict police for their illegal acts, judges rarely disbelieve even incredible police testimony, and allegations of police abuse often lead to more severe treatment of the accuser.[88]

There are ways in which the pernicious effects of the code of silence can be mitigated. First, the department must make clear that officers who fail to report and provide information regarding unlawful actions of fellow officers will be subject to serious discipline. To be effective, these sanctions should be directed at supervisory officials who abet the code by uncritical acceptance of reports that demonstrate a pattern of silence. Particular attention should be paid to cases in which the allegations of the complainant are sustained either in internal proceedings or in court, and where officers who observed the incident have either not come forward or have supported the false testimony of the offending officer.

Second, the courts should recognize liability both for officers who fail to file truthful police reports or who remain silent concerning abuses that they have witnessed and for municipalities on a theory that a department's failure to take steps to deal with the code of silence constitutes a municipal policy under *Monell*.[89]

E. Racially Motivated Conduct

The use of racially derogatory language towards the Rafts is strong evidence that at least some of the officers' misconduct was racially motivated. Such conduct is actionable under Section 1983 (and other civil rights acts),[90] although once again the burden of proof is significant. No independent witnesses could confirm the remarks; the police would maintain that they were firm but polite during the search of the house; and most jurors would be disinclined to believe that the police acted out of racial motivation.[91]

---

[88] Anthony G. Amsterdam, *The Supreme Court and The Rights of Suspects in Criminal Cases*, 45 N.Y.U. L. Rev. 785, 787–89 (1970).

[89] *See supra* note 46.

[90] *See, e.g.*, Johnson v. Morel, 876 F.2d 477, 479 (5th Cir. 1989) (en banc). Racially motivated police misconduct is also actionable under 42 U.S.C. §§ 1981 and 1982.

[91] Of course, if the police are as openly racist as they were in Los Angeles in the Rodney King incident, police radio transmissions or other recorded statements may provide additional proof of racially motivated abuse.

The racism reflected in the derogatory remarks made to the Raft family is a legacy of our Nation's history of racial discrimination. Racially motivated conduct is hurtful in any form, but where it infects police practices the risks to the victim are particularly great. Historically, police abuse against minorities has been the single most cited cause for the deep distrust and suspicion that inhere in virtually all police-minority community contacts and that have led on several occasions to rebellions and riots.[92]

Even today, police tactics that would not be countenanced in middle-class suburban communities are the norm in poorer urban areas where minorities make up the majority of the residents. It is not uncommon for the police to conduct sweeps of certain neighborhoods, to stop or arrest persons without individual suspicion, and to conduct searches like the one conducted at the Raft home.[93] The LAIC's report of virulent racism in the Los Angeles Police Department should give pause to those who believe that we have eliminated overt racial prejudice from the criminal justice system.[94] The police justify their differential treatment of minority communities by exploiting the universally shared fear of crime. But people whose lives are threatened daily by criminal activity should not be subjected to police abuse as a price of police protection.

As long as racial discrimination exists in our culture, it will necessarily impact the criminal justice system.[95] However, we

---

[92] See, e.g., NATIONAL ADVISORY COMMISSION ON CIVIL DISORDERS, REPORT 157–68 (Government Printing Office 1968) [hereinafter KERNER COMMISSION REPORT].

[93] See, e.g., City of Los Angeles v. Lyons, 461 U.S. 95 (1983); Hall v. Ochs, 817 F.2d 920 (1st Cir. 1987); Spring Garden United Neighbors v. City of Philadelphia, 614 F. Supp. 1350 (E.D. Pa. 1985); Sheri Lynn Johnson, Race and the Decision to Detain A Suspect, 93 YALE L.J. 214, 225–37 (1983).

[94] The LAIC reviewed police transmissions and found "an appreciable number of . . . racial remarks," including

"Well . . . I'm back over here in the projects, pissing off the natives."
"I would love to drive down Slauson with a flame thrower . . . we would have a barbeque."
"Sounds like monkey-slapping time."
"Oh always dear . . . what's happening . . . we're huntin wabbits."
"Actually, muslim wabbits."
"Just over here on this arson/homicide . . . be careful one of those rabbits don't bit you."
"Yeah I know. . . . Huntin wabbits is dangerous."

LAIC, supra note 6, at 72.

[95] See McCleskey v. Kemp, 481 U.S. 279, 286–87 (1987) (discussing racial bias in death penalty prosecutions in Georgia); MAUER, supra note 11, at 10; MAUER 1992 UPDATE,

have the capacity to reduce the incidence of racially motivated misconduct. First, police departments must impose serious disciplinary sanctions for racist conduct. Second, departments must continue to integrate their forces both racially and sexually. Third, significant changes must be made in the training of officers with a view toward broadening their respect for persons of different races, sexual orientations, national origins and cultures.[96] Finally, police departments must address their failure to assure minorities quality assignments and equal opportunities for promotions.[97] It is remarkable that *all* of the officers involved in the Rodney King beating were white. While no one would suggest that minority officers do not commit abuses, their presence would assuredly provide some deterrence to overt racism.

F. Institutional Obstacles

There are other significant barriers to judicial vindication of the rights of victims of police misconduct. First, victims are not assured access to counsel. There is probably a very small civil rights bar in Metropolis; most lawyers would not be interested in a contingent fee case against the police or the city, even with the possibility of court-awarded attorney's fees if the suit is successful.[98] Second, many civil rights plaintiffs are burdened by characteristics that may prejudice juries against them. They are often poor, or members of racial minorities, or uneducated or inarticulate; some have criminal records. Jurors tend to dismiss their allegations, often awarding them less than a full measure of compensation.[99]

Third, release agreements can be insidious obstacles to the vindication of civil rights in police abuse cases: if they are validated by the courts, they will add to the arsenal of those interested in

---

supra note 16, at 11–12. The drug war has had a highly disproportionate effect on racial minorities, particularly Blacks and Latinos. *See, e.g.*, Lisa Belkin, *Airport Drug Efforts Snaring Innocents Who Fit 'Profiles'*, N.Y. TIMES, Mar. 20, 1990, at A1; E.J. Mitchell, Jr., *Has Drug War Become a War Against Blacks?*, DETROIT NEWS, Apr. 26, 1990, at A1; Rose Marie Arce, *Crimes, Drugs and Stereotypes*, NEWSDAY, Dec. 2, 1991, at 5; Minnesota v. Russell, 60 U.S.L.W. 2425 (Dec. 13, 1991).

[96] *See, e.g.*, LAIC, *supra* note 6, at 91–92, 136.

[97] *See, e.g.*, KERNER COMMISSION REPORT, *supra* note 92, at 166; LAIC, *supra* note 6, at 78–91.

[98] *See* Amsterdam, *supra* note 88, at 787; Caleb Foote, *Tort Remedies for Police Violations of Individual Rights*, 39 MINN. L. REV. 493, 500 (1955).

[99] Foote, *supra* note 98, at 500–08.

covering up police misconduct. In the Metropolis hypothetical, Raft agreed not to sue the police or the city in return for the dismissal of the criminal charges against him. There is a distinct possibility that this agreement would bar Raft's claims. In *Town of Newton v. Rumery*,[100] the Supreme Court ruled that a release agreement is valid if it is "the product of an informed and voluntary decision,"[101] and if "enforcement of [the] agreement would not adversely affect the relevant public interests."[102] Where a prosecutor played a role in the release negotiations, he must have "an independent and legitimate reason to make this agreement directly related to his prosecutorial responsibilities."[103] The burden of "establish[ing] that the agreement was neither involuntary nor the product of an abuse of criminal process" rests upon civil defendants.[104] If the prosecutor's motivation was simply to protect the police from a civil damages action, the public policy prong of *Rumery* would probably be violated.[105]

Fourth, it is very possible that the individual officers would be judgment proof.[106] If they are, and if there is no provision for

---

[100] 480 U.S. 386 (1987).

[101] *Id.* at 393.

[102] *Id.* at 398.

[103] *Id.*

[104] *Id.* at 399 (O'Connor, J., concurring in part and concurring in the judgment of the plurality).

[105] *See id.* at 400. *See also* Lynch v. City of Alhambra, 880 F.2d 1122, 1127 (9th Cir. 1989); Seth F. Kreimer, *Releases, Redress, and Police Misconduct: Reflections on Agreements to Waive Civil Rights Actions in Exchange for Dismissal of Criminal Charges*, 136 U. PA. L. REV. 851, 934 (1988).

[106] Local and state governmental units differ significantly in their provisions for the defense and indemnification of officers in civil rights suits. Some municipalities provide counsel, subject to case-by-case determinations regarding possible conflicts of interest with the municipality itself. *See, e.g.*, Dunton v. County of Suffolk, 729 F.2d 903 (2d Cir. 1984), *vacated in part on other grounds*, 748 F.2d 69 (2d Cir. 1984); Kevlik v. Goldstein, 724 F.2d 844 (1st Cir. 1984). In some jurisdictions, insurance carriers will provide counsel, while in others, the department may retain outside counsel to represent the officer or provide funds for the officer to do so.

Practices also differ with respect to payment of settlements or judgments. The municipality may pay such awards or provide indemnification to the officer. Insurance may cover the settlement or judgment. In some jurisdictions, recovery may be limited to the pocket of the individual defendant, who may be judgment proof.

These varying practices serve different interests. Where the municipality pays the costs of litigation (including counsel) and any monetary awards, the plaintiff is assured of payment, but there is virtually no deterrent value with respect to the officer (particularly where the city does not otherwise discipline or retrain the officer). Where the officer is responsible for payment, deterrence is better served, but at the possible cost of depriving the plaintiff of compensation. For extended discussions of these important competing interests, see PETER H. SCHUCK, SUING GOVERNMENT: CITIZEN REMEDIES FOR OFFICIAL WRONGS (1983); Ronald A. Cass, *Damage Suits Against Public Officers*, 129 U. PA. L.

indemnification, recovery must be sought directly from the municipality. But under Section 1983, municipal liability can be established only where a city policy, practice or custom has caused the constitutional violation; there is no respondeat superior liability.[107]

IV. An Agenda for Reform

If the analysis I have made of the judicial and administrative responses to the misconduct involved in the Metropolis hypothetical is correct, the measures necessary for reform are fairly obvious. In the judicial arena, the Supreme Court must make significant doctrinal adjustments with respect to constitutional litigation. These changes should be tailored to the political and administrative realities of policing, and must take explicit account of the systemic nature of most forms of police abuse.

The Court consistently considers operational exigencies of governmental law enforcement in its adjudication of Fourth and Fifth Amendment claims. In those cases, in the balancing of interests, weight has always been given to the "realities" and dangers of policing.[108] Recognizing the realities only on the governmental side has created a jurisprudence of consistent deference to law enforcement officials and an array of procedural obstacles to the vindication of personal liberties.[109] It is the politics of the Court, and not immutable legal doctrine, that will foreclose appreciable change in the Court's approach to police misconduct in the foreseeable future.[110]

Individual damage suits may continue to generate incremental changes in policy, particularly where the aggregate amounts in any particular locale become so large as to create a political issue concerning the public fisc. Similarly, if the courts develop the doctrinal kernel of *City of Canton* and require municipalities to adequately train, supervise and discipline police, we are likely to

---

REV. 1110 (1981); and Daniel J. Meltzer, *Deterring Constitutional Violations By Law Enforcement Officials: Plaintiffs and Defendants As Private Attorneys General*, 88 COLUM. L. REV. 247, 283–86 (1988).

[107] *See* Monell v. New York Dep't of Social Servs., 436 U.S. 658, 658–59 (1978).

[108] *See, e.g.*, Maryland v. Buie, 494 U.S. 325 (1990); New York v. Quarles, 467 U.S. 649 (1984); Michigan v. Summers, 452 U.S. 692 (1981); Terry v. Ohio, 392 U.S. 1 (1968).

[109] *See supra* notes 72–81.

[110] *Cf.* Payne v. Tennessee, 111 S. Ct. 2597, 2619 (1991) (Marshall, J., dissenting: "Power, not reason, is the new currency of this Court's decisionmaking.").

see at least some police departmental response to seriously flawed procedures.

However, it is unrealistic to rely on judicial intervention as a source of fundamental change. Regardless of the judiciary's response, we must focus attention on other alternatives. The most important factor in the control and reduction of abuse is organizational accountability. All other remedies will ultimately fail if not accompanied by a system of training, supervision and discipline that is structured to ensure that departmental policies relative to use of force and other restrictions on the arbitrary use of power are implemented and enforced. The numerous commissions and studies which have examined the problems of police abuse are unanimous in their recommendations: only a dramatic change in the enforcement of new norms of behavior by the police will dislodge the deeply entrenched culture that currently prevails.[111]

There are several possible ways in which the culture can be modified and in which practices that are more respectful of the normative limitations on police power can be created. The processes of reform involve different institutions in our society; to be successful, they must be mutually reinforcing.

A. Police Administration and the Politics of Change

Despite the formidable obstacles, there is some hope for internally generated police reform. There have been significant advances in recent years in the scope and quality of police training and in the development of official policies and practices. Most departments are managed by professionals who understand the harm to policing that is inflicted when communities are alienated from the police because of patterns of abuse. In part in response to court-imposed sanctions for the violation of rights—including exclusion of evidence from criminal prosecutions and monetary damages against police and municipalities—police departments have developed extensive training programs on the constitutional limits on critical police practices in the arrest, search, interrogation and other investigation areas. However, reliance on judicial inter-

---

[111] See LAIC, supra note 6, at 151–81; Kansas City Task Force, supra note 63, at 45–49; Boston Police Report, supra note 63.

vention as a source of basic change is unrealistic.[112] Of course, as the Supreme Court continues to restrict constitutional rights of suspects, these important incentives for training and supervision will be reduced accordingly.

Further, in some areas the police have taken the responsibility for changing abusive practices. For example, in the 1970s and 1980s public concern over the unjustified use of deadly force led several departments to reconsider their regulations on this practice.[113] Years before the Supreme Court ruled that deadly force could be used to stop a fleeing felon only where the suspect posed an imminent threat of serious physical harm, many police departments had limited deadly force to such situations. As a result, the number of shootings decreased dramatically without any increase in harm to the police.[114]

The reasons for the police initiative on this issue were several, not the least of which was the political pressure of community groups and others concerned with the illegitimate use of such force.[115] Not only did the official rules change,[116] but so did the

---

[112] Imposition of municipal liability under *Owen* and *Monell* has prompted some changes in police practices. A study conducted pre-*Monell* found that suits against individual officers had little impact on institutional policies. *See* Lant B. Davis, John H. Small & David J. Wohlberg, Project, *Suing the Police in Federal Court*, 88 YALE L.J. 781, 809–18 (1979). More recent studies credit the threat of municipal liability as an incentive to police departments to better train, supervise and discipline officers. *See* Candace McCoy, *Enforcement Workshop: Lawsuits Against Police—What Impact Do They Really Have?*, 20 CRIM. L. BULL. 49, 50–53 (1984); Wayne W. Schmidt, *Section 1983 and the Changing Face of Police Management, in* POLICE LEADERSHIP IN AMERICA 226, 235 (William Geller ed., 1985). *See also Report Says Tighter Policies Reduce Killings by the Police*, N.Y. TIMES, Oct. 20, 1986, at A20 (attributing police leadership in new restrictive shooting policies, in part, to the financial influence of civil litigation). The deterrent effect of civil damage payments by municipalities on the conduct of individual officers, however, remains highly questionable. *See* Meltzer, *supra* note 106, at 285–86. *See also* discussion *infra* note 141 and accompanying text.

[113] *See* James J. Fyfe, *Police Use of Deadly Force: Research and Reform*, 5 JUST. Q. 165 (1988) [hereinafter *Deadly Force*]; James J. Fyfe, Garner *Plus Five Years: An Examination of Supreme Court Intervention into Police Discretion and Legislative Prerogatives*, 14 AM. J. CRIM. JUST. 167 (1990); Albert J. Reiss, Jr., *Controlling Police Use of Deadly Force*, 452 ANNALS AM. ACAD. POL. & SOC. SCI. 122 (1980). *See also* Tennessee v. Garner, 471 U.S. 1 (1985).

[114] Fyfe, *Deadly Force*, *supra* note 113, at 181, 186–88. *See also Justice Department Battles Against Conflicts Between Police and Minorities*, N.Y. TIMES, Nov. 13, 1983, at A30.

[115] *See, e.g.*, Richard Higgins, *Debate Over Deadly Force*, BOSTON GLOBE, Sept. 8, 1983, at A1; Judith Miller, *New Questions Arise on Policing Police*, N.Y. TIMES, Apr. 3, 1983, at 4.

[116] *See, e.g.*, Joel J. Smith, *Gun Use—A Dilemma for Police*, DETROIT NEWS, Oct. 22, 1981, at A1 (describing policy changes in Detroit, Beverly Hills and Dearborn, Michigan); Arnold Markowitz, *Chiefs Revise Deadly Force Rules in Dade*, MIAMI HERALD, Dec. 15, 1983, at D1.

police culture. Violations of the policy resulted in discipline and retraining (and in some cases prosecution).[117] Police officers soon understood that their departments were serious about the new policies and adjusted their conduct accordingly.[118] That the new rules were imposed internally on a "voluntary" basis no doubt played a part in their overall acceptance. Indeed, the change in policy was so successful that, when the Court ultimately was faced with the constitutional issue, professional police organizations urged the Court to discard the broad and easily-abused fleeing felon rule.[119]

Other areas of police duties are equally amenable to significant internal change in norms and conduct. There is no reason why specific practices, for example, the use of police dogs,[120] non-deadly weapons,[121] and the control of public demonstrations[122]

---

[117] See Justice Department Battles Against Conflicts Between Police and Minorities, supra note 114, at A30.

[118] For example, in 1980 in Philadelphia, after a mayoral campaign that focused in large part on the brutality of the city's police force, the new administration adopted strict limitations on the use of deadly force, and made it known that it was serious about enforcement. See SKOLNICK & FYFE, supra note 10. An officer told this author at the time that word had gone out in the department that "if you shoot, you had better be right."

[119] Fyfe, Deadly Force, supra note 113, at 200 (brief of amici curiae against Tennessee and Memphis Police Department in Garner was filed by the Police Foundation and joined by nine associations of police and criminal justice professionals, the chiefs of police associations of two states, and 31 law enforcement chief executives).

[120] The city of West Palm Beach, Fla., has been held liable for its failure to adequately train and supervise its canine police unit. Kerr v. City of West Palm Beach, 875 F.2d 1546 (11th Cir. 1989). The LAIC reported citizen complaints that Los Angeles police officers ordered their dogs to attack minority suspects who were already in police custody or under control. LAIC, supra note 6, at 77–78.

[121] Attention was focused on the use of electric stun guns in 1985 when three New York City police officers were accused and convicted of using the devices to torture confessions from four men arrested on minor drug charges and other minor offenses. Joseph P. Fried, Ex-Sergeant's Release Ordered in Stun-Gun Case, N.Y. TIMES, Sept. 16, 1990, at 35; Robert D. McFadden, Youth's Charges of Torture By an Officer Spur Inquiry, N.Y. TIMES, Apr. 22, 1985, at B3. Electric stun guns deliver a 40,000-volt charge without inflicting permanent injury and leave only a pair of small burn marks on the skin. New York City Police Officers Convicted in 'Stun Gun' Case, CRIM. JUST. NEWSL., May 15, 1986, at 7, 8. At the time of the incident, many police departments across the country regularly used electric stun guns. Alleged Torture Brings Focus on Police Use of Stun Guns, CRIM. JUST. NEWSL., May 15, 1985, at 3.

[122] On the night of August 6, 1988, a demonstration of 150 to 200 people protesting the closing of Tompkins Square Park in Manhattan degenerated into four hours of fighting between the crowd and the officers policing the event. Todd S. Purdum, Melee in Tompkins Square Park: Violence and Its Provocation, N.Y. TIMES, Aug. 14, 1988, at A1. There were almost 100 complaints of police brutality; 44 civilians and police officers were injured. Id. The police violence was attributed to poor planning, tactical errors, the youth and inexperience of the officers and a shortage of sergeants and lieutenants. David E. Pitt, Roots of Tompkins Sq. Clash Seen in Young and Inexperienced Officer Corps, N.Y. TIMES, Aug. 25, 1988, at B7; Purdum, supra, at A1. As a result of the police riot, the N.Y.C. Police

cannot be subjected to careful study and control in a manner that limits possibilities for the abuse of power. As evidenced by the dramatic results achieved across the country in the difficult field of hostage takings,[123] training of special units that incorporate as a basic tenet the use of all means to save human life can produce remarkable improvements in police work. Over the years, the professionalization of this aspect of policing has substantially reduced the number of persons killed or injured in these volatile situations.[124]

Not all potentially abusive practices are as amenable to administrative efforts at reform. The patterns of harassment, indignities and violence that attend the everyday work of investigation, searches and arrests are far more resistant strains of misconduct, which emanate from a strong police subculture reinforced by political demands such as the "war on crime." If part of the community is seen as a deadly enemy, law enforcement tactics are bound to reflect that conception. If the resulting abuses are to be contained, more fundamental structural change will be required.

One promising development is the practice of community-oriented policing. This model is built on the premise that there are mutual community and police interests and that reciprocal respect for these concerns and interests will provide a more effective and progressive means of policing. Community policing relies less upon the practices of the past three decades which emphasized proactive, aggressive policing aimed at apprehension and prosecution; rather, it stresses the principle of police-community cooperation by increasing foot patrols, supporting community citizen patrols, and developing mutually acceptable goals for particular communities.[125]

Of course, the case for community-oriented policing can be overstated, and there should be no expectation that it alone will generate progressive change. If the police view this concept merely as a matter of labeling, as opposed to one of substantive change in which they have a voice and a stake, the program will not

---

Department instituted "sweeping improvements in training, command structure and equipment." Pitt, *supra*, at B7.
   [123] See SKOLNICK & FYFE, *supra* note 10; Robert W. Taylor, *Hostage and Crisis Negotiation Procedures: Assessing Police Liability*, TRIAL, March 1983, at 64.
   [124] SKOLNICK & FYFE, *supra* note 10.
   [125] LAIC, *supra* note 6, at 95–106; Boston Police Report, *supra* note 63, at 29–53.

succeed.[126] A necessary corollary to police understanding and acceptance of community policing as a new philosophy is the willingness of community leaders to support effective and fair policing, while at the same time condemning excesses and abuses. The community should not be held hostage to a pattern of abuse as a quid pro quo for police protection.

Civilian review of the police is a necessary component of a system of accountability.[127] There has been bitter debate about the concept of civilian review of police, but it is now firmly established in varying forms in thirty of our fifty largest cities.[128] The success of civilian review will depend in large part on the proper allocation of power between police and civilians. It is essential that the civilian oversight include the full power to investigate complaints, conduct hearings, subpoena witnesses, including police officers, and issue reports or findings on the complaints. If the civilian review board does not have authority to impose sanctions, its recommendations for discipline should be given careful consideration by the police commissioner. Civilian review procedures should also include the authority to make policy recommendations and to gather statistical data relevant to patterns of abuse.

The early intervention initiative utilized by an increasing number of police departments provides a related means of breaking the cycle of abuse. Statistical studies within various departments show a disturbingly disproportionate number of complaints regarding excessive force against relatively few officers.[129] The fact that these numbers are as high as they are points to significant deficiencies in the monitoring and disciplining process. But even if internal discipline is effective, many officers reject findings made against them in adversary administrative or judicial proceedings as the illegitimate products of a system that fails to understand the pressures and dangers facing the officer on the street. The officers

---

[126] Indeed, the Boston Police Department tried to implement a community policing program in March 1991. It has been widely recognized as a failure because the Department merely added community policing onto existing policies, rather than radically rethinking its philosophy of protection as a whole. Boston Police Report, *supra* note 63, at 39, 44–51.

[127] *See id.* at 128–33.

[128] Samuel Walker & Vic. W. Bumphus, *Civilian Review of the Police: A National Survey of the 50 Largest Cities, 1991*, in FOCUS: CRIMINAL JUSTICE POLICY 1, No. 91-3 (Dept. of Criminal Justice, Univ. of Neb., 1991).

[129] *See, e.g.*, LAIC, *supra* note 6, at 31–65; George Jones, *Police to Track Brutality Charges Against Officers*, N.Y. TIMES, Nov. 7, 1991, at B2; Don Terry, *Kansas City Police Force Go After Own 'Bad Boys,'* N.Y. TIMES, Sept. 10, 1991, at A1.

may moderate their conduct for fear of sanctions, but their own standards and world view remain unchanged.

For some officers who repeatedly engage in abusive conduct, an early intervention program based on principles of non-punitive retraining may be a more effective means of reducing unnecessary violence in police confrontations with citizens. These programs include a mix of retraining on rules governing use of force, role playing, psychological interviews and improving oral communication skills. In an experiment in Oakland, California, a police violence prevention unit used a peer review approach on street officers who, on average, had engaged in physical confrontations with citizens at a rate nearly four times that of non-participating officers. Over time, the officers who participated in this program reduced their violent incident records by more than fifty percent.[130]

B. Federal Intervention

In light of the nationwide scope of the problem, consideration should be given to federal intervention. The power of the federal government in enforcing the constitutional rights of citizens against local police officials has been bitterly disputed.[131] Historically, the Department of Justice has generally refrained from investigation and prosecution of local police abuse. The limits on federal authority are largely self-imposed, although a narrow statutory authority is also a contributing factor. The magnitude of the abuse problem calls for a substantial change of direction.

The federal government has authority to bring criminal prosecutions against state officers who violate or conspire to violate the civil rights of citizens.[132] These criminal statutes require the government to prove that the defendant specifically intended to

---

[130] See HANS TOCH & J. DOUGLAS GRANT, POLICE AS PROBLEM SOLVERS 242–43 (1991).
[131] The traditional argument against intervention is deeply ingrained. For example, John Dunne, Assistant Attorney General in charge of the Civil Rights Division of the Justice Department, stated during Congressional hearings on police brutality in the wake of the Rodney King incident: "We are not the 'front-line' troops in combatting instances of police abuse. That role properly lies with the internal affairs bureaus of law enforcement agencies and with state and local prosecutors. The federal enforcement program is more like a 'backstop' to these other resources." John Dunne, Statement to the House Subcommittee on Civil and Constitutional Rights of the House Judiciary Committee (March 20, 1991) [hereinafter Dunne Statement], quoted in HUMAN RIGHTS WATCH, POLICE BRUTALITY IN THE UNITED STATES 4–5 (July 1991).
[132] 18 U.S.C. §§ 241, 242 (1988).

deprive the victim of a constitutional right,[133] a factor that is often cited by the Justice Department as the reason why there are so few police abuse prosecutions.[134] It is unlikely that the failure of the federal government to prosecute police can be so easily explained. It is far more likely that the reasons behind the lack of federal prosecutions are the same as those explaining the paucity of state prosecutions: prosecutors do not like prosecuting fellow law enforcement officers (with whom they work on a day to day basis); evidence of such misconduct is often shielded by the code of silence; victims are more readily subject to impeachment (prior records, life styles, etc.); and juries are inclined to give the benefit of the doubt to the police.[135]

On the civil side, the Justice Department lacks authority to bring injunctive actions even where police abuse is alleged to be widespread.[136] Congress can give the Attorney General the power to bring litigation to protect against widespread violations of constitutional rights. Congress has authorized injunctions in cases of employment discrimination,[137] discrimination in public accommodations,[138] deprivation of voting rights[139] and, for persons in prisons, mental institutions and nursing homes, where "egregious or flagrant conditions which deprive . . . persons of any rights, privileges or immunities secured or protected by the Constitution or laws of the United States."[140]

Without the availability of private or public enforcement of constitutional rights in this area, local governments are free simply

---

[133] *See, e.g.*, United States v. Guest, 383 U.S. 745, 760 (1966).

[134] The FBI investigates approximately 2500 complaints of police abuse per year. Dunne Statement, *supra* note 131, at 5. However, very few of these result in prosecution. Mr. Dunne has stated that in the three years preceding the Rodney King incident, there were 98 prosecutions in this area. *Id.* Yet, in the City of Los Angeles, despite documented cases of serious abuse, no prosecutions had been initiated in several years. Hoffman, *supra* note 65, at 4–5. The jurisdictional confines of the federal law have provided a rationalization for not doing so.

[135] *See supra* notes 60, 83–85, 88, 91, 99 and accompanying text.

[136] In *United States v. City of Philadelphia*, 644 F.2d 187 (3d Cir. 1980), the Justice Department sought an injunction against the police department of the City of Philadelphia to end the department's "practice of violating the rights of persons they encounter on the streets and elsewhere in the city," a departmental policy "implemented with the intent and the effect of inflicting abuse disproportionately on black and Hispanic persons." *Id.* at 190. The Court of Appeals for the Third Circuit refused to recognize an implied power in the federal government to bring an action to enjoin violations of constitutional rights. *Id.* at 192–201.

[137] 42 U.S.C. § 2000e-6 (1988).

[138] 42 U.S.C. § 2000a-3 (1988).

[139] 42 U.S.C. § 1971 (1988).

[140] 42 U.S.C. § 1997a (1988).

to pay as they go for the violation of the rights of their people without any possibility of judicial intervention to prevent abuses before they occur. In Los Angeles, even the payment of more than $10 million in police abuse judgments in 1990 alone (more than $1,000 per sworn officer in the LAPD) has had no perceptible impact on these problems.[141]

Legislation introduced in Congress in the wake of the Rodney King incident would allow greater federal intervention. The Attorney General and aggrieved individuals would be authorized to bring pattern or practice suits.[142] In recommending these provisions, the House-Senate conference proposed the use of injunctions to meaningfully address patterns of police abuse.[143]

The bill would also require the Department of Justice to compile and publish data on the use of excessive force by police officers.[144] The lack of information on the incidence of excessive force and other forms of police abuse is a significant barrier to both political and legal reform.[145] Without credible information on the scope and pervasiveness of the problem, the public is left with the impression that the abuses are more aberrational than systemic. Significant changes on the national level will not occur unless there is detailed evidence that the abuse is not isolated or local in nature.

The federal government has a large program of assistance to local law enforcement agencies under the Office of Justice Pro-

---

[141] John L. Mitchell, *$11.3 Million Paid in 1990 to Resolve Abuse Cases*, L.A. TIMES, Mar. 29, 1991, at A1. In other cities, payment of similarly high figures as compensation for police abuse does not seem to deter such activity. *See, e.g.*, Sean Murphy, *City Paid $3.4 Million in Civil Suit Settlements in '88*, BOSTON GLOBE, May 14, 1989, at 29 (police misconduct cases cost city $1.1 million out of total $3.4 million paid). Part of the reason stems from the fact that, in most cases, the police officer faces no financial risk or other disciplinary sanctions if his conduct leads to a civil suit. *See* discussion *supra* note 106. Even being sued repeatedly does not necessarily hinder promotion or assignment to elite training or narcotics units. Bill Wallace, *San Francisco Pays in Many Suits Against Cops*, S.F. CHRON., May 30, 1990, at A1. Provisions for municipal payment of settlements and judgments may suffice to compensate victims of police abuse, but unless taxpayers are offended by the amounts paid or police departments consider such judgments in disciplining their officers, there will be little deterrence of individual officers' behavior from these payments.

[142] *See* H.R. 2972, 102d Cong., 1st Sess. (1991). This proposal has been incorporated in part by the Senate-House conferees on the "Violent Crime Control and Law Enforcement Act of 1991." H.R. CONF. REP. NO. 405, 102d Cong., 1st Sess. 97 (1991).

[143] H.R. CONF. REP. NO. 405, 102d Cong., 1st Sess. at 97.

[144] *Id.*

[145] HUMAN RIGHTS WATCH, *supra* note 131, at 8.

grams.[146] It is appropriate for the federal government to establish standards for the use of force, including the proper use of weapons, and for internal review of police performance. Further, meaningful and institutionalized respect for constitutional rights should be a condition of the receipt of federal funds for law enforcement.[147]

V. Conclusion

On April 29, 1992, as this Article was about to go to press, a jury without any African-Americans (drawn from a conservative suburban community) returned a verdict of not guilty as to all the officers charged with beating Rodney King. This shocking verdict touched off widespread protests and rioting in Los Angeles and other cities around the country. While the reasons behind the jury's conclusion are not yet clear, the verdict unfortunately confirms the thesis of this Article: the law and order mentality that has pervaded the consciousness of America, coupled with strong elements of racism, lead many to believe that the police should retain a free hand in order to protect "us" from "them."

The Rodney King incident demonstrates once again the tragic consequences of our failure as a society to respond to the systemic and institutional aspects of police abuse. Official misconduct endures in large part because we respond to its many manifestations in an episodic manner. As long as the courts and both federal and state government treat police abuse as a series of isolated incidents, or as a regrettable by-product of the war on crime, the Monroes, Rafts and Rodney Kings will continue to pay an unconscionable price for our misguided policies. Police violence will be contained only if we challenge fundamental aspects of police culture and hold the police politically and legally accountable. Experience teaches that structural problems require structural remedies. We ignore that lesson at the peril of individual victims of abuse, the core values and institutions of constitutional government and the very integrity of our society.

---

[146] For example, the Bureau of Justice Assistance Grant Programs can make direct grants to local law enforcement agencies for the acquisition of equipment and other programs dedicated to improving the criminal justice system. 42 U.S.C. § 3751 (1988).

[147] It is a common device under federal law to condition a grant upon compliance with some other provision of federal law, and it is already used in the federal law enforcement assistance programs. Under 42 U.S.C. § 3789(d) (1988), for example, a federal grant for local law enforcement may be suspended if it is found that the local body has discriminated in employment on the basis of race, religion, nationality or gender.

American Journal of Police Vol. 12, No. 2 1992   *1*

INTEGRATING DISTINCT MANAGERIAL STYLES: THE CHALLENGE FOR POLICE LEADERSHIP

Malcolm K. Sparrow

Harvard University

The spread of "community policing" throughout the United States leaves many police officers frustrated, resentful, even bewildered. From their practical experience, they know the urgency of life-threatening emergencies. They understand the continuing need for coordinated military-style action in public order situations. They still believe in the deterrent effect of highly visible mobile patrols.

However rational and intelligent the arguments for community and problem-solving policing, the message that some officers think they hear clashes with their own operational experience. They feel that the emerging strategies of policing pay inadequate attention to the continuing demand for emergency services, and thus reduce public safety (Skolnick & Bayley, 1988; Larson, 1990). They worry that community policing would not or could not support swift, effective response to public disorder situations to prevent escalation into riots. They hear what seems to be a diminution in the importance being attached to serious crime (Murphy, 1991; Pisani, 1992).

Often, when the philosophy of community policing is being considered, some officers worry that adoption "on a department-wide scale" would leave absolutely zero capacity for rapid response, or for centrally coordinated interventions (Larson, 1990:3). They imagine a department disregarding important criminal activities just because there was no particular community group upset by them. They also worry that a problem-solving approach to policing might ignore specific instances of very serious crimes just because they did not fit into any discernible pattern, or "problem."

Experienced police officers have genuine and well-motivated concerns that some proponents of new strategies, given free rein, would destroy valuable aspects of existing police service. They worry that police departments may end up filled to the brim with thoughtful and academically well-qualified problem solvers who would be quite incapable of making tough operational decisions quickly when someone's life depended on it.

Officers are also mindful of political and economic realities that seem to demand that attention be paid to serious but unsolvable crimes, and to bank robberies and financial frauds, whether or not any community group regards them as priorities. And they know that police departments will continue to pay an extremely high price in terms of public support when someone dies because they were "too late" getting to a road accident, a domestic dispute or a street fight.

There are apparent philosophical differences between the positions taken by community policing advocates and rapid-response advocates. Community policing and the traditional, more militaristic, styles of policing have at their core fundamentally different ideas about what is being policed. Community policing sees the object of policing as people: communities, institutions, individuals, families. But a "patrol" force is traditionally accustomed to patrolling spaces. Controlling spaces and influencing behaviors are quite different goals.

A friend of mine recently claimed to have the answer to the crime problem. He said he knew how to exclude crime altogether from a room of whatever size I chose. Curious, I asked how. He said he'd fill it with concrete!

An absurd idea, but an interesting one. It's interesting because it epitomizes an extreme version of the "controlling space" idea. At the same time it is absurd because it is not usefully extensible, and because we know that the social fabric with all its latent criminality would simply bend around precluded spaces, finding alternative locations for all of its activities.

Organizing for rapid response clearly promotes the geographical, or spatial, approach. The object is to be able to get an officer to any place within defined geographical space as soon as possible.

On the other hand, organizing for community policing promotes division of labor and allocation of resources according to the structure of the social fabric; that is, according to the needs of people. Officers are allocated to communities, or neighborhoods—the emphasis being upon the integrity and characteristics of the community groups that dwell there, rather than on the accompanying geographical divisions (Sparrow et al., 1990). Moreover, within a framework of problem-solving policing, officers spend much of their time assigned for working on a particular problem or problems, working on the problems of the people (Goldstein, 1990).

There are thus two distinct domains for police action: space, and society. Emerging strategies of policing appear to be placing more emphasis on policing society and less on policing spaces.

The issue that then emerges is how far policing can, or should, move in shifting from one domain to another. If it were possible to police society well enough, how much policing of spaces would still be required? Is it theoretically possible (or desirable) to exercise such control over people, and their behaviors, that we would no longer need to patrol highways, parks or subway stations in an organized way? Can community policing produce such levels of harmony within neighborhoods that round-the-clock patrolling of those areas becomes unnecessary?

The practical answer seems obvious. Police cannot expect to abandon twenty-four-hour coverage, shift work or rapid response. They have to continue operating in the domain of space as well as in the domain of society. Yet all the academic and pragmatic arguments supporting community policing and problem solving suggest that greater effectiveness in policing comes by doing more of the latter and less of the former.

The point to be made here is that police must continue to operate in both domains. They always have operated in both, and they probably always will. The balance may change, as may ideas about which methods are the key technologies. But both kinds of policing will remain.

This aim of this paper is to show that the need to operate simultaneously in these two quite distinct modes and to integrate the resulting activities within one coherent organization presents very special managerial challenges for policing. They are challenges unique to the policing profession. They are challenges that will probably lie at the heart of the debate over policing styles and operations for the next decade.

THE PERSISTENCE OF THE NEED
FOR EMERGENCY RESPONSE

No amount of preventative or proactive work is going to eradicate traffic accidents, mechanical failures, drunkenness, or violence. Levels may be reduced through appropriate pre-disaster interventions, but the requirement for post-disaster responses at one level or another is an inevitable fact of life.

Nor are the rapid responses required purely medical in nature. At the scene of emergencies someone has to prevent further danger (e.g., by controlling traffic flow), coordinate the activities of different agencies, take care of personal property, preserve evidence about the cause of the incident and the culpability of participants, identify witnesses, begin whatever investigations are appropriate, and generally figure out what happened and why—all traditionally the responsibilities of police. There is, therefore, much to be done that could not simply be left to emergency medical crews.

Therefore, whatever organizational forms eventually emerge in support of community and problem-solving policing have to take account of the persistent requirement for emergency response.

The persistence and inescapable urgency of emergency response often appears to hamper the development of departmental commitment to community and problem-oriented policing. Thus, it is very tempting to propose that all emergency rapid-response functions be hived off into a separate unit, leaving the bulk of the department free to grapple with the more complex, longer term and potentially more important business of building community rapport and developing strategies for addressing deep underlying problems.

But segregation of the rapid response function from whatever turns out to be the mainstream of police business has to be rejected. Segregation would deny the grounds upon which the new philosophies are based. The theoretical foundation of community policing and problem-solving policing is the realization that the day-to-day disasters and victimizations that befall individuals—despite their apparent unpredictability—are inextricably linked with the patterns, norms, values, traditions, feelings and well-being of the broader population. It is because of this link that police leaders have turned their attention to these new styles of policing. It would be an extraordinary about-face, in implementing these new strategies, if the connection were severed.

Moreover, if the rapid-response functions were segregated it would not be long before the units responsible for emergency cover started rediscovering the truths that underpin the present changes. They would discover that their emergencies formed patterns, and that crimes were most effectively solved and prevented within a cooperative public partnership. They would soon be running to the "problem-solving unit" asking for help.

Likewise, the problem-solving or community policing units, devoid of responsibility for emergency intervention, would gradually lose their way. The motivation for pursuing these styles of policing lies in the contribution they make to relieve human misery and suffering, and the enhancement to the quality of life in the cities. Cut off from the tangible evidences of disharmony, strife and victimization, proactive or preventative units would slowly lose touch with their *raison d'etre*.

Preserving rich information interchange and close cooperation between the emergency and proactive functions seems to be essential to the effectiveness of both.

THE PERSISTENCE OF THE NEED
FOR SPATIAL APPROACHES

In general, proactive or preventative police functions operate mostly upon people, whereas reactive and emergency functions are organized mostly around spaces. But there are interesting exceptions to this rule. It is worth noting that community and problem-solving policing do continue to operate, where appropriate, in the spatial domain—not always, but sometimes.

In Tampa, Florida, the Police Department took a highly imaginative problem-solving approach to the growing threat of open drug dealing within the city (Kennedy, 1991). The QUAD (Quick Uniform Attack on Drugs) squads set up to focus on the problem, developed tactics that were heavily concentrated around the idea of retaking control of particular spaces—sixty to eighty specific locations identified as drug dealing spots. The Tampa Police Department could have organized their operations by dealer, but they chose to organize them, in this case, by location. The reason for the choice was that police could create a shortage of comfortable drug-dealing locations (thus destroying the market) whereas they could not create any damaging shortage of drug dealers.

Another example: within the New York subway system one tactic adopted to reassure passengers of their safety was the establishment of "safe areas"—well-lit and closely monitored pieces of subway platforms where waiting passengers could feel relatively safe (Kelling, 1991). It could be argued that policing subway systems should remain essentially a problem of controlling spaces, because the spaces are relatively small, the density of people relatively great, and the population relatively transient when compared with the task of policing city neighborhoods.

In Philadelphia, citizen groups worked in cooperation with police to take back street corners from drug dealers (Kennedy, 1990). It was a community policing success. But the division of labor and allocation of resources was street corner by street corner, and shift by shift.

So adoption of progressive policing strategies does not at all seem to preclude organization and operation in the spatial domain. Nor does it preclude organizing the public to operate that way. That style of operation remains an option. So it is an advantage for police departments to remain good at it. But defining the units of work in terms of place and time, under the new strategies, becomes just one option among many. There should no longer be the presumption that operating in squads, by areas and in shifts is necessarily the best way to tackle any particular problem.

DIFFERENT MANAGERIAL CONSEQUENCES

Modern police departments must accept that there will be occasions when their effectiveness depends upon their thoughtfulness, their skill at eliciting community perceptions and opinions, their open-mindedness in framing issues for analysis, their versatility and creativity in generating and implementing a wide range of solutions, their salesmanship in procuring community support, and their articulateness and rationality in giving an account for their actions.

But there will also be occasions when the department's effectiveness depends upon the speed with which they can assess an emergency situation, the accuracy of the initial assessment, the effectiveness of central control, the reliability and speed of the communication system, the degree of coordination of disparate resources, the ability to marshal officers and equipment, and the ability (on occasions) to formulate and execute military-style manoevres.

But the choice is not "either-or." There remains a need for both. Therein lies the special managerial challenge for policing. Maintaining the ability to function in these two very different styles imposes a certain organizational schizophrenia on police departments. It is a schizophrenia that reaches many parts of the organization, because these two different styles of operation demand very different types of organizational support.

For example, they require different qualities from patrol officers, different forms of command and control, different ideas of what it means to be "in-service," different forms of analytical support, different roles for middle managers, and different qualities and qualifications for officers of all ranks.

QUALITIES FOR PATROL OFFICERS

During the most recent miner's strike in Britain (in the early 1980s) the idea of a standardized public order police squad was conceived. Called a "Police Support Unit", each comprised 20 constables, two sergeants, and an Inspector (in charge). Equipped with riot shields, they travelled around the country from coal field to coal field in minibuses. The principle of "mutual aid" between separate county forces was also formalized, so that a pit head picket in Yorkshire could easily be policed by Police Support Units (PSUs) from all over the country. When one county needed manpower assistance, the only relevant question was "how many PSUs, and for how long?"

The demand for PSUs was so high that officers were taken away from many other types of police duty. Detectives found themselves in uniform crouched behind riot shields. So did rural beat officers. It was the village "bobbies" who found the transition most difficult. One day they were talking with their parishioners, all of whom they knew personally, dealing with problems that had histories. The next day they were stripped of their individuality, required to operate as a small cog in a large machine, under the command of a Sergeant or Inspector they might never have seen before.

Switching from role to role on a daily or weekly basis brought home to many the psychological strains of playing such different roles. Many beat officers found it extremely difficult to settle back into their communities once the miner's dispute was over.

Community policing and problem-solving policing demand of officers the following skills, among others: the ability to manage one's time, weighing short-term obligations against longer term projects; communication and negotiation skills; the ability to mobilize and motivate others; analytical problem-solving skills; public speaking; the ability to construct effective liaisons with other public agencies; knowledge of crime prevention techniques, and many more.

But other, more militaristic or emergency-oriented roles require a very different set of abilities: commanding physical presence; ability to drive fast and safely; navigation under pressure; acute spatial awareness; physical strength; physical courage; accurate shooting; instant obedience to orders; quick thinking; the ability to function as a part of a team.

So which of these two sets of skills are most important? It is, not surprisingly, impossible to say. Different situations require different abilities. Clearly the emerging policing strategies are putting more emphasis on the first set, and less on the second. And it is with respect to the first that most departments have had the most obvious deficiencies in the past. But we should not imagine that policing can survive if the second set is ignored or disregarded. Modern police departments need both.

In making personnel assignments, and in conducting performance appraisals, notice has to be taken of officers' varying talents. Few officers offer the whole range of skills. Some officers are much better suited to some functions than others.

The question is how police departments can make progress in developing the more thoughtful analytic skills while continuing to give appropriate recognition to the more traditional quasi-military and rapid-response capabilities. The message that existing skills remain valuable is too frequently construed as an excuse not to take seriously the need for change. It is extremely difficult to preserve some measure of quasi-military capability without also preserving the impediment of a quasi-military culture (Sparrow et al., 1990; Wasserman & Moore, 1988).

COMMAND AND CONTROL

Community and problem-solving policing require much less centralized control than reactive emergency response functions. The new strategies shift the emphasis to precinct-level control, localized and flexible priority setting, and beat officer discretion. In their mature forms the new styles produce less rank-conscious, more professional, cultures, similar to those of lawyers in a legal practice or physicians in a hospital. Advice is given or received on the basis of specialization, experience and expertise, not rank.

But responses to genuine emergencies still need to be centrally administered, and response times kept to a minimum. The ability to move police units around a city like pins on a pin map must be preserved. It should not, however, remain the normal mode of operation for routine police business (Sparrow, 1991).

Within a reactive mode of operation a unit that is "in service" is a unit that is doing nothing! Simply being available is important work within the emergency response operation. But within the problem-solving framework, "in service" would more naturally mean away from the car, doing something intelligent. They are very different ideas about what is important.

Again, the department does not have to choose. It has to recognize both. The challenge is setting an appropriate balance and achieving the requisite integration.

ANALYTICAL SUPPORT

Herman Goldstein has laid out in considerable detail the range of "problems" that can be nominated for police attention. He suggests some useful definitions of "problem"—as "a cluster of similar, related, or recurring incidents rather than a single incident," "a substantive community concern," and as "the unit of police business" (Goldstein, 1990:66).

He makes it quite clear that such problems may or may not be crime related. He also points to several different dimensions in which incidents may be clustered: they might reveal common types of behavior; they might all occur in some particular geographic location or territory; they might all involve a particular type of offender, or a particular type of victim, or a repeat offender or a repeat victim; or they might be clustered around some particular time of day or week or season (Goldstein, 1990:67-68).

Traditional police departments, when asked to invent "crime analysis" and to start doing it, move very naturally to conducting analyses in the same domain in which they have done their patrolling in the past:

that is, they naturally start examining the distribution of crimes in time and space. To support such analysis many modern computer-aided dispatch systems offer some kind of analytical clustering capability.

But geographic and temporal patterns cover only a small subset of Goldstein's list. All the other kinds of patterns—offender class, victim class, behavior type, weapon type and so on—focus on people or groups of people or behaviors. Thus, in order to be able to conduct problem-solving analyses across the whole spectrum of problems, departments will require the facility to aggregate and disaggregate incident data along one, or any combination, of these several different dimensions. That requires flexible database structures with versatile access and analytic capabilities. The required analytic capabilities are not fully prescribed either by the reactive or the proactive approach, but by a combination of the two.

ROLE OF MIDDLE MANAGEMENT

The new strategies of policing are defining new roles for middle management. Under community and problem-oriented policing, middle managers become responsible for bringing together power over resources with knowledge of community problems. Mid-level managers encourage street-level officers to identify substantial community (or client) problems, help street officers win organizational acknowledgment of the importance of such problems, and bring appropriate organizational expertise and energy to bear upon them.

Middle managers are also required to produce a professional atmosphere conducive to creativity, experimentation, and problem-solving; to stimulate the production and dissemination of ideas; to craft cooperative partnerships sufficient to tackle weighty and complex problems.

They also become the appropriate ears for concerns of community groups that transcend the responsibility of individual beat officers, but which fall short of being department-wide. Thus they become project managers and problem solvers in their own right.

These new roles differ markedly from tradition. The military influence on policing is perhaps most clearly visible in pervasive middle-management styles that emphasize tight supervision and control and reveal an intolerance for error. Such managerial styles have been quite closely associated with the more traditional functions of policing.

The police rank structure, like all tall rank structures, was created in order to enable large tasks to be broken down into smaller pieces, through several intermediate stages of aggregation. The role of middle manager always used to be parceling out pieces of a well-defined job.

Several police functions still remain that require middle managers to operate in this mode. Crowd control still requires middle managers who can bark orders and procure instant obedience; who can move officers around in units without losing control, or respect. Maintaining emergency response capabilities requires middle managers to coordinate shifts, equipment, and deployments. VIP protection and policing large public events require similar managerial skills.

But community and problem-solving policing demand very different managerial skills. Once again, the challenge is not to choose, but to balance and integrate the competing demands of different police functions.

THE UNIQUENESS OF THE CHALLENGE

There are few, if any, other professions which have to integrate strong commitments to both reactive and proactive work styles within a single organization. Fire departments are organized principally around rapid response. Welfare departments do much people-oriented family-centered problem solving, but little emergency response.

Perhaps the closest equivalent is medicine, in which a similarly strong link between emergencies and preventative health care exists. But medicine enjoys the luxury of separate, dedicated emergency response teams (ambulances and paramedics). They also enjoy the fact that, except in emergencies, most of their clients come to them rather than vice versa.

It is difficult to determine exactly where the interface between reactive medicine and preventative medicine lies. Hospital emergency rooms act as emergency entry points into the hospital system. But most of what hospitals do could be classified as reactive, albeit with varying degrees of urgency. Most patients who go to hospitals are already sick, at least to some degree.

There is also clear feedback between proactive and reactive medical care that passes through the general medical community and its literature, and through studies aided or conducted by academics. Correlations between human behaviors (diet, exercise, sexual practices etc.)

and resultant diseases or traumas are the fodder of medical research. Breakthroughs in medical research—reports linking human habits with increased or decreased chances of disease—frequently make front page news. The general public now take for granted the fact that the medical profession is conscientiously studious over the early causes, early detection and the prevention of disease. (The same claim can hardly be made for the profession of policing with respect to crime).

But the most effective interface between reactive and proactive medicine lies within the medical profession's equivalent of the community beat officer. It is the family practitioner, more readily found in rural communities than big cities, who automatically and naturally links what he or she learns about local family and community life with the resulting medical conditions. It is these generalists who are best placed to respond to medical emergencies in context.

The medical profession, like the police profession, has practiced effective preventative care for years—but has done so most naturally through small practices in rural communities. General practitioners are harder to find in large American cities than in British or Canadian cities, or throughout rural America. The abundance of medical high-technology in American cities, supporting specialists and specialization, appears historically (and somewhat ironically) to have driven out much of the generalist, preventative care. It is as if the concentration of so much knowledge and expertise makes general practitioners look ignorant.

But the role of a general practitioner requires a valuable and particular type of knowledge. They need to know which specialists to call, and when. They do not need to know everything the specialists know. The value of generalists lies in the combination of their accessibility with their knowledge of the organizational resources available to them. Their function is to spot emerging problems, and to know the most appropriate forms of support to call forward.

Within the police profession, just as within medicine, provision of generalist, accessible, preventative service is least natural within the largest (and therefore most specialized) departments. The greater the opportunity for functional specialization, the greater the distance between emergency response and its social context. The greater the extent to which promotional paths lie through high-status specialities, the lower the status of generalists.

The "general practitioners" of policing must to be accessible; and must know which specialist organizational resources to bring to bear on a problem. Preferably they will also be willing and able to procure specialist capabilities from all the other departments of urban government when appropriate.

Medicine, like policing, faces a major challenge in the cities—the challenge of re-integrating the reactive and proactive styles on an organization-wide basis. In both professions, the advent of technology and functional specialization appears largely responsible for creating the rift.

SETTING THE TARGET, PAYING THE PRICE

Much has been said here about the need to shift balances. Community policing and problem-solving policing place greater emphasis on proactive and preventive work than on reactive work, and more emphasis on policing society than on policing spaces.

Many departments, embracing the new strategies, are determined to adjust some balances. There are two important things they need to bear in mind.

First, they need to think hard about where the ideal balance lies. They need to set the goal. Too much of the recent debate over apparently conflicting policing styles has centered on making choices, rather than on choosing appropriate balances. Adoption of community policing, department wide, cannot mean zero resources available for rapid response. What does it mean? How many, if any, officers are going to spend their time being prepared for emergencies?

Few departments will actually have to specify a precise answer in the immediate future. That is because the balance slides only very slowly, and we know which way it has to move for now! But talking, or thinking, about setting realistic targets might give peace of mind to, and procure more cooperation from, officers who fear decimation of their response capacity as a result of adoption of community policing.

Second, they need to acknowledge that there is a capital cost to moving the balance in favor of proactive work. Proactive work takes time to produce fruit. There is a definite lag—of months, sometimes of years—in its effect. In the meantime, the level of reactive effort required remains undiminished. So, during the process of shifting the balance, some duplication of efforts is required.

Seeing programmatic or strategic change as a capital investment is a strange idea, especially foreign to the public sector. But there are many occasions when changing a system turns out to have capital consequences.

An analogy may help: suppose your traditional practice is to buy goods with a credit card, and then pay off the credit card bill when it comes due six weeks later. Then, one day, you change to a system of immediate payment in cash for everything you buy. During the change, for one six-week period, you will be apparently paying double. The capital cost of changing the system is equal to six weeks worth of expenses.

But the money is not gone. It can be recouped. If, at some later stage, you change back you enjoy a six week period with zero cash outflow. Hence the capital nature of the cost. It represents an investment in a change of system.

Moving from reactive to proactive work—whether in medicine or policing—produces an interim period of doubled effort. It costs. It is hard to find the resources to finance such changes, because government exhibits a marked reluctance to regard expenditures as capital unless they can see the money invested in bricks and mortar, or in substantial and resalable pieces of equipment. So persuading a city to fund something as intangible as a change of policing style, to bear with the police chief through trials and experiments, to wait for results, is somewhat difficult; more so given the lingering uncertainty of the payoffs from proactive work.

The argument for increasing the level of proactive work is that it should be a more effective policing strategy in the long run. But making the change, or shifting the balance, remains expensive in the short run.

CONCLUSION

The aim of this paper was not to define the appropriate balances to be struck between reactive and proactive policing; between control of spaces and influence over behaviors; between directed patrols and community intervention; or between deployment of squads and of neighborhood beat officers. Defining the requisite balances is work for each department to do. Some need to move much further than others in the new balances they set. Some police departments, such as those that police dockyards or subway systems, might ultimately need to remain largely in the "control of spaces" business. Different police organizations will certainly vary in the speed with which they can dismantle old ideas, reallocate resources, and introduce new skills.

But hopefully this paper, unambitious in the sense that it does not seek to give precise prescriptions, will help police executives understand the nature of the managerial challenges they face. These are uncommon challenges, unique to policing. Answers developed in other professions and easily transferable to policing just do not exist. Nor are there police departments (yet) that can claim to have solved these problems completely. Ready-made solutions are unavailable.

Police executives and managers intent on implementing the best of the new ideas about policing, and equally intent on preserving valuable capabilities that their departments already have, must pay attention to these issues—issues that have the potential to be extraordinarily damaging to prospects for change. Executives need to frame these questions of balance and integration precisely enough to be useful in the context of their particular department. They need to generate the appropriate debate about them, both inside their departments and with their external constituencies. There needs to be a process for prescribing both eventual and transitional goals in answer to those questions.

The object of this paper is to point out that this work has yet to be done, and hopefully to reduce some of the unproductive antagonism generated by insufficiently thoughtful debate about contrasting styles of policing.

REFERENCES

Goldstein, H. (1990). *Problem-Oriented Policing.* New York: McGraw-Hill.

Kelling, G. (1991). "Reclaiming the Subway." New York: *The City Journal,* 1(2).

Kennedy, D. (1990). "The Philadelphia Anti-Drug Coalition." Case no: C16-90-937.0. Case Program. Cambridge, MA: John F. Kennedy School of Government. Harvard University.

Kennedy, D. (1991). "Closing the Market: Controlling the Drug Trade in Tampa, Florida." Case Program. Cambridge, MA: John F. Kennedy School of Government. Harvard University.

Larson, R. (1990). "Rapid Response and Community Policing: Are They Really in Conflict?" *Community Policing Series*, No. 20. Lansing, MI: National Center for Community Policing, School of Criminal Justice, Michigan State University.

Murphy, D. (1991). "When Cops go Back on the Beat." Los Angeles, CA: *Los Angeles Times*, August 27.

Pisani, A. (1992). "Dissecting Community Policing: Part I." *Law Enforcement News*, May 15.

Skolnick, J. and D. Bayley (1988). *Community Policing: Issues and Practices Around the World*. Washington, DC: National Institute of Justice, U.S. Department of Justice.

Sparrow, M., M. Moore and D. Kennedy (1990). *Beyond 911: A New Era for Policing*. New York: Basic Books.

Sparrow, M. (1991). "Information Systems: A Help or Hindrance in the Evolution of Policing?" *Police Chief*, April.

Wasserman, R. and M. Moore (1988). "Values in Policing." *Perspectives on Policing*, No. 8. Washington, DC: National Institute of Justice, U.S. Department of Justice.

0091-4169/94/8501-0241
THE JOURNAL OF CRIMINAL LAW & CRIMINOLOGY
Copyright © 1994 by Northwestern University, School of Law

Vol. 85, No. 1
Printed in U.S.A.

CRIMINOLOGY

THE INFLUENCE OF THE *GARNER* DECISION ON POLICE USE OF DEADLY FORCE

DR. ABRAHAM N. TENNENBAUM

ABSTRACT

In March of 1985, the Supreme Court in *Tennessee v. Garner* held that laws authorizing police use of deadly force to apprehend fleeing, unarmed, non-violent felony suspects violate the Fourth Amendment, and therefore states should eliminate them.

This paper investigates the impact of that decision on the number of homicides committed by police officers nationwide. The investigation shows a significant reduction (approximately sixteen percent) between the number of homicides committed before, and after the decision. This reduction was more significant in states which declared their laws regarding police use of deadly force to be unconstitutional after the *Garner* decision.

Evidence suggests that the reduction is due not only to a reduction in shooting fleeing felons, but also to a general reduction in police shooting. This paper discusses a mechanism that can explain the unique *Tennessee v. Garner* dynamic.

I. INTRODUCTION

People have criticized use of deadly force ever since police officers began carrying guns. In 1858, a New York Times editorial about a case in which a police officer shot and killed a fleeing suspect stated:

The pistols are not used in *self-defence*,—but to stop the men who are running away. They are considered substitutes for swift feet and long arms. Now, we doubt the propriety of employing them for such a purpose. A Policeman has no right to shoot a man for running away from him. . . .

But what right have Policemen to carry revolvers at all? . . . We doubt very much the policy of arming our Policemen with revolvers.[1]

Similar arguments have persisted to the present day as the public has consistently denounced civilian homicides by police officers. People have accused officers of shooting arbitrarily, or unjustifiably,[2] and most frequently of exhibiting racism in such situations.[3] These accusations have been supported by numerous empirical studies showing that police officers kill African-Americans at a disproportionately higher rate than whites.[4]

In March of 1985, the United States Supreme Court, in *Tennessee v. Garner*,[5] held that laws authorizing police use of deadly force to apprehend fleeing, unarmed, non-violent felony suspects violate the Fourth Amendment, and therefore states should eliminate them. This paper investigates the impact of the *Garner* decision on homicides committed by police nationwide. However, before estimating the influence of the decision, it is appropriate to describe the different policies that existed prior to *Garner*, and the changes in the law resulting from *Garner*.

A. POLICIES AND LEGAL SITUATION BEFORE GARNER

Prior to *Garner*, laws controlling police use of deadly force fell into one of four groups: The Any-Felony Rule; The Defense-of-Life Rule; The Model Penal Code; The Forcible Felony Rule.[6] At one extreme of the spectrum was the Any-Felony Rule. English common law authorized officers to use any means necessary to arrest felony suspects or prevent them from fleeing. In the United States, courts interpreted this rule as legal permission to shoot an unarmed felony suspect in flight.[7]

---

[1] *Police with Pistols*, N.Y. TIMES, Nov. 15, 1858, at 4.

[2] An early study claims that from the incidents that were checked by the author, only two-fifths were justifiable, one-fifth was questionable, and two-fifths were not justifiable. Arthur L. Kobler, *Police Homicide In A Democracy*, 31 J. Soc. ISSUES 163, 165 (1975).

[3] *See, e.g.*, Paul Takagi, *A Garrison State In "Democratic" Society*, 5 CRIME & Soc. JUST. 27, 29-30 (1974).

[4] Mark Blumberg, *Police Use of Deadly Force: Exploring Some Key Issues, in* POLICE DEVIANCE 219, 229 (Thomas Barker & David L. Carter eds., 2d ed. 1991); James J. Fyfe, *Blind Justice: Police Shootings in Memphis*, 73 J. CRIM. L. & CRIMINOLOGY 707, 720 (1982); William A. Geller & Michael S. Scott, *Deadly Force: What We Know, in* THINKING ABOUT POLICE: CONTEMPORARY READING 453 (Carl B. Klockars & Stephen D. Mastrofske eds., 2d ed. 1991); David B. Griswold & Charles R. Massey, *Police and Citizen Killings of Criminal Suspects: A Comparative Analysis*, 4 AM. J. POLICE 1, 6 (1985).

[5] 471 U.S. 1 (1985).

[6] GEOFFREY P. ALPERT & LORIE A. FRIDELL, POLICE VEHICLES AND FIREARMS: INSTRUMENTS OF DEADLY FORCE 70-71 (1992). *See also* Mark Blumberg, *Controlling Police Use of Deadly Force: Assessing Two Decades of Progress, in* CRITICAL ISSUES IN POLICING: CONTEMPORARY READINGS 442, 442-43 (Roger G. Dunham & Geoffrey P. Alpert eds., 1989).

[7] See ALPERT & FRIDELL, *supra* note 6, at 70; Lawrence W. Sherman, *Execution Without*

At the other end of the spectrum was the Defense-of-Life Rule. Under this doctrine, the only justification for using deadly force was to protect human life, either the police officer's own life or a civilian's life.[8] The only justification for risking loss of life was the preservation of another life. Following this rationale, police shooting of an unarmed fleeing suspect was unjustifiable, and unacceptable. Until recently, this was the official policy of the FBI.[9]

The other two policies, the Model Penal Code (MPC) and the Forcible-Felony Rule, tried to balance the two extremes. Ultimately, however, they had the same practical result. The American Law Institute drafted the MPC to guide states that want to modify their criminal statutes and procedures.[10] The Code offered two conditions to the use of deadly force: (1) The crime involved the use or threatened use of deadly force; and (2) There is a substantial risk that the suspect will cause death or serious bodily harm if his apprehension is delayed.[11]

States enacting the Forcible-Felony Rule have defined specific felonies as "forcible felonies." Those states allow police to use deadly force only against people suspected of committing those felonies. Usually, forcible felonies include murder, arson, rape, kidnapping, and armed robbery.[12]

Critics have directed most of their criticisms towards the Any-Felony Rule, commenting that this rule is not adequate for modern times.[13] Indeed, when the English Common Law developed this rule, the courts recognized only a few felonies, and the penalty for them was capital punishment. Moreover, police did not have firearms, so the permission to use "any means" meant actual physical force, or, at most, perhaps a sword. Ultimately, England has eliminated the rule, perhaps recognizing its inadequacy in today's world.

In the United States, many people have argued that the Any-Felony Rule is unconstitutional. They have claimed that it violates the Fourth Amendment's protection against illegal search and seizure, the Eighth Amendment's prohibition of cruel and unusual punish-

---

Trial: Police Homicide and the Constitution, 33 VAND. L. REV. 71, 74-79 (1980).

[8] ALPERT & FRIDELL, *supra* note 6, at 71.

[9] WILLIAM A. GELLER & MICHAEL S. SCOTT, DEADLY FORCE: WHAT WE KNOW, A PRACTITIONER'S DESK REFERENCE ON POLICE-INVOLVED SHOOTINGS 267-275 (1992) [hereinafter DEADLY FORCE: PRACTITIONER'S DESK REFERENCE].

[10] ALPERT & FRIDELL, *supra* note 6, at 70.

[11] MODEL PENAL CODE § 3.08(2)(b)(i),(iv) (Proposed Official Draft 1962).

[12] ALPERT & FRIDELL, *supra* note 6, at 71; J. Paul Boutwell, *Use of Deadly Force to Arrest a Fleeing Felon—A Constitutional Challenge, Parts I & III, in* READINGS ON POLICE USE OF DEADLY FORCE 65, 73 (James J. Fyfe ed., 1982).

[13] Blumberg, *supra* note 6, at 443-44. Sherman, *supra* note 7, at 97.

ment, and the Fourteenth Amendment's guarantee of due process.[14]

Despite long standing criticism, the Any-Felony Rule was the law prior to *Garner* in at least twenty-four states, while some combination of the other three policies existed in the other states.[15] However, police departments usually follow their internal guidelines rather than the state's laws. Further, many of these guidelines are more restrictive than the state law. Thus, the actual police departments' policies before *Garner* varied significantly not only from state to state, but also within each state.[16]

B.   *TENNESSEE V. GARNER*

Most jurisdictions considered police use of deadly force for all felonies to be legitimate until the Supreme Court decided *Tennessee v. Garner*. In that case, Garner brought a wrongful death action under the federal civil rights statute against a police officer and his respective department for the fatal shooting of Garner's son as he fled the scene of a burglary. Garner's son was unarmed at the time of the shooting. Justice White wrote for the majority, in a monumental decision: "We conclude that such force may not be used unless it is necessary to prevent the escape and the officer has probable cause to believe that the suspect poses a significant threat of death or serious physical injury to the officer or others."[17]

Although scholars agree that *Garner*-type shootings are unconstitutional,[18] they disagree on what the phrase "the suspect poses a significant threat of death or serious physical injury" means. Some believe that the decision "created a constitutional right to run for many felony suspects;"[19] others argue that it gave police officers the right to use deadly force only to protect life.[20]

---

[14] *See* Boutwell, *supra* note 12; Floyd R. Finch, Jr., Comment, *Deadly Force to Arrest: Triggering Constitutional Review*, 11 Harv. C.R.-C.L. L. Rev. 361 (1976); Sherman, *supra* note 7, at 97.

[15] While the Supreme Court lists 24 states where the 'Any Felony' rule was in existence before *Garner*, others claim different numbers. Professors Fyfe and Walker show surprise at that number, and claim some inaccuracy. James J. Fyfe & Jeffery T. Walker, Garner *Plus Five Years: An Examination of Supreme Court Intervention Into Police Discretion and Legislative Prerogatives*, 14 Am. J. Crim. Just. 167, 177 (1990). This article uses the 22 states mentioned by Professors Fyfe and Walker as the sample for the states influenced by *Garner*, and all the rest as states that were not. *See id.* at 177-78, table 1.

[16] For the variety of policies, see Geller & Scott, *supra* note 9, at 247-75.

[17] Tennessee v. Garner, 471 U.S. 1, 3 (1985).

[18] Ginny Looney, *The Unconstitutional Use of Deadly Force Against Nonviolent Fleeing Felons:* Garner v. Memphis Police Department, 18 Ga. L. Rev. 137, 163 (1983); John Simon, Tennessee v. Garner: *The Fleeing Felon Rule*, 30 St. Louis U. L.J. 1259, 1277 (1986).

[19] Michael D. Greathouse, *Criminal Law—The Right to Run: Deadly Force and the Fleeing Felon:* Tennessee v. Garner, *105 S. Ct. 1694 (1985)*, 11 S. Ill. U. L.J. 171, 184 (1986).

[20] David B. Griswold, *Controlling the Police Use of Deadly Force: Exploring the Alternatives*, 4

It seems that the Supreme Court equivocated. It severely restricted the Any-Felony Rule, but did not limit the use of deadly force to self-defense. Its language is similar to the MPC, but demands less by not requiring a life-threatening crime. As a result, most commentators agreed that the Court's decision in *Garner* would not significantly affect police conduct,[21] because the creation or modification of laws has never effectively modified police behavior.[22]

Professors Fyfe and Walker conducted a nationwide study which examined the impact of the *Garner* decision on policy-makers.[23] They examined legislative changes, activities of state attorneys general, and subsequent federal case law, and found that of the twenty-two states that *Garner* apparently affected, only four have amended their statutes to comply with the Court's holding.[24] In the remaining eighteen states, only two state attorneys general have officially advised the police of the decision. Fyfe and Walker attribute this response to legislators' fear that complying with *Garner* would cause voters to view them as being "soft on crime."[25] However, their study did not deal with the empirical question of whether *Garner* influenced the number of homicides committed by police.

The primary focus of this article is to fill that void, and investigate empirically the effect of the *Garner* decision on the number of homicides police officers commit nationwide.

II.   RESEARCH METHODOLOGY

A.   DATA SET

Law enforcement agencies that report criminal homicides on the basic Uniform Crime Report (UCR) form are requested (but not required) to submit a Supplementary Homicide Report (SHR) for each month.[26] Agencies do not submit SHRs for months in which police do not receive any reports of homicides. The form is incident-oriented—*i.e.*, if more than one murder occurred during the same incident, the agency fills out only one form, which covers each of the homicides. Each form details the age and race of the offenders and

---

AM. J. POLICE 93, 102 (1985).

21 *See* ALPERT & FRIDELL, *supra* note 6, at 69; James J. Fyfe, *Police Use of Deadly Force: Research and Reform*, 5 JUST. Q. 165, 199 (1988).

22 James J. Fyfe & Mark Blumberg, *Response to Griswold: A More Valid Test of the Justifiability of Police Actions*, 4 AM. J. POLICE 110, 111 (1985). *See also* William B. Waegel, *The Use of Lethal Force By Police: The Effect of Statutory Change*, 30 CRIME & DELINQ. 121, 136 (1984).

23 Fyfe & Walker, *supra* note 15.

24 *Id.* at 178.

25 *Id.* at 179.

26 FEDERAL BUREAU OF INVESTIGATION, UNIFORM CRIME REPORT HAND BOOK 63, 63-65 (1984).

victims (if known), and the weapon used. The form also details the circumstances and background of the incident, using terms such as "love triangle," "killed by babysitter," "brawl under alcohol," "argument over money," "killed while robbery," "killed while rape," "justifiable homicide-civilian," and "justifiable homicide-police."[27]

The data sources for this research are SHR files for the years 1976 through 1988, as processed by the Inter-University Consortium for Political and Social Research (ICPSR) from the original SHR master tapes provided by the FBI.[28] While the SHR has clear limitations, the problems are not significant for the general question being tested,[29] and are similar to the problems in data sets used in previous research about deadly force.[30]

B.   THE STATISTICAL METHOD

The empirical analysis discussed in this article relies on "interrupted time series analysis," which estimates the impact of a specific event of social behavior. Analysts have used it to estimate the effect of political changes on the stock market, to measure the effect of installing a service fee on the number of phone calls to directory assistance, and to test and measure the impact of experimental psychological treatment. The most intensive use, however, has been to test the influence of new laws on changing public behavior.[31]

Under this method, analysts measure the average number of ob-

---

[27] Marc Riedel, *Nationwide Homicide Data Sets: An Evaluation of the Uniform Crime Reports and the National Center for Health Statistics Data*, in MEASURING CRIME: LARGE-SCALE, LONG-RANGE EFFORTS 175, 178 (Doris L. MacKenzie et al. eds., 1990)[hereinafter MEASURING CRIME].

[28] Two states, Florida and Kentucky, were not included because of flawed data.

[29] The validity of the UCR is a question beyond the scope of this paper. *See generally* Yoshio Akiyama & Harvey M. Rosenthal, *The Future of the Uniform Crime Reporting Program: Its Scope and Promise*, in MEASURING CRIME, *supra* note 27, at 49-74; Victoria W. Schneider & Brian Wiersema, *Limits and Use of the Uniform Crime Reports*, in MEASURING CRIME, *supra* note 27, at 22-48; Paul H. Blackman & Richard E. Gardener, Flaws in the Current and Proposed Uniform Crime Reporting Programs Regarding Homicide and Weapons Use in Violent Crime (1986) (Paper Presented at the Annual Meeting of the American Society of Criminology). Concerning the SHR, Professor Maxfield points to some flaws in the data caused largely by law enforcement agencies filling out the forms inappropriately. *See* Michael G. Maxfield, *Circumstances in Supplementary Homicide Reports: Variety and Validity*, 27 CRIMINOLOGY 671, 685-92 (1989). The main problem in the "circumstances" variable seems to be that the same circumstances can be interpreted in more than one way. *See generally* Colin Loftin, *The Validity of Robbery-Murder Classifications in Baltimore*, 1 VIOLENCE & VICTIMS 191, 191-204 (1986).

[30] On the general question of measuring homicides by police officers, see Lawrence W. Sherman & Robert H. Langworthy, *Measuring Homicide by Police Officers*, 70 J. CRIM. L. & CRIMINOLOGY 546 (1979). For a comprehensive review on the SHR measure of police homicides, see DEADLY FORCE: PRACTITIONER'S DESK REFERENCE, *supra* note 9, at 32-37.

[31] DAVID MCDOWALL ET AL., INTERRUPTED TIME SERIES ANALYSIS 10-11 (1980).

---

servations in a time unit, before and after a specific event. If the event influenced social behavior, these averages should be different. However, some trends which are not correlated to the tested event may influence the time series' behavior. For example, some commentators have suggested that, even before *Garner*, the trend in justifiable homicides by police was declining.[32] Thus, any conclusion based only on average differences may be incorrect.

One way to avoid this is to build a mathematical model which takes into account trends and correlations in the data. After controlling for those, analysts may properly measure the averages and calculate the influence of the event.

The most popular way to estimate the effect of a specific event for this purpose is through the use of Auto Regressive Integrated Moving Average (ARIMA) models.[33] The advantage of ARIMA models (compared with regression models) is that they are more sensitive to the data, rather than the specific variables chosen by theory. One problem, however, is that the ARIMA models may not be sensitive enough to find a correlation between two variables. If, however, researchers do find a correlation, they can rely on it conservatively.

An accurate model using ARIMA requires researchers to first identify the reasonable model, then estimate the parameters for that model, and then conduct an appropriate diagnosis of the model.[34] Once an appropriate model is built, analysts may add the intervention component and test its influence on the model.

Using an ARIMA model, the influence of *Garner* on the number of homicides committed by police nationwide was tested.[35] Also, *Garner*'s influence on various states was tested. The author divided the data into two groups: states whose deadly force laws were declared unconstitutional ("unconstitutional states"); and states whose laws

---

[32] *See generally* LAWRENCE W. SHERMAN ET AL., CITIZENS KILLED BY BIG CITY POLICE 1970-84 (1986).

[33] For details on ARIMA, see GEORGE E.P. BOX & GWILY M. JENKINS, TIME SERIES ANALYSIS: FORECASTING AND CONTROL 12, 73-78, 87-103 (1976). On the specific question of intervention in time series, see Douglas A. Hibbs, Jr., *On Analyzing the Effects of Policy Interventions: Box-Jenkins and Box-Tiao vs. Structural Equation Models*, SOCIOLOGICAL METHODOLOGY 137 (1977); Richard McCleary & David McDowall, *A Time Series Approach to Causal Modeling: Swedish Population Growth, 1750-1849*, 10 POLITICAL METHODOLOGY 357 (1984); RICHARD MCCLEARY ET AL., APPLIED TIME SERIES ANALYSIS FOR THE SOCIAL SCIENCES (1980); DAVID MCDOWALL ET AL., INTERRUPTED TIME SERIES ANALYSIS (1980).

[34] SPSS INC., SPSS-X USER'S GUIDE 385 (3d ed. 1988). Technically, the author identifies the model using the auto-correlation-function (ACF) and the partial-auto-correlation-function (PACF). The parameters must lie within the bounds of stationarity-invertability, and be statistically significant, to be considered adequate. Two tests are usually applied to verify the estimated model; the residuals of the ACF must describe white noise (without spikes in key lags), and the Q-statistic must be insignificant.

[35] The study examined a total of 4733 cases from January 1976 to December 1988.

were adequate before *Garner* ("constitutional states"). The study measured *Garner's* influence on each of these groups to determine whether it was greater on one than on the other.[36]

C. VERIFICATION TESTS

To avoid the possibility that a variable which is unrelated to *Garner* affected the results, the author first determined the total number of homicides (including justifiable) committed by police during the same time period. If the measurement process is accurate, the number of total homicides before and after *Garner* should not differ. Also, the author measured the influence of *Garner* on the ratio of police homicides to the total number of criminal homicides. If the data were faulty, the ratio between them would be influenced to a lesser extent than the individual categories.[37]

These two validations are important because of the correlation between the number of police homicides and the number of criminal homicides.[38] If, despite this connection, the number of police homicides decreased, while the number of criminal homicides remained constant, the *Garner* decision most likely influenced that reduction.

III. FINDINGS

A. THE REDUCTION IN POLICE HOMICIDES

Graph 1[39] shows the incidence of police homicides over time. The line in the middle is the intervention point (the month of the *Garner* decision). As the graph indicates, the data does not contain an outlier.

---

[36] The study actually looks at the influence of *Garner* on police shooting in general and not only at cases that resulted in death. However, the number of homicides is a direct result of the number of shootings. According to the SHR, from the total of 4733 police homicides used for this study, 4670 (98.67%) were the results of shooting.

[37] *See generally* THOMAS D. COOK & DONALD T. CAMPBELL, QUASI-EXPERIMENTATION: DESIGN & ANALYSIS ISSUES FOR FIELD SETTINGS (1979). For a short summary, *see* Thomas D. Cook, *Clarifying the Warrant for Generalized Causal Inferences in Quasi-Experimentation, in* EVALUATION AND EDUCATION: AT QUARTER CENTURY 115 (Milbrey W. McLaughlin & D.C. Phillips eds., 1991).

[38] *See* James J. Fyfe, *Geographic Correlates of Police Shooting: A Microanalysis,* 17 J. RES. CRIME AND DELINQ. 101 (1980); Richard R.E. Kania & Wade C. Mackey, *Police Violence as a Function of Community Characteristics,* 15 CRIMINOLOGY 27 (1977). *But see* Robert H. Langworthy, *Police Shooting and Criminal Homicide: The Temporal Relationship,* 2 J. QUANTITATIVE CRIMINOLOGY 377 (1986). For the connection between police homicides and violent crime in general, see David Jacobs & David Britt, *Inequality and Police Use of Deadly Force: An Empirical Assessment of a Conflict Hypothesis,* 26 SOCIAL FORCES 403, 412 (1979).

[39] Looking at graphs alone is not an accurate way to reach conclusions, and can sometimes be misleading. It is recommended, however, to avoid outlying points. *See generally* F.J. Anscombe, *Graphs in Statistical Analysis,* 27 AM. STATISTICIAN 17 (1973).

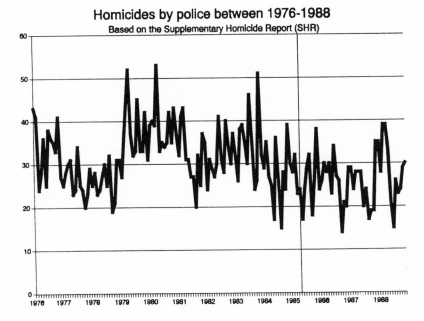

GRAPH 1

Homicides by police between 1976-1988
Based on the Supplementary Homicide Report (SHR)

As stated, analysts cannot add the intervention component until they identify the right statistical model for the data. As Graph 2, which shows the auto-correlation-function (ACF), and Graph 3, which shows the partial-auto-correlation-function (PACF) of the original data illustrate, the most appropriate model is the auto-regressive model of order 1. Graph 4 shows the auto-correlation-function (ACF), and Graph 5 shows the partial auto-correlation-function (PACF) of this model.

The model passes the diagnostic stage because there are no significant values in key lags in any graphs; the parameter estimates are within the permitted boundaries; and the Q-test is not significant.[40] Thus, this model is appropriate to test the intervention—*i.e.*, the effect of the *Garner* decision on police homicides.

Table 1 includes the parameters for the intervention model for the number of police homicides each month ("police" variable), and the ratio of police homicides to criminal homicides ("ratio" variable).

---

[40] The Q-statistic is distributed as a chi-square statistic. At the 0.05 level, the critical value (with 23 degrees of freedom) is 35.17. If the Q-test is more than the critical value (as in Graph 2), the model does not fit the assumption about non-auto-correlation of the residuals. If this is the case, the model is inappropriate.

GRAPH 2

ACF VARIABLE IS POLICE.
MAXLAG IS 25. LBQ./

FIRST CASE NUMBER TO BE USED	=	1
LAST CASE NUMBER TO BE USED	=	156
NO. OF OBS. AFTER DIFFERENCING	=	156
MEAN OF THE (DIFFERENCED) SERIES	=	28.1026
STANDARD ERROR OF THE MEAN	=	0.5430
T-VALUE OF MEAN (AGAINST ZERO)	=	51.7513

AUTOCORRELATIONS

1-12	.35	.20	.27	.21	.10	.02	.22	.18	.14	.20	.20	.15
ST.E.	.08	.09	.09	.10	.10	.10	.10	.10	.11	.11	.11	.11
L.-B. Q	20.	27.	38.	46.	47.	47.	55.	60.	63.	70.	77.	80.

13-24	.06	0.0	−.05	−.01	0.0	−.06	.02	.05	.02	−.15	−.13	0.0
ST.E.	.11	.11	.11	.11	.11	.11	.11	.11	.11	.11	.11	.12
L.-B. Q	81.	81.	81.	81.	81.	82.	82.	83.	83.	87.	90.	90.

25-25	−.01
ST.E.	.12
L.-B. Q	90.

PLOT OF AUTOCORRELATIONS

```
          -1.0   -0.8   -0.6   -0.4   -0.2   0.0    0.2    0.4    0.6    0.8    1.0
LAG   CORR.  + - - - + - - - + - - - + - - - + - - - + - - - + - - - + - - - + - - - +
                                                  I
  1   0.353                                       +    IXXX+XXXXX
  2   0.205                                       +    IXXX+X
  3   0.269                                       +    IXXXX+XX
  4   0.211                                       +    IXXXXX
  5   0.103                                       +    IXXX +
  6   0.025                                       +    IX    +
  7   0.215                                       +    IXXXXX
  8   0.176                                       +    IXXXX+
  9   0.138                                       +    IXXX +
 10   0.197                                       +    IXXXXX
 11   0.198                                       +    IXXXXX
 12   0.148                                       +    IXXXX+
 13   0.058                                   +       IX       +
 14  -0.001                                   +       I        +
 15  -0.054                                   +      XI        +
 16  -0.010                                   +       I        +
 17   0.004                                   +       I        +
 18  -0.059                                   +      XI        +
 19   0.023                                   +       IX       +
 20   0.045                                   +       IX       +
 21   0.018                                   +       I        +
 22  -0.155                                  +XXXXI           +
 23  -0.125                                   + XXXI          +
 24   0.000                                   +       I        +
 25  -0.010                                   +       I        +
```

Show the ACF for the variable 'police' (police homicides), and the Q statistic. As can be seen, the ACF has significant value in all the first four lags, and the Q statistic is significant (Q distribution here is like chai-square distribution with twenty-five degrees of freedom).

GRAPH 3

PACF VARIABLE IS POLICE.
MAXLAG IS 25./

FIRST CASE NUMBER TO BE USED	=	1
LAST CASE NUMBER TO BE USED	=	156
NO. OF OBS. AFTER DIFFERENCING	=	156
MEAN OF THE (DIFFERENCED) SERIES	=	28.1026
STANDARD ERROR OF THE MEAN	=	0.5430
T-VALUE OF MEAN (AGAINST ZERO)	=	51.7513

PARTIAL AUTOCORRELATIONS

1-12	.35	.09	.20	.07	−.03	−.08	.21	.05	.07	.08	.04	0.0
ST.E.	.08	.08	.08	.08	.08	.08	.08	.08	.08	.08	.08	.08

13-24	−.05	−.12	−.11	.03	.01	−.08	.04	0.0	0.0	−.19	−.06	.09
ST.E.	.08	.08	.08	.08	.08	.08	.08	.08	.08	.08	.08	.08

25-25	.15
ST.E.	.08

PLOT OF PARTIAL AUTOCORRELATIONS

```
              -1.0    -0.8    -0.6    -0.4    -0.2    0.0    0.2    0.4    0.6    0.8    1.0
LAG   CORR.    + - - - + - - - + - - - + - - - + - - - + - - - + - - - + - - - + - - - + - - - +
                                                       I
  1   0.353                                     +     IXXX+XXXXX
  2   0.091                                     +     IXX +
  3   0.197                                     +     IXXX+X
  4   0.065                                     +     IXX +
  5  -0.029                                     +   XI    +
  6  -0.078                                     + XXI    +
  7   0.208                                     +     IXXX+X
  8   0.053                                     +   IX    +
  9   0.067                                     +   IXX  +
 10   0.081                                     +   IXX  +
 11   0.040                                     +   IX    +
 12   0.001                                     +   I     +
 13  -0.046                                     +   XI    +
 14  -0.118                                     +XXXI    +
 15  -0.114                                     +XXXI    +
 16   0.028                                     +   IX    +
 17   0.011                                     +   I     +
 18  -0.079                                     + XXI    +
 19   0.036                                     +   IX    +
 20  -0.002                                     +   I     +
 21  -0.003                                     +   I     +
 22  -0.188                                     X+XXXI    +
 23  -0.058                                     +   XI    +
 24   0.093                                     +   IXX  +
 25   0.149                                     +   IXXXX
```

Shows the PACF for the variable 'police' (police homicides).

GRAPH 4

ACF VARIABLE IS OUTR.
MAXLAG IS 25. LBQ./

FIRST CASE NUMBER TO BE USED	=	2
LAST CASE NUMBER TO BE USED	=	156
NO. OF OBS. AFTER DIFFERENCING	=	155
MEAN OF THE (DIFFERENCED) SERIES	=	−0.0688
STANDARD ERROR OF THE MEAN	=	0.5087
T-VALUE OF MEAN (AGAINST ZERO)	=	−0.1353

AUTOCORRELATIONS

1-12	−.05	0.0	.19	.12	.03	−.09	.19	.08	.02	.11	.11	.09
ST.E.	.08	.08	.08	.08	.08	.08	.09	.09	.09	.09	.09	.09
L.-B. Q	.30	.30	6.1	8.5	8.6	9.9	16.	17.	17.	19.	21.	22.
13-24	.02	0.0	−.07	0.0	.04	−.08	.03	.05	.08	−.15	−.10	.05
ST.E.	.09	.09	.09	.09	.09	.09	.09	.09	.09	.09	.09	.09
L.-B Q	22.	22.	23.	23.	24.	25.	25.	25.	26.	30.	32.	33.

25-25	.04
ST.E.	.09
L.-B Q	33.

PLOT OF AUTOCORRELATIONS

```
            -1.0   -0.8   -0.6   -0.4   -0.2    0.0    0.2    0.4    0.6    0.8    1.0
LAG  CORR.    + - - - + - - - + - - - + - - - + - - - + - - - + - - - + - - - + - - - +
                                                    I
 1  -0.047                                     +   XI    +
 2   0.002                                     +   I     +
 3   0.190                                     +   IXXX+X
 4   0.121                                     +   IXXX+
 5   0.028                                     +   IX    +
 6  -0.090                                     + XXI     +
 7   0.185                                     +   IXXX+X
 8   0.078                                     +   IXX +
 9   0.024                                     +   IX  +
10   0.114                                     +   IXXX+
11   0.106                                     +   IXXX+
12   0.095                                     +   IXX +
13   0.020                                     +   I   +
14  -0.004                                     +   I   +
15  -0.068                                     + XXI   +
16   0.003                                     +   I   +
17   0.042                                     +   IX  +
18  -0.084                                     + XXI   +
19   0.026                                     +   IX  +
20   0.048                                     +   IX  +
21   0.077                                     +   IXX +
22  -0.149                                     +XXXXI    +
23  -0.095                                     +  XXI    +
24   0.054                                     +   IX  +
25   0.039                                     +   IX  +
```

Shows the ACF and the Q-statistic for the residuals of 'police' (police homicides) for the autoregressive first-order model.

GRAPH 5

PACF VARIABLE IS OUTR.
MAXLAG IS 25./

FIRST CASE NUMBER TO BE USED	=	2
LAST CASE NUMBER TO BE USED	=	156

1PAGE 7 2T POLICE HOMICIDES

NO. OF OBS. AFTER DIFFERENCING	=	155
MEAN OF THE (DIFFERENCED) SERIES	=	−0.0688
STANDARD ERROR OF THE MEAN	=	0.5087
T-VALUE OF MEAN (AGAINST ZERO)	=	−0.1353

PARTIAL AUTOCORRELATIONS

1-12	−.05	0.0	.19	.14	.04	−.13	.13	.08	.07	.09	.06	.06
ST.E.	.08	.08	.08	.08	.08	.08	.08	.08	.08	.08	.08	.08
13-24	.01	−.07	−.15	−.04	.04	−.06	0.0	0.0	.08	−.14	−.14	−.02
ST.E.	.08	.08	.08	.08	.08	.08	.08	.08	.08	.08	.08	.08
25-25	.16											
ST.E.	.08											

PLOT OF PARTIAL AUTOCORRELATIONS

```
                -1.0    -0.8    -0.6    -0.4    -0.2    0.0     0.2     0.4     0.6     0.8     1.0
LAG   CORR.     + - - - + - - - + - - - + - - - + - - - + - - - + - - - + - - - + - - - + - - - +
                                                        I
  1  -0.047                                      +   XI   +
  2   0.000                                      +    I   +
  3   0.190                                      +    IXXX+X
  4   0.145                                      +    IXXXX
  5   0.044                                      +   IX   +
  6  -0.132                                      +XXXI    +
  7   0.126                                      +    IXXX+
  8   0.077                                      +   IXX  +
  9   0.072                                      +   IXX  +
 10   0.090                                      +   IXX  +
 11   0.064                                      +   IXX  +
 12   0.056                                      +   IX   +
 13   0.014                                      +    I   +
 14  -0.071                                      + XXI    +
 15  -0.154                                      XXXXI    +
 16  -0.044                                      +   XI   +
 17   0.036                                      +   IX   +
 18  -0.060                                      + XXI    +
 19   0.002                                      +    I   +
 20   0.003                                      +    I   +
 21   0.076                                      +   IXX  +
 22  -0.137                                      +XXXI    +
 23  -0.145                                      XXXXI    +
 24  -0.025                                      +   XI   +
 25   0.160                                      +   IXXXX
```

Shows the PACF for the residuals of 'police' (police homicides) for the auto-regressive first-order model.

The estimate for the first order component relating to the police variable is 0.2804 with a T-ratio of 3.60. The mean (before the intervention) is 29.43 police homicides a month with a 35.8 T-ratio. The intervention component is -4.75 with a -3.15 T-ratio.

TABLE 1

	'Police'	'Ratio'
First third mean:	29.54	1.95
Second third mean:	29.88	1.90
Third third mean:	24.88	1.68
Model Type:	Autoregressive order 1	Autoregressive order 1
Parameter:	0.28	0.32
T-Ratio:		
(of the parameter)	3.60	4.19
Intervention:	-4.75	-0.26
T-ratio:		
(of the intervention)	-3.15	-2.56
Mean:	29.43	1.91
T-ratio:		
(of the mean)	35.88	34.57
Reduction:	-16.13%	-13.61%

Summarizes the results for the variables 'police' (number of police homicides) and 'ratio' (the ratio between police homicides and criminal homicides).

Model type:	is the ARIMA model which fitted the data.
Parameter:	is the first order parameter.
Intervention:	is the size of the intervention (reduction) component.
Mean:	is the mean of the variable before the intervention point.
Reduction:	is the size of the reduction in percentage.

Based on the first order component for the police variable, the full equation is:

$$Ht = 29.43 + Ht\text{-}1*0.28 - 4.7*I + At$$

where I is a dummy variable representing the time before and after the intervention, and At is the random component.

These results indicate that police homicides decreased from 29.43 per month to 24.68 following the Court's decision in *Garner*. This is a monthly average of 4.75, a reduction of approximately sixteen (16.15) percent.

Table 1 also includes the parameters for the "ratio" variable, which represents the ratio between police homicides and criminal homicides. The estimate for the first order component is 0.32, with a T-ratio of 4.19. The mean of the ratio between police homicides and criminal homicides is 1.91. The intervention component is -0.26, with a T-ratio of -2.56. This means that after *Garner*, the percentage of police homicides that contributed to the total number of homicides fell by approximately 0.26%. As before, the full equation is:

Ratio t = 1.91 + Ratiot-1*0.32 - 0.26*I + At

The total reduction of the "ratio" variable between police homicides and criminal homicides decreased by 13.55% following the *Garner* decision.

The difference between the police homicide reduction (16.15%) and the ratio reduction (13.55%) is due to variation in the criminal homicides number and not in the police homicides number. As Table 1 illustrates, the mean of police homicides in the first-third of the third period (29.54) is almost the same as in the second-third (29.88), while the ratio mean went down from 1.95 in the first-third to 1.90 in the second-third. In both cases, however, the big reduction occurred in the third-third (each third represents 52 months out of the sample of 156. The intervention point is seven months after the beginning of the third-third).

B.   "CONSTITUTIONAL" AND "UNCONSTITUTIONAL" STATES

Table 2 summarizes three intervention variables in addition to the "police" and "ratio" variables.

The first variable is the total number of criminal homicides ("total" variable). The results in Table 2 show that the T-ratio of the intervention is -0.72, so even the small reduction of 2.9% is not valid. This suggests that there was no significant intervention in the total homicides as reported in the Supplementary Homicide Report, and therefore, the results of this study are not an outcome of measurement variability.

TABLE 2.

	Size of intervention component	T-ratio of intervention component	Mean before intervention	Reduction in precent
Total:	−46.28	−0.72	1576	−2.9%
State	−2.16	−3.66	9.072	−23.80%
Notstate:	−2.64	−2.47	20.37	−12.96%

Summarizes the results of the intervention for five other variables: 'Total'—the number of criminal homicides. 'State'—the number of police homicides in states whose laws were influenced by the Garner decision. 'Notstate'—the number of police homicides in states whose laws were not influenced by the Garner decision. Size of intervention component indicates the number of homicides reduced by the decision. A mean before intervention is the mean predicted by the model in the assumption that the intervention made a difference.

Table 2 indicates that the *Garner* decision influenced both the constitutional and unconstitutional states. In the unconstitutional states (termed "State" in Table 2), the reduction was an average of

2.16 homicides following the *Garner* decision; in constitutional states (termed "Notstate"), the reduction was 2.64 homicides following *Garner*. Clearly, however, the decision in *Garner* had a greater influence on the unconstitutional states than the constitutional ones. Because of the differences in the number of police homicides to start with, the percentage reduction was different. In the constitutional states, the number of homicides declined by approximately thirteen percent (-12.96%). In the unconstitutional states the reduction was approximately twenty-four percent (23.80%).

C.   SUB-CIRCUMSTANCES

Another variable in the data set is called sub-circumstances. Sub-circumstance is defined only for the cases where the "circumstances" variable value is "justifiable homicide—police" or "justifiable homicide—civilian." In cases of criminal homicide, it has a zero value. This variable has seven values (the values are defined by the SHR itself, and this is how they appear in the code book):

1. Felon attacked police officer
2. Felon attacked fellow police officer
3. Felon attacked civilian
4. Felon attempted flight from a crime
5. Felon killed in commission of crime
6. Felon resisted arrest
7. Not enough information to determine

Unfortunately, the sample is too small to use ARIMA for each category (or even a combination of categories). However, the mean values in each category before and after the *Garner* decision reveal as indicated in Table 3, that the sub-category of shooting felons who attacked police officers increased slightly from an average of 10.91 police homicides per month before *Garner* to 11.489 per month after *Garner*. Also, attempted flight went down from 2.135 to 1.044 per month (a reduction of 51%), the number of felons killed in the commission of a crime decreased by 29% (from 8.847 police homicides per month to 6.267), and cases of resisting arrest went down from 3.874 cases a month to 2.644 (a reduction of approximately 32%).

This reduction has to be viewed cautiously for two reasons. First, comparing averages alone is not generally a good measure for estimating impact.[41] Second, it is not surprising that police officers tend to report shootings differently when the norms have been changed. Professor Fyfe reported that after a new New York City Police Department policy banned warning shots, the number of police shootings re-

---

[41] *See supra* note 33 and accompanying text.

TABLE 3.

Code	Description	Total-Before	Mean-Before	Total-After	Mean-After
1	Felon attacked police officer	1211	10.910	517	11.489
2	Felon attacked fellow police officer	211	1.901	41	.911
3	Felon attacked a civilian	69	.622	36	.800
4	Felon attempted flight from a crime	237	2.135	47	1.044
5	Felon killed in commission of a crime	982	8.847	282	6.267
6	Felon resisted arrest	430	3.874	119	2.644
7	Not enough information to determine	417	3.760	134	2.978
	SUM OF ALL	3557	32.050	1176	26.133

Table 3 shows the total and monthly means for each sub-circumstances category.

ported as "accidental" jumped from 4.5% to 9.2%.[42] The Memphis Police Department reported similar results. Professors Sparger and Giacopassi reported that after a policy change, the number of shootings classified as "apprehend suspect" declined by 58.6% while the rate of "defend life" increased 91.5%.[43] These changes in Memphis occurred despite the fact that there was no reduction in the total amount of police shootings.

IV. DISCUSSION

A. THE FACTS

Three conclusions seem to be self-evident from the data presented here. The first, and most important one is that *Garner* had a clear effect on justifiable police homicides. It reduced the total number of police homicides by approximately sixty homicides a year (more than sixteen percent). Second, *Garner* had an influence in both unconstitutional states and constitutional states. The magnitude of the reduction, however, was greater in unconstitutional states. Finally, *Garner* influenced not only a reduction in the number of police shootings of fleeing felons, but of all shootings, even those that are not correlated to defending life. This conclusion, however, needs more empirical support before it can be unequivocally accepted.

---

[42] James J. Fyfe, *Administrative Interventions On Police Shooting Discretion: An Empirical Examination*, 7 J. CRIM. JUST. 309, 318 (1979).

[43] Jerry R. Sparger & David J. Giacopassi, *Memphis Revisited: A Reexamination of Police Shootings After the* Garner *Decision*, 9 JUST. Q. 211, 218 (1992).

B. WHY DID THE GARNER DECISION HAVE SUCH AN IMPACT?

The impact of *Garner* is surprising. Even before *Garner*, many police departments had already restricted their guidelines, and repealed the Any-Felony Rule. Accordingly, observers did not expect *Garner* to have such a dramatic impact.[44]

A recent study on the influence of the *Garner* decision on the Memphis Police Department (MPD) may explain this phenomenon. Sparger & Giacopassi investigated MPD shootings in three different periods: 1969-1974; 1980-1984; 1985-1989.[45] They concluded that *Garner* definitely reduced police shootings.[46] Even though Memphis' policy before *Garner* was consistent with the Supreme Court's decision, the police restricted the policy even further after the decision. In fact, the policy after *Garner* emphasized "that deadly force should be used only as a last resort to protect life, not merely to apprehend fleeing dangerous felons."[47]

This tendency by police departments to restrict their shooting guidelines beyond legal requirements is not a new one. Kenneth Matulia, who conducted a survey among fifty-seven big city police departments, wrote that "the individual police department rules . . . generally place a more restrictive standard of conduct than permitted by law."[48] Professors Geller and Scott also described a tendency in law enforcement agencies to move towards guidelines which were more restrictive than *Garner* required.[49]

Thus, the adoption of more restricted policies by police departments nationwide after the Court's decision in *Garner* seems to have caused the reduction in police homicides. This is consistent with the evidence that restricted policies can reduce police shootings, and therefore police homicides.[50] The magnitude of the change can explain the differences in reduction between the unconstitutional states (23.8% reduction in police homicides), and the constitutional states (12.96% reduction). The modifications which should have been made in department policies were higher in states that had the Any-Felony Rule than in states which did not. As a result, *Garner*'s influence was more accentuated in the unconstitutional states.

---

[44] See *supra* note 22 and accompanying text.

[45] *See generally* Sparger & Giacopassi, *supra* note 43.

[46] *Id.* at 224.

[47] *Id.* at 214.

[48] KENNETH J. MATULIA, A BALANCE OF FORCES: MODEL DEADLY FORCE POLICY AND PROCEDURE 17 (2d ed. 1985).

[49] DEADLY FORCE: A PRACTITIONER'S DESK REFERENCE, *supra* note 9, at 256.

[50] *Id.* at 257-67; *see also* Gerald I. Uelmen, *Varieties of Police Policy: A Study of Police Policy Regarding the Use of Deadly Force in Los Angeles County*, 6 LOY. L.A. L. REV. 1 (1973).

The self-restrictions on police behavior concerning deadly force were not only the result of good will but were also a political necessity. Police shootings of civilians have huge social costs, including riots.[51] This has happened not only in the United States but in other nations too,[52] and it is almost anticipated in some neighborhoods. Aside from public disturbances, police use of deadly force often spawns civil lawsuits.[53] The fear of riots and law suits may explain why mayors and police chiefs prefer to severely limit the instances in which their officers may use deadly force.

In sum, the *Garner* decision seems to have reduced police homicides directly (by reducing police shooting at fleeing felons), and indirectly (by influencing police departments to reduce and modify their guidelines beyond *Garner* to appear just and sensitive to the public). As a result, all police shooting unrelated to protecting life seems to be declining.

C.   SOME UNDESIRABLE OUTCOMES

Until the 1960s, the number of homicides in the United States was relatively stable.[54] There were fewer homicides then there are today, and the percentage of homicides which qualified as justifiable (by police or civilians) was much higher than today. As Professor Brearley wrote in 1932, "it may be safely concluded that justifiable homicides comprise from one-fourth to one-third of the total number of slayings."[55]

These statistics suggest that the more society views police and civilian homicides as justifiable, the more criminals these homicides deter. Professor Cloninger investigated the connection between police homicides and the crime rate in fifty cities.[56] He found that non-homicide violent crime rates are inversely related to the police's lethal

---

[51] For a list of occasions where shooting or other incidence between police officers and civilians caused rioting, see DEADLY FORCE: A PRACTITIONER'S DESK REFERENCE, *supra* note 9, at 1-14.

[52] Any incident where a police officer causes some unnecessary harm to civilians can cause riots. For example, on July 17, 1992, in Bristol, England, two local men died in a collision with a police car after they had stolen a police motorcycle. Their death immediately caused three days of rioting and looting. Maurice Chittenden & Christopher Lloyd, *Police Say Infiltrators Organised Bristol Riots*, THE TIMES (LONDON), July 19, 1992, at 3.

[53] *See generally* Michael M. Kaune & Chloe A. Tischler, *Liability in Police Use of Deadly Force*, 8 AM. J. POLICE 89 (1989).

[54] Margaret A. Zahn, *Homicide in the Twentieth Century: Trends, Types, and Causes, in* VIOLENCE IN AMERICA 216, 222 (Ted R. Gurr ed., 1989).

[55] H.C. BREARLEY, HOMICIDE IN THE UNITED STATES 63 (1932). *See also*, Zahn, *supra* note 54, at 221-22.

[56] Dale O. Cloninger, *Lethal Police Response As A Crime Deterrent*, 50 AM. J. ECON. & SOC. 59-69 (1991).

response rate, and concluded that police use of deadly force has a deterrent effect on the crime rate.[57]

Further, police officers believe that the threat of deadly force deters felony criminals, and that harsh statutory limitations on police discretion is dangerous.[58] In fact, some officers have already complained that the *Garner* decision, and resulting restrictive practices, have made their work frustrating and more dangerous.[59]

Arguably, Justice O'Connor recognized this concern in her dissenting opinion: "I cannot accept the majority's creation of a constitutional right to flight for burglary suspects seeking to avoid capture at the scene of the crime."[60] The majority of the Court considered this concern, but decided that the deterrent effect does not justify the risk of unnecessary police homicides. While the data is not sufficient to answer the empirical questions, the possibility that the Court's decision in *Garner* eroded the deterrent effect of police homicide should be considered in any evaluation of *Garner*'s influence.

D. SUMMARY

Despite suspicion about the ability of the Supreme Court to change police discretion,[61] the *Garner* decision demonstrates that a decision can have a strong effect on police behavior. However, more research is needed on the local level to determine whether police departments have changed their policies to comply with *Garner*. This would provide a better understanding of the types of policies that can influence police use of deadly force.

---

57 *Id.*

58 A.L. Rodez, Deadly Force As a Deterrent to Felony Crimes Against Property: An Analysis of Michigan Police Officer Attitudes Toward Statutory Limitations On Their Use of Discretion (1980) (unpublished Ph.D. dissertation, Michigan State University); Abraham N. Tennenbaum, *Police Officers' Need For Self-Defense Causes Brutality, in* POLICE BRUTALITY 100-01 (Bruno Leone ed., 1991).

59 Gordon Witkin et al., *Cops Under Fire,* U.S. NEWS AND WORLD REP., Dec. 3, 1990, at 32, 38.

60 Tennessee v. Garner, 471 U.S. 1, 32-33 (O'Connor, J., dissenting).

61 *See generally* GERALD N. ROSENBERG, THE HOLLOW HOPE: CAN COURTS BRING ABOUT SOCIAL CHANGE? (1991).

American Journal of Police, Vol. XI, No. 1 1992   *1*

POLITICAL PRESSURES AND INFLUENCES ON POLICE EXECUTIVES: A DESCRIPTIVE ANALYSIS

Kenneth D. Tunnell
Larry K. Gaines
Eastern Kentucky University

The purpose of this study was to examine the degree of political interference or pressure exerted on police chief executives by public and private officials, the location or areas of political interference, and their impact on police executives. Additionally, we examined the level and source of pressure on predecessor chiefs and the predecessors' longevity to determine average tenure of police chiefs.

Although scant, the literature, relative to political interference on police chiefs by public and private officials, has developed accordingly: the political nature of local government; the process of becoming a police chief; the effects of community structure and values on police organizations; and the relationship between political officials and police executives. Informed by this literature, we collected and analyzed survey data from Kentucky police chiefs relative to the political processes and pressures that they experience. The findings from this research speak to the quality and quantity of political interference on police chiefs by public and private officials.

POLICE EXECUTIVES AND THE POLITICAL PROCESS

Because official government is the nucleus of both politics and political activities in our society, it follows that the police—the component of government that wields legitimate force—and how they are managed, are influenced by and through various political processes.

323

Indeed, this situation has long been recognized by concerned public officials who periodically have attempted to eliminate, or at least reduce, the influence of politics on law enforcement and its potential for corruption. In 1929, for example, President Hoover appointed the National Commission on Law Observance and Enforcement to study police problems. As a result, a variety of state and local commissions, such as those in New York City across the years, have examined the problems resulting from politics and policing (see, e.g., Fogelson, 1977).

The National Commission on Law Observance and Enforcement (1931) found that partisan politics played a key role in police corruption, police inefficiency, and the use of police as pawns to supplant community interests for those of politicians. The political reins on police departments prevented them from effectively performing the critical functions that the citizenry expected of them. The Commission concluded that politics should be absent from policing. Research since the Commission found that numerous citizens believed police in many cases were nothing more than adjuncts to political machines, and that police reform not only improved policing, but also attacked the infrastructure of political machines (Fogelson, 1977).

The effects of politics on police personnel administration historically have been devastating. For example, in 1917 a newly elected Republican Mayor in Louisville, Kentucky dismissed over 300 officers from a force of 429 (Fosdick, 1972). Likewise, in Salt Lake City, police attrition after an election ran as high as 85 percent. And in Indianapolis, politicians attempting to remedy the constant turmoil, dictated that all police ranks be equally divided between Republicans and Democrats. The police chief and everyone in the department were scrutinized by politicians eager to provide political patronage to their supporters and punish their foes.

Given that American law enforcement was dominated by politics and political machines during the early decades of this century, it is astonishing that police chiefs now have any independence. And indeed, some jurisdictions never have been able to dislodge the shackles imposed by political machines. Chicago, for example, arguably is little different today than it was at the turn of the century (Robinson, 1975).

A contemporary study examined political "interference" or "intrusion" in 24 police departments (Mastrofski, 1988). Numerous factors were discovered that mediate the degree and type of interference exerted on police executives. Some of the most telling included community size, the community's social class, the size of the department, and its dominant values. Furthermore, the study suggested that levels of interference may vary as a result of the personalities of individuals involved in governance, the political culture, the degree of police bureaucratization, and the community power structure (Mastrofski, 1988).

Undoubtedly, politics have not been removed from policing. Although just as prevalent today, political influences are qualitatively different than those during the earlier part of this century. Political influences are much more subtle; they affect policy issues as opposed to affecting people and events. They also tend to involve a greater plurality of citizens and interest groups, as opposed to political demagoguery (e.g., Mills, 1956; Dahl, 1961; Gilbert, 1967; Manley, 1983). This is not to say that politics have been eliminated from policing, but that the political situation in many jurisdictions is "better" or less intrusive than in years past. For example, many of the conditions found in police departments earlier this century, and detailed in earlier work (e.g., Fosdick, 1972; Fogelson, 1977), are not as prevalent in those departments today.

One of the most noticeable changes in police administration as a result of political reforms has been the increasing influence of the professional police chief. One facet of this development may be that police chiefs in some locales have more independence than their predecessors. Although a number of policy boundaries or parameters remain, many of today's chiefs have more decision-making latitude than their predecessors. Comprehending the subtle differences in executive independence among police chiefs is imperative if police administration is to be thoroughly understood.

Our study sheds light on the political processes of government and business as they interfere with or affect police chiefs. We describe both qualitative and quantitative categories of political interference and how they influence police executive decision making. Police chiefs frequently find themselves in situations where their autonomy is limited by "bounded rationality" (Simon, 1961). That is, they are not always allowed to select and implement their definitions of optimal solutions for the problems confronting their agencies; political boundaries sometimes prohibit such actions. In an effort to clarify the tenuous positions of chiefs in the political arena, we describe the relationships between chiefs and political representatives within government.

325

THE POLITICAL RELATIONSHIP BETWEEN CHIEFS AND POLITICAL OFFICIALS

Understanding the nature of the relationship between police executives and government officials is fundamental for understanding the nature of political interference and its impact on policing. By illuminating these relationships and the nature of political interference, we situate them within a context of political dynamics.

Although literature on the relationships between police chiefs and politicians is scarce, early research focused on politicians' dysfunctional interventions into police administration (e.g., O'Brien, 1978). From his study, O'Brien delineates three types of dysfunctional politicians: the misfeasors, the nonfeasors, and the malfeasors. The misfeasors are motivated by their fears of being accused of inefficiency and thus believe it is imperative to be involved in police administrative matters. The nonfeasors are those who stay detached from everyday police matters (i.e., "out of the loop") to remain isolated from negative consequences that may result from both enforcement and nonenforcement decisions. Finally, the malfeasors are those who are both corrupt and intent on using their office as a means of manipulating the police for their own benefit. These three types of political officials seldom exist in a pure form.

Regardless of their attitudes or inclinations, police chiefs must work with public officials. Indeed, a former Commissioner of the New York City Police Department and President of the Police Foundation readily concedes that politicians have a legitimate stake in areas such as the prioritization of police problems, the facilitation of media relations, municipal policy making, and the deployment of personnel (Murphy, 1985). He admonished potential police chiefs to negotiate not only the terms of their contracts, but also where ultimate authority in specific police policy areas rests. Andrews (1985:7) likewise supports the notion that relationships should be formally negotiated.

> Without clear bounds of legally established authority, clear day-to-day relationships cannot be established, and consequently much personal and organizational energy must be expended on each issue or event as it develops to define the power and the working and the authority relationships. Such

continuing uncertainty does not improve either city government or police organization stability or success.

If relationships are not articulated and understood clearly, not only will
a great deal of individual and organizational energy be expended, but
ultimately the relations between the police and government officials
may disintegrate to the point that the chief is replaced. This is especially poignant in cases where there is a veteran chief and a new city
manager is hired, a new mayor is elected, or new council members assume office. Once new public officials assume office, chiefs are advised to develop a plan or course of action to control various aspects of
their jobs and to delineate duties and responsibilities (Scott, 1986).
Such a plan seemingly would minimize problems between police chiefs
and these new officials.

Considerable effort from the police chief and the political official
is required for a meaningful working relationship. For example, Regoli
et al. (1989a; 1989b) found that the most important factors contributing
to police chief job satisfaction were autonomy, job security, salary, and
job conditions regardless of department size. However, police chiefs
must be mindful that total autonomy is seldom attainable, and that job
security, salary, and job conditions are dependent on the relationships
forged with governmental leadership. A former Minneapolis Mayor
advises that many law enforcement matters require careful planning
and cooperation between the chief and executive, and if this cooperation does not exist, both are doomed to failure (Fraser, 1985). And a
former Superintendent of Police in Chicago notes that,

> . . . the chief's ability to serve as a major municipal policy
> maker and even his ability to run a police department free
> from the most outrageous kinds of partisan political incur-
> sions is largely dependent on local idiosyncrasies rather than
> on the scientific application of immutable principles con-
> cerning the police chief-mayor relationship (Brzeczek,
> 1985:55).

It becomes clear then, that even good working relationships may not
always shield the police chief or prevent unwholesome interferences
into police departments. With this in mind, this research was under-

327

taken to examine political interference in police administration and to understand the relationship between the police executive and governmental officials.

RESEARCH METHODS

Within the context of this research, political pressure, as a concept, is used to delineate subjective political pressure, as opposed to objective pressure, on the police executive. By subjective pressure, we mean those perceived pressures (e.g., Blumer, 1969). Objective pressures are represented by acts of power performed to alter police executives' decisions or actions. The degree of subjective pressure on police chiefs is predicated on their definitions of such pressures and their magnitude rather than actual events or conditions.

We use subjective interpretations rather than objective pressures because we were interested in the levels of pressures perceived by police executives. For example, a politician or significant other may exert pressure but the recipient may not define it as such, it may be inane, or the police executive may possess sufficient political powers to rebut the pressure. In another example, a politician or significant other may make benign or innocent statements, but due to the existing political environment or the police executive's previous experiences, these statements might be interpreted as an exertion of political pressure. Thus, the subjective interpretations are of interest to us and represent the dependent variable in this study. Similar general terms have been used by other researchers to describe subjective pressure. For example, Mastrofski (1988) examined "political interference" or "intrusion" and Regoli et al. (1990) examined "community influence." In an effort to better understand or place contextual constraints on these interpretations, respondents were asked to report on both the sources of pressures and the areas where pressures were exerted.

The focus of this study was on Kentucky police chiefs. An exhaustive list of chiefs was obtained from the Kentucky Department of Criminal Justice Training. A questionnaire was constructed and mailed to all municipal and county police chiefs in Kentucky regardless of the size of their departments. Thus, chiefs were mailed a survey whether their department employed one or several dozen officers. A total of 277 questionnaires was mailed with a letter requesting cooperation. Although we did not mail a follow-up letter and requested that each chief state where he was employed, surprisingly 115 (42%) surveys were returned. Although requesting such information may have negatively affected the response rate, we believe it was necessary to perform jurisdiction-specific comparisons and to determine which chiefs, indeed, lost or quit their jobs after mayoral elections.

The questionnaires were mailed in November 1989, which preceded the mayoral elections across the state. Every four years all mayors in Kentucky are elected and are then free to make political appointments to the office of police chief. This generally results in a significant turnover of police chiefs the following year. We timed the mailing this way to identify the current chiefs before new mayors assumed office. Therefore, the questionnaires were completed by chiefs who were acutely aware of the political limitations on their tenure.

FINDINGS

Police Chief and Departmental Characteristics

Based on the 115 responses from police chiefs, we found that they had held their present position for an average of 5.5 years and that they had been employed with their respective departments an average of 12.1 years. More recent studies indicate that the average tenure of police chiefs range from 5.5 years (Witham, 1985) to 5.68 years (Enter, 1986). However, 23 percent of the respondents (N=26) had served only one year as police chief, and 64 percent of the respondents had been chief for five years or less. This finding is similar to national data which report that 50 percent of police executives have fewer than four years tenure while only 26 percent have eight years or more (IACP, 1975).

We were interested in whether tenure and political pressure were related. In an effort to investigate this concern, we examined the relationship between the chiefs' tenure and the amount of political pressure they encountered. We found a mild, inverse relationship between tenure and political pressure. Although the direction of the relationship was expected, we anticipated that this relationship would have been stronger than that found here ($r= .136$, $p=.153$).

The police departments represented in our sample averaged 15.8 full-time officers (sd=37.1). There were several larger departments in the sample which skewed this mean. The chiefs in our sample averaged a yearly salary of $20,000 to $25,000. Finally, the respondents served jurisdictions with an average population of 11,184 (ranging from 500 to 230,000).

Perceived Effectiveness of Previous Chiefs

The survey contained questions about predecessor chiefs. These questions were included in an effort to better understand the effectiveness, popularity, and ultimate demise of the former police chief in each jurisdiction. We intuitively believed that current chiefs would have better insights about their predecessors than they would about themselves. We also believed that because the former police chiefs' careers had been completed, details about their careers (especially their cessation) would yield more pertinent information than details of current chiefs.

Table 1 provides data on predecessor police chiefs vacating their positions—data based on the recollections and assertions of current chiefs.

From the current chiefs' recollections, it is clear that their predecessors left under some degree of political pressure. A total of 44 percent of the predecessor chiefs left their positions as a result of political pressure, and an additional nine percent were demoted. These findings indicate that political pressure contributes significantly to police chief nonsurvival. An additional 30 chiefs, or 26 percent, left for personal reasons.

Although a number of reasons could account for their decision to resign, it is very conceivable that politics may have played a role in some of these cases.

The respondents were asked to rate their predecessors in terms of their performance. They were asked their perceptions of how the communities, governments, and rank-and-file officers would have rated their predecessors' performance. On a Likert scale ranging from one (poor performance) to seven (outstanding performance), the respondents' perceptions were that the rank-and-file officers would have ranked the predecessor chiefs an average of 3.3; the community an average of 3.6; and the local government an average of 3.1. Hence, the responses indicate that the community, rank-and-file officers, and the government would have rated the previous chief as somewhat less than adequate.

Table 1
REASONS GIVEN FOR PREDECESSOR CHIEFS'
DEPARTURE FROM THE DEPARTMENT

Reason	Number	Percent
Retired after successful service	20	17.7
Retired due to political pressure	11	9.7
Resigned due to political pressure	19	16.8
Terminated by the government	20	17.7
Personal reasons	30	26.5
Demoted within the department	10	8.8
Died	3	2.7

Finally, the relationships between why their predecessors left their departments and their ratings were examined. The various reasons for leaving the department which related to political pressure and the absence of political pressure were collapsed into a dichotomous variable. Analyses of variance were computed using the rank-and-file ratings, community ratings, and governmental leaders' ratings as the dependent variables. As depicted in Table 2, those chiefs who left for reasons other than political pressure uniformly had significantly higher ratings than did those chiefs who departed under political pressure.

Table 2

ANALYSIS OF VARIANCE BETWEEN THE SUPPORT
OF VARIOUS GROUPS AND THE PRESSURES OF POLITICAL
INTERFERENCE IN DECISIONS TO LEAVE THE DEPARTMENT

Support Group	F-value	p-value
Rank-and-file		
Police Ratings	7.70	.0069*
Community Ratings	8.79	.0040*
Government Leaders		
Ratings	24.15	.0001*

* In each instance, those chiefs who left as a result of political pressure had significantly lower ratings than those who left under no pressure.

Political Pressures Exerted on Current Chiefs

The police chiefs were asked to provide information about the types of political pressures they presently encounter from the mayor, city council members, local business leaders, and state politicians. The respondents were asked specifically to rate the relative amount of political pressure that they encounter in their decisions: to (1) hire officers; (2) promote or demote officers; (3) arrest offenders or enforce specific laws; (4) make unnecessary changes in personnel assignments such as transfers to and from specialized units; and (5) provide special or unusual services to individuals or groups within the community. As illustrated in Table 3, the respondents reported that they had some pressure in each of these areas from the mayors and city council members but little from business leaders. The participants reported virtually no pressure from state politicians.

First, regarding personnel decisions, 21 percent of the participants reported that their mayors pressured them in decisions to hire or terminate officers and 22 percent reported that city council members pressured them in this area. Ten percent of the respondents reported some pressure in hiring decisions from business leaders. Also, 16 percent of the chiefs reported pressure from the mayor in promotion decisions, 16 percent reported pressure from city council members in this area, and none reported pressure from business leaders in this area. Finally, 23 percent of the chiefs reported pressure from the mayor in making special personnel assignments, 17 percent reported this pressure from city council members, and 6 percent reported that business leaders attempted to influence them in this area. Thus, it appears that personnel decisions are not necessarily autonomous decisions residing within the purview of the chief's authority.

Second, regarding political pressure in police operations, 28 percent of the chiefs reported pressure from the mayor in arrest or enforcement decisions, 29 percent reported pressure in arrest and enforcement decisions from city council members, and 6 percent claimed business leaders attempted to influence their decisions in this area. Twenty-seven percent of the police chiefs reported being asked by mayors to provide unusual or special services, 29 percent of the chiefs were asked for these services by city council members, and 13 percent of the chiefs recounted some pressure in this area. Thus, it appears that the local politicians have a direct effect on operational decisions in almost one-third of the police agencies.

Table 3
POLICE CHIEF SELF-REPORTING ON TYPE
AND LOCATION OF POLITICAL PRESSURE: BY PERCENT

Source	Personnel Decisions	Promotion Decisions	Personnel Assigns.	Arrest & Enforce.	Special Services
Mayor	21.0	15.8	23.0	28.0	27.0
City Council	21.6	16.5	17.1	29.0	29.1
Business Leaders	10.0	0	6.3	6.3	12.6

Third, we conducted further analyses to assess whether political pressure patterns exist. The rating patterns of the mayors and city council members were intercorrelated to determine if similar patterns existed for each. Business leaders and state politicians were not used in the analyses because they were reported to interfere considerably less than mayors and city council members. Again, pressure in the following areas was assessed: (1) hiring and firing officers; (2) promoting and demoting officers; (3) arresting offenders or enforcing specific laws; (4) making unnecessary changes in personnel assignments such as transfers to and from specialized units; and (5) providing special or unusual services to individuals or groups within the community. We generally found that those chiefs who were pressured in one area by the mayors were pressured in other areas by the mayors as evidenced by high correlation coefficients. The intercorrelations among the areas range from a low of r=.553 (p=.0001) to a high of r=.739 (p=.0001). Again, these correlations indicate that if a mayor exerted pressure in one area, he or she was likely to in another. Next, the intercorrelations for the city council members were examined, and the range of correlations was from r=.379 (p=.0001) to a high of r=.736 (p=.0001). These significant correlations indicate that officials, when exerting pressure on police chiefs, do so across a wide area rather than only one area. It is also interesting that city council members seemingly exert more pressure than mayors except in personnel assignments, contrary to Mastrofski's (1988) findings that city council members are rarely involved in daily police activities. Perhaps this difference lies in part in the size of jurisdictions. Mastrofski's jurisdictions were much larger than those used here.

Kentucky's cities are classified into six classes based on size. We investigated whether city size had any impact on the political pressure exerted on chiefs. The relationship between city size as measured by the city's class and the amount of self-reported political pressure (a question about general political pressure using a Likert scale) resulted in a correlation coefficient of r=.034, (p=.725). This insignificant correlation indicates that city size has no appreciable effect on the amount of political pressure exerted on chiefs. Thus, it appears that governmental officials, regardless of city size, are equally guilty of this practice.

Finally, the respondents were questioned about general pressure they encounter while performing their jobs as police chief, and 56 percent reported that they encounter political pressure. As alarming as this is, interestingly, they believe they are under less pressure than their predecessors. We cannot be certain if they actually experience less pressure than their predecessors, but most importantly, they perceive that they experience less. This may indicate that they believe they are in better control of their political environments and that politics is playing a less important role in policing than in the past. Even so, several respondents volunteered written comments describing the need for better insulation and protection from the politicians and the need for job security, perhaps in the form of civil service protection. The following two comments exemplify the chiefs' desire to have some form of job protection.

- I believe it's time to have some protection for police chiefs from the threat of being fired by some individual, that is the mayor [who] does not agree with the decisions the chief might have to make. We have the policeman's bill of rights and the chiefs should be included in this hearing process before being dismissed by politicians. It's time we stood up for our rights in this matter. (From a 30-year veteran who has been chief for 22 years of a city of 8,000).

- Police chiefs throughout the state need some type of protection to assist them in upgrading old and outdated ways small departments have been run, without fear of losing their jobs. I am appointed on a yearly basis which makes it difficult to stand up for the department, citizens, and very much needed training without fear of not being reappointed each year. (From a chief who has been with the department three years, two of which as chief. The department has five full-time officers in a town of 6,000 population.)

The following two comments indicate the nature and extent of political pressure placed on police chiefs.

- I need to explain, political interference is different. For example, a council member received a ticket and funding for a new building was blocked, same council member opposes salary increases. Instead of voicing support for police from council members, you get no comment. (From a Chief with a force of 75 officers serving a city of 51,000.)

- In my case, I have consistently been subjected to more pressure from the city manager than from all other sources combined. Obviously, on some occasions, he was speaking for politicians or other community leaders but they were not identified. More often, he was expressing his view on the administration of the police department. (From a chief with 48 officers serving a population of 27,000. He has been chief approximately seven years.)

The following two comments are indicative of the respondents' concerns about the then-approaching mayoral elections and the potential effects on their tenure and autonomy.

- With the current mayor and council, no interference. But with the election next month, we are looking at interference from the new members. (From a chief serving a city of 13,000 population and with less than two years experience as chief.)

- The current mayor is not seeking re-election. After the election on November 7, I expect every answer on this study to change. (From a chief serving a city of 7,500 with 13 officers. He has been chief for one year and reported little pressure at the time of the study.)

In support of their concerns, the Kentucky Department of Criminal Justice Training reported that 24 percent (N=66) of Kentucky police chiefs left their jobs during 1990, the year immediately following elections and the new mayors assuming office. Undoubtedly, many of these were either dismissed or demoted.

CONCLUSIONS

The data indicate that Kentucky police chiefs must cope with varying levels of political pressures and interference, some legitimate and some illegitimate. Our study, for the most part, agrees with earlier findings. We found that political pressures are exerted from a variety of directions, and as a result, over 50 percent of the police chiefs in our study who had left their jobs were forced out by governmental politicians (see Table 1). We have no measure as to how many of these removals were justified.

What is becoming increasingly clear however, is that we know very little about this political process. The literature abounds with anecdotes on the problems of police executives, but offers little beyond these descriptive illustrations. We must initiate attempts at quantifying, better understanding, and controlling these relationships if policing is truly to become free of political interference. We also realize that this is a double-edged sword. Recent events in Los Angeles point to a problem where the police chief possessed too much autonomy. However, there are numerous other examples in which chiefs have been unable to ensure that their departments provided the best possible service because of a lack of political autonomy. As Goldstein (1977) has noted, it is extremely difficult to maintain a working balance between police responsiveness and political accountability. At this point, police administration, at least in Kentucky, is severely bounded by these relationships, which removes a large degree of management discretion from police administrators.

NOTE

An earlier version of this paper was presented to the Annual Meeting of the American Society of Criminology, Baltimore, Maryland, November 1990. We are grateful to the anonymous reviewers and journal editor for their critical comments on our work

REFERENCES

Andrews, A. (1985). "Structuring the Political Independence of the Police Chief." In W. Geller (ed.) *Police Leadership in America: Crisis and Opportunity.* New York: Praeger Press.

Blumer, H. (1969). *Symbolic Interactionism: Perspective and Method.* Englewood Cliffs, NJ: Prentice-Hall.

Brzeczek, R. (1985). "Chief-Mayor Relations: The View from the Chief's Chair." In W. Geller (ed.) *Police Leadership in America: Crisis and Opportunity.* New York: Praeger Press.

Dahl, R. (1961). *Who Governs?* New Haven: Yale University Press.

Enter, J. (1986). "The Rise to the Top: An Analysis of Police Chief Career Patterns." *Journal of Police Science and Administration,* 14(4):334-346.

Fogelson, R. (1977). *Big-City Police.* Cambridge, MA: Harvard University Press.

Fosdick, R. (1972). *American Police Systems* (Reprint Edition). Montclair, NJ: Patterson Smith.

Fraser, D. (1985). "Politics and Police Leadership: The View from City Hall." In W. Geller, (ed.) *Police Leadership in America: Crisis and Opportunity.* New York: Praeger Press.

Fraser, D. (1985). "Politics and Police Leadership: The View from City Hall." In W. Geller, (ed.) *Police Leadership in America: Crisis and Opportunity.* New York: Praeger Press.

Gilbert, C. (1967). "Some Trends in Community Politics: A Secondary Analysis of Power Structure Data from 166 communities." *Social Science Quarterly,* 48:373-381.

Goldstein, H. (1977). *Policing a Free Society.* Cambridge, MA: Ballinger.

IACP Police Chief Executive Committee (1975). *Police Chief Executive.* Washington, DC: U.S. Government Printing Office.

Manley, J. (1983). "Neopluralism: A Class Analysis of Pluralism I and II." *American Political Science Review,* 77:368-383.

Mastrofski, S. (1988). "Varieties of Police Governance in Metropolitan America." *Politics and Policy,* 8:12-31.

Mills, C. (1956). *The Power Elite.* New York: Oxford University Press.

Murphy, P. (1985). "The Prospective Chief's Negotiation of Authority with the Mayor." In W. Geller (ed.) *Police Leadership in America: Crisis and Opportunity.* New York: Praeger Press.

O'Brien, J. (1978). "The Chief and the Executive: Direction or Political Interference?" *Journal of Police Science and Administration,* 6(2):394-401.

Regoli, R., J. Crank, & R. Culbertson (1989a). "The Consequences of Professionalism Among Police Chiefs." *Justice Quarterly,* 6(1):47-67.

_____ (1989b). "Police Cynicism, Job Satisfaction, and Work Relations of Police Chiefs: An Assessment of the Influence of Department Size." *Sociological Focus,* 22(3):161-171.

Regoli, R., R. Culbertson, J. Crank & J. Powell (1990). "Career Stage and Cynicism Among Police Chiefs." *Justice Quarterly,* 7(3):593-614.

Robinson, C. (1975). "The Mayor and the Police: The Political Role of the Police." In G. Mosse (ed.) *Police Forces in History.* Beverly Hills, CA: Sage Publications.

Scott, M. (1986). *Managing for Success: A Police Chief's Survival Guide.* Washington, DC: Police Executive Research Forum.

Simon, H. (1961). *Administrative Behavior.* New York: Macmillan.

Witham, D. (1985). *The American Law Enforcement Chief Executive: A Management Profile.* Washington, DC: Police Executive Research Forum.

DOES ANYONE REMEMBER TEAM POLICING?
LESSONS OF THE TEAM POLICING
EXPERIENCE FOR COMMUNITY POLICING

Samuel Walker
University of Nebraska at Omaha

Does anyone remember team policing? In all of the discussions of community policing, there are almost no references to this earlier experiment. This silence is particularly surprising because there are so many apparent similarities between the two concepts. Both focus police services at the neighborhood level, decentralize decision-making authority within the police department, call for a high level of community input into decision making, and, in different ways, redefine the police role.

Given these similarities, one would expect to find in the community policing literature considerable attention to the "lessons" of the earlier team policing experience. Team policing failed, or at least is reputed to have failed. One would expect the advocates of community policing to examine closely the causes of that failure in order to avoid repeating them. Instead, however, there is a near-total silence about the subject.

There are several possible explanations for this silence. One is the passage of time. Team policing reached its peak in the early 1970s and then faded away quickly.[1] There are today many officers in middle management positions of responsibility with fewer than twenty years on the job. None would have had any firsthand experience with team policing. At best, team policing for them is "history," something they might have heard or read about.

A second reason may be related to team policing's reputation as a failure. No one likes to talk about failure, particularly if the failure is somewhat close to home. It simply raises too many difficult questions when someone points out that "we tried a neighborhood-focused approach to policing back in the seventies, and it failed." Any high-ranking officer who was directly involved in a team policing experiment might be tainted by the association.

A third reason may be that we have a very limited experience in learning from past experiments in policing. We are now in a new phase of police history. For the first time, we have available to us a body of research that includes independent evaluations of previous experiments. The 1960s witnessed a burst of research, creative thinking, and experimentation. Earlier reform efforts were based on hope, unverified assumptions, and ideologically driven ideas (Walker, 1977). The efforts of the period from the mid-1960s onward were the first to be based on empirical research and, in many instances, to be evaluated. We are only just beginning to learn how to use this accumulated knowledge and experience.

A promising beginning in this direction has already begun. Some of the leading advocates of community policing have drawn heavily on the accumulated body of knowledge. Wilson and Kelling's (1982) seminal article on "Broken Windows" drew heavily upon the available research on what works and what does not. Other community policing advocates (Moore & Kelling, 1983; National Institute of Justice, 1988-1990) have pursued this line of inquiry.

This article argues that we can and should inquire into the team policing experience to see what lessons, if any, it has for community policing.

A BRIEF HISTORY OF THE BRIEF HISTORY OF TEAM POLICING

Like a shooting star, team policing appeared suddenly in American policing, burned brightly, and quickly vanished. The concept received its first authoritative endorsement in 1967 when the report of the President's Crime Commission, citing some English experiments, recommended that police departments experiment with it (President's Commission, 1967:118). This was an obvious response to the urgent police-community relations crisis. The summer of 1967 marked the third of four straight summers of urban racial violence (National Advisory Commission, 1968). The idea quickly captured the imagination of reform-minded police chiefs and a number of experiments were quickly launched. By 1974 it was estimated that as many as 60 police departments were operating something they called "team policing" (Schwartz & Clarren, 1977:2). It is doubtful, however, that many of these projects contained the central elements of team policing. Many, and possibly even most, were simply a new label for traditional operations.

In the mid-1970s, somewhere between 1974 and 1976, team policing died. Suddenly, it was no longer the exciting panacea to the problems of policing. References to it virtually vanished. Even worse, it acquired a bad name, and fell into the category of reforms that had "failed."

The Aftermath: Towards Community Policing

The collapse of team policing coincided with the end of a more general period of reform in American policing. In the 1960s, the police-community relations crisis, the President's Crime Commission, and the advent of federal monies stimulated a burst of research and reform. By the mid-1970s, that movement had run its course. Many of the promising reforms, such as team policing, had not effected any major changes. The accumulating research on police and police experiments tended to cast doubt on the possibilities for change. The advent of police unions greatly limited the power of police chiefs, the traditional engines of reform (Walker, 1977). Police reform entered a period of uncertainty and lack of direction.

A "second wave" of police reform was eventually launched. The pivotal events were the publication of two provocative articles: Herman Goldstein's (1979) "Problem-Oriented Policing" article in 1979 and James Q. Wilson and George L. Kelling's (1982) "Broken Windows" piece in 1982. They are the seminal articles in the current community policing/problem-oriented policing movement (Greene & Mastrofski, 1988). Both articles made heavy use of the accumulated body of police research. The combined use of police history and the major findings of police research is particularly evident in the National Institute of Justice-Harvard University Perspectives on Policing series (National Institute of Justice, 1988-1990) which gave a strong endorsement to community policing.

LEARNING FROM HISTORY

This essay reexamines the team policing experience with an eye toward identifying any lessons that might be relevant for current experiments in community policing. It relies primarily on the team policing evaluation literature, including the 1973 Police Foundation report, *Team Policing: Seven Case Studies* (Sherman, Milton, & Kelly, 1973) and the Foundation's evaluation of team policing in Cincinnati (Schwartz & Clarren, 1977). There is also a prescriptive Justice Department report on *Neighborhood Team Policing* (National Institute of Justice, 1973) and a few other published items. Some interviews are also used.

For purposes of this discussion, community policing and problem-oriented policing will be treated as the same. There are some differences between two, but certain common elements are sufficient to permit generalization. Generalization is hazardous in any event. While there was some general agreement on what the key components of team policing should be (National Institute of Justice, 1973), in practice there were many variations. Few of the experiments had all of the key elements (Sherman, Milton, & Kelly, 1973) and "community policing" has many variations (Greene & Mastrofski, 1988).

TEAM POLICING AND COMMUNITY POLICING COMPARED

Common Features

Team policing and community policing share several important features.

Neighborhood Focus

Both team policing and community policing have a community or neighborhood focus (National Institute of Justice, 1973; Greene & Mastrofski, 1988). This represents a break with the dominant ethos of American police administration which has emphasized centralized command and control. The police professionalization movement early in this century emphasized the closing of neighborhood precinct stations, the hiring of experienced administrators as police chiefs, and the application of modern management techniques. All of these measures were designed to enhance centralized control over police operations (Walker, 1977). O.W. Wilson, who was the leading authority on police management from the 1950s through the early 1970s also stressed centralized control (Wilson & McLaren, 1977). Neighborhood-level influence on policing, it should be stressed, was associated with corruption.

Many critics of American policing in the 1960s and early 1970s saw the centralized police bureaucracy as the source of many separate police problems. It made police departments rigid and inflexible, incapable of responding to social change, and damaged the morale of rank-and-file police officers. All of these factors, in turn, contributed to poor police-community relations. The popularity of team policing was due in large part because it was seen as a solution to the police-community relations crisis. Community policing views the neighborhood focus as a means of responding to the long-term causes of neighborhood deterioration.

Decentralized Decision Making

In team policing and community policing, a key component of the neighborhood focus is decentralized decision-making authority within the department. In both cases, policies are to be developed on the basis of the special needs of the neighborhood. This involves enhanced decision making by relatively low-ranking officers on the basis of a high level of community input. This also represents a direct challenge to the traditional, O.W. Wilson style of police management (Wilson & McLaren, 1977). In the Cincinnati team policing experiment, for example, the planning task force was told to "ignore division policies" and draft its own SOP manual for the experimental district (Schwartz & Clarren, 1977:50). The team policing experiment in the Venice section of Los Angeles was described as functioning "to a great degree as if it were a separate small police department" (Sherman, Milton, & Kelly, 1973:51). In New York City, officers in the initial CPOP experiment were required to maintain beat books in which they would indicate the major problems in their assigned area and the strategies and tactics they planned to adopt in response to them (Walker, 1985; Farrell, 1988).

343

Community Input

The emphasis on community input in the development of programs also deviates from the traditional O.W. Wilson style of decision making (Wilson & McLaren, 1977). Insulation from the public was both an unintended and intended consequence of police reform. It was an unintended consequence of bureaucratization and the adoption of the patrol car (Walker, 1977). But it was also an intended element of an anti-corruption strategy, designed to eliminate the close police ties with community leaders that led to corruption (Goldstein, 1975).

In the Los Angeles team policing experiment, officers had personal contact with an estimated 12,000 of the 35,000 residents of the neighborhood (Sherman, Milton, & Kelly, 1973:50). In the Newport News, Virginia problem-oriented policing experiment, the program officer surveyed neighborhood residents as part of the planning process (Eck & Spelman, 1987:68).

A New Police Role

Second, both team policing and community policing involve a different conception of the police role. Officers at the rank-and-file level are expected to behave differently than traditional police officers.

Community policing is more explicit on this point than was team policing. The role of community policing officers is frequently defined in terms of "planning," "community organizing," "brokering" government services, and "problem solving" (Eck & Spelman, 1987; Greene & Mastrofski, 1988). These terms are utterly alien to the vision of professional policing advanced by O.W. Wilson (Wilson & McLaren, 1977).

In the case of team policing, the conception of a different role tended to emphasize means rather than ends. Team policing officers were to plan programs tailored to their assigned neighborhoods, to do so through a collegial decision-making process, and to seek community input. This was far different from the traditional role of the street-level patrol officer, which emphasized following departmental procedures, responding to citizen calls for service, and initiating contact with citizens where appropriate. But the larger goal was still the traditional one of improved crime fighting. The *Seven Case Studies* report concluded that "Team Policing projects have one broad goal—to improve the control of crime through better community relations and more effective police organization" (Sherman, Milton, & Kelly, 1973:61).

The question of the goals of team policing and community policing is an extremely important one, to which we now turn our attention.

Major Differences

Basic Objectives

The basic goals of community policing differ radically from team policing. As we have already suggested, team policing was conceived largely as a means to an end: improved crime fighting. The *Seven Case Studies* report concluded that "[t]eam policing projects have one broad public goal—to improve the control of crime through better community relations and more effective police organization" (Sherman, Milton, & Kelly, 1973:61). In one instance (Syracuse), the Crime Control Team experiment was launched as a crime control program (Sherman, Milton, & Kelly, 1973:35). Improved police-community relations was intended to enhance the flow of information to the police that would be useful in crime-fighting. The Cincinnati COMSEC experiment, on the other hand, gave the goals of reducing crime and improving community relations equal weight (Schwartz & Clarren, 1973:1).

Community policing, on the other hand, represents a fundamental redefinition of the basic police role. It explicitly rejects the "crime attack" model of policing in favor of an emphasis on order maintenance and quality of life problems. This reorientation has a substantial empirical base.

Some of the most important contributions to the police "research revolution" of the 1960s and 1970s emphasized the limited capacity of changes in routine patrol to reduce the incidence of crime (Kelling et al., 1974), the limited capacity of the police to improve clearance rates (Greenwood, et. al., 1975), and the limited impact of faster response time on either crime or community satisfaction (Spelman & Brown, 1984). The Newark Foot Patrol Experiment (Police Foundation, 1981) found that while additional foot patrol did not reduce crime it did reduce citizen fear of crime.

Wilson and Kelling (1981) summed up this body of research in their influential "Broken Windows" article and suggested that further concentration on improved crime fighting was a dead end. They cited the Newark Foot Patrol Experiment's finding about fear of crime (Police Foundation, 1981), together with other research on neighborhood quality of life problems, and argued that police services should be redirected toward problems of order and disorder.

Organization and Delivery

There are considerable variations in how team policing and community policing are organized. Generalization is particularly difficult because of the many variations within each concept. Nonetheless, a few important points stand out.

In important respects, team policing represented a radical restructuring of the police organization. As we have indicated, this was a response to the police-community relations crisis and the argument that the centralized police bureaucracy was itself the problem (Angell, 1971). Generally, team policing experiments converted entire areas to team policing, but only certain areas. From one perspective, then, team policing was not an "add-on," or a supplement to basic police operations, as was the case with most police-community relations programs (Klyman & Kruckenburg, 1979). One of the central goals of team policing was to integrate all police services (patrol, investigation, etc.), with team members functioning as "generalists."

The organizational restructuring that team policing entailed was the source of several problems. Primarily, it created an anomaly within the larger organization: most of the department carried on traditional policing, while one part was operating according to very different principles. One practical problem that arose involved the dispatching technology, which had evolved into the highly centralized "nerve center" of the modern police department. Observations of police patrol work had found that patrol officers were frequently dispatched to calls outside their assigned area (Reiss, 1971). Problems related to the dispatching system were cited as one of the three major obstacles to team policing by the Police Foundation evaluation (Sherman, Milton, & Kelly, 1973:94-96). The Cincinnati COMSEC experiment addressed this problem by creating a separate radio channel for District 1 (Schwartz & Clarren, 1977:51).

To date, community policing represents a number of variations related to organization and delivery of basic police services. In many experiments, community policing is an "add on." CPOP officers in

New York City are assigned to precincts along with officers performing traditional police services (Farrell, 1988; Walker, 1985). By 1992, when community policing had been expanded to the entire city, there were still only 800 CPOP officers in a department of about 27,000 sworn officers. Other community policing or problem-oriented policing experiments involved a small number of officers operating specialized programs within a traditional framework. Houston, on the other hand, at one point converted its entire department to community policing.

THE LESSONS OF TEAM POLICING

The *Seven Case Studies* report identified three major obstacles to team policing (Sherman, Milton, & Kelly, 1973:91-96). In addition, a number of other actual and potential problems can be identified in the text of that report and in the evaluation of the Cincinnati team policing experiment (Schwartz & Clarren, 1977).

The Three Major Obstacles

Opposition From Middle Management

Opposition from middle management officers was a serious problem. Captains and lieutenants resented their loss of authority as greater responsibility was placed on sergeants and police officers. Their resistance was manifested in the form of (1) failure to deal with organizational problems that arose, (2) "bad-mouthing" the experiment, and (3) directly confronting top management with their opposition (Sherman et al., 1973:91-92).

This opposition was largely a consequence of the attempt to alter the formal structure of the police organization and the consequent threat to the authority of middle managers. Because community policing generally does not involve the same kind of organizational restructuring, it may avoid this particular problem. Nonetheless, opposition from within the department can be anticipated. The source of this opposition may arise not from threats to decision-making authority but from opposition to the substance of community policing itself. Opposition is likely to be aroused by the radical redefinition of the police role. Many officers may find the idea of being "planners," "community organizers," and "brokers" unappealing or even threatening. An evaluation of Neighborhood-Oriented Policing (NOP) in Houston, arguably one of the most comprehensive community policing programs to date, found that "Many officers seem entrenched in their opposition to the program, perceived as a public relations gimmick" (Cresap, 1991:NOP-2).

The "lessons" of team policing on this point appears clear and unequivocal. Planning and training are crucial to success. Officers who are affected, even indirectly, by the new program need to understand its goals and where they fit into the future of the organization. In the two greatest successes reported in the *Seven Case Studies*—Los Angeles and Holyoke—planning and training were indistinguishable. It noted that "[i]n Holyoke, the planning process was the training process" (Sherman, Milton, & Kelly, 1973:68). Involvement in the planning process of those officers who will be expected to implement the experiment appears to be crucial. Training, meanwhile, needs to be more than just a pre-implementation process. The apparent success of team policing in Los Angeles was due in part to the fact that "training was, in a sense, continuous" (Sherman, Milton, & Kelly, 1973:51).

Trial By Peers

The second major obstacle identified by the Police Foundation evaluation was "trial by peers" (Sherman, Milton, & Kelly, 1973:93-94). Where it was a success, or reputed to be a success, there was resentment on the part of other officers. In some instances, resentment was the result of a lack of communication. Other officers were never fully informed about the experiment and did not understand its goals or procedures. The problem of resentment and jealousy arose in both those cities were where all officers in a given neighborhood were members of the team policing experiment and those where team policing officers and regular patrol officers worked the same neighborhoods simultaneously.

Some of the resentments were the result of unequal workloads. In some instances a sophisticated workload analysis was used for team policing areas but not other areas. The result was that team policing areas appeared to be overstaffed, with other officers resenting their colleagues lighter workload (Sherman, Milton, & Kelly, 1973:96).

The problem of resentment by other officers would appear to be potentially serious for community policing. Community policing has already acquired a very positive reputation and officers not included in it may resent the publicity and glamour enjoyed by the officers who are included. The evaluation of Neighborhood-Oriented Policing in Houston found that some sergeants and lieutenants were "negative leaders" who did not "support officer initiative" (Cresap, 1991:NOP-3).

The issue of unequal work-loads—or, even more important, perceived inequality—is potentially very serious. Because community policing involves a radical new approach to the police role, other officers may quickly feel that the community policing officers are not doing "real" police work, or any work, for that matter. This matter touches on a larger problem that will be discussed at length below. The nontraditional role that is the core element of community policing creates a number of potentially serious problems for everyone: the officers in the project, their supervisors, other officers in the department, and the community.

Problems With Dispatching Technology

Team policing encountered serious problems because the patrol car dispatching technology remained centralized, in conflict with the decentralized orientation of team policing (Sherman, Milton, & Kelly, 1973:94-96). This served to erode the integrity of team policing's neighborhood focus. In New York City team members spent as much as half their time outside of the team area, while in Detroit they were outside their areas as much as one-third of the time (Sherman, Milton, & Kelly, 1973:31, 46, 94-96).

The impact of the dispatching technology on community policing depends heavily on the exact form that community policing takes. In New York City it may not be a major threat. CPOP officers are a distinct unit within each precinct, with regular patrol officers responsible for calls for service. In cities where all officers in a given neighborhood are community policing officers, the dispatching technology does raise the same threat that it raised in team policing.

Unless measures are instituted to screen out a large number of calls or insulate some officers from responsibility for responding to calls, there is good reason to fear that the sheer pressure of calls for service could erode the integrity of community policing. This threat is highlighted by another problem encountered by team policing: the tendency of the experiments to evolve into a form of policing that was little different from traditional police work (Sherman, Milton, & Kelly, 1973:73, 80). This issue is another consequence of the radical role redefinition embodied in community policing. Unless community policing officers have a clear sense of what they are supposed to do and receive the necessary support from their supervisors (who presumably also know what this new role involves) the tendency to drift back into a traditional role will be very great.

OTHER POTENTIAL PROBLEMS

Unclear Definition of Goals

Perhaps the most important lesson from the team policing experience involves problems associated with unclear definition of goals. The *Seven Case Studies* report found that in most cities, team policing never achieved its organizational goals of decentralization and neighborhood stability. More worrisome is the fact that even where these organizational goals were achieved, "It was not long, however, before the team members noticed that their team policing hardly differed from the 'policing' they had done before" (Sherman, Milton, & Kelly, 1973:73).

A number of factors contributed to this problem. In part it was a consequence of inadequate planning, training, and supervision. Several aspects of policing, however, contribute to that tendency. The dispatching technology, as we have already noted, tended to pull officers not just out of their areas, but away from team policing generally. Yet some officers apparently left their areas on their own initiative, out of boredom with the lack of activity. This is another way of saying they did not have a clear definition of what kinds of "activity" in which they were supposed to be engaged (Sherman, Milton, & Kelly, 1973:74).

Unclear goals left projects vulnerable to conflicting pressures from community residents, peer group officers, and supervisors. For example, some thought team policing meant a "nice guy" approach to policing, with an emphasis on enhanced informal relations between officers and community residents. Others thought team policing meant a "tough guy" approach to policing, meaning aggressive crime control tactics (Sherman, Milton, & Kelly, 1973:108).

The problem of unclear goals is probably greater in community policing than in team policing. As we have already noted, team policing was generally seen as an innovative means to a traditional end: crime control. Community policing, as we have noted, represents a radical role redefinition, eschewing crime control in favor of attention to problems that have traditionally been defined as not part of the police role. The evaluation of Houston's Neighborhood-Oriented Policing (NOP) found that "The limits of the officer's responsibilities under NOP have not been clearly delineated . . . Officers must understand where their problem-solving advocacy responsibilities end, and where those of others, such as the Planning Department and City Council begin" (Cresap, 1991:NOP-3).

The evaluation of the Houston NOP program was itself a symptom of a lack of understanding or consensus about the nature of community policing. The report by the Cresap management consulting firm was highly critical of the innovative NOP program. In part, this was due to the fact that the consultant's perspective reflected a traditional orientation toward crime-fighting and rapid response to citizen calls for service. Inevitably, it criticized a community policing program that de-emphasized these activities (Cresap, 1991:NOP-7, 21).

Redefining the police role in such a radical fashion introduces a number of problems. The most important is socializing the various actors and publics into the new role. Resocializing police officers is a major challenge. The initial CPOP experiment in New York City solved this problem by utilizing only officers who volunteered (Farrell, 1988). Expanding a community policing program to an entire department, however, poses a very serious challenge.

Equally difficult is the task of resocializing the public. Erroneous public expectations are equally serious. The "most important" obstacle encountered by the team policing experiment in Dayton, Ohio was "the lack of understanding within the department and in some segments of the community" of the true purposes of the project. Some community people saw it as a "left-wing liberal attempt(s) to undermine law and order in the city" (Sherman, Milton, & Kelly, 1973:20).

In this respect, the police have to undo much of what they have done over the years. The public has come to define the police role primarily in terms of immediate response to requests for service. The police created this expectation themselves by introducing the telephone, the dispatch system, and the patrol car and then encouraging citizens to call (Walker, 1984). The net result was a seemingly insatiable demand for police services. Finally, in the late 1970s, some experts began to think seriously about reducing that demand by resocializing the public into not expecting a response to every call (McEwen, Connors, & Cohen, 1986).

It is not clear that the public will immediately accept the idea of police officers as "problem solvers" and "community organizers." On the one hand, it is inconsistent with what they have come to expect about the police. At the same time, as some critics have already pointed out, the community organizer role could easily inject the police into a highly political role (Bayley, 1988).

Clearly, one of the most important lessons of the team policing experience is that acceptance of community policing requires careful planning and training. For the police officers, this includes the involvement of all officers, pre-implementation training, and continued training (Sherman, Milton, & Kelly, 1973).

The Danger of Goal Displacement

The lack of clear goals creates the danger that the goals will be displaced. In the case of community policing, the danger is that they will shift back to a traditional form of policing.

The *Seven Case Studies* report hints at the goal displacement problem but does not discuss it in detail. Even in experiments in which the purely *organizational* goals (i.e., stable geographic assignment) were achieved, policing on the street proved to be little different from traditional policing. The report found that "It was not long, however, before the team members noticed that their team policing hardly differed from the 'policing' they had done before" (Sherman, Milton, & Kelly, 1973:73). In short, what started out as a major reorientation of police work ended up as a conventional form of policing. Reversion to traditional practice may explain why one veteran of the New York City team policing experiment told this author that "no one knows when team policing ended" (Walker, 1985). There was no memo announcing the formal end of the experiment. Perhaps that was because there was nothing distinctive left to terminate.

Goal displacement is a particularly serious threat to community policing, given the current social and political context. The principal threat is that community policing will be seen by the public as a new approach to crime-fighting. There is already considerable evidence to that effect. A 1990 *New York Times* editorial endorsing community policing defined it entirely in terms of "reclaiming the streets" (*New York Times*, 1990). Ironically—and somewhat ominously—this editorial appeared opposite an article by Herman Goldstein explaining that community policing did not involve traditional law enforcement (Goldstein, 1990). During the same time period, a proposed 5,000 officer increase in the size of the New York City police department was justified almost entirely on the grounds that the additional officers would be used in community policing and that this would help to reduce crime (*New York Times*, 1990). And when New York City reported a reduction in crime for 1991, some officials and some of the press wanted to attribute it to community policing (*New York Times*, 1992). Finally, the proposed 1991 Violent Crime Control and Law Enforcement Act included financial assistance to police departments adopting community policing. The explicit purpose was to "put more cops back on the beat" (House of Representatives, 1991).

In the current climate of great public concern about crime, drugs and gangs, community policing may well become viewed entirely as a crime control strategy. This is entirely different from the goals originally defined by Goldstein (1979, 1990b) and Wilson and Kelling (1982). Under public pressure for quick results in crime reduction, police officials may be forced to play two of the traditional games in police administration: first, treating high-profile programs merely as public relations efforts; and, second, playing with crime data to "prove" the success of community policing.

Successful implementation, then, requires specific guidelines for officer behavior. They need specific instructions on what problems they might address, which ones if any might not be appropriate, what actions are appropriate to achieve their goals and which ones are inappropriate.

In this regard, there is an important distinction between "problem-oriented policing," as proposed by Herman Goldstein (1979, 1990b) and many, if not most, of the published writings on community policing. Problem-oriented policing is essentially a planning process. It lists a number of problems that might be addressed and outlines a planning process for dealing with them. A police department is free to pick and choose from among many possible problems. Most of the literature on community policing, on the other hand, tends to be vague and hortatory. There tends to be a lot of rhetoric about "community,"

353

"order," and "fear reduction," but not much detail on exactly how these goals are to be achieved.

The Conflicting Demands of Control and Autonomy

As attempts to decentralize decision making within the department, both team policing and community policing confront the inherent tension between the goals of control and autonomy. This tension was most clearly exposed in the Cincinnati team policing experiment. The evaluation report noted that, as the experiment progressed, "senior officers feared that with the promised autonomy and reduction in central control, their officers might become less productive or even corrupt. To many senior staff officers, autonomy and control were competing issues" (Schwartz & Clarren, 1977:7).

The central trend in the history of police administration has been in the direction of greater control. We should not dismiss this as some form of mindless bureaucratization, serving only the interests of power-hungry administrators. Centralized control, largely through standardized procedures and written rules, has been the principal tool for achieving accountability of rank-and-file police officers. This has served extremely important legal and social policy goals. The best examples are the control of police use of deadly force (Fyfe, 1988), response to domestic violence (Cohn & Sherman, 1987), high-speed pursuits (Alpert & Dunham), and the reduction of corruption (Goldstein, 1975).

The attempt to control discretion can be seen as the central theme not just of recent police history but of the history of the entire criminal justice system (Walker, 1993). Reducing or weakening centralized controls, without putting into place some effective alternative, threatens to undermine a generation of police reform. The is a crucial problem for community policing precisely because it places so much emphasis on flexibility and the creativity of rank-and-file officers. If community policing has the potential for unleashing the untapped creativity of officers on the street, it also has the danger of allowing them to revert to the gross abuses of a previous era in policing.

This danger is particularly acute in the current social and political climate. There is probably no greater invitation to disaster than to send officers out onto the street with a vague and ill-defined mandate to "reduce fear" or "improve the quality of life." Permitting or even encouraging rough street justice could be far worse. Wilson and Kelling's (1982) original "Broken Windows" article did raise the specter of "kick ass" policing.

The Hazards of Success

Another lesson from team policing is that early success, or the reputation of success, can be a disaster. When an innovative and promising program acquires a reputation for success, there is often a mad rush to adopt it without adequate understanding of its true nature and without proper planning.

The initial team policing experiment in Los Angeles was probably the greatest success reported in the *Seven Case Studies* (Sherman, Milton, & Kelly, 1973:45-53). The planning and training were the most extensive, particularly in terms of involving officers in the planning and maintaining training on a continuous basis. This achievement is all the more impressive in light of the department's reputation for having the most centralized and tightly run bureaucracy in all of American policing. Many observers might have considered it the least likely candidate for meaningful decentralization. Yet decentralization was achieved.

This success, however, was destroyed when the department decided to implement team policing citywide. The politics of this decision are extremely important. Chief Ed Davis developed a proposal to increase the size of the department from about 6,900 officers to 8500 ("Plan 8500," as it was called). Needing to persuade city council to make a substantial increase in the police budget, he seized on the success of team policing as a way of promising an improved form of policing. As as result, he expanded team policing citywide overnight. Officers received absolutely no training for their new roles (Curtsinger, 1991).

A similar process occurred with New York City's community policing experiment. CPOP began slowly, on an experimental basis in 1984. The experiment included careful planning, monitoring and evaluation by the Vera Institute. By 1985-86 CPOP had acquired a very positive reputation; residents loved it, according to all reports. About the same time, however, Police Commissioner Ben Ward found himself in political hot water because of a number of different problems. To save himself, he seized on the popular CPOP program and expanded it citywide. Some observers felt that the expansion was too sudden and precluded the necessary planning and training (Walker, 1985).

Community policing faces a very serious problem in this regard for two reasons. First, it has received an enormous amount of publicity and a bandwagon effect has already begun. As a result, many of the discussions of it are entirely uncritical. Second, there is enormous public pressure to do something about crime. Police chiefs are under great pressure to do something, or at least to appear to be doing something about crime. Given the publicity surrounding community policing, the easiest thing for a chief to do is to announce that it is being adopted. There is strong evidence that this is in fact occurring.

Hasty adoption not only results in poor planning and implementation, but also sets the stage for a negative backlash. This is the final lesson from the team policing experience. When team policing failed to transform policing as promised, disillusionment quickly set in. This accounts for the swift demise of team policing and its disappearance from the reform agenda in the mid-1970s.

Community policing could easily suffer the same fate. If anything, the expectations surrounding it are even higher than was the case in team policing. The backlash could be stronger as well. It would be a tragedy if a similar reputation for "failure" developed. An essential part of the planning process, then, probably involves curbing expectations and making it clear that community policing is not a "quick fix" that will suddenly reduce crime and disorder.

The Hazards of Inflated Expectations

Community policing became an enormously popular concept in the late 1980s. Many hailed it as the advent of a new era in policing (National Institute of Justice, 1988-1990). This popularity was due in part to its reputation as a "success." It is important, therefore, to take a close look at exactly what these successes were.

Perhaps the most widely cited program was the "fear reduction" project in Houston. Specific programs to reduce fear included neighborhood community stations, a program to encourage informal contacts between officers and community residents, a victim recontact program, a community newsletter, and other programs. An evaluation found that while some of these programs were apparently successful, in the sense that residents reported that they were aware of the program and that their attitude toward the police improved, they were more successful among whites, middle-income people, and homeowners than among racial minorities, low-income people, and renters (Brown & Wycoff, 1986; Pate, 1986). These findings were disturbingly similar to the results of other evaluations of community crime prevention programs which have found that they work best among those people and in those neighborhoods that are already relatively stable (Skogan, 1990). In short, even where it is successfully implemented, community policing may not be able to "save" neighborhoods that have reached a serious level of deterioration. Unfortunately, the literature on team policing does not help us on this point. Most of the experiments were relatively short, and the evaluations covered an even shorter time frame. This does not permit any inferences about the impact of team policing on long-term neighborhood deterioration.

On another point regarding inflated expectations, there is some sobering evidence in the community policing literature. As we have indicated, community policing places a heavy burden of responsibility on rank-and-file officers to develop creative, neighborhood-specific programs. This is an enormous burden indeed and the unpleasant truth may be that it is unrealistic to expect that much creativity among the police rank and file. Herman Goldstein reached this pessimistic conclusion in the final volume of his report on an early problem-oriented policing experiment in Madison, Wisconsin (Goldstein, 1978). In the end, officers did not come up with marvelously creative ideas to deal with drunk driving enforcement or repeat sex offenders. Team policing placed a similar burden of responsibility on rank-and-file officers. And yet, in the end, actual policing was generally not a great deal different from what had occurred before (Sherman, Milton, & Kelly, 1973).

SUMMARY

The team policing experience was an important event in American police history. It represented an ambitious attempt to refashion the organization and delivery of police services in order to deal with a number of problems. The experience offers a number of potentially valuable lessons for the currently popular concept of community policing. The goals of neighborhood-focused policing and decentralized decision making are similar. In addition, there is available a body of evaluation literature on team policing. We are not forced to rely on folklore about what happened. Yet this experience has been almost entirely ignored in the literature on community policing. It would be a tragedy if valuable lessons were ignored and, as a consequence, community policing were robbed of its potential. This article has attempted to sketch the most obvious lessons. There is much more to be said on the subject. Let the dialogue begin.

NOTE

1. Both the Police Foundation's evaluation of seven team experiments' (Sherman, 1973) and a Justice Department report on Neighborhood Team Policing (National Institute of Justice, 1973) were published in 1973. That date was probably the high point of the team policing movement.

REFERENCES

Alpert, G. and R. Dunham (1990). *Police Pursuit Driving*. Westport, CT: Greenwood Press.

Angell, J. (1971). "Toward an Alternative to the Classic Police Organizational Arrangements: A Democratic Model." *Criminology*, 9:185-206.

Bayley, D. (1988). "Community Policing: A Report From the Devil's Advocate." In J. Greene and S. Mastrofski (eds.), *Community Policing: Rhetoric or Reality?* Westport, CT: Praeger Publishers.

Cohn, E. and L. Sherman. *Police Policy on Deadly Force, 1986: A National Survey*. Washington, DC: Crime Control Institute.

Cresap (1991). *Houston Police Department: Draft Final Report*. Washington, DC: Cresap Management Consultants.

Curtsinger, C. (1991). Interview.

Eck, J. and W. Spelman (1987). *Problem-Solving: Problem-Oriented Policing in Newport News*. Washington, DC: Government Printing Office.

Farrell, M. (1988). "The Development of the Community Patrol Officer Program: Community Policing in the New York City Police Department." In J.

Greene and S. Mastrofski (eds.), *Community Policing: Rhetoric or Reality?* Westport, CT: Praeger Publishers.

Fyfe, J. (1988). "Police Use of Deadly Force: Research and Reform." *Justice Quarterly,* 5 (June):165-205.

Goldstein, H. (1990a). "Does Community Policing Work?" *The New York Times,* December, 30.

Goldstein, H. (1990b). *Problem-Oriented Policing.* New York: McGraw-Hill.

Goldstein, H. (1982). *Experimenting With the Problem-Oriented Approach to Improving Police Service.* Madison, WI: University of Wisconsin Law School.

Goldstein, H. (1979). "Improving Policing: A Problem-Oriented Approach." *Crime and Delinquency,* 25 (April):236-258.

Goldstein, H. (1975). *Police Corruption: A Perspective on its Nature and Control.* Washington, DC: The Police Foundation.

Greene, J. and S. Mastrofski (1988). *Community Policing: Rhetoric or Reality?* Westport, CT: Praeger.

Greenwood, P. et al., (1975). *The Criminal Investigation Process.* Santa Monica, CA: RAND Corporation.

House of Representatives (1991). *Violent Crime Control and Law Enforcement Act of 1991.* Washington, DC: U.S. Government Printing Office.

Kelling, G., T. Pate, D. Dieckman and C. Brown (1974). *The Kansas City Preventive Patrol Experiment: A Summary Report.* Washington, DC: The Police Foundation.

Klyman, F. and J. Kruckenburg (1979). "A National Survey of Police-Community Relations Units." *Journal of Police Science and Administration,* 7 (March):73-79.

McEwen, J., E. Connors and M. Cohen (1986). *Evaluation of the Differential Police Response Field Test.* Washington, DC: Government Printing Office.

Moore, M. and G. Kelling (1983). "To Serve and Protect: Learning From Police History." *The Public Interest,* 7 (Winter):49-65.

National Advisory Commission on Civil Disorders (1968). *Report.* New York: Bantam Books.

National Institute of Justice (1988-1990). *Perspectives on Policing* (Thirteen Volumes). Washington, DC: U.S. Government Printing Office.

National Institute of Justice (1973). *Neighborhood Team Policing.* Washington, DC: U.S. Government Printing Office.

New York Times (1992). "Cheery Crime Data: Was It Community Policing?" March 27, 1992.

New York Times (1990). "First, Reclaim the Streets." Editorial, December 30.

Pate, A. (1986). *Reducing Fear of Crime in Houston and Newark: A Summary Report.* Washington, DC: The Police Foundation.

Police Foundation (1981). *The Newark Foot Patrol Experiment.* Washington, DC: The Police Foundation.

President's Commission on Law Enforcement and Administration of Justice (1967). *The Challenge of Crime in a Free Society.* Washington, DC: U.S. Government Printing Office.

Reiss, A. (1971). *The Police and the Public.* New Haven, CT: Yale University Press.

Schwartz, A. and S. Clarren (1977). *The Cincinnati Team Policing Experiment: A Summary Report.* Washington, DC: The Police Foundation.

Sherman, L. (1975). "Middle Management and Police Democratization: A Reply to John E. Angell." *Criminology,* 12 (February):363-377.

Sherman, L., C. Milton and T. Kelly (1973). *Team Policing: Seven Case Studies.* Washington, DC: The Police Foundation.

Skogan, W. (1990). *Disorder and Decline: Crime and the Spiral of Decay in American Neighborhoods.* New York: The Free Press.

Walker, S. (1993). *Taming the System: The Control of Discretion in Criminal Justice, 1950-1990.* New York: Oxford University Press.

Walker, S. (1985). Personal Observations of CPOP Program, 72nd Precinct. New York.

Walker, S. (1984). "Broken Windows and Fractured History: The Use and Misuse of History in Recent Police Patrol Analysis." *Justice Quarterly*, 1 (March):75-90.

Walker, S. (1977). *A Critical History of Police Reform*. Lexington, KY: Lexington Books.

Wilson, J. and G. Kelling (1982). "Broken Windows: The Police and Neighborhood Safety." *Atlantic Monthly*, 249 (March):29-38.

Wilson, O. and R. McLaren (1977). *Police Administration* (Fourth Edition). New York: McGraw-Hill.

American Journal of Police Vol. XI, No. 4 1992   1

THE EFFECTIVENESS OF CIVILIAN REVIEW: OBSERVATIONS ON RECENT TRENDS AND NEW ISSUES REGARDING THE CIVILIAN REVIEW OF THE POLICE

Samuel Walker
University of Nebraska at Omaha

Vic W. Bumphus
Michigan State University

Civilian review of the police has been a controversial issue in policing for nearly forty years (Terrill, 1991). The concept is defined as a procedure under which citizen complaints against police officers are reviewed at some point by persons who are not sworn officers. Virtually all proposals for civilian review were defeated in the 1960s, but in the last few years the concept has spread rapidly among big-city police departments. By 1992 over two-thirds (68%) of the police departments in the 50 largest cities had some form of civilian review (Walker & Bumphus, 1991; Walker, 1992). This paper reports the findings of a survey of the 50 largest cities and discusses the important new questions raised by this data.

The central issue regarding civilian review has traditionally been the question of whether it is appropriate for citizens to be involved in the complaint process. The police have opposed civilian review on the grounds that the concept intrudes on their professional autonomy, that persons who are not police officers are not competent to evaluate police actions, and out of fear of greater scrutiny of police behavior. The civilian review issue has also been a civil rights issue, pitting the African-American community against predominantly white police departments.

To a great extent, these traditional issues have been settled. The city councils in two-thirds of the largest cities have, in effect, made a legislative finding that some form of civilian review is an appropriate response to the problem of police misconduct. This development shifts the ground to a different set of questions. The central question concerns the effectiveness of civilian review. Does it work? Or, more precisely, is one form of complaint review more effective than others? This raises a host of subsidiary questions. How is effectiveness defined? What measures of effectiveness are appropriate? How useful is official data on citizen complaints and the disposition of complaints? This paper examines these and other new questions raised by the recent developments in the area of civilian review.

THE 50-CITY SURVEY: FINDINGS

Methodology

In the spring of 1991 a survey was conducted of citizen complaint procedures in the 50 largest cities in the United States (Walker & Bumphus, 1991). An initial telephone inquiry determined whether the police department had any form of citizen input in the complaint process. If the answer was yes, the respondent was asked to describe the process and also to forward official documents describing the complaint process. On the basis of the telephone interviews and the official documents, citizen complaint procedures were then analyzed and categorized according to a three-part classification system.[1]

Principal Findings

The survey found some form of civilian review in 30 of the 50 police departments. Between April, 1991 and October, 1992, civilian review procedures were adopted in four additional cities, bringing the total to 34, or 68 percent of the total (Walker, 1992).[2] The survey also found an accelerating trend toward civilian review. Nineteen of the 34 (55.8%) have been established since 1986, with eight established between 1990 and 1992 alone. An earlier survey (West, 1988) identified a total of 15 civilian review, or external review procedures in the entire country by 1987.

There is some ambiguity regarding the exact date some civilian review procedures were created. In some instances, city councils passed an ordinance creating a new procedure in one year but did not actually begin its operation until the following year. In some cities (New York City [Kahn, 1975], Chicago, Milwaukee) preexisting units or agencies were revised several times over the years. The survey defined the effective creation date as the point when non-sworn persons gained some involvement in the complaint process.[3]

Civilian review appears to be a nationwide phenomenon, with no geographic region underrepresented. The demographic characteristics of cities also do not appear to be a factor. Civilian review procedures exist in cities with small African-American populations (Indianapolis, Minneapolis) as well as those with large minority populations (Detroit, Atlanta). The trend toward civilian review also appears to be an international phenomenon, at least in English-speaking countries, with the establishment of new procedures in England, Canada and Australia in the 1980s. The United Kingdom created a national system, the Police Complaints Authority (PCA) in 1985 (Goldsmith, 1991).

Types of Civilian Review Procedures

The survey also found considerable variation among civilian review procedures in terms of the degree of civilian input and operating procedures. The degree of civilian input is the crucial factor in civilian review. "Degree" in this context refers to the exact point in the complaint process at which non-sworn persons participate. The three key points are: (1) the initial fact-finding investigation; (2) the review of investigative reports and the power to recommend action by the chief executive; (3) the review of decisions already taken by the chief executive. The survey developed a three-part classification system (Walker & Bumphus, 1991). This closely resembled classification systems developed by Kerstetter (1985) and Petterson (1991).[4]

Class I systems are those in which the initial fact-finding investigation is done by individuals who are not sworn police officers. Their reports go to a person (or persons) who is also not a sworn officer, and who makes a recommendation to the chief executive for action. Class II systems are those in which the fact-finding investigation is done by sworn officers, but the recommendation to the chief executive is made by a person (or persons) who is not a sworn officer. Class III systems are those in which the initial fact-finding and recommendation are done by sworn officers; if the complaining party is unsatisfied with the disposition of the complaint, he or she may appeal that decision to a person who is not a sworn officer, or group of persons that includes at least some non-sworn persons.

Since the 1991 survey was conducted, two cities (Seattle and San Jose) have created "auditor" systems that do not fit neatly into any of the three classes. Under these systems, a non-sworn person has the authority to oversee the complaint process, and may make recommendations to police investigators, but has no power to make recommendations for discipline. The auditor approach fits the classification system created by Petterson (1991:276).

General Features

Several features are common to all existing civilian review procedures. First, none have the power to impose discipline on a police officer and can only make recommendations to the police chief executive (Petterson, 1991).[5] Granting a civilian review agency the power to impose discipline would require a change in existing civil service laws, as well as collective bargaining contracts in most cities.

Second, 26 of the 30 procedures identified in 1991 were established by municipal ordinance or state statute. This represents a significant change from the pattern in the 1950s and 1960s in which the first two important procedures, in Philadelphia (Coxe, 1965; Hudson, 1972; Terrill, 1988; Walker, 1990) and New York City (Kahn, 1975), were created by executive order. Because they did not represent a decision by a majority of the elected representatives, they were politically and administratively vulnerable. The Philadelphia Police Advisory Board (PAB) was abolished by the executive order of a subsequent mayor. An expanded and more civilian version of the New York City CCRB was abolished by referendum. Thus, current civilian review procedures are on more solid legal footing and represent a broader community consensus than earlier procedures.

The extent of this community consensus is indicated by a 1992 public opinion poll that found broad public support for civilian review. The Louis Harris (1992) organization surveyed 1,248 adults and found that 80 percent favored review of citizen complaints by mixed teams of police and non-sworn investigators; 15 percent supported investigations by non-sworn persons only, while only four percent supported the traditional approach of having citizen complaints reviewed entirely by police officers. Third, the survey revealed some of the problems involved in the commonly used terminology. The public and the media generally refer to these groups as "civilian review boards."

The national survey of civilian review procedures also found that the term civilian review *board* is a misnomer. Not all of the existing review procedures involve a multi-member board. Several are municipal agencies with a single director (Walker & Bumphus, 1991). The generic term "civilian review *procedure*" is a more accurate descriptor than civilian review board.

The term "independent" is also extremely ambiguous and the source of much misunderstanding. The Cincinnati Office of Municipal Investigations is independent in the sense that it is an agency separate from the police department. The Professional Standards Section of the Detroit Police Department, on the other hand, is under the jurisdiction of the Board of Police Commissioners and, thus, might be viewed by some observers as not independent (Littlejohn, 1981). However, the investigative fact-finding in Detroit is done by persons who are not sworn officers. Consequently, the 50-city survey deemed it independent. The Kansas City Office of Citizen .omplaints (1983) is a separate municipal agency, with a director .10 is not a sworn officer and an office in a building separate from police headquarters. However, the fact-finding in Kansas City is done by sworn officers in the internal affairs unit. This makes the review of complaints in Kansas City much less independent of the police department than the procedure in Detroit.

UNANSWERED QUESTIONS

Explaining the Patterns of Growth

The recent growth of civilian review procedures has not received close attention by police scholars. With the exception of Terrill (1991) and West (1988), there is no general overview of this rapidly changing area of policing. There is a detailed analysis of the creation of only one of the current systems (Littlejohn, 1981). Occasional surveys of various agencies are conducted by private organizations (New York Civil Liberties Union, 1993) but the resulting reports often lack important data and do not reach a wide audience.

The agenda for future research on civilian review includes, at a minimum, explaining the recent growth of the phenomenon and developing more detailed comparative data.[6]

Some observations about the history of civilian review suggest the direction that research might take. In the 1960s, the two major civilian review procedures were abolished. Both had been created by liberal Republican mayors in response to the demands by civil rights forces and both were abolished primarily as a result of pressure from local police unions (Hudson, 1972; Terrill, 1988). In the case of New York City, a union-sponsored referendum abolished the civilian-dominated CCRB, leaving in place a board not dominated by civilians (Kahn, 1975). Because of the success of the police unions, many observers concluded that civilian review was essentially dead as a possible reform measure. A change evidently occurred in 1974, with the creation of two important review procedures (Detroit, Chicago). They were followed by twelve others over the next decade.[7] Since 1986, the spread of civilian review has been very rapid. The momentum of this trend appears to be accelerating, with the 1991 Rodney King beating and its aftermath providing an additional boost. No systematic data exists on cities smaller than the fifty largest. Impressionistic evidence suggests that there is increasing interest in civilian review in medium-sized cities.[8]

The trend of events suggests a significant change in the balance of power in the context of municipal politics. The most obvious possible explanation would be the growth of African-American political power, particularly in those cities where blacks constitute a majority of voters and where black mayors have been elected. Black political leadership was undoubtedly a factor in the creation of civilian review procedures in Detroit (Littlejohn, 1981) and Atlanta. Yet this cannot account for the creation of civilian review in cities with relatively small black communities (Indianapolis, Minneapolis, Seattle) and the absence of civilian review in some cities with relatively large black communities (Philadelphia). Nor is the election of a black mayor the critical variable, in and of itself. Philadelphia and Los Angeles have both elected black mayors but remain without civilian review procedures.

Many observers argue that the creation of a civilian review procedure requires a well-organized political effort by a coalition of community groups. This was the case in Indianapolis (Gradison, 1989) and Minneapolis, but it fails to account for the absence of civilian review in cities with similar community coalitions, such as Los Angeles

(Ripston, 1991) and Philadelphia (Coxe, 1988).   A well-organized coalition has had great difficulty in strengthening the existing system in New York City (Siegel, 1991). In short, a well-organized demand for civilian review is probably a necessary condition, but not itself a sufficient one.

One major factor has been the apparent decline in the power of police unions, at least on this issue. Police unions were the principal force in defeating civilian review proposals in New York City (Kahn, 1975) and Philadelphia (Terrill, 1988) in the 1960s. Yet they have been increasingly unsuccessful in most cities. In fact, with the two most recently created review procedures, Seattle (Taylor, 1991) and Denver (Law Enforcement News, 1992), the police union either actively supported the proposal or chose not to oppose it. In both cases, the police union concluded that some form of civilian review would be adopted in any event and that it could live with the present proposal.

Generally speaking, police chiefs do not appear to be active opponents of civilian review. This represents a significant change from the 1960s when the International Association of Chiefs of Police adopted a official statement opposing civilian review (Police Chief, 1964). The attitude of the big-city chiefs is best indicated by the official position of the Police Executive Research Forum (1981), which has urged police departments to establish and maintain effective systems of discipline. Although it has not endorsed civilian review, PERF has not officially opposed the concept either.

A case-study approach could serve to illuminate the process by which civilian review procedures are established. In virtually every city, creation of a procedure is the result of some immediate controversy (usually a shooting or physical force incident). In each case, however, there had been a number of similar incidents in the past, each usually followed by a proposal for civilian review (Gradison, 1989; Taylor, 1991). The relevant question, then, becomes what changes led to the creation of a civilian review procedure? A case-study approach could identify whether the most important change or changes involved: (1) new mayoral leadership; (2) a new composition on city council; (3) a new police chief; (4) changes in the strategy and tactics of civilian review advocates; (5) some other relevant factor.

The Effectiveness of Civilian Review

The most frequently asked question about civilian review is whether it works. At present, it is impossible to provide a definitive answer to that question. There are no thorough, independent evaluations of the effectiveness of any procedure, much less any comparative studies. Studies by Hudson (1972) and Perez (1978; 1992) are limited by serious conceptual and methodological problems. An evaluation of the New York City CCRB by the Vera Institute (1989a, 1989b, 1988) addressed a limited range of issues.

The question of effectiveness raises a number of problems. First, there is no single entity known as "civilian review." As the 50-city survey found, there are three general categories and a number of variations within each category (Walker & Bumphus, 1991). Any attempt to measure effectiveness needs to take into account the possibility that one form of civilian review may prove to be more effective than other forms. Common sense suggests that procedures with greater resources (e.g., number of staff) and powers (e.g., subpoena power) are more likely to be effective than other systems. By the same token, it would be dangerous to compare procedures solely on the basis of their formal structure and powers. One procedure that appears to be more "independent" on paper may be undermined through administrative resistance and thus be less effective than another system which is nominally less "independent."

Second, defining effectiveness is problematic. There are several possible measures of effectiveness that are related to the different objectives of the concept. Maguire (1991:186) identifies four distinct objectives of civilian review. They include: (1) maintaining effective discipline of the police; (2) providing satisfactory resolution of individual complaints; (3) maintaining public confidence in the police; and (4) influencing police management by providing "feedback from consumers." A comprehensive evaluation of effectiveness would take into account all four of these dimensions of civilian review.

In the minds of its advocates, the primary objective of civilian review is to provide a more independent review of citizen complaints (ACLU, 1966). The assumption has been that persons who are not sworn police officers are likely to conduct a more thorough investigation of a complaint than a fellow officer. The so-called "blue curtain" and the tendency of officers to cover up the misconduct of fellow officers has long been recognized as a phenomenon of the police officer subculture (Westley, 1970; New York Civil Liberties Union, 1990) and a barrier to effective discipline. Advocates of civilian review have assumed that the review of complaints by non-sworn officers will result in more disciplinary actions and an improvement in on-the-street police behavior (ACLU, 1966).

The Ambiguity of Official Data

One of the major problems confronting any attempt to evaluate the police complaint process (whether internal or external) is the ambiguous nature of official data on the number of complaints, the complaint rate (complaints per population or complaints per officer), the rate at which complaints are sustained, and the ultimate disciplinary actions taken, if any.

The number of complaints may reflect administrative procedures rather than police performance. In the wake of the Rodney King beating in March, 1991, some observers noted that San Francisco had more citizen complaints than did the much larger Los Angeles police department (New York Times, 1991). It is entirely possible that the existence of an strong civilian review procedure in San Francisco brings forth more citizen complaints. In fact, a study by the ACLU in Los Angeles in 1992 found that the police department was actively discouraging citizen complaints (ACLU-Southern California, 1992). In New York City, the number of complaints increased tenfold between the mid-1960s and the mid-1970s. This enormous increase appears to be associated with administrative changes that made the complaint process more open and more accessible to the public (Kahn, 1975).

Two comments on this phenomenon are in order. First, a higher rate of complaints could be viewed as an indicator of success: it reflects that fact that citizens are more confident that they will receive a fair hearing and therefore file their complaints (ACLU, 1992; Crew, 1991). The New York Civil Liberties Union (1990:29-33) attributed the 50 percent decline in the number of complaints filed with the CCRB between 1985 and 1989 to declining public confidence in the CCRB itself. Second, police departments face the unpleasant fact that the better they do the worse they will look. A more open and responsive complaint system will probably generate more complaints.

The impact of administrative changes on the number of complaints is extremely complex. In Detroit the creation of a more inde-

pendent review procedure produced an immediate increase in complaints, followed by a reduction (Littlejohn, 1981). A similar pattern
was reported in Kansas City (Kansas City, Office of Citizen Complaints, 1983) and New York City (Kahn, 1975; New York Civil Liberties Union, 1990). The initial increase in complaints could be the result of greater public confidence in the complaint process. The subsequent decline could be the result of either citizen disillusionment with
the process or a genuine improvement in police conduct, with the
civilian review procedure functioning as a genuine deterrent to misconduct. The interplay of complaint procedures and the volume and rate of
complaints is, in short, highly complex and complicates any attempt at
evaluation.

The official data on the number and rate of complaints is problematic because we do not have any baseline data on the actual number of
incidents of police misconduct. This issue is a highly political question, with some people arguing that misconduct is pervasive, while others argue that it is a relatively infrequent event. The available research
on this question is suggestive at best. Albert Reiss (1968; 1971) found
that police officers used "undue force" relatively rarely: in only 37 of
3,826 observed police encounters. This represented a rate of 5.9 for
every 1,000 white citizens and 2.8 for every 1,000 black citizens. The
New York City Civilian Complaint Review Board (1990:45-51) reported citizen complaints at rates ranging from a high of five per
10,000 to a low of one per 10,000 documented encounters between officers and citizens, depending on the neighborhood. These data suggest
that excessive force is a statistically rare event. Reiss (1971:151),
however, pointed out that instances of police abuse accumulate over
time, creating the perception of police harassment. Official data on
complaints has consistently indicated that racial minority males are
disproportionately represented among complainants (New York City
Civilian Complaint Review Board, 1990). Thus, the perception of a
pattern of police harassment is a major factor in conflict between the
police and racial minority communities.

The Police Services Study (PSS), which included a more representative sample of police agencies, used a victimization survey and
found that 13.6 percent of all respondents felt that they had been the
victim of police mistreatment in the previous year (Whitaker, 1982). In
certain respects this might appear to reflect a very high rate of police
misconduct. A study of 911 calls in Minneapolis, for example, found
that only 40 percent of the addresses in the city had any contact with

the police (Sherman, 1987). Assuming for the moment that 13 percent of the population experienced some mistreatment, then a disturbingly high percentage of those with any contact at all would be the victim of misconduct. These observations are entirely speculative; it is dangerous to make estimates by combining the results of two unrelated surveys. Nonetheless, these observations are designed to highlight the absence of any systematic victimization data regarding police misconduct.

Only 30 percent of the PSS respondents who claimed to have been mistreated by the police filed a formal complaint about the incident (Whitaker, 1982). This figure bears a striking similarity to the 37 percent rate of reporting crimes to the police. Moreover, the reasons given for not filing complaints are very similar to the reasons for not reporting crimes (e.g., "wouldn't do any good," which was given by 43 percent of the respondents) (Whitaker, 1982; U.S. Department of Justice, 1991). Extrapolating these estimates to New York City (1990), one might estimate that even in the high complaint rate precincts there is some misconduct in 15 out of every 10,000 encounters. It is reasonable to conclude that official complaints received by police departments represent about one-third of all incidents of alleged police misconduct. An important research question involves whether the complaining/reporting rate is higher in some cities than others and whether the differences are associated with differences in the complaint process.

Even the raw number of citizen complaints is problematic. It is a truism that official police data on crime often reflect administrative practices rather than the actual behavior it purports to measure. An unknown number of crimes reported by citizens are unfounded by police. The recording of arrests also varies widely by department (Sherman & Glick, 1984). With respect to citizen complaints, a number of problems arise. First, there is evidence that some departments actively discourage the filing of complaints (ACLU-Southern California, 1992; Kahn, 1975). Second, commonly used terms are not standard across departments. The San Francisco Office of Citizen Complaints (1991) distinguishes between "complaints" and "allegations." One complaint may involve several different allegations against one or more officers. In 1990, the New York City Civilian Complaint Review Board (1990:9) received 3,377 complaints involving 5,554 separate allegations. Clearly, then, comparisons in the absence of standardized definitions are problematic. Imagine an event in which three officers verbally and physically abuse one citizen. One department might record this as "one" incident or complaint, while another might record it as "six" complaints.

Police departments report very different rates at which citizen complaints are sustained. A citizen complaint may result in one of several outcomes. It is "substantiated" or "sustained" if the department agrees with all or some of the citizen's complaint. The officer is "exonerated" if the department agrees with the officer's version of the incident. The complaint is "not sustained" or "unfounded" if the investigation is unable to resolve the matter in the favor of either. Finally, many complaints are "dismissed" or "dropped," frequently because the complaining party fails to pursue the complaint or cooperate further with the investigation (New York, CCRB, 1990; San Diego, 1990).

The fact that a department sustains a relatively higher rate of complaints may be a result of the fact that it receives relatively few complaints. The smaller number of complaints would presumably include a relatively higher proportion of more serious instances of misconduct that are presumptively more likely to be sustained. By the same token, a relatively low rate of sustaining complaints in a department may be a product of receiving a high volume of complaints, which presumably includes a relatively lower percentage of more serious instances of misconduct.[9]

Any attempt to evaluate the effectiveness of a complaint review process needs to be incident-specific and seriousness-specific. Aggregate data on complaints and dispositions fail to take into account relevant distinctions between incidents. Common sense suggests that the unjustified use of physical force is far more serious than mere discourtesy. The use of racial or ethnic slurs is more serious than a neutral expression of discourtesy. A number of existing civilian review procedures, however, do divide complaints into two categories, according to seriousness (San Diego, 1990; Kansas City, 1983).

An important but hidden aspect of the complaint disposition process involves the lack of subsequent cooperation by the complaining party. In New York City, 35.4 percent of the complaints (1,197 out of 3,377) were dropped because the complaint was formally withdrawn or the complainant was unavailable or uncooperative (New York City, 1990:16). Critics of the CCRB characterized these data as "alarming" (New York Civil Liberties Union, 1990:28). The high rate of non-cooperation is not entirely surprising. Failure of the victim to cooperate is one of the major reasons why criminal cases are dismissed. With respect to complaints about the police, however, the reasons for withdrawal or non-cooperation may reflect the behavior of the investigators. Complaint processing officials may discourage citizens through indifference, rudeness, or failure to act on complaints in a timely fashion. A telephone survey conducted by the Southern California ACLU (1992) found that Los Angeles Police Department officials actively subverted the complaint process, rarely providing the caller with the department's official toll-free telephone number for complaints. Even when cases are investigated, investigators from the police department's internal affairs unit or the civilian complaint agency make only a half-hearted attempt to locate the complaining party or potential witnesses.

In any event, an officially recorded disposition of "complainant unavailable" cannot be taken at face value. Advocates of civilian review argue that non-sworn investigators are likely to be more aggressive in following up on complaints and less hostile to complainants. While there are abundant *a priori* reasons for assuming this to be true (particularly the literature on the "blue curtain," [Westley, 1970]), there is at present no empirical evidence to support it.

This discussion highlights the point that the key element in the effectiveness of any complaint review system, whether internal or external, is the vigor of the investigative process. Presumably, this could be measured in terms of the number of witnesses contacted, the timeliness of the investigation, or other possible factors. At present, however, such data is not readily available. The formal administrative structure of any procedure (internal vs. external, independent vs. not independent, etc.) does not necessarily determine the vigor or the quality of investigations.

A study of the bias crimes unit of the New York City Police Department, however, does suggest that there is some relationship between the level of organizational commitment, the vigor of investigations, and case outcomes (Garofalo, 1991). The existence of a bias crimes unit reflected an organizational commitment to investigating hate-motivated crimes. Over 90 percent of the incidents investigated by the unit resulted in three or more follow-up investigative reports. Meanwhile, 76 percent of a comparable sample of non-bias crimes produced no investigative reports; only seven percent received three or more. The arrest rate for bias crimes was two and one-half to three times that of the non-bias crimes sample. In short, a greater formal organizational commitment produced more actual work that resulted in a measurable difference in outcomes.

Public Opinion About the Police

Because one of the purposes of civilian review is to enhance public confidence in the police, surveys of public opinion offer a potential evaluation technique. The simplest approach would be to compare citizens' attitudes toward their local police department in cities with different complaint procedures (e.g., cities with civilian review vs. those without). Previous surveys of public opinion indicated some city-by-city variations in citizen evaluations of local police departments (U.S. Department of Justice, 1977). Significantly, white and black attitudes tend to move in the same direction, suggesting that persons of different races evaluate their local police department on the basis of roughly the same criteria. It would be possible to correlate such differences with complaint procedures. In some instances, it might be possible to identify changes in public opinion about a local police department that is associated with the creation of, or the revision of, a civilian review procedure.

Police complaint procedures could also be evaluated through surveys of public knowledge about the complaint process (e.g., the existence of a complaint procedure; where complaints could be filed). One could reasonably hypothesize that a relatively higher level of public awareness reflects a more effective job of facilitating complaints on the part of the police department. A low level of citizen knowledge about the complaint procedure might suggest that the police department is actively discouraging the filing of complaints.

Another possible measure of effectiveness would be the satisfaction of citizens who have filed complaints. Douglas Perez (1978; 1992) adopted this approach, surveying citizens who had filed formal complaints, comparing the responses in cities with civilian review and cities without it.[10] His data indicated a higher level of satisfaction in the complaint process in those cities with civilian input, including citizens whose complaints were not sustained. Unfortunately, the extremely small number of cases in his study raises serious questions about the reliability of his findings. He had only ten respondents in Berkeley, California, 19 in Kansas City, and 22 in San Jose (Kerstetter, 1985:168-169). The technique, however, appears to be a viable one.

The Vera Institute (1989b) surveyed a sample of 371 citizens who had filed complaints with the New York City CCRB. Significantly, it found a much lower rate of satisfaction among those whose complaints were fully investigated (16%), compared with those who withdrew their complaints (62%), and those who accepted conciliation (59%). Vera concluded that "the investigative process itself has a significant negative influence" on citizen satisfaction. Dissatisfaction was associated with the length of time the complaint process took, the lack of contact with and information about the subject officer, and the final outcome. Not surprisingly, those whose complaints were substantiated were more satisfied than other complainants.

One of the important findings of the Vera study involved the conciliation option. Under the CCRB procedures, the complainant may be offered conciliation if the evidence is weak, the alleged misconduct not serious, and the subject officer does not have a long record of prior complaints (Vera, 1989b:3). Vera found that a minority of complainants (20%) desired severe punishment for the officer(s). Most (61%) had "moderate" objectives: an apology for themselves and/or a reprimand of the officer(s). The desire for a direct encounter with the subject officer(s) was "pervasive" and "significantly associated with complainant satisfaction" (Vera, 1989b:11).

The Vera study suggests a refinement of the objectives of civilian review. Many civilian review advocates conceptualize it in terms of a criminal trial, with a formal public hearing, presentation of evidence and cross-examination, and a formal adjudication. The Vera study suggests that evaluating the effectiveness of civilian review needs to be approached from the standpoint of a variety of possible procedures and outcomes, with each tailored to the seriousness of the alleged offense and the expressed desires of the complainant.

The literature on civilian review has to date neglected a large body of literature by social psychologists on the question of procedural justice. Lind and Tyler (1988) conclude that people who seek justice through some formal mechanism (e.g., the courts) are at least as concerned with the procedure itself as with the outcome. The result is not necessarily as important as the process of interaction—of getting a hearing and having a sense of being heard. This is consistent with the findings of the Vera (1989b) study of complainants in New York City. Future research on the effectiveness of civilian review needs to take into account the insights emerging from the work on procedural justice.

Review Board Determinations vs. Police Determinations

Another potential measure of effectiveness would be the extent to which the determinations made by civilians in a complaint process differ from the determinations made by the police department. This approach would be particularly relevant in Class II systems (Walker & Bumphus, 1991) where a board or civilian agency director reviews investigative reports completed by the police internal affairs unit. Several of the current civilian review procedures publish data that provide some suggestive, although not definitive, leads on this matter. In 1990, the San Diego Citizens' Review Board disagreed with internal affairs findings in only seven of 297 Category I incidents (the most serious allegations of misconduct). This represented 2.3 percent of all Category I cases. The Review Board disagreed with internal affairs in only three of 138 Category II allegations (or 2.1% of all cases) (San Diego, 1990). In New York City, the pattern of disagreement was far more complex. The CCRB disagreed with 98 recommendations of its investigative staff (composed of both sworn officers and non-sworn investigators). This represented 8.4 percent of the 1,153 completed investigations in 1990. It disagreed with ten findings of "substantiated," reducing them to some lesser category for which no discipline would be recommended (New York CCRB, 1990:17). The ten originally substantiated cases were from a total of between 150 and 200 substantiated cases. The reporting of the data in the CCRB's *Annual Report* is not clear on this point. The CCRB also disagreed with 65 findings of "unsubstantiated," raising 28 (or 43%) to a finding of "substantiated." Only one other finding was raised to a finding of "substantiated." Thus, the CCRB raised the finding to a level at which formal discipline would occur in 29 of 98 disagreements (or 30%). In sum, the CCRB (which in 1990 did not include a majority of persons not employed by the police department) was more likely to recommend discipline than the investigative staff only rarely (slightly less than three percent of all completed investigations).

Several commentators have noted that civilian review procedures sustain citizen complaints at very low rates, rates that are not significantly higher than those reported by internal affairs units. The New York City CCRB substantiated only 3.8 percent of all complaints filed in 1988 and 2.8 percent in 1989. This appears to be an international phenomenon. Maguire (1991:187) found that the new Police Complaints Authority (PCA) substantiated only 8.2 percent of all fully investigated complaints, a rate that was "similar" to the previous and less independent procedure.

In some situations it may be possible to compare the record of the civilian complaint procedure with the police internal affairs unit. In some cities there is concurrent or overlapping jurisdiction over certain kinds of complaints. Hudson (1972) compared the activities of the Philadelphia Police Advisory Board (PAB) with the police internal affairs unit for several years in the 1960s. He found that the internal affairs unit was more likely to recommend discipline. Yet, this was a result of the fact that the two procedures were handling very different kinds of misconduct. Internal affairs generally handled corruption charges and violations of departmental policy. Such incidents are likely to involve less ambiguity about the facts of the case than are citizen complaints about excessive physical force or offensive language as to the facts—incidents that are often "swearing matches" that cannot be resolved through physical evidence or objective witnesses.

Several comments about these data are in order. First, they suggest that citizens do not substantially disagree with the judgment of police complaint investigators. This suggests that police officer fears that a civilian review process will be a "kangaroo court" are unfounded. At the same time it also suggests that civil rights leaders are likely to be disappointed that a civilian review procedure does not produce more findings of police misconduct. Second, the low rate of disagreement may be a result of the fact that the fact-finding is done by sworn officers. This would be a Class II system according to Walker and Bumphus (1991). The Citizens' Review Board has available to it only the information generated by the internal affairs investigation. The Review Board does have the power to request further investigation (San Diego, 1990), but the possibilities for covering up misconduct obviously remains.

Finally, it should not be forgotten that in all but a handful of cities, the ultimate disciplinary power remains with the police chief executive (Petterson, 1991:287-289). Civilian review procedures have the power to recommend disciplinary action. The effectiveness of a civilian review procedure, therefore, depends upon the extent to which such recommendations are accepted and acted upon. The most "independent" review procedure imaginable would be rendered irrelevant if most recommendations were rejected. The data from the San Francisco Office of Citizen Complaints (1991) is not encouraging on this point. According to the OCC's 1991 statistical report, the police chief did not impose any discipline in about one-third of the cases sustained by the OCC.

These data suggest a number of issues related to the effectiveness of civilian review. What is the rate at which recommendations are accepted by the chief executive? Assuming a relatively high rate of nonacceptance, what factors explain that pattern? Are their problems associated with the quality of the investigations and recommendations of the civilian review agency? Is there a highly antagonistic relationship between the civilian review agency and the chief executive? If so, is this antagonism the product of institutional conflict, particular personalities, or some other factors?

Civilian Review as a Policy-Making Agency

Some advocates of civilian review argue that the procedure can serve as a monitor or maker of police department policy. Maguire (1991:186, 192-193) defines this as the "feedback" function of civilian review. Only a few of the existing civilian review procedures in the United States have this function as part of their official role. Most are limited to the review of individual citizen complaints on a case-by-case basis. The Philadelphia Police Advisory Board (PAB), however, had the authority to make recommendations about general police policy (Coxe, 1965). The current civilian review procedures in Tucson, Arizona and Berkeley, California have similar authority (Walker & Bumphus, 1991). Possibly even more important, the Tucson Citizens' Police Advisory Committee has the authority to undertake investigations on its own initiative, without having to wait for a citizen to file a complaint.

Advocates of this particular role argue that it can serve an effective preventive role, making corrections in general police operations in a way that might reduce the number of complaints in the future (ACLU, 1992). An evaluation of this dimension of effectiveness could identify specific policy recommendations, determine whether they were implemented, and whether there was any reduction in complaints that might be attributed to the change.

Civilian Review as a Data Source

A recent manual on fighting police misconduct argues that a civilian review procedure could serve as an important source of data on police practices (ACLU, 1992). This addresses the traditional problem of the closed police bureaucracy and the difficulty in obtaining even the most rudimentary information about police practices, citizen complaints, and the disposition of complaints. Although researchers have had considerable success in recent years gaining access to police files on the use of deadly force (Fyfe, 1979; Geller & Karales, 1981), police departments have not been similarly forthcoming with respect to the use of physical force or other forms of misconduct. According to the proposed strategy (ACLU, 1992), the effectiveness of a civilian review procedure would be indirect. Instead of recommending discipline in particular cases, it would provide data that elected officials, community activists, and the news media could use to bring pressure on the police department to make needed changes. The strategy assumes that a civilian review agency would be less defensive about the implications of certain data and would be legally empowered to obtain and publish it.

Some already available data suggest how data generated by a civilian review agency could be used as a part of a strategy for improving police performance. One of the most important results of the Rodney King incident was a dramatic increase in public concern about police misconduct, as represented by official investigating commissions and investigative reporting by journalists.

Perhaps the single most important finding has been the fact that a small number of officers generate a disproportionate percentage of all complaints. This phenomenon had previously been documented by the U.S. Civil Rights Commission (1981). The Commission recommended that departments establish "early warning systems" to identify officers involved in an excessive number of citizen complaints and to take appropriate action to remedy the problem. The phenomenon of the "high complaint rate" officers (referred to colloquially as the "bad boys") has also been found in the Los Angeles police department (Independent Commission, 1991), the Los Angeles County Sheriff's Department (Kolts, 1992), Boston (1992), and Kansas City (New York Times, 1991).

A civilian review agency could generate such data on a routine basis, alerting both responsible police administrators and members of the public to the existence of problem-prone officers. There are certain problems with such a strategy that would have to be overcome. Police unions would oppose the identification of "problem" officers by name. They would have a valid claim that using unsubstantiated complaints for such identification would represent a form of punishment without adequate due process. This problem might be overcome if officers were identified by a code number (e.g., Officer #1, etc.). This would protect the privacy and due process rights of the individual officer, while at the same time alerting responsible officials and the public to the existence of certain problem officers. It would be useful to know, for example, whether there were many such officers or only a handful; whether the number of problem officers had declined over previous years; whether the number of complaints involving the seemingly worst officers was declining over previous years.

Data published by existing civilian review agencies already provide valuable data on patterns of police misconduct. The New York City Civilian Complaint Review Board (1990) confirms the fact that racial minority citizens and low-income neighborhoods are disproportionately represented among citizen complaints. As expected, younger officers are involved in more complaints than senior officers. Younger officers are more often assigned to patrol duty in high-crime areas and on the evening shift, assignments that are presumptively more likely to generate conflict-filled encounters between the police and citizens (Fyfe, 1981).

With respect to officer race, however, the New York City data indicated that officers were represented as the subject of complaints at rates equal to their presence in the department. This is consistent with Reiss' (1968; 1971) earlier finding that excessive use of force did not follow a clear pattern of racial discrimination—although they may accumulate over time among low-income and racial minority males. The data also indicate that, with perhaps one exception, officers were no more likely to use force against citizens of one race compared with another. The exception was that Hispanic officers were involved in a higher rate of complaints from Hispanic citizens. Female officers, meanwhile, were the subject of complaints at only half the rate of their presence in the department. This finding is supported by the fact that in other departments female officers have not been identified as among those officers who are the subject of a high rate of complaints (Independent Commission). Subsequent research could be directed to investigating whether the low rate of complaints against female officers reflects gender-related differences in on-the-street behavior or some other causal factor.

CONCLUSIONS

For several decades, controversy over the concept of civilian review of the police has primarily involved the question of whether such a procedure should be established in a particular community. To a great extent, that question has been settled. Over two-thirds of the 50 largest cities in the United States have created some form of civilian review. These actions represent a legislative finding that the concept is an appropriate response to the problem of police misconduct.

The recent spread of civilian review introduces a new era in the history of this subject and raises a new set of questions. The important issues involve questions of effectiveness. What works? What kinds of systems are more effective than others? What kinds of procedures and resources are associated with success? How should success be measured? What kind of data is necessary for meaningful evaluations? This article has attempted to identify some of the problems facing any attempt to undertake a meaningful evaluation of the effectiveness of civilian review.

NOTES

1. A valuable but non-systematic collection of information on civilian review procedures in found in International Association of Civilian Oversight of Law Enforcement (IACOLE), Compendium of Civilian Oversight Agencies (Evanston, IL, revised periodically). The Compendium is particularly valuable for information on civilian review procedures outside the United States. The data is summarized in Petterson (1991).

2. The four new cities are Virginia Beach, VA; Seattle, WA; Denver, CO, and San Jose, CA. In 1992 the mayor of Boston also created a limited civilian review procedure by executive order. Author's notes and conversations.

3. Because of the number of changes over the course of nearly 40 years (Kahn, 1975), the New York City CCRB presents an almost impossible

situation with respect to effective starting date. The authors of the survey determined that the changes made in 1987 constituted an important turning point in the history of the agency.

4.   Kerstetter's categories are: civilian review, civilian input, and civilian monitor.

5.   On this point, there is some ambiguity regarding the powers of the Milwaukee Police and Fire Commission, the Baltimore Complaint Evaluation Board and the Chicago Police Board.

6.   There is considerable literature on the early history of civilian review in Philadelphia (Terrill, 1988) and New York City (Kahn, 1975).

7.   These data are consistent with the findings of West's (1988) national survey conducted in 1987.

8.   This evidence consists largely of the author's telephone conversations with journalists and community activists.

9.   The assumption here is that more serious incidents, such as physical force, are more likely to be taken seriously by both complainant and investigators and more likely to involve physical evidence, such as injury requiring medical attention, that can help to verify the allegation. Less serious incidents, such as verbal abuse, are particularly difficult to verify.

10.   The Perez data is more readily available in Kerstetter (1985:162-163, 168-169).

REFERENCES

ACLU (1992). *Fighting Police Abuse: A Community Action Manual.* New York: Author.

ACLU (1966). *Police Power and Citizens' Rights: The Case For an Independent Police Review Board.* New York: Author.

ACLU-Southern California (1992). *The Call for Change Goes Answered.* Los Angeles, CA: Author.

Boston (1992). *Report of the Boston Police Department Management Review Committee.* Boston, MA: Office of the Mayor.

Boston Globe (1992). "Wave of Abuse Claims Laid to a Few Officers." (October 4).

Coxe, S. [Former Executive Director, Philadelphia ACLU] (1988). Interview with author.

Coxe, S. (1965). "The Philadelphia Police Advisory Board." *Law in Transition Quarterly* 2:179-185.

Crew, J. [Staff Counsel, Northern California ACLU] (1991). Interview with author.

Fyfe, J. (1981). "Who Shoots? A Look at Officer Race and Police Shooting." *Journal of Police Science and Administration*, 9:367-382.

Fyfe, J. (1979). "Administrative Interventions on Police Shooting Discretion." *Journal of Criminal Justice*, 7(Winter):309-323.

Garofalo, J. (1991). "Racially Motivated Crimes in New York City." In M. Lynch and E. Patterson (eds.), *Race and Criminal Justice*. New York: Harrow and Heston.

Geller, W. and K. Karales (1981). *Split-Second Decisions*. Chicago, IL: Chicago Law Enforcement Study Group.

Goldsmith, A. (1991). *Complaints Against the Police: The Trend to External Review*. Oxford, England: Clarendon Press.

Gradison, M. [Former Executive Director Indiana ACLU] (1989). Interview with author.

Harris, L. (1992). "Public Solidly Favors Mixed Police/Civilian Review Boards." *Law Enforcement News*, (October 31, 1992).

Hudson, J. (1972). "Organizational Aspects of Internal and External Review of the Police." *Journal of Criminal Law, Criminology, and Police Science*, 63 (September):427-432.

Independent Commission on the Los Angeles Police Department (1991). *Report*. Los Angeles, CA: Author.

International Association for Civilian Oversight of Law Enforcement (1989). *Compendium of International Civilian Oversight Agencies*. Evanston, IL: Author.

Kahn, R. (1975). "Urban Reform and Police Accountability in New York City: 1950-1974." In R. Lineberry (ed.), *Urban Problems and Public Policy*. Lexington, MA: Lexington Books.

Kansas City, Office of Citizen Complaints (1983). *Annual Report*. Kansas City, MO: Author.

Kerstetter, W. (1985). "Who Disciplines the Police? Who Should?" In W. Geller (ed.), *Police Leadership in America: Crisis and Opportunity*. New York: Praeger.

Kolts, J. (1992). *The Los Angeles County Sheriff's Department: A Report*. Los Angeles, CA: L.A. County Sheriff's Department.

Law Enforcement News (1992). "Denver Presses Ahead With High-Powered Civilian Review Panel." (September 30).

Lind, E. and T. Tyler (1988). *The Social Psychology of Procedural Justice*. New York: Plenum.

Littlejohn, E. (1981). "The Civilian Police Commission: A Deterrent of Police Misconduct." *University of Detroit Journal of Urban Law*, 59 (Fall):5-62.

Maguire, M. (1991). "Complaints Against the Police: The British Experience." In A. Goldsmith (ed.), *Complaints Against the Police: The Trend to External Review*. Oxford, England: Clarendon Press.

New York City, Civilian Complaint Investigative Bureau (1990). *Annual Report*. New York: Author.

New York Civil Liberties Union (1993). *Civilian Review Agencies: A Comparative Study*. New York: Author.

New York Civil Liberties Union (1990). *Police Abuse: The Need for Civilian Investigation and Oversight*. New York: Author.

New York Times (1991a). "Police Attacks: Hard Crimes to Uncover, Let Alone Stop." (March 24):IV:4.

New York Times (1991b). "Complaints About Police Declining in New York." (March 27):B12.

New York Times (1991c). "Kansas City Police Go After Their 'Bad Boys.'" (September 10).

Perez, D. (1992). *Civilian Review of the Police.* (Advance copy of manuscript).

Perez, D. (1978). "Police Accountability: A Question of Balance." Berkeley, CA: Ph.D. Dissertation, University of California at Berkeley.

Petterson, W. (1991). "Police Accountability and Civilian Oversight of Policing: An American Perspective." In A. Goldsmith (ed.), *Complaints Against the Police: The Trend to External Review.* Oxford, England: Clarendon Press.

Police Chief (1964). "Civilian Review Boards" (Summer).

Police Executive Research Forum (1981). *Police Agency Handling of Citizen Complaints: A Model Policy Statement.* Washington, DC: Author.

Reiss, A. (1971). *The Police and the Public.* New Haven, CT: Yale University Press.

Reiss, A. (1968). "Police Brutality—Answers to Key Questions." *Transaction,* 5 (July-August):10-19.

Ripston, R. [Executive Director Southern California ACLU] (1991). Interview with author.

San Diego, Citizens' Review Board (1990). *Annual Report.* San Diego, CA: Citizens' Review Board.

San Francisco (1991). *Office of Citizen Complaints: 1991 Year-End Statistical Report.* San Francisco, CA: The Police Commission.

Sherman, L. (1987). *Repeat Calls to the Police.* Washington, DC: Crime Control Institute.

Sherman, L. and B. Glick (1984). *The Quality of Police Arrest Statistics.* Washington, DC: The Police Foundation.

Siegel, N. [Executive Director, New York Civil Liberties Union] (1991). Interview with author.

Taylor, K. [Executive Director Washington (State) ACLU] (1991). Interview with author.

Terrill, R. (1991). "Civilian Oversight of the Police Complaints Process in the United States: Concerns, Developments, and More Concerns." In A. Goldsmith (ed.), *Complaints Against the Police*. Oxford, England: Clarendon Press.

Terrill, R. (1988). "Police Accountability in Philadelphia: Retrospects and Prospects." *American Journal of Police*, 7:79-99.

U.S. Civil Rights Commission (1981). *Who Is Guarding the Guardians?* Washington, DC: U.S. Government Printing Office.

U.S. Department of Justice (1991). *Criminal Victimization in the United States, 1989*. Washington, DC: U.S. Government Printing Office.

U.S. Department of Justice (1977). *Public Opinion About Crime*. Washington, DC: U.S. Government Printing Office.

Vera Institute (1989a). *The Processing of Complaints Against Police in New York City: The Perceptions and Attitudes of Line Officers*. New York: Vera Institute (September).

Vera Institute (1989b). *Processing Complaints Against Police in New York City: The Complainant's Perspective*. New York: Vera Institute (January).

Vera Institute (1988). *Processing Complaints Against Police: The Civilian Complaint Review Board—Executive Summary*. New York: Vera Institute (January).

Walker, S. (1992). *Update: The Current Status of Civilian Review*. Omaha, NE: University of Nebraska at Omaha, unpublished notes.

Walker, S. (1990). *In Defense of American Liberties: A History of the ACLU*. New York: Oxford University Press.

Walker, S. and V. Bumphus (1991). *Civilian Review of the Police: A National Survey of the 50 Largest Cities, 1991*. Omaha, NE: University of Nebraska at Omaha.

West, P. (1988). *Police Complaints Procedures in the USA and in England and Wales: Historical and Contemporary Issues*. Ann Arbor, MI: Unpublished M.S. Thesis, Michigan State University. University Microfilms International.

Westley, W. (1970). *Violence and the Police*. Cambridge, MA: MIT Press.

Whitaker, G. (1982). *Basic Issues in Policing*. Washington, DC: U.S. Government Printing Office.

Community Policing in
Small Town and Rural America

Ralph A. Weisheit
L. Edward Wells
David N. Falcone

Community policing has become a popular approach. Discussions of community policing have focused on urban and suburban departments, generally ignoring rural and small town police organizations. Ironically, many of these departments have a history of practices that correspond directly to the principles of community policing. For example, officers in these agencies typically know the citizens personally, have frequent face-to-face contact with them, and engage in a variety of problem-solving activities that fall outside of law enforcement. In neglecting small town and rural police, researchers have denied themselves an important natural laboratory for studying community policing.

In recent years, American policing has seen the emergence of a new vocabulary and, some would argue, a new philosophy of policing. The *idea* of community policing has swept the country, although in practice the term has been defined in many ways, some of them seemingly contradictory. At the heart of community policing is the idea that police departments must be more responsive and connected to the communities they serve, that policing is properly a broad problem-solving enterprise that includes much more than reactive law enforcement, and that individual line officers on the street and in the community should have a major role in this process.

Community policing by no means represents an isolated development. Rather, it seems to have emerged as a correlate of various social trends and movements, particularly the victim's rights and civil rights movements, each of which has organized citizens to demand that police be more accountable

RALPH A. WEISHEIT: Professor, Department of Criminal Justice, Illinois State University, Normal, IL. L. EDWARD WELLS: Associate Professor, Department of Criminal Justice, Illinois State University, Normal, IL. DAVID N. FALCONE: Associate Professor, Department of Criminal Justice, Illinois State University, Normal, IL.

This manuscript was prepared with the support of the National Institute of Justice (Grant No. 92-IJ-CX-K012). The views presented here are those of the authors and do not necessarily reflect those of NIJ. An earlier version of this article was presented to the Academy of Criminal Justice Sciences' Annual Meeting in Chicago on March 10, 1994.

CRIME & DELINQUENCY, Vol. 40 No. 4, October 1994 549-567

to the public (Karmen 1990). Similarly, such grassroots organizations as Mothers Against Drunk Driving (MADD) have focused on monitoring criminal justice agencies and have demanded that they be more accountable to the public for their decisions. The interest in community policing among police administrators also parallels general management trends that have emerged in the business world. Total quality management (TQM), for example, concerns itself with reducing layers of bureaucracy, empowering line employees, and increasing responsiveness to customers (e.g., Walton 1986)—ideas that have figured prominently in discussions of community policing. Health care and medicine have shown parallel developments, particularly in the growing trend toward medicine as proactive wellness production, rather than simply reactive disease treatment. The result is an emphasis on holistic, coproductive, general practitioner, and family practice medicine, as contrasted with segmented, specialty-oriented medicine. Given the developments in policing's recent past, the greater organization of citizens, and management trends more generally, it would have been surprising if some form of community policing had *not* become a dominant philosophy among police administrators.

Although community policing clearly has roots in earlier police strategies, as an organizational philosophy, its boundaries, implications for specific programs, and the circumstances under which it might be effective are still being explored. This article examines the idea of community policing by considering the fit between police practices in rural areas and the philosophy of community policing as an urban phenomenon. We suggest that experiences in rural areas provide examples of successful community policing, but the comparison also raises questions about the simple applicability of these ideas to urban settings.

WHAT IS COMMUNITY POLICING?

Although a relatively new idea, the concept of community policing has already generated a sizable and rapidly growing body of literature (e.g., Brown 1989; Goldstein 1987; Greene and Mastrofski 1988; Moore 1992; Trojanowicz and Bucqueroux 1990; Wilson and Kelling 1989). Although there is agreement on some broad dimensions of the concept, there is substantial variability in the types of program activities included under this conceptual umbrella and in the presumed central focus of the approach. Some discussions depict community policing as primarily a matter of reorganizing the nature of *police work*, from reactive law enforcement to proactive policing (in the classical sense of that term), order maintenance, and problem solving.

At other times, the emphasis is on the implications of community policing for the *organizational structure* of police agencies as formal organizations. These discussions suggest that community policing is primarily a move from segmented, hierarchical, paramilitary bureaucracies that flatter, to more participatory and flexible organizations. Still other discussions of community policing stress the *community* half of the term and center on the idea that social order is most effectively a coproduction by police and the community, where police-citizen connections and cooperation are essential to doing the job effectively and properly.

The focus here is not on the organizational structure of police departments, although the rural setting does provide opportunities to study the issue of formal organization variability. Most rural municipal police departments are small and have simple organizational structures; however, it is possible for sheriff's departments to be rather large and organizationally complex while still serving a predominantly rural area. Rather than organizational structures, this study focuses on the relationship between the community and the police in rural areas and how this relationship affects police practices.

It is possible to extract three broad themes from the literature on community policing that are relevant to the relationship. The first has to do with the police being *accountable* to the community as well as to the formal police hierarchy. The second is that police will become more *connected* with and integrated into their communities, which means that police will interact with citizens on a personal level, will be familiar with community sentiments and concerns, and will work *with* the community to address those concerns. A third and final theme requires that police will be oriented to *solving general problems*, rather than only responding to specific crime incidents. The discussion that follows reflects each of these broad themes and how it plays out in rural areas. First, however, we will describe the existing literature that can also be used to build our arguments.

EXISTING EVIDENCE

We begin with the simple observation that community policing looks and sounds a great deal like rural and small town policing, as it has been practiced for a long time. Although there have been no studies that directly examine the extent to which rural policing reflects many key elements of community policing, there are many scattered pieces of evidence with which one can make this case.

In his study of tasks regularly performed by police in 249 municipal agencies of differing sizes, Meagher (1985) found that small agencies were more concerned with crime prevention, medium-sized agencies showed the greatest concern for providing noncrime services, and large agencies focused on enforcing criminal laws and controlling crime through arrests. Similarly, Flanagan (1985) examined public opinion data about the police role. He found that the larger and more urban the community, the more citizens were likely to believe that police should limit their role to enforcing criminal laws. Conversely, people from smaller communities were more likely to want police to perform a wide variety of problem-solving and order-maintenance functions. Gibbons (1972) also saw evidence of this emphasis on order maintenance in his study of "crime in the hinterland." In the sheriff's department in rural Pine County (a pseudonym), Decker (1979) observed that

> the police were called upon and *expected* to render services for a wide variety of irregular occurrences, only a few of which were statutorily defined as law enforcement responsibilities. For example, the deputies complied with a request to inspect a boundary line between two farmers' property that was only accessible by tractor. In a related incident, the same mode of transportation was used to check on a foundered cow. Many instances required the symbolic presence of a sheriff's deputy to legitimate its occurrence in the citizen's eyes. (p. 104)

In many rural areas, police *must* provide a wide range of services because other social services are either nonexistent or are more remote than the police. Marenin and Copus (1991) observed that in rural Alaska, where all types of social services are scarce, traditional law enforcement is a relatively small part of the service police are expected to perform: "Village policing is not normal policing, in the sense of law enforcement or crime control, but is much more of a social work kind of job" (p. 16), which includes fire fighting, emergency medical services, and rescue operations.

A number of researchers have observed that styles of policing are partly a reflection of the relationship between police and the community. Although police in many urban areas may be viewed as outsiders, in rural areas they are viewed as an integral part of the community (Decker 1979). In interviews with officers from one rural department and several urban departments, Kowalewski, Hall, Dolan, and Anderson (1984) found that whereas officers in rural and urban departments had many similar concerns, they differed in several interesting respects. Urban officers thought they were less respected and less supported by citizens, whereas police in rural communities felt more public support for being tough, particularly with juveniles. Dealing with juveniles is an important function for rural police because this is often a major concern for rural community members (Decker 1979).

Consistent with the greater informality of social interaction processes in rural areas, rural and urban officers believed they were given public respect for different reasons (Decker 1979). In urban areas, respect went to the *position*, the role, or the badge, and it was believed that a good way to improve public respect was through professionalizing the department. In contrast, respect was thought to be given to rural officers as *individuals*, who had to prove that respect was *personally* deserved. This was often done by establishing a reputation for toughness and fairness early in their career.

Given the nature of rural culture and of social interactions in rural areas, police-community relations probably will be very different in rural and urban departments. In rural areas, officers are likely to know the offenders, the victims, and their families, just as the officer and his family will be known by the community. Rural officers are also more likely to know and appreciate the history and culture of an area and to use that information in their work, something observed by Weisheit (1993) in his study of rural marijuana growers. Given the close social ties between police and the community, it should be expected that rural officers will use policing styles that are responsive to citizens in their area and that, in turn, local residents should be supportive of the police. In fact, a 1991 Gallup survey found measurable rural-urban differences in the support that citizens show for the local police. In urban areas, 54% of the citizens reported having a great deal of respect for the local police, contrasted to 61% of rural citizens. The differences were even more pronounced when asked about police brutality and the discretionary use of force by police. In the survey, 59% of urban residents thought that there was police brutality in their area, but only 20% of rural residents believed this to be the case ("Americans Say Police Brutality Frequent" 1991).

The same features of rural policing that compel officers to be more responsive to the public also mean that rural police may have relatively less discretion because their work is more visible to the public:

> A major explanation for the high degree of police discretion found in urban areas is the *low visibility* of police actions. In smaller communities the actions of police officers are known to most of the population thanks to the effectiveness and extensiveness of informal communication networks; there they are more highly visible. As a result, small town police enjoy less latitude in deviating from dominant community values. (Eisenstein 1982, p. 117)

Consistent with this idea, Crank (1990) found that organizational and community factors had a different impact on the adoption of a legalistic police style in rural and urban areas. In urban areas, characteristics of the police organization, such as the number of ranks or the ratio of administrators to sworn officers, were better predictors of police style than were characteristics of the community, such as percentage Black or level of economic distress. In rural areas, these relationships were reversed, with community factors being more important than organizational ones. As might be expected, Crank's data suggested that rural departments are more responsive to the local community, whereas urban departments may be more sensitive to the dynamics of the police organization. Or, as a publication of the International Association of Chiefs of Police (IACP) put it, "The urban officer answers to the police department. The rural or small town officer is held accountable for his actions by the community" (IACP 1990, p. 9).

In many ways, rural departments are positioned to be the very embodiment of community policing. According to the IACP document,

> Rural and small town police are closer to their community than are urban police. Rural and small town police are a part of the local culture and community, whereas urban police tend to form a subculture and move apart from the community. . . . Urban police tend to be efficient; rural police tend to be effective. (IACP, 1990, p. 8)

These scattered pieces of evidence suggest it would be fruitful to more fully examine the link between rural policing and community policing. They also suggest that rather than modifying rural departments to fit an urban definition of good policing, or of community policing, urban departments might well look to rural areas for insights into policing in general and community policing in particular.

THE STUDY

The information presented here is drawn from a larger study of rural crime and rural policing funded by the National Institute of Justice. The larger study involves collecting and reviewing relevant literature, conducting a focus group with rural sheriffs, locating and cataloging data sets relevant to rural crime, and, finally, interviewing officials familiar with rural crime and rural policing. This article is based on information from interviews conducted to date. The larger study was not specifically designed to study community policing but to consider rural crime and rural policing issues more generally. In the course of reviewing the literature and in interviews with rural police, we were continuously presented with ideas that paralleled those raised in discussions of community policing in urban areas. Thus what follows explores one dimension of a larger study which is itself exploratory. The purpose is not to reach definite conclusions but to stimulate thinking and suggest patterns that merit further study.

Although over 100 people from a variety of perspectives have been interviewed thus far, this discussion is based on interviews with 46 rural sheriffs and with 28 police chiefs in small towns. Of these 74 interviews, 13 (18%) were face-to-face, and the remainder were by telephone. Although we wanted to include jurisdictions of varying sizes, the focus was on the most rural jurisdictions. Among interviewed municipal chiefs, their community ranged in size from 900 to 50,000 people, with an average of 7,500 persons. Departments ranged in size from 1 to 66 uniformed officers, with an average of 17 officers. The departments of the interviewed county sheriffs ranged in size from 1 to 182 uniformed officers, with an average of 23 officers. This figure is a very rough approximation because sheriff department size is difficult to compute due to sometimes high numbers of part-time employees, jail staff who are sometimes also sworn officers, and some counties having a large number of reserves. The county populations served by these sheriffs ranged from 2,100 to 712,000 people, with only 8 of the 46 sheriffs working in a county of more than 50,000.

As an exploratory study, locating subjects for interviews focused on identifying individuals from the widest possible range of social and physical environments, rather than on studying "average" rural settings. Indeed, the differences across rural areas are so substantial that speaking of averages is probably misleading and is certainly of limited use for policy. Rural Montana and rural Delaware, for example, probably are as dissimilar as they are similar. To capture as much of this range as possible, we selected police officers from across the country, attempting to include every state, while giving particular attention to the 18 states identified as predominantly rural by the federal General Accounting Office (1990).

Because we are engaged in an exploratory study, we felt it important to use largely unstructured interviews. Appreciating rural variation, and always keeping it in mind, we were still interested in identifying common themes. Thus we used the available literature and information gathered from a series of preliminary interviews to develop a list of question areas to be covered in the course of the interviews, but we also encouraged subjects to explore other areas they thought were important. Question areas included crime concerns, police-citizen interactions, police practices, and the working relationship between police and other criminal justice agencies. The length of interview ranged from 20 minutes to 2 hours but was typically about 40 minutes long.

OBSERVATIONS

There was general agreement among the interviewed rural police that their long-standing police practices fit well into what has been termed community policing. However, the concept of community policing is a broad one, encompassing a variety of ideas. Consequently, we focus here on more specific ways in which rural police practices seem to mirror the principles of community policing.

Community connections. A key element of community policing is police-citizen familiarity and interaction. For example, having officers walk through neighborhoods and talk with people means that more citizens will know officers personally, and, at the same time, officers will come to know many individuals in a neighborhood. The bonds between rural police and the community are also strengthened by the practice of hiring local citizens in police agencies. Thus the officers not only know the community and share many of the values of its members, they are also members of that community and are often involved in community activities. As Decker (1979) noted:

> All members of the sheriff's department had biographies not uncommon to those of the community. The sheriff and his three deputies were all born and educated in the county. Prior to joining the force, every member was involved in an agricultural form of employment, the dominant form of employment for the county. There is evidence of integration into the community in other ways. Each member participates in an important community function; i.e., the softball team, Jaycees, Rotary, Elk's Club, etc. (p. 105)

Many urban departments have recently tried, with varying degrees of success, to induce individual officers to live in their work area, sometimes even providing financial incentives for them to do so. Living in the areas they patrol, however, has been a long-standing practice in rural and small town agencies that has occurred naturally and without special effort. Through increased citizen-police interactions, it is believed that citizens will be more likely to cooperate with the police, and police, in turn, will be more sensitive to the community.

Sheriffs and chiefs with whom we spoke frequently saw what they had been doing in rural areas as community policing and believed they were well ahead of urban areas in this regard. One sheriff's comments are typical:

> Yes, there's far more community policing taking place in rural agencies than urban. We have been doing community policing since time began, I believe. We have always stopped and talked with the ranchers, the businessmen. We have walked the streets, rattled doors, and checked on sick folks. We know the various workers in the community and what they do. We see the kid delivering papers at 6:00 a.m. and talk with him. We have always done that. We are much closer to the people. Consequently, your whole mode of operation changes. Our method of gathering information derives from our personal contact on a day-to-day or minute-to-minute basis. In an urban setting, you're out "devel-

oping informants." We do that too, but the vast majority of our information comes from regular folks on a regular basis. I'm a believer in scanners. That would cause cardiac arrest in a lot of agencies. We have gotten more help from folks that have heard us out on a chase and we have lost the guy. They call up and say, "He's two blocks away going down this street." Plus, it tells them we are on the job, what we're doing.

This illustration shows how a strong bond between police and the community in rural settings is helpful in enforcing the law. It is also true, however, that rural police themselves act differently when such a bond exists:

> You cannot call somebody an SOB on the street here because the next day you could be buying tires from him or going in to eat in his restaurant. You've got to know these people because you deal with them day after day. I worked in Fort Worth, Texas. You get into a row with some guy down there—he's smart mouthing you, bad mouthing you. You can give it right back because you're not going to see that man again, except in court. After court, you'll never lay eyes on him again. Here, he's the cousin of the deputy who works the night shift.

Knowing their citizens well also allows rural officers greater latitude in disposing of cases informally:

> The street officer sees ol' Joe on the street and waves to him. When Joe gets drunk and gets into a row, he can just grab him and stuff him into the car. If he doesn't need to go to jail, he can just take him home and turn him over to Martha. She's going to straighten him out.

> In smaller communities, particularly with juveniles, which is most of the crime problem in small communities, in my experience, the parents were not some faceless, mythical creatures from the middle of nowhere. I could grab up little Johnny by the scruff of his neck or whatever and we would go talk to Mommy and Daddy, who also knew me. We could work things out a lot easier, without having to get involved in the formal justice system. . . . The small communities, at least where I worked, generally if we had to make an arrest, it was the exception rather than the norm. We almost looked at arrests as a last resort. Everything else either has not worked or will not work. If I had to make an arrest, it was almost as if I'd done something wrong further back down the line.

These close personal interactions also mean that citizens expect more of their police, both in the range of services offered and in the personal attention that will be paid to individual cases:

> The city residents expect the man in blue to come by and be very perfunctory, a Joe Friday. We're expected to do the follow-up and a lot more caring. People expect caring from rural law enforcement. We're not there to just take the reports of crimes; we also scoot the kiddies across crosswalks. It's an obligation. We have to wave at everybody we pass by. We have to be more caring.

We've had a lot of examples. An officer might go to a domestic one night and he'll stop by the next night and see how things are going. It's not uncommon for an officer, where a couple of juveniles have gotten into trouble, the next day he's got off to go get 'em and take them fishing. They try and get involved personally and make a difference.

In rural areas, police are highly visible members of the community, and it is not unusual for citizens to know individual officers by name. It also appears rather common for a citizen to consider a particular police officer *his* or *her* officer and to request him or her by name when problems arise. Although this also happens to some extent in urban areas, it appears to be far more common in rural communities.

These examples illustrate how close police-citizen interactions in rural areas shape the nature of police work in those areas. For the most part, the features of rural policing described above arise quite naturally and spontaneously and are not the result of formal policies or of specific community policing *programs*.

General problem solving. Another central characteristic of community policing is the focus on general problem solving, rather than more narrowly on reactive law enforcement. That is, officers not only respond to specific criminal incidents, but, more importantly, they recognize and respond to more general problems that set the stage for specific criminal acts. These problems are not be limited to "crimes" and the solutions need not involve arrests.

This lady just recently passed away. We've changed light bulbs for people. She called up, she's old, she's not very mobile, she's scared. The power went off, and now she's hearing things. Tell us the name, we know we're going to change a light bulb, talk to her for five or ten minutes and everything's fine. That is a service that fortunately we can still do—spend the time, especially on some of the older residents. Everything is OK, we're here. You call, we're going to be there.

When asked about the kinds of problems to which his department was expected to respond, one small-town chief responded:

Everything, including the kitchen sink. I've had people in here to counsel families on their sex life because they think I'm the Almighty and can do that. I've had people come in who are having problems making ends meet, and we intercede for them in getting assistance, helping them file for welfare. We do a lot of service-oriented work. I consider it non law enforcement. Somebody needs a ride, like an elderly lady needs a ride to the doctor. We'll take her to the doctor or go get her groceries for her.

Because they are closer to the public they serve, and because they are often the only 24-hour service providers in rural areas, rural police receive calls for a wide range of services. If they respond to a wider variety of non-police problems than do urban police, it is not because they are required to do so by statute or because written departmental policies demand it. Rather, it is because they define police work differently, perhaps because the people they serve are neighbors and fellow community members, rather than nameless, faceless citizens. As such, it is not a conscious formal decision but a necessity arising from the social context.

Rural versus urban policing. We found some of the most telling evidence that rural and urban policing styles are very different in the experiences of rural sheriffs and chiefs who had previously worked outside of rural areas or who hired officers with such experiences:

> Their [police and citizens'] kids go to the same school. You see them on the street. You see them in the grocery store. It isn't like a city. In fact, I've worked with several cities and their officers are cold. They treat the good people the same way they treat the bad people. They are callous.

> If you hire somebody from a larger agency who has been in a situation where they specialized, they tend to look at a "hay seed" operation and say things need to be done in a different way . . . We've had some real problems with them having personality conflicts with the public in general because they are used to dealing with people as faces and not as neighbors or friends or relatives.

> I'm willing to be shown that I'm wrong, but it's a lot harder being a sheriff of a small rural county than it is to be the sheriff of [a city] with a population of 250,000 because everybody in that [rural] county—they want to be able to pick up that phone, whether it be Saturday night at 2:00 in the morning and they have a problem. They want to be able to pick up that phone and call that sheriff. They don't want to talk to a deputy, or the dispatcher. They want the sheriff, "I have a problem." It may be dogs barking.

One officer who had worked in an urban department and then moved to a rural part of Alaska declared:

> If there's a bar fight and I get involved, and somebody comes toward me with the intent of attacking me, I've had several bar patrons jump on them and take them down and even put their hands behind their back so I can handcuff them. It's not like a bar in the lower 48. You still have to watch your back, but we're a part of the community here more than you are there. In an urban area, the police officer is not part of the community. Here, a police officer is a part of the community. We live here, we work here, our kids run around with their kids, date their kids, and go to basketball games. I encourage my officers, and I do it by example, to participate as much as possible in all community functions. . . . But we just don't have problems that we can't take the time to sit down and talk it over with them. In the lower 48, I never had time. At the end of my shift, I was handing call cards out for burglaries in progress and rapes to the following shift. I had already worked 2 hours overtime and I

couldn't get to all of them. But here, we have time to take care of the problems. I don't know if they would even use it [the time] if they had it in the lower 48.

Another chief who was asked if he thought rural police had to be more sensitive to the public than urban police responded:

Absolutely. I come from a bigger agency. In the bigger agencies, you lose that personal day-to-day touch with the actual citizenry, unless you're there for a specific reason. Here, we're very close to these people. There's not too many of us, so they all get to know you. They come in all the time with their problems, and not just law enforcement-related problems. Yes, we're extremely sensitive. It's a very close-knit operation.

These comments repeat many of the contrasts between rural and urban policing noted in earlier sections. Routine personal contact between the police and the policed changes the relationship between the two. And the fact that many rural officers live in the communities they police seems to further strengthen the ties between the two groups.

Effectiveness. Aside from being good public relations, it has also been argued that community policing is more effective. The idea that rural departments may be more effective is not consistent with stereotypes of rural police, and there may be some disagreement about what constitutes effective. One bit of evidence about the relative effectiveness of rural police comes from the *Uniform Crime Reports,* which report the percentage of crimes cleared by arrest by size of the community served. As Table 1 shows, agencies in rural counties have consistently higher clearance rates than departments in cities of 250,000 or more. This pattern holds for every index crime except rape, for which the clearance rates are essentially the same.

The gap in clearance rates between rural and urban areas shown in Table 1 is particularly marked for violent crimes. Some of the rural-urban differences might be attributable to differences in reporting and recording practices. Rural police might, for example, be less likely to write up a report on a larceny if there are no suspects. However, this cannot explain the very large rural-urban difference in clearance rates for homicides. Homicides will almost certainly be recorded regardless of whether there are suspects. It is also possible that the close social networks in rural areas make it easier to solve crimes. One police chief told us:

You've got a specific number of kids who are committing things and it's very easy after a crime to determine who did it here. The closeness of the community and the wide variety of MOs, when something happens they usually leave enough of a telltale sign that we know exactly who committed it. We only have one school that we have to listen to for rumors and things. We've got a lot of

TABLE 1:   Percentage of Index Crimes Cleared by Arrest, 1992

Crime Type	Cities 250,000+	Rural Counties
Violent	38.5	60.7
Murder	59.6	74.5
Rape	53.4	53.0
Robbery	21.4	38.1
Aggravated Assault	53.2	63.4
Property	14.3	18.4
Burglary	11.3	16.4
Larceny	16.9	18.3
Vehicle theft	10.3	32.4
Arson	9.2	21.8
All Index Crimes	18.8	23.0

SOURCE: *Uniform Crime Reports* 1992, Table 25, Pp. 208-9.

> law-abiding kids that let us know what they are hearing. We solved almost
> every one of our crimes here. For every one of our thefts, burglaries, we know
> who has done it.

A county sheriff echoed this view by noting:

> For example, my secretary's husband owns the tire store. His tire store got
> burglarized. People know him and they know her, so they come and tell me "I
> know who did it." All we have to do is prove it. In some place like Fort Worth
> [Texas], that's not going to happen—ever. The people on the street don't know
> the cop; the cop doesn't know the person on the street. They don't intermix too
> much.

Finally, when one chief was asked if knowing people in the community made
his job easier, he replied:

> Yeah, I'll give you an example. I live on a road, and when I heard on the squawk
> box here of a burglary at a neighbor's house three doors down, I immediately
> called my neighbor across the street, because I knew the two girls were home
> at that time. I just asked them, "Did you see anything?" They said, "Yeah, I
> saw this person that was passing around." We picked them up and recovered
> the goods. Because we are small, my neighbors saw the car and recognized the
> person, the thief. It happens with some frequency because of the fact that people
> know each other.

The circumstantial evidence presented here suggests that rural police are
more effective than urban police, and that effectiveness may be related to the
close bonds among community members and between the community and
the police. This was also suggested by Cordner (1989), who found that rural

departments were more effective investigators, and this was in part due to the close social networks in those areas:

> Consider two small police departments, one located in a rural area and the other in a metropolitan area. Although the residential populations served by the two agencies may be the same size, the investigators in the rural departments have some natural advantages. They actually know, by name, by sight, and/or by reputation, a much greater proportion of the people in their jurisdiction and its surrounding area than the metropolitan agency investigators know of theirs. The witnesses that they deal with are much more likely to have recognized suspects they observed. Also, the rural investigator has only a few neighboring jurisdictions to keep in contact with, whereas the metropolitan investigator may have a dizzying array of other police departments in close proximity. (p. 153)

Factors in the rural environment that seem to make rural police more effective are those interpersonal networks that community policing tries to foster in urban areas. Thus a better understanding of how rural departments use these networks may have implications for community policing in urban areas.

Other issues. Looking at policing in rural areas leads one to think about community policing in other ways, particularly to adopt a more elaborate conception of *the community* than is common in discussions of community policing. For example, community policing discussions often allude to the community in terms of lay citizens or nonpolice agencies that might be helpful to citizens. In the rural environment, however, the community in which the police officer works includes not only citizens but other criminal justice officials as well. As one sheriff describes it:

> I tell the guys, we are as much social workers as we are law enforcement officers—community policing. We are expected to work for solutions for these people—what brought them to our attention. When these cases are brought to court, myself, the state public defender, the chief deputy, the prosecutor, and the judge have all set [sic] around a table and discussed what actions we're going to do to this guy, what treatment program we can come up with to keep him from becoming a repeater. I think that's probably unusual, even in rural areas. We take an interest. At court time, it's not unusual for the officer working the case, the prosecutor, and the public defender to go over here to the restaurant and get in the back corner where you have some privacy, and try to work out a solution to the case. What's best for him and what's best for the community?

It is easy to see how this informal approach can be a two-edged sword. In many cases it can render justice in the very best sense of the word. At the same time, however, it is less clear what happens to justice when the defendant is an outsider, such as a migrant worker, or an insider who is simply disliked, or when rural officers do not use good sense or sound judgment.

Accordingly, it is easy to see why some critics are concerned that community policing can shift away from something that is *for* the good of the public to a technique for manipulating the public and doing things *to* it (see Bayley 1988). After all, the development of the formal, militarized style of modern urban police was itself a response to corruption and misbehavior by police, arising from informality that also meant a lack of control (Klockars 1988). Although our study was not designed to examine misconduct or corruption among rural police, such a study would provide insights into problems that arise when the police and the community are *too* close.

Policing in rural areas can also illustrate the idea of decentralizing police department activities. One municipal chief, who previously had been a police officer in a large city, suggested that as generalists, rural police do not simply involve themselves in a variety of nonpolice functions, but they also have to be generalists within policing:

> In a rural area, you do everything yourself. You do the fingerprinting, the pictures, the interviews, the crime scene, everything. In a big department in an urban area, you specialize. As a patrolman in an urban area, I would simply secure the scene of a crime. Once the detective arrived, it was theirs. The detective called in whoever they [sic] needed. Here, there's one officer on duty; he's the primary officer. If he calls for a backup and I come out, he is still the primary officer. The future of policing is where a complete, mature, well-rounded police officer can step into a situation and handle it, or call for the necessary elements to handle it. The day will come in this country . . . where all police officers, no matter where they are stationed, they're it. . . . There won't be chiefs and things like that. There might be supervisors, but they'll be stationed in one place where they can respond to many, many officers from many, many areas.

Rural police practices also raise questions about the nature of police accountability to the public and highlight the difference between *formal* and *informal* accountability. Formal accountability is more explicit but less direct, being concentrated through specific established channels of communication and authority within the organization. In contrast, informal accountability is diffused through multiple channels spread throughout the community, which are also more direct. For example, under formal accountability, the officer is accountable through the organization, and citizens make their complaints through formal channels. Their complaints are processed and eventually fed back to the officer. In contrast, informal accountability means that officers are more directly and immediately aware of citizen concerns and may hear about those concerns from a variety of people, both inside and outside the police organization, in a variety of social settings.

We have argued throughout that as a result of close social ties between police and community in rural settings and in the absence of organizational buffers in small rural departments, rural police are more accountable and responsive to local citizens than are urban police. Although this appears to be true of rural police as a group, rural sheriffs with whom we spoke were emphatic that, as *elected* officials, they were compelled to be much more sensitive to citizen concerns than were municipal chiefs. *If* their perceptions are accurate, and *if* accountability to the public is a worthwhile goal, then it is interesting to speculate what might happen if municipal departments shifted to a system in which chiefs were elected officials.

DISCUSSION

We have argued that modern community policing draws heavily on ideas and practices that have long been traditions in rural areas, although this link is rarely made explicit. It is important to understand the rural dimensions that matter most. What makes the rural community unique in the examples given here is not simply low population density, but also relatively dense social networks. Even among rural areas there is variation in the density of these networks, and it is possible to police rural areas without having the kinds of experiences described here. State police, for example, may operate in rural areas but have relatively little connection to local social networks. As one sheriff observed about his own prior experience as a state trooper:

> I was in 11 stations in 25 years with the state police. I worked all over the place. You see a group of young state troopers come in, they work there for a very short period of time, they go out, they don't care about the individual population. They're statistically oriented—A, B, C—so they are out to make numbers. I think your [sheriffs'] deputies are there for life. They develop a better relationship with the people, on the whole, where they are *their* cop.

Similarly, one may be an officer whose background and/or personality make it difficult for him or her to fit in with the local culture—and it is our experience that such officers have a particularly difficult time doing their work. Thus a rural area is not simply a physical place but a *social place* as well. This is something community policing advocates in urban areas recognize when they suggest that beats cover *natural* (i.e., social) neighborhood boundaries, rather than those created for bureaucratic expediency. Of course, the social characteristics of crime and policing in rural areas are shaped by the size of the population and the size of the department. We do not know the threshold size for either departments or communities, that is, the size at which they cease to be clearly *rural*. However, we did encounter a number of departments in which rapid population growth had transformed their rural conditions and eroded the police-community networks that once characterized their community:

> That is the one thing that I'm crying about. We are now responding to in excess of 3,000 calls for service in a year. We are losing some of that personal contact. [His city] and some of the urban areas are having to limit the types of calls they will respond to, such as whether they will do funeral escorts. It's a Catch 22; when you become incident driven, the community plays a less active role, and its a downward spiral.

Although we have gone to great lengths to show themes common to community policing and rural policing, we would argue that community policing is *not* simply and invariably identical to rural policing. Rather, community policing is a formalized and rationalized version of small town policing—where the purpose is to introduce accountability and provide a measure of legal rationality to what, in rural areas, is a much more spontaneous and informal process. Thus community policing and rural policing are not identical. Community policing is small town policing set in a rational framework that attempts to formalize the spontaneous acts of good sense and good citizenship found in many rural officers into a *program* that can be taught and that can be monitored and evaluated. This observation suggests a fundamental paradox of community policing—in many ways it is the formalization of informal custom and the routinization of spontaneous events.

It is also true that rural policing is not homogenous across the country. One implication of this is that, to be effective, there can be no *one* program of community policing. Effective community policing must be tailored to the needs and wishes of each individual community, just as rural police tailor their activities to their local communities.

Further, what we have learned about community policing in rural departments suggests there are elements of the model that chiefs and line officers in urban departments might *not* find attractive or acceptable. For example, the closeness between citizens and police in rural areas may have many benefits for both groups, but it also comes at the expense of the privacy of rural chiefs and line officers. We have observed there are very few rural chiefs or rural sheriffs whose home telephone numbers are unlisted—and many reported that citizens were more than willing to call them at home at any hour, even regarding minor problems. In many communities, line officers could also expect to routinely be contacted at home on police business. One rural chief provided a particularly telling example, an example that is unlikely to be duplicated by any large urban chief:

> In a small town you lose your private life, too. It has taken a toll on my wife and our kids. Two years ago on Thanksgiving we had our family over and then

we had a domestic that ended up on my front porch. The husband came over to tell me the problem and then she came over. . . . It was pretty embarrassing. I have since put a sign up on my porch that says this is not the police department, it is our home. Dial 911 if you have an emergency. It hasn't worked. The amount of calls that you get at your house, and . . . if you get an unlisted number, they will come by your house. I would rather have them call me.

This chief, and a number of others, also observed that when off duty they could not have a beer at the local bar without starting rumors in the community. In such cases it is not unusual for chiefs, sheriffs, and their officers to go to nearby towns if they wish to have a quiet evening or if they wish to have a drink. How many urban chiefs and line officers are willing to "live" their jobs to this extent?

Another feature common to rural policing that may not be welcomed by urban officers is the high level of community involvement expected of rural officers. In most rural areas, officers live in the community in which they work. Beyond that, it is our impression that rural police are more involved in civic organizations than are urban police. In most rural communities this is voluntary. One sheriff was more explicit, expressing his philosophy this way:

I tell them [deputies] before they are ever employed that I want my people involved in the community in some way. It may be a service club, a fraternal organization, your church—I don't care what it is. But I don't want you and your partner to just work together all day and drink together all night. When you deal with the rear end of society, and the majority of our work deals with those kinds of people, it's awful easy to build a negative, horrible attitude where everybody is a SOB or a jerk. . . . Some kind of community activity, but in some way to deal with real people, just like themselves and see that they are not all criminals. If they'll do that, then they try to make their community a better place rather than just through law enforcement.

In summary, rural policing presents an *ideal type* example of community policing. A more extensive study of rural policing should allow us to determine which aspects of the rural police experience can be applied to urban models of community policing. At the same time it is important to determine if there are key elements of successful rural policing that will *never* fit the urban setting. By improving our understanding of these contrasting areas, the study of rural policing can also provide a better understanding of community policing's potential and its limitations.

REFERENCES

"Americans Say Police Brutality Frequent." 1991. *The Gallup Poll Monthly* 306:53-56.

Bayley, David H. 1988. "Community Policing: A Report From a Devil's Advocate." Pp. 225-37 in *Community Policing: Rhetoric or Reality*, edited by J. R. Greene and S. D. Mastrofski. New York: Praeger.

Brown, Lee P. 1989. *Community Policing: A Practical Guide for Police Officials*. Washington, DC: National Institute of Justice.

Cordner, Gary W. 1989. "Police Agency Size and Investigative Effectiveness." *Journal of Criminal Justice* 17:145-55.

Crank, John P. 1990. "The Influence of Environmental and Organizational Factors on Police Style in Urban and Rural Environments." *Journal of Research in Crime and Delinquency* 27:166-89.

Decker, Scott. 1979. "The Rural County Sheriff: An Issue in Social Control." *Criminal Justice Review* 4:97-111.

Eisenstein, James. 1982. "Research on Rural Criminal Justice: A Summary." Pp. 105-43 in *Criminal Justice in Rural America*, edited by S. Cronk, J. Jankovic, and R. K. Green. Washington, DC: U.S. Department of Justice.

Flanagan, Timothy J. 1985. "Consumer Perspectives on Police Operational Strategy." *Journal of Police Science and Administration* 13:10-21.

General Accounting Office. 1990. *Rural Drug Abuse: Prevalence, Relation to Crime, and Programs*. Washington, DC: U.S. General Accounting Office.

Gibbons, Don C. 1972. "Crime in the Hinterland." *Criminology* 10:177-91.

Goldstein, Herman. 1987. "Toward Community-Oriented Policing: Potential, Basic Requirements, and Threshold Questions." *Crime & Delinquency* 33:6-30.

Greene, Jack R. and Stephen D. Mastrofski, eds. 1988. *Community Policing: Rhetoric or Reality*. New York: Praeger.

International Association of Chiefs of Police (IACP). 1990. *Managing the Small Law Enforcement Agency*. Dubuque, IA: Kendall/Hunt.

Karmen, Andrew. 1990. *Crime Victims: An Introduction to Victimology*, 2nd ed. Pacific Grove, CA: Brooks/Cole.

Klockars, Carl B. 1988. "The Rhetoric of Community Policing." Pp. 239-58 in *Community Policing: Rhetoric or Reality*, edited by J. R. Greene and S. D. Mastrofski. New York: Praeger.

Kowalewski, David, William Hall, John Dolan, and James Anderson. 1984. "Police Environments and Operational Codes: A Case Study of Rural Settings." *Journal of Police Science and Administration* 12:363-72.

Marenin, Otwin and Gary Copus. 1991. "Policing Rural Alaska: The Village Public Safety Officer (VPSO) Program." *American Journal of Police* 10:1-26.

Meagher, M. Steven. 1985. "Police Patrol Styles: How Pervasive is Community Variation?" *Journal of Police Science and Administration* 13:36-45.

Moore, Mark Harrison. 1992. "Problem-Solving and Community Policing." Pp. 99-158 in *Modern Policing*, edited by M. Tonry and N. Morris. Chicago: University of Chicago Press.

Trojanowicz, Robert and Bonnie Bucqueroux. 1990. *Community Policing: A Contemporary Perspective*. Cincinnati, OH: Anderson.

Walton, Mary. 1986. *The Deming Management Method*. New York: Perigee.

Weisheit, Ralph A. 1993. "Studying Drugs in Rural Areas: Notes from the Field." *Journal of Research in Crime and Delinquency* 30:213-32.

Wilson, James Q. and George L. Kelling. 1989. "Making Neighborhoods Safe." *Atlantic Monthly* 263:46-52.

POLICE FORUM

Academy of Criminal Justice Sciences Police Section

VOLUME 2 NUMBER 2   JUNE 1992

MAKING THE POLICE PROACTIVE:
An Impossible Task for Improbable Reasons

Frank P. Williams, III
Carl P. Wagoner
California State University-San Bernardino

The standard position today, heard from both the public and the police, is that our crime problem is getting out of hand. Begging the question of whether we actually have a crime wave or a media-based crime-reporting wave (Fishman, 1977), we propose to discuss the issue of what society can do about crime in the context of police reform and police services. With some ideological exceptions, those who study crime and the police are fairly well agreed that police can be expected to have very little direct effect on crime and criminality and that, further, preventing crime is not really the function of the police.

Unfortunately, neither the public nor their quasi-elected officials share this opinion regarding the function of the police. Their position is grounded in a conservative ideology which stresses deterrence and "taking the handcuffs off police," in addition to advocating the adding of more police and more technological innovation, in order to increase the apprehension of offenders. However, there is abundant evidence to the effect that crime is not reduced nor apprehension increased by adding police or, for example, by eliminating the exclusionary rule (Walker, 1989).

This resistance to evidence that police, by themselves, can do little about crime is itself an interesting situation. As noted above, we suspect that it is based in the current conservative mentality and movement, the political utility of crime in providing a "mantle of law and order" and, ironically, the police themselves. This latter source is intriguing because both the rise and fall of crime rates have long been used as a political ploy by law enforcement to gain access to greater resources (Weis and Milakovich, 1974). The latent function of such a ploy, however, is that police departments then invite the public to hold them accountable for crime itself.

The connection between "doing something" about crime and recent calls for proactive policing has created an expectation

that police should, indeed, engage in proactive crime prevention. Historically, there is some merit to this expectation. The origins of modern policing lie in the private forces created by the Bow Street merchants of London and the Thames River police of the West Indies Merchants Association. These forces were clearly proactive in their approach to "crime." Yet, as police forces became public entities, they became more reactive in approach and lost their direct connection to citizens. This is further illustrated by the changing nature of the police role in the movement from mechanical to organic solidarity, and the corresponding changes in the nature of criminals and the increasing rates of crime (Lundman, 1980).

In short, police forces evolved concurrently with the state's emergence under the social contract in the dual role of victim and enforcer of restitution. This process resulted in a police role as chief enforcer of the social contract and, in modern times, placed the police directly as a servant of the government, not as a servant of the people. The point here is that modern police are reactive in nature and respond directly to government rather than to the citizenry. Indirectly, of course, police do respond to the people through the representatives of government.

This is not to suggest that the police are completely devoid of an ability to be proactive. It is the case that both in law enforcement situations and in order maintenance situations police can take the initiative. However, when they do so it is usually in response to internal pressure from top administration, which is often acting in response to external pressure.

When a call is issued to "do something about crime," government (local or otherwise) instructs its law enforcement agent to respond, either with action or with explanations. Unfortunately, the police are not for the most part, designed as proactive agents. This is illustrated in the limited success of community crime prevention programs ("neighborhood watch," "operation identification," and home security surveys) have had (Currie, 1985; Turk and Grimes, 1992). Even more problematic from our viewpoint is that the type of response which is demanded from law enforcement, and the form of response generated, varies by the type of "public" making the demand.

A common observation is that power (or potential power) defines the type of public and the form of response. Thus, demands that the police respond to crime take various forms and precipitate commensurate demands for change in police philosophy and structure.

The primary intent of this essay is to critique proactive policing and calls for police change. To do this, we will explore the relationship between crime, proactive policies, and three "ideal types" of public, which we will refer to as citizens, interest groups, and elites. A secondary intent is to stimulate discussion on the issue of police change in a proactive direction. As a result, we have chosen to eschew an objective and carefully documented approach in favor of a more subjective and controversial one.

Public Power, Proactive Policing and Change

Proactive Policing

Our first concern is to determine the type of response that would be required in order to generate proactive policing under our three types of publics. A demand from citizens requires a more diffuse and broader response(s) than from the other types of publics. In fact, for such a demand to be made is itself an extraordinary event, since the "public" is not often united or does not often see the world through the same colored glasses, particularly in an heterogeneous, urban/industrial society. In keeping with the nature of the demand, the police response will likely result in substantial resource expenditure (if this is possible in an era of steady state or decreasing resources), perhaps even requiring major structural and philosophical changes. The likelihood of such changes is minimal since, as we will note later, law enforcement organizations are particularly resistant to change.

Demands from interest groups, on the other hand, are commonplace and often require little adaptation on the part of the police, other than the shifting of focus and resources from one area of concern to another. Our form of government is well-adapted to interest groups and, thus, one might even argue that police structure and philosophy are currently products designed to meet this form of public demand. The chief characteristic we expect here is that the demands are individualistic and specific.

The elite demand requires a non-specific response by the police. In fact, the nature of the response is unlikely to be directly generated by the police themselves. Instead, the response is likely to be in the form of police reaction to new laws or political philosophies. Such responses can be profound and far-reaching, but will tend to produce new enforcement strategies and/or directions of activity aimed at particular segments of society rather than changes in police philosophy or organizational structure. In short, we see citizen demands as resulting in a return to a more mechanical style of policing (as opposed to a contemporary organic style), interest group responses as service-oriented, and elite demands as selective repression.

Change

Because of the changing nature of society, as well as the changing nature and increased amount of crime, many have argued that change of the police is both desirable and/or eminent (Currie, 1985; Germann, 1985; Wilson, 1985; Goldstein, 1979). If so, our second concern is to describe the form that changes might take under our three types of publics. Under the citizen type of demand we believe that any police change would be toward development into a more citizen-responsive force, and oriented to a closer relationship with the community. Such a change, if real rather than superficial, would require a substantial increase in new resources and recommitment of current resources, significant changes in philosophy, and potentially massive restructuring of police organizations.

The term interest group as used here refers to associations and coalitions of persons with a common concern which binds them together. Their effectiveness is determined by the degree of pressure they can bring to the police directly or indirectly through other governmental agencies. It needs to be noted that many such interest groups are transitory in nature, and are often issue specific. Interest-group demands would produce change oriented toward specific services such as peace-keeping and enclave protection. Further, because the nature of interest groups is both pluralistic and individualistic, change to meet their demands would entail a certain amount of decentralization in order to quickly respond to shifting priorities and allegiances. Critical variables influencing the extent of change are the degree of resources dispersed among the interest groups, the form of those resources, and the temporal nature of those resources.

Elite demands would result in selective repression of those who constitute a threat to the existing social order. Thus, change in policing requires a reordering of priorities and, potentially, some degree of new organizational structure. Because some older parts of the structure can be dispensed with, structural changes may merely mean a reshuffling of resources and reorganization. Centralized authority and the chain of command would remain important due to the necessity of ensuring the transmission of the new priorities and the preparation for, and the development of, new attitudes on the part of the rank and file in regard to the "new" threat. Critical variables here include the extent of police agreement with the values to be defended, perceptions police have of the newly criminalized community, and the relative threat to the existing social order.

The Irony of Change

Given these potential avenues of change, the question is not what police organizations will become but in what directions have the police already responded? A few brief examples will serve to demonstrate an irony that the triad of publics does indeed affect the nature of policing and, at the same time, produces conflict that results in little actual change.

Citizen-based Change

The clearest example of reaction to this power source is the development of community policing. Although by 1990 more than 300 police departments in the United States had reported some form of community policing, there remains today a relative lack of understanding as to what constitutes community policing (Strecher, 1991). At times it has been substituted for what is still a community-relations approach, at times it has been synonymous with "problem-oriented policing," and at times foot patrol has been equated with community policing (Trojanowicz and Bucqueroux, 1990).

Instead, community policing requires a substantial change in both structure and form, including attitudinal, organizational, and subcultural change. It represents a "new" philosophy of policing whereby police officers and the community work together to solve community problems of crime and related social ills. This means giving citizens of the community a direct say in the solutions and activities that regulate crime. Community policing also requires an organizational structure which is flattened, with horizontal as well as vertical communication. Centralized authority is minimized, with area captains becoming "mini-chiefs" with full decision-making authority, and with individual community-policing officers sharing decision making, particularly on their own beat. Police officers are given authority to not only create their own solutions to problems but also contact and request assistance from other governmental agencies and private entities. In short, police officers become citizens of their own neighborhoods and combine with residents to produce a healthy neighborhood.

Thus the problems here are that real community policing requires a radical restructuring of police organizations and a new sense of function. All we know of organizational theory tells us that such change will be resisted. A project manager of one of the five sites for the national community policing experiment aptly described the adaptations required of police

officers and the organization as "traumatic" (McPherson, 1992). Further, as Van Horn and Van Meter (1977), among others, have noted, the predisposition of the people in the agency to support the implementation of new policy is a crucial variable in determining the success of the policy.

Other governmental agencies also play a key role in the success of this transformation. If they have different agendas, or see the "citizen mandate" as conflicting, responses to the requests of individual community police officers will be problematic. These agencies can defeat community policing philosophies either by failing to participate or simply by dragging their feet on requests. The probability of all affected government agencies buying into the same citizen-oriented philosophy is exceedingly low.

Similarly, because police officers will come and go in neighborhoods (and of course there will be several shifts involved), officers themselves cannot be responsible for community policing — the community itself must be. Getting a community to realize this in today's specialized world is no small feat, in and of itself. In effect, the ultimate feasibility and success of community policing is beyond the control of the police. The five-site national experiment has demonstrated the way in which these difficulties have combined to effectively disassemble the citizen-oriented approach. Only one of the sites (San Diego) remains committed to community policing and that site had an existing heritage of a community orientation. The other four have not only fallen by the wayside, but in one case the experiment caused the downfall of the chief of police (McPherson, 1992).

Interest Group-based Change

Reactions to this power source require the ability to make swift responses to potentially immediate concerns of changing interest groups. We suggest this can result in the creation of decentralized teams to police and protect the various interest groups. In operation such decentralized teams (such as an anti-gang task force with the responsibility of quickly moving into an area, conducting a sweep for possible law violators and then moving out) may be responding to interest groups such as the "public at large" or to the organized interests of a particular neighborhood. Further, such interest groups may demand or require other than purely law enforcement activities on the part of police. Wilson (1968) has written at length on the "interests" of particular communities centering around service functions.

While this service orientation may share appearances, and even some techniques, with community based-policing, or with problem-oriented policing, the reality is that the police organization is merely responding to various pressures brought about by various special-interest groups. Therefore, the result is policy based on short-term decisions and assignments, with ever-increasing resources devoted to immediate problems. Such a situation leads to relative chaos and the inability of police to respond to changing conditions in the community at large.

With squandered resources and a lack of organized policy and planning, a reasonable expectation is that geographic enclaves derived from the more powerful and long-term interest groups will develop. We refer to these as "enclaves" because the concept of enclaved and walled communities, whether based on cultural factors or on environmental design, is an excellent exemplar. Residents identify with the area and non-residents are seen as intruders and potential criminals. Emergent police responses to the enclave movement are concerned with maintaining the enclave community at the expense of the larger community. Examples of the form of policing required here include stopping of blacks who are in an enclave where they "do not ordinarily belong" (e.g., Jamal Wilkes, former Los Angeles Lakers basketball star being detained "on suspicion" while driving his Rolls Royce in the "Wilshire Corridor" in Los Angeles; an episode of LA Law where a black attorney jogging in an upper-class neighborhood was accosted and arrested by police).

Neighborhood Watch programs exemplify the response of police organizations to this source of governmental power. In a real sense, these programs are not oriented toward protecting citizens of the general community, but rather are a method of focusing service on selective areas. Those who have been in police departments operating neighborhood watch programs tell us that, when a "neighborhood" is advised of a possible displacement effect on crime, the invariable response from residents is that they don't care, they just want *their* neighborhood safe from crime. This is analogous to the NIMBY (Not In My Back Yard) phenomenon which routinely occurs in prison site selection.

The irony here is that as services are continually focused on the interest group enclaves, the proactive nature of police crime prevention can serve to displace crime into the larger non-enclaved community, thus creating a "battle-ground" and greater demands of protection from the enclaves. The cycle of demand for protection and focus of resources has the potential to render impotent the police organization and to destroy the enclaves themselves.

Elite-based Change

Changes in police derived from this power base require selective enforcement of laws, proliferation of special-interest laws, and order maintenance exerted on the masses. All are based on a re-emphasis of basic (elite) values in society and the emergence of a strident conservatism. A number of current modifications of police structure are predicated on the drug war and are, in some sense, a reorientation of the

earlier war on crime of the 1970s. For example, resource allocations from the federal government, designed to encourage and reward police departments for their crime-fighting efforts, were moved into drunken-driving campaigns and now have been moved into the drug war. Police departments, as a result, have eliminated some older crime-fighting units and substituted drug enforcement programs.

This most recent phase, the war on drugs, has once again succeeded in connecting drug use with crime, thus providing a rationale for police to adopt the ideology of the new drug war. In addition, the war has succeeded in criminalizing (and thus delegitimizing) a major portion of those who might threaten the elite value system. In part because drug use has been associated with the liberal values of the 1960s, elite conservative values have been able to dominate the present era. Moreover, both an emphasis on the repression of drug-users and the advent of work place drug-testing have been used to resolve elite concerns about societal productivity.

It is likely that in a democratic society there will ultimately be a reaction, and there will be attempts to shift power (at least momentarily) in efforts to liberalize the laws concerning drug possession and use. Thus, it could be argued that repression contains the seeds of its own overthrow and may ultimately result in image problems for the police, as well as distrust and greater regulation of police activity. The police themselves have been placed in a quandary of having to eliminate a large number of otherwise desirable recruits because of a history of drug use. A recent recruiting solution has been to ask about the kind of drugs and make selective decisions while ignoring the presumptive illegality of all drug use.

Conclusions

While some change is undoubtedly taking place among police and in police organizations, the current situation leads us to believe that nothing substantial is taking place except, perhaps, in idiosyncratic circumstances and isolated instances. Further, our separation of the public into three types is misleading in the sense that each appears to be acting independently. Actually, all three types act in concert, with the more powerful having the greatest potential effect. Each one, however, tends to offset the others and dissipates the entire effect of change. The most probable approach to police change is that there will be a mixture of all these variations, in response to the mixture of the public types. This means that none of the potential approaches above will become commonplace, none will be logically and systematically approached, and in the end police will not become proactive. We predict that the police will maintain their current paramilitary form and bureaucratic structure. In the face of conflicting masters and differential demands, informal organizational goals serving survival will yield resistance to change and no viable new alternatives will emerge. We do not, however, rule out incremental change, particularly that change associated with larger societal concerns.

The most likely scenario is that crime will decrease by the turn of the century, largely due to demographic changes. The decrease in crime will, in turn, take pressure off the police to "do something about it." Thus, through the end of this decade, there will be minor modifications in policing, all of which will be strongly resisted, or modified to such an extent that the consequences will be minimal or nonexistent.

This, however, belies the function of the police and takes as granted the fact that police can effect crime. We believe there is sufficient evidence to support the assertion that any reduction of crime must come from outside the police. Therefore, the real question is not whether the police can prevent and control crime but, instead, whether and how efficiently and effectively the police can react to crime. Our constructed scenarios for proactive police roles are all unlikely, or else undesirable, in our present society. We would do well, then, to focus on the police as a reactive force and, if enhancement of this function is desirable, find methods of stripping proactive pretense from police organizations. If we must have a specific proactive force to control and prevent crime, a far better choice is to create an agency specifically responsible for that function and empower it to respond to crime on a far larger scope. Such an agency would presumably engage in the improvement of education, health, recreation, community renovation, and the myriad of other factors associated with the emergence of crime in our society. The police, however, should simply be assigned the task of reacting in crime as, or after, it is committed.

References

Currie, E. (1985). *Confronting Crime: An American Challenge.* New York: Pantheon Books.

Fishman, M. (1977). Crime waves as ideology. *Social Problems,* 25: 531-543.

Germann, A.C. (1985). "Law Enforcement: A Look Into the Future." In *The Ambivalent Force: Perspectives on the Police,* Abraham Blumberg and Elaine Neiderhoffer (eds.), 3rd ed. New York: Holt, Rinehart and Winston.

Goldstein, A. (1979). Improving the Police: A Problem-Oriented Approach. *Crime and Delinquency,* 25: 236-258.

Inciardi, J. (1992). *The War on Drugs II.* Mountain View, CA: Mayfield Publishing Company.

McPherson, N. (1992). "Problem Oriented Policing in San Diego." Comments made during panel presentation at the annual meeting of the Western Society of Criminology, San Diego, CA.

Strecher, V.G. (1991). Histories and futures of policing: Readings and misreadings of a pivotal present. *Police Forum,* 1(1): 1-9.

Trojanowicz, R. and Bucqueroux, B. (1990). *Community Policing: A Contemporary Perspective.* Cincinnati: Anderson Publishing Company.

Turk, A.T. and Grimes, R. (1992). "Neighborhood Watch Committees: Participation and Impact." Paper delivered at the annual meeting of the Western Society of Criminology, San Diego, CA.

Van Horn, C.E. and Van Meter, D.S. (1977). "The implementation of inter-governmental policy." In *Policy Studies Review Annual,* Vol. 1, S.S. Nagel (ed.). Beverly Hills, CA: Sage.

Walker, S. (1989). *Sense and Nonsense About Crime: A Policy Guide.* 2nd ed. Pacific Grove, CA: Brooks-Cole Publishing Company.

Weis, K. and Milikovich, M.E. (1974). Political misuses of crime rates. *Transaction,* 11(5):27-33.

Wilson, J.Q. (1968). *Varieties of Police Behavior.* Cambridge, MA: Harvard University Press.

_____ (1985). *Thinking About Crime.* Rev. ed. New York: Vintage Press.

Acknowledgments

Barlow, David E. and Melissa Hickman Barlow. "Cultural Sensitivity Rediscovered: Developing Training Strategies for Police Officers." *Justice Professional* 8 (1994): 97–116. Reprinted with the permission of Wyndhal Hall Press.

Blankenship, Michael B. and James M. Moneymaker. "Unsafe at Any Speed: The Utility of Police Pursuits." *American Journal of Police* 10 (1991): 53–59. Reprinted with the permission of the *American Journal of Police*.

Bracey, Dorothy H. "Police Corruption and Community Relations: Community Policing." *Police Studies* 15 (1992): 179–83. Reprinted with the permission of MCB University Press Ltd.

Brandl, Steven G., James Frank, Robert E. Worden, and Timothy S. Bynum. "Global and Specific Attitudes Toward the Police: Disentangling the Relationship." *Justice Quarterly* 11 (1994): 119–34. Reprinted with the permission of the Academy of Criminal Justice Sciences.

Crank, John P. "Watchman and Community: Myth and Institutionalization in Policing." *Law and Society Review* 28 (1994): 325–51. Reprinted with the permission of the Law and Society Association.

Greene, Jack R., Geoffrey P. Alpert, and Paul Styles. "Values and Culture in Two American Police Departments: Lessons from King Arthur." *Journal of Contemporary Criminal Justice* 8 (1992): 183–207. Reprinted with the permission of the *Journal of Contemporary Criminal Justice*.

Hirschel, J. David, Ira W. Hutchinson, Charles W. Dean, and Anne-Marie Mills. "Review Essay on the Law Enforcement Response to Spouse Abuse: Past, Present, and Future." *Justice Quarterly* 9 (1992): 247–83. Reprinted with the permission of the Academy of Criminal Justice Sciences.

Jackson, Pamela Irving. "The Police and Social Threat: Urban Transition, Youth Gangs, and Social Control." *Policing and Society* 2 (1992): 193–204. Reprinted with the permission of Harwood Academic Publishers.

Klockars, Carl B. "The Legacy of Conservative Ideology and Police." *Police Forum* 3 (1993): 1–6. Reprinted with the permission of Northern Kentucky University.

Manning, Peter K. "Violence and Symbolic Violence." *Police Forum* 3 (1993): 1–6. Reprinted with the permission of Northern Kentucky University.

Lumb, Richard C. "Standards of Professionalization: Do the American Police Measure Up?" *Police Studies* 17 (1994): 1–19. Reprinted with the permission of MCB University Press Ltd.

Martin, Susan E. "The Effectiveness of Affirmative Action: The Case of Women in Policing." *Justice Quarterly* 8 (1991): 489–504. Reprinted with the permission of the Academy of Criminal Justice Sciences.

Marx, Gary T. "When the Guards Guard Themselves: Undercover Tactics Turned Inward." *Policing and Society* 2 (1992): 151–72. Reprinted with the permission of Harwood Academic Publishers.

Pursley, Robert D. "Local Government Fiscal Scarcity: Its Context and an Examination of the Productivity Issue Among Municipal Police Departments." *Journal of Crime and Justice* 16 (1993): 109–38. Reprinted with the permission of the Anderson Publishing Company.

Rudovsky, David. "Police Abuse: Can the Violence Be Contained?" *Harvard Civil Rights-Civil Liberties Law Review* 27 (1992): 465–501. Permission granted. Copyright 1992 *Harvard Civil Rights-Civil Liberties Law Review,* and by the President and Fellows of Harvard College.

Sparrow, Malcolm K. "Integrating Distinct Managerial Styles: The Challenge for Police Leadership." *American Journal of Police* 12 (1993): 1–16. Reprinted with the permission of MCB University Press Ltd.

Tennenbaum, Abraham N. "The Influence of the *Garner* Decision on Police Use of Deadly Force." *Journal of Criminal Law and Criminology* 85 (1994): 241–60. Reprinted with the special permission of the Northwestern University School of Law, *Journal of Criminal Law and Criminology.*

Tunnell, Kenneth D. and Larry K. Gaines. "Political Pressures and Influences on Police Executives: A Descriptive Analysis." *American Journal of Police* 11 (1992): 1–16. Reprinted with the permission of MCB University Press Ltd.

Walker, Samuel. "Does Anyone Remember Team Policing? Lessons of the Team Policing Experience for Community Policing." *American Journal of Police* 12 (1993): 33–55. Reprinted with the permission of MCB University Press Ltd.

Walker, Samuel and Vic W. Bumphus. "The Effectiveness of Civilian Review: Observations on Recent Trends and New Issues Regarding the Civilian Review of the Police." *American Journal of Police* 11 (1992): 1–26. Reprinted with the permission of MCB University Press Ltd.

Weisheit, Ralph A., L. Edward Wells, and David N. Falcone. "Community Policing in a Small Town and Rural America" *Crime and Delinquency* 40 (1994): 549–67. Reprinted with the permission of Sage Publications.

Williams, Frank P. III and Carl P. Wagoner. "Making the Police Proactive: An Impossible Task for Improbable Reasons." *Police Forum* 2 (1992): 1–5. Reprinted with the permission of Northern Kentucky University.